# Constit

## Do You Have Any?

by

Phil Hart

First edition 2000
Second edition 2001
Third edition 2005, 2nd printing 2008
Third Printing 2010

Printed in the United States of America



Cover by Ms. Stephanie Corley

ISBN: 978-0-9711880-3-7

Library of Congress Control Number: 2001118711

Alpine Press
Post Office Box 1988
Hayden, Idaho 83835

**www.constitutionalincome.com**

Printed by: Morris Publishing
3212 East Highway 30
Kearney, NE 68847
1-800-650-7888

# NOTICE

Much of the information presented in this work is taken directly from the Congressional Record, court case opinions and court files. The information has been provided in this format to give the reader a new perspective on the income tax, based upon the intent of those who debated the issue at the time the 16th Amendment was offered for ratification. The author sees himself as only a messenger bringing forward information from established legal authorities.

The reader should realize that defending one's rights is risky, especially against big government. The right to pursue happiness has been denied to many Americans who have found themselves destitute after entanglements with the tax collector. How the reader uses the information in this book, either directly or indirectly, is not the responsibility of the author.

Proclaim Liberty throughout all the Land and to all the Inhabitants there of.
Leviticus 25:10

# Dedication

This book is dedicated to my daughter, Sarah Hart, and her friends, who have been born into a feudal system: may they live in Freedom.

## About the author

Phil Hart received a bachelor's degree in Civil Engineering from the University of Utah and a master's degree in Business Administration from the Wharton School at the University of Pennsylvania. He makes his living as a licensed structural engineer. As an athlete, Phil qualified for the U.S. Cycling Nationals the first time he rode a 25 mile trial, and later came within 6 seconds of the American record for the 10 mile time trial. He was also the winner of two World Cup races on the masters FIS alpine ski racing series. In 2004, Phil was elected to the Idaho Legislature. Phil was re-elected to the Legislature in 2006 and 2008. Phil serves on the Judiciary Rules Committee, the Revenue and Taxation Committee and the Transportation and Defense Committee.

# Contents

## Chapter 4



## Chapter 5



## Chapter 6

## Chapter 7



## Chapter 8



## Chapter 9



## Chapter 10

# Introduction

Writing a book is not something I planned to do. Writing this book was motivated by my own entanglements with the Internal Revenue Service. I used to think the IRS was an agency of our national government. That was when I was young and uninformed. It was also when I thought I had a legal duty to pay an annual tax to the IRS. In my research I have not been able to figure out who the IRS is. The community where I live has hired Waste Management, Inc. to collect the garbage. In the same way, it appears that the IRS is a contractor to the United States government for the purpose of collecting taxes. Well, it's not really only taxes they collect, but payments to offset the obligations of the bankrupt federal government, the citizenry being the collateral for the bankruptcy. That is a subject for another book.

Being frustrated with the literature out in the public realm on the tax issue, I began to do my own research. I found the statutes and regulations, all 19,000 pages of them, to contain much smoke and mirrors of a complex nature. I decided instead to investigate the foundational underpinnings of the Congress' authority to levy an income tax. In the first seven chapters of this book you will not find a single statute quoted out of Title 26, the Internal Revenue Code. Instead you will find an analysis of the history and the legal authority behind the income tax amendment to the Constitution.

I believe this approach will provide a more easily understood body of material that can be used to unravel the income tax issue. What I discovered was the entire income tax issue to be complex primarily because there are too many taxes which wear the label of "income tax" which are actually not income taxes at all. The effect of this is to make the entire income tax issue to appear more complicated than it needs to be. Of course this plays into the hands of those who benefit from the tax and hurts those who end up paying the tax.

With all the purported "income taxes" segregated into their appropriate "pigeon holes," I think this book will allow a person of reasonably good intelligence the opportunity to more clearly understand the income tax issue. But you'll still have to work at it as no one can be spoon-fed on such a complex subject.

It is my opinion that about three quarters of Americans don't have "constitutional income." But most Americans have unknowingly declared themselves to have "statutory taxable income." Through sleight of hand, virtually all of us have been entrapped into creating a "legal duty" for ourselves to pay this tax. A friend of mine said it is similar to getting your shirt caught in a piece of machinery. Generations of Americans have gone to the battlefields of the world believing they were fighting for freedom, yet at home they live under a form of economic tyranny where the spies and the informers report financial crimes. The goal of the bureaucracy seems to be political and social control, and the deception of the American people has been wonderfully clever.

It is my hope that this book will allow the reader to understand his constitutional duty to pay taxes. I believe Supreme Court Justice Oliver Wendell Holmes was right when he said "Taxes are what we pay for a civilized society." Furthermore, I also believe that a balanced income tax is a desirable tax and should be part of the revenue collection apparatus of the federal government. I hope I will have sold the reader on this latter point by the end of the book, as I have proposed a replacement for the 16th Amendment. This proposed amendment has the same purpose of the 16th Amendment, yet uses unambiguous terms not subject to manipulation. The original theory behind the income tax is good. That being the taxation of only that property which was economically productive. In the vernacular of the day, it was a tax on "accumulated weath."

Under the rule of law, all men are equal. Throughout the history of mankind there has been a pattern where the strong and the rich did not pay taxes, only the weak and poor did. The general rule of history is that the rule of law does not prevail most of the time. There is another general rule; that anyone who subverts the truth is always ultimately exposed when the "rule of law" returns. Only with the "rule of law" do we have "liberty and justice for all." Unfortunately, this is not the case in America today. The strong are those who are on the inside and understand the intricacies of the Internal Revenue Code and escape taxation. Whereas the weak are those, like most of the rest of us, who are ignorant as to what is going on and pay because we think paying the income tax is the right thing to do.

This book will serve to narrow the issues in the income tax debate. What will no longer be debated after this book circulates is:

1.) The 16th Amendment, the income tax amendment, did not create an exception to the constitutional rule of apportionment nor an exception to the constitutional rule of uniformity for the levying of taxes allowed by the original organic handwritten Constitution of 1787. All parts of the Constitution are still in harmony.

2.) The 16th Amendment **does not** provide authority for the levying of a direct tax in the nature of an income tax.

3.) The 16th Amendment **does** provide authority for the levying of an indirect tax in the form of an income tax.

4.) The income tax authorized by the 16th Amendment is an excise tax, a species of indirect tax.

Unraveling the income tax issue is like reverse engineering a UFO that has landed in your front yard. Trial and error and theorizing are involved. In order to collect the greatest amount of money and fool the greatest number of people, Congress has intentionally written the Internal Revenue Code to be deceptive while at the same time refusing to answer our questions on the matter. Don't blame the IRS, it is Congress that has the power to levy and collect taxes. Congress is the villain. The American People never consented to an unapportioned direct tax on their wages and salaries. Write your Congressman and tell him: **No Taxation Without Our Consent.**

This book applies primarily to America and the taxation authority delegated to Congress by the Constitution. But the principles of this book apply to people everywhere as the foundational arguments spring from the inalienable rights granted to man by " the laws of Nature and Nature's God."

If this is an issue you want to take on, understand the task is a difficult one, and the risks are great. Anyone who tells you otherwise is lying to you. Please understand that you have a human and moral duty to stand for truth and to speak for those who can not speak for themselves. Your children, the Posterity referred to in the Preamble of the Constitution, are among the latter. You may have to wait until the afterlife for your reward.

If you think the courts of this country administer justice, you are naive. We have the government we are willing to accept. It won't get better until enough Americans at the grass roots level determine to make it so.

"If the People will lead, the leaders will follow." This is a realistic slogan to describe politics in America.

And lastly, I am not an attorney and this book does not offer legal advice. You must make your own determination on whether or not you have a tax that you owe. I hope when you do pay taxes in the future that you will understand what you are doing, and that you will pay taxes for the support of government in order that we might live in a civilized society. Up to now you have probably been paying taxes because you have been duped into paying off a debt created by the mismanagement of our unconstitutional monetary system and the phony bankruptcy associated with it.

**Phil Hart,**
**Coeur d'Alene, Idaho**
**February 2004**

**Note:** Throughout the book, I have used the capitalization style used by our original handwritten Constitution when referring to the American People in their Sovereign capacity. There are a few other words and terms to which I have applied this rule. **(PH)**

## Foreword

By the late 1800s and up until the passage of the 16th Amendment, in 1913, many Americans were demanding that their legislators levy an income tax on accumulated wealth. This was because families such as the Carnegies and the Morgans, although virtually untaxed, had gained ever-increasing influence and control over the American political system using their vast fortunes. By reading the Congressional Record, House and Senate documents, newspapers, magazines, law journal articles of the time and the writings of the people who were intimately involved in the development of the 16th Amendment, Phil Hart proves beyond doubt that the intent of the federal income tax was to tax the annual profit from businesses and the net annual income from investment. Wages and salaries from labor were not considered income within the original meaning and intent of the 16th Amendment, known to some people as the Income Tax Amendment.

Hart's book provides compelling evidence that taxes on labor, as currently collected by the IRS as an "income" tax, cannot be described as anything other than a direct tax. Senator Norris Brown from Nebraska, the man who wrote the 16th Amendment, defined clearly what income was and what the income tax was intended to accomplish. Not once did Sen. Brown, in any of his writings, mention that Congress intended to pass an amendment that would grant the federal government a new power to directly tax the wages or salaries of working people.

The historical record shows that the Republicans of the early 20th century, acting as agents for those who had monopolized the American economy, set the "wages-are-income" concept into motion by language placed into the federal tax code after the 16th Amendment was passed. The first statute threw all sorts of "sources of income" into the mix including wages. Other statutes then "benevolently" exempted the first $4,000 of a person's "income." Since the average American family's earned income was about $500 a year at the time, it wasn't until after World War II, when this nation's economy was really booming and national pride was peaking, that Americans really began paying taxes on their wages. In post-World War II America, Americans took for granted that they could trust the federal government and the average person had long since forgotten the debates of the income tax issue, as well as what the law considered "income" to be.

We have been conditioned since kindergarten to believe that wages and salaries generated from our labors are "income" for federal tax purposes, yet this book provides testimony in direct opposition to such conditioning. The federal government knew what it was doing then and it knows what it is doing today. The Constitution recognizes two kinds of taxes: direct and indirect. Congress does not have the constitutional authority to lay direct taxes against the people unless the tax burden is equally apportioned by population among the Several States. Congress does have the authority to lay indirect taxes on privileges, events and activities. Excise taxes on cigarettes, alcohol and gasoline are examples of constitutional indirect taxes. An excise tax on a corporate dividend is a tax on a privilege, as a corporation is a privileged entity created by government. There is no intelligent way to argue that a tax on a man's labor is anything but a direct tax. We work, get paid for our work and then get taxed according to the amount of money we are paid. If you don't work, you don't eat and you die. Whereas you can choose not to consume cigarettes, alcohol, gasoline or other products subject to excise taxes. A tax on wages is a tax on our right to exist, in many ways similar to the feudal systems of old. Through threats, coercion, and "brown shirt" tactics, the federal government deceives the American public regarding the constitutional limitations of their taxing authority, leading to trillions of dollars being confiscated from the American People through questionable means. In effect, we are being taxed without our consent because, as Hart points out in this book, consent was given according to the intent of the laws passed, not to the deceitful levels commandeered by the contemporary federal tax enforcement apparatus.

My own entry into this battle began as an IRS Criminal Investigation Division Special Agent, sworn to support and defend the United States Constitution. After being exposed to claims that there might be legal problems with the manner in which the IRS administered and enforced the federal income tax system, I set out to investigate those claims myself because I knew I had a moral, ethical and legal duty to do so. During my own investigation, I also encountered disparities and inconsistencies with the manner in which the IRS enforced the federal income tax system, similar to those described by Hart in this fine book. I attempted to clarify these disparities and inconsistencies with my IRS supervisors but rather than address my concerns, I was encouraged to resign from my position. I did resign from my special agent position on February 25th, 1999, eerily coinciding with February 25th, 1913, the day that the 16th Amendment was proclaimed to be ratified.

I am so grateful to Phil Hart for dedicating so much of his life to showing the American public what the federal income tax is all about from its inception. Phil's book will provide you with a "big picture" view of the federal income tax, rich with history and incontrovertible facts. I know this book will be instrumental in educating the American public about the limits to federal taxing power, an education that is critical to re-harnessing an out of control federal tax enforcement apparatus.

**Joseph R. Banister**
**Former IRS Criminal Investigation Division Special Agent**

# Chapter 1
## Constitutional Taxation

**"On every question of the construction of the Constitution, let us carry ourselves back to the time when the Constitution was adopted, recollect the spirit manifested in the debates, and instead of trying what meaning may be squeezed out of the text, or invented against it, conform to the probable one in which it was passed."**

***—Thomas Jefferson, Letter to William Johnson, Supreme Court Justice, 1823.***

The issue of income taxes is a complicated one. Those who levy and collect this tax have purposely made it complex in order that the masses will be unable to comprehend just how the tax code works. The purpose of this book is to raise the awareness of the American People on the income tax issue so that the People will be better equipped to keep the government within its constitutional boundaries with respect to its powers of taxation.

The best way to start this task is to state the conclusions of this book in Chapter 1. This way readers will know what to look for as they read the material and will have a clearer understanding of the government's taxation authority.

The title of this book is *Constitutional Income: Do You Have Any*? Why is it necessary to understand what the term "constitutional income" means? It is necessary because there are various types of "income."

This book is primarily concerned with two: "constitutional income" and "statutory taxable income." These are not always the same. "Statutory taxable income" is whatever the legislature says it is. On the other hand, "constitutional income" means what **We the People** say it means. Any word or term used in the Constitution has the meaning the People intended that word or term to mean at the time the Constitution was ratified. Or, in the case of an amendment to the Constitution, we use the words therein as the American People understood them to mean at the time the amendment was ratified by the several States. In this book we are concerned with what the word "income" means within the context of the 16th Amendment. So, naturally we will want to know what the People understood that word to mean at the time the 16th Amendment was ratified.

To understand what the meaning of the word "income" is, we must examine the history of income taxes in America prior to the ratification of the 16th Amendment. This history has a legislative/political component and a judicial component, in addition to its common meaning in everyday speech. We must also remember that our Constitution is unique to this country. The way in which taxes are levied under our Constitution depends upon whether the tax is a "direct tax" or an "indirect tax." How other countries levy an income tax is immaterial to America; they aren't bound by our Constitution.

According to our national Constitution, direct taxes must be apportioned among the several States, and indirect taxes must be uniform throughout the United States.

As we go through the history of income taxation in America, we will develop a test to determine whether a tax is a *direct tax* or an *indirect tax*. In America, such a test is necessary to determine the appropriate way any tax is to be levied. Does a tax have to be uniform throughout the United States? Or, does it have to be apportioned among the several States? In creating this test, we can only function as researchers. This, too, is all the Supreme Court can do on the issue. For it is the People, at the time of the ratification of the Constitution and the 16th Amendment, who have already made the determination on what the terms "income" and "direct tax" mean. Our job is to discover what this is.

The law is based upon words. If words were to have variable meanings, then it would be impossible to have the "rule of law;" instead we would have the "rule of men." Those who defined what the words meant would rule. Some words have a tendency to change meaning over time and generations, but the meanings of words used in law need to have consistent definitions, otherwise we have evolutionary law. Such law benefits only tyrants at the expense of the citizenry.

Moreover, for the purposes of any given law, the words used therein can be, and often are, defined strictly for the purposes of that particular law. Words written by lawyers can, and often are, subtle and sophisticated in their peculiar meaning. We might call this "wordsmithing."

"Wordsmithing" occurs when, for the purpose of a statute, words, or groups of words known as "terms," are given unique meanings that apply only to that particular statute. Usually these words or terms are commonly used in everyday speech. Their use in a statute can have a meaning different than that normally associated with the word or term when used by nonlawyers. For example, the familiar term "United States" has approximately 450 different and unique definitions within the entire body of state and federal law. Now that you know this, never assume you know what the term "United States" means when you see it used in a statute or on a government form.

Definitions, therefore, are extremely important in determining whether or not you have "constitutional income." As the

Congressional Record reflects:

> **[w]e have tolerantly permitted the habitual misuse of words to serve as a vehicle to abandon our foundations and goals. House Congressional Record, June 13, 1967, pg. 15641.**

In order to understand this book, you will need to know at least three definitions. These are the definitions for "direct tax," "indirect tax," and "apportionment." You should also realize from the beginning that there are many species of income taxes. Not all income taxes belong in the same pigeon hole. Failure to place the various types of income taxes in their appropriate pigeon holes will result in confusion.

> **"The Supreme Court of the United States has thus held that certain kinds of income taxes are indirect, that certain other kinds of income taxes are direct, and that still other kinds of income taxes are invalid, irrespective of whether they are direct or indirect." Edwin R.A. Seligman, The Income-Tax Amendment, 25 Political Science Quarterly 193, 197 (1910).**

The basic premise of this book is as follows:

1. The 16th Amendment created no new classification of taxes under the Constitution, and we are therefore still left only with direct and indirect taxes.

2. The 16th Amendment provides taxation authority only for income taxes that are inherently indirect. Such taxes must be levied according to the constitutional rule of uniformity.

3. The 16th Amendment does not provide an exception to the constitutional rule of apportionment for direct taxes.

4. Any income tax which is inherently a direct tax is outside (without) the scope of the 16th Amendment, and therefore must be apportioned among the several States according to population.

5. Income taxes on wages and salaries are direct taxes and must be apportioned among the several States. The taxation clauses of the United States Constitution provide:

**"Representatives and direct taxes shall be apportioned among the several States which may be included within this Union, according to their respective Numbers of free Persons, including those bound to Service for a Term of Years, and excluding Indians not taxed, three fifths of all other Persons." Article 1, Section 2, Clause 3.**

**"The Congress shall have Power to lay and collect Taxes, Duties, Imposts and Excises, to pay the Debts and provide for the common Defense and general welfare of the United States; but all Duties, Imposts, and Excises shall be uniform throughout the United States." Article 1, Section 8, Clause 1.**

**"No Capitation, or other direct, Tax shall be laid, unless in Proportion to the Census or Enumeration herein before directed to be taken....No Tax or Duty shall be laid on Articles exported from any State. Article 1, Section 9, Clauses 4 and 5.**

**"The Congress shall have power to lay and collect taxes on incomes, from whatever source derived, without apportionment among the several States, and without regard to any census or enumeration." 16th Amendment.**

The taxation authority of Congress is plenary. This means it is total and complete, able to reach any article or person with its taxing power. It has been this way from the beginning, that is from 1789 when the Constitution was ratified. However, there is one exception: Congress can not tax exports.

When levying any tax, Congress must follow one of two rules. The first rule is that direct taxes must be apportioned among the several States according to population. This means that Congress will determine the total amount of tax they want to collect. Next, Congress will divide up the amount of the tax due among the States in a way such that each citizen will have to pay the same dollar amount of the tax. In other words, the tax will be apportioned according to population. The states would actually be responsible for collecting the money for Congress. The states then collect the tax from the citizens of the state. It would be up to the states to determine how to collect the tax and/or what to levy. There would be no direct contact between the citizen and the national government. Only if the states failed to perform would the federal government step in and collect the tax. This is how "apportionment" was meant to work.

The term "indirect tax" does not actually appear in the Constitution. You might say it means "any tax that is not direct." For after all, there are only two types of taxes: "direct taxes" and "indirect taxes." It is similar to, "You're either pregnant or you're not."

Indirect taxes are "Duties, Imposts, and Excises." Duties and imposts are tariffs collected on the importation of goods into our country. Sometimes a duty is a "required action," like payment of a stamp duty. Of duties, imposts and excises taxes, the Supreme Court said in the case of *Flint v. Stone Tracy Company* that:

> **"Duties and imposts are terms commonly applied to levies made by governments on the importation or exportation of commodities. Excise taxes are those laid upon the manufacture, sale or consumption of commodities within the country, upon licenses to pursue certain occupations, and upon corporate privileges." Flint v. Stone Tracy Co., 220 U.S. 107, 151 (1910).**

Indirect taxes can be avoided or passed on. No one has to pay an indirect tax if they don't want to. Indirect taxes are therefore voluntary. Hence the word "indirect."

The tax on a pack of cigarettes is an avoidable excise tax. You can choose not to smoke and avoid the tax. Or you can grow your own tobacco for your own personal use and avoid the tax. The excise tax on tires is avoidable. So is the excise tax on gasoline. You can choose to ride your bicycle. If you are a bus company, you have to pay the excise tax on both tires and gasoline, but you pass this cost onto the patrons who ride your bus in the form of higher ticket prices. You, therefore, are not the ultimate payer of the excise tax, your patrons paid it **indirectly.**

A direct tax cannot be avoided. It cannot be passed on. If you owe it, you pay it. There is nothing you do that causes you to owe the tax. For example, if you get a license to manufacture alcohol, you pay an excise tax on this privilege. You pay this tax because you made the choice to get into this business. You could choose to do something else for a living and avoid the tax. There are no choices you make which causes you to owe a direct tax. You must pay a direct tax for the simple reason that you exist and the tax is levied on you. A direct tax is direct.

> **"Any tax when placed on the right of the man ... to live is a capitation tax and as direct as any tax can be." Brief for appellant, Flint v. Stone Tracy Co., 220 U.S. 107, 119 (1910).**

One example of a direct tax is a tax on land because of ownership. The government levies the tax on the land solely because the land exists. It is immaterial what the land is used for, whether or not the land is economically productive, or who owns it. The tax is on the land and the owner of the land pays the tax.

There are a variety of direct taxes as the framers of the Constitution used the phrase "or other direct," when identifying the apportionment rule. It is worth noting that the requirement to apportion direct taxes is the only provision mentioned twice in the Constitution. The framers obviously understood the inherent appetite government had for revenue.

The framers also well understood the difference between an indirect tax and a direct tax. A reading of the congressional debates over the taxation issue from 1796 to 1798 will reveal much dialog on the issue. The nature of direct or indirect taxes was not debated, but only which of the two was the more desirable.

**"History, Mr. Williams said, informed them of the annihilation of nations by means of direct taxation. He referred gentlemen to the situation of the Roman Empire in its innocence, and asked them whether they had any direct taxes? No. Indirect taxes and taxes upon luxuries and spices from the Indies were their sources of revenue; but, as soon as they changed their system to direct taxation, it operated to their ruin; their children were sold as slaves, and the Empire fell from its splendor. Shall we then follow this system? He trusted not." Annuals of Congress, 4th Congress, 2nd Session, pg. 1898 (Jan. 1797).**

Professor Seligman of Columbia University, quoted on page 4, was right when he said that some income taxes were direct and some income taxes were indirect. There is a boundary line which separates the two. An indirect income tax is either a tax on a privilege, measured by income, or it is a tax on unearned income or profit which diminishes only the income and leaves the source of the income whole.

Income tax levied on a privilege, i.e., doing business in corporate form, is an indirect tax. Such a tax may be measured by either gross income or net income. The tax is on the privilege and the amount of the income is used to measure the amount of tax due. An income tax that diminishes only the income and leaves the source whole takes its bite out of only the severable income and does not touch the underlying capital. For example, a tax on the interest income from a savings account diminishes only the interest and does not touch the original principle.

A direct income tax is a tax on gross income that can not be placed on any privilege. If a man works and only makes enough money to barely meet his needs and the needs of his family, any tax on his wage or salary is a direct tax. Since the tax makes it more difficult for the man to feed, clothe and shelter his family, the tax is therefore a direct tax. The man is diminished by the tax. The tax is on the man's right to exist as it makes his existence more difficult. It is not a tax he can avoid or pass on to someone else. Adam Smith wrote that taxes on the revenue of the people are capitation taxes.

Congress is still bound by these constitutional provisions when levying taxes. Not until the Constitution is further amended, or the Nation is conquered by a foreign foe, can these rules be ignored. We will see how, through slight of hand and clever "wordsmithing" of statutes, Congress has done something they are otherwise not permitted to do. Even though the courts have repeatedly determined that substance rules over form, the bureaucracy excels at collecting a tax it is not permitted by the Constitution to collect.

Although the effect of the income taxation statutes are far removed from what the American People intended when they ratified the 16th Amendment, the statutes themselves are constitutional. They just don't mean what you and I think they mean in a simple reading of them. Years ago the *Wall Street Journal* claimed it took someone with the intelligence of a triple Ph.D. to understand the Internal Revenue Code in a first reading of it. Let's not kid ourselves; we're not free if our liberty and property are at risk because of such a complex and convoluted law that only a few understand.

This book presents the income tax issue without going into the statutes and regulations. These being so complex, it is nearly an endless task to unravel them in order to actually determine who and what is being taxed. Instead, this book looks at the question from a constitutional standpoint. We will determine what is permitted by the Constitution and what is not in so far as the taxation of "incomes" is concerned.

The conclusions drawn by this book are supportive of what other researchers are discovering as they unravel the statutes and regulations. That being that the income tax is an excise tax on activities and privileges. It is an indirect tax. Please realize that having "passive income" is a privilege one enjoys due to the existence of civil government. Having "earned income" is not a benefit of civil government. You would have it even if civil government didn't exist. The statutes, regulations and internal IRS documentation support this conclusion.

If you are still not clear on what the meanings of "direct tax," "indirect tax" and "apportionment" are, reread this chapter or consult the glossary at page 348. However, be careful as to what you read elsewhere about the definition of "direct tax;" there is some misinformation out there. You won't fully benefit from the rest of the book unless you understand these terms.

We will also see that there is no foundation for the government's position that the word "income" as used in the 16th Amendment includes wages and salaries of a American working in the private sector and living in the several States of the Union. The government's position is based on the Supreme Court's statement in the *Eisner v. Macomber* case where they said:

> **"Income may be defined as the gain derived from capital, from labor, or from both combined." Eisner v. Macomber, 252 U.S. 189, 206 (1919).**

The *Eisner Case* was a stock dividend case; that is a stock from a corporation. It relied on two other cases for this statement, that of *Stratton's Independence v. Howbert*, 231 U.S. 399 and *Doyle v. Mitchell Bros. Co.*, 247 U.S. 179. These latter two cases were cases relating to corporations. An examination of court's Transcript of Record for these three cases will show that there is no foundation to the government's position that the Supreme Court determined that wages and salaries equal income. That a corporation may derive income from labor as it utilizes labor in pursuit of profits is entirely correct. But, to say that income may be derived from labor is entirely different than saying that labor equals income. The question has never been directly before the Supreme Court.

In examining the history of the debate and ratification of the 16th Amendment, we will also see that there is no evidence upon which the government can rely for their claim that the American People desired to have their wages and salaries taxed. No evidence can be found in the law journals of the time, not in the journals on political economy or economics, not in the Congressional Record, nor in any of the newspapers of record of the time. In other words, the government's position that wages and salaries equals income within the meaning of the 16th Amendment is **"wholly without foundation."**

Wages and salaries will be "income" within the constitutional meaning of the term only when **We the People** determine this to be so.

Today our politicians justify America's involvement with the "peacekeeping" efforts of the New World Order when they tell us we must make the world safe for democracy. But when was there ever a democratic process whereby the American People determined that they wanted their wages and salaries taxed? Where is the evidence that proves that the American People lobbied Congress and their state legislatures demanding there be levied a constitutionally direct tax on their wages in lieu of an indirect tax on their consumption? The historical record is void of any evidence that such a democratic process ever took place. It was never the intention of the American People for the 16th Amendment to confer the new power upon Congress that the bureaucracy says it has. There is no evidence to support this contention. We are therefore the world's biggest hypocrite as our government takes one-third of the earned income of the American People without our consent while promoting democracy throughout the rest of the world.

Although this argument has been around for some time, it has never been substantiated by the information and evidence presented in this book. The remaining chapters will prove the assertions made in this first chapter.

# Chapter 2
## A Brief History of "Income" Taxation in the United States of America

In Adam Smith's famous work, *Wealth of Nations*, we discover:

> **"Capitation taxes, so far as they are levied upon the lower ranks of people, are direct taxes upon the wages of labour, and are attended with all the inconveniences of such taxes."**
>
> ***—Adam Smith, Wealth of Nations, book V, 541 (1776), Prometheus Books, Amherst, New York, 1991.***

## Origins

During America's colonial period there was no income tax as we understand such a tax today. This was a more primitive time for the new world as many people were carving out their existence from the raw materials provided by nature. Money was scarce in the interior areas but circulated more freely in the coastal cities. This naturally made it difficult to measure one's earnings as there was no universal measuring device like the "dollar" as we have today. Adam Smith wrote in his *Wealth of Nations* in 1776:

> **"The impossibility of taxing the people, in proportion to their revenue, by any capitation, seems to have given occasion to the invention of taxes upon consumable commodities. The state not knowing how to tax, directly and proportionably, the revenue of its subjects, endeavors to tax it indirectly by taxing their expense, which, it is supposed, will in most cases be nearly in proportion to their revenue. Their expense is taxed by taxing the consumable commodities upon which it is laid out." id. at 541.**

At the beginning of the colonial period, when valuing property for purposes of taxation, the key element was not location, but instead production. Survival was the dominate criteria and a productive property was more valuable. Taxes were also levied on personal property. Early colonial taxation generally looked only to the land itself and the extent of its improvements, i.e., its productivity. No concern was given to the personal condition of the landowner. Although it is the person who pays the tax, the *object* of the tax was tangible property, real or personal. All early taxes fell upon the property itself, the estimated income that the property was thought to produce, or in later years, on the value of the property at sale. Back then, many of the colonies also had what they called a "faculty tax."

> **"Here for the first time we have the definition of faculty or ability. Just as the faculty of the property owner is seen in the produce of his estate, so that of 'artists' and 'tradesmen' is to be found in their 'returns and gains.' Of course, since the property value of an estate is approximately equal to the capitalization value of the annual produce, the faculty of the property owner can be measured by the value of the property, that is, by the value of his 'estate'; but when there is no property, the assessors are compelled to fall back on the 'returns and gains.'" E.R.A. Seligman, The Income Tax, 369 (The MacMillan Co., New York 1911).**

The "faculty tax" was a personal tax but not a tax on the person. Instead it was a tax on his profession. It was the third prong of a three pronged colonial approach to taxation. The other two prongs were taxes on land and taxes on personal property, all three being direct taxes. The faculty tax was imposed upon the estimated returns, gains, profits, or increase of the laborer or craftsman, at a *fixed rate* based upon his particular craft. This "faculty" tax was, specifically, for those who owned no real property. Since labor is property, this tax was a direct tax upon property. Persons were assessed in groups depending on their trade, craft and the number of years of experience they had in their profession. It did not take into consideration the specific circumstance of the person. There were no deductions. The faculty tax was considered a direct tax. This fact is important to our question as to the meaning of "constitutional income" as we will see later that direct taxes are without the authority of the 16th Amendment.

> **"[D]irect taxes are such as are levied with reference to the *ability* of the taxpayer, as indicated by his property or income, while indirect taxes are such as are levied without reference to the ability of those who may pay them." Kossuth K. Keenan, Income Taxation, Burdick & Allen Publishers, p. 17 Milwaukee (1910).**

The faculty tax was a forerunner to the "income" tax in the modern sense. A modern "income" tax is a tax upon the personal "income" of an individual. It is a tax "on income," not a tax on things. The faculty tax can best be described as a primitive "income" tax on the *estimated gross revenue of a person*. Today, allowance is made for indebtedness or other factors affecting the personal situation of the taxpayer. But, the "faculty" tax was not levied on the total "income" of the individual. *It was a tax, not on actual profits, but on assumed profits*. Just as articles of personal and real property were listed at fixed rates, so too the individuals subject to the "faculty" tax were not required to make returns of their earnings, but were assessed by the "listers" at *fixed amounts*. The "faculty" tax was simply a classified product tax in which different employments and classes within each employment were rated at fixed amounts. For example, all tinsmiths with 20 years experience in the art would pay a fixed amount of tax, while those with only 10 years experience would pay a fixed but lesser amount of tax. Because it bore little relation to actual income, the "faculty" tax became so grievous that it fell into disuse.

Later, the taxes of the eighteenth century were closer to true "income" taxes because they were not set to assumed profits of certain classes as was the faculty tax, but have been levied on the actual, total income of the taxpayer. The entire colonial tax system evolved over time—first there was the land tax levied on net production; then there was a tax on personal property; then came the building tax levied on rental value of buildings; then came the tax on capital levied on the yield of capital. All of these taxes were upon the income of *things*—land, buildings, or capital. Finally, there was sometimes imposed a tax on the only remaining source, that is the professions and employments, which are levied upon salaries or compensation. Just like the faculty tax, all these taxes are upon *things*, not persons and all were considered direct taxes.

## National Taxation

In July 1776, America declared its independence from Great Britain and became a sovereign Nation. Today Americans think that something magical happened on that day, but this is wrong. The colonies had already been on the battlefield for one year and three months by then. It would be another seven years before Great Britain respected our Declaration of Independence. Much blood and treasure would be expended to bring force and effect to those words that

Thomas Jefferson penned in July of 1776. Then on March 4, 1789, America commenced operation of its new government under the newly ratified Constitution.

In 1791, the first Secretary of the Treasury, Alexander Hamilton, encouraged Congress to impose taxes on distilled spirits and carriages "more as a measure of social discipline than as a source of revenue." Subsequently, the first "commissioner of the revenue" was appointed on May 18, 1792.

In 1794, Congress enacted legislation which levied a tax on carriages, "whether for personal or commercial use." Daniel Lawrence Hylton of Virginia owned a carriage and the tax was assessed against him accordingly. He decided to challenge the validity of the statute on the grounds that the tax was a direct tax subject to the constitutional requirement of apportionment among the several States.

Under the Judiciary Act of 1789, to commence a lawsuit in the Circuit Court, the matter in dispute must have exceeded "the sum of $500." And, in order to appeal to the Supreme Court, following final judgment in the Circuit Court, the matter at controversy had to exceed $2,000. Because Hamilton [no longer Secretary of the Treasury] and Attorney General William Bradford were eager to secure a decision from the Supreme Court on the constitutionality of the carriage tax, both parties falsely stipulated that Hylton owned not one, but 125 carriages! (*The Law That **Always** Was*, by Vern Holland, pg. 93, 1987.) Moreover, they stipulated that the alleged tax of $2,000 could be settled by the payment of $16. It was an entirely staged lawsuit. Later you will see that this charade has had an enormous impact on taxation in America. It is also worthy to note that Hamilton was a leading federalist. That is, one in favor of a strong central government. Hamilton also objected to all direct taxation at the constitutional convention. It is likely he had a related hidden agenda in prosecuting the Hylton case, after all it was a staged lawsuit and he was being paid to win.[1]

Thus, an action for debt was brought by Alexander Campbell, United States Attorney for the District of Virginia, against Daniel L. Hylton for recovery of $2,000. Both parties waived the right of trial by jury and argument began in Circuit Court at Richmond on May 27, 1795, before James Wilson, Associate Justice of the Supreme Court, and Cyrus Griffin, federal District Judge. Counsel for the United States was Alexander Hamilton, William Bradford and John Wickham, a prominent Virginia lawyer. Hylton's counselor was a Mr. Taylor. One wonders if having a jury would have added an uncontrollable variable to the process.

The argument centered around the sole, pivotal question: Was the carriage tax a "direct tax" or an "indirect tax?" During trial, considerable reference was made to Adam Smith's *Wealth of Nations*, which had been published in 1776 and was well known in both Europe and America and which certainly influenced America's Founding Fathers.

Following entry of judgment against Hylton on June 2, 1795, the United States retained Hamilton and Charles Lee as counsel, in anticipation of taking the case to the Supreme Court on a writ of error. The case did go to the Supreme Court. Remarkably, the government also employed counsel on *Hylton's* behalf—Jared Ingersoll, and Alexander Campbell, United States Attorney for Virginia! Thus, Alexander Campbell, *the very attorney who had prosecuted Hylton in the lower Court was paid by the government to represent him in the Supreme Court.*[2] Oral argument began on February 23, 1796, and continued through the 25th.

Judgment was rendered on March 8, 1796, holding that a tax on carriages was *not* a direct tax, but was an indirect duty. The entire decision was based upon the *presumption*, argued by Hamilton, that the only direct taxes are capitation or poll taxes; taxes on lands or buildings; and general assessments upon the *whole* property of individuals or their *whole* real or personal property. Of course, this *presumption* was not sustained by the evidence. In the *dicta* of the three

Supreme Court judges concurring in the limitation of "direct taxes" to a tax on land and capitation taxes, it is clear that they did so with doubts. Justice Patterson said it was a "questionable point." Justice Chase said "I am inclined to think, but of this I do not give a judicial opinion." Justice Iredell said "Perhaps a direct tax can mean nothing but a tax on land." (*The Law That Always Was*, pg. 102-3.) Such comments in guarded language out of the dicta of a case are simply not authoritative. Yet today, through sleight of hand, the guarded dicta of *Hylton* is now fraudulently the stare decisis of today.

In *Cohens v. Virginia*, 6 Wheaton, 264, 399, Chief Justice Marshall said, "It is a maxim not to be disregarded, that general expressions, in every opinion, are to be taken in connection with the case in which those expressions are used. If they go beyond the case, they may be respected, but ought not to control the judgement in a subsequent suit when the very point is presented for decision." Rehearing - Brief for Appellant at 11, Pollock v. Farmers' Loan and Trust Co., 158 U.S. 601 (1895).

In *Hylton,* according to Judge Curtis, all "that the Court had to decide was, whether the tax on carriages is a 'duty;' and they held it to be so, because it is an indirect tax falling on consumption or expense." Although "a tax on a carriage, (because of ownership)...is no less direct than a tax on an acre of land", some "other element of discrimination is therefore to be sought." "If it is to be regarded as sound law, it must be accepted as having established, in our constitutional law, as one of the grounds of distinction between a direct and an indirect tax, that the latter is of such a quality that it reaches to consumption or expense, while the former has no relation to consumption or expense."[3]

Mr. Curtis, himself a federal judge and respected legal author, found some "of the reasoning of Judge Chase" to be "fallacious." Chase's opinion that "a tax on carriages can not be laid by the rule of apportionment without very great inequality and injustice" simply missed the point; when the tax is direct and apportioned, the States can levy the tax on any articles which they may see fit to select—they don't have to levy it on carriages!

Within thirty days of the *Hylton* decision Congress directed the Secretary of the Treasury, Oliver Wolcott, Jr., to "report a plan for laying and collecting direct taxes by apportionment among the several States agreeably to the rule prescribed by the Constitution; adapting the same, as near as may be, to such objects of direct taxation and such modes of collection as may appear by the laws and practice of the States, respectively, to be most eligible in each."[4] (April 4, 1796) Wolcott's report was exhaustive and included recommendations as to direct taxation much broader in scope than the narrower dicta of the *Hylton Case*.

If Congress had thought that the *Hylton Case* had definitely settled the definition of direct taxes, the report would have been meaningless! On December 14, 1796, Mr. Wolcott delivered his Report on Direct taxes to the House of Representatives of the 4th Congress, 2nd. Session. (American State Papers, Finance, Vol. 1, pgs. 414-441) On page 439 of this report, under the heading "Taxes on the profits (net income) resulting from certain employments", Mr. Wolcott distinctly pointed out that "taxes of this nature cannot be considered as of that description which the constitution requires to be apportioned among the States." A tax upon the profits of business were, therefore, considered (and later held to be) indirect taxes. A tax on the profits of employments is not the same as a tax on employments. The former is a tax on "net income," the latter is a tax on "earned income."

Then, "in 1813—notwithstanding the dicta of the judges in the case of *Hylton v. The United States*, expressing the opinion that direct taxes are only taxes on land, improvements to land (i.e., houses), and capitation taxes—Congress ruled that an *ad valorem* tax on slaves was a direct tax..." "In 1815 Congress laid an *ad valorem* tax on slaves as a direct tax, by expressly denominating it a direct tax, and laid it by the rule of apportionment." (Harper's, *supra*, p. 358, Act of January 9, 1815) Although Congress "doubtless felt themselves bound, or authorized, by the judicial decision of 1796, to treat a specific tax on carriages as an indirect tax...they did not feel themselves bound, or authorized, by the extrajudicial opinions of the judge's *dicta*, to treat an *ad valorem* tax on slaves as anything but a direct tax." A tax on a slave is a tax on labor—a direct tax. Thus, while the suggestion that direct taxes include only taxes on lands, improvements to land and capitation taxes was widely known, it was *not accepted by Congress*. Until 1861, taxes on lands, improvements to land, capitation taxes and *ad valorem* taxes upon personal property, without reference to consumption, were considered by Congress to be direct taxes while taxes on specific articles of consumption or expense were considered to be indirect taxes.

It is upon those doubtful expressions of judicial opinion in *Hylton*, the *dicta*, that subsequent decisions of the Supreme Court relied. (*Insurance Co. v. Soule*, 7 Wall. 443 (1868) (taxes on the receipts of insurance companies from premiums were indirect taxes); *Veazie Bank v. Fenno,* 8 Wall. 533 (1869) (taxes on circulating notes of State banks are indirect taxes); *Scholey v. Rew*, 23 Wall. 331 (1874) (inheritance taxes were indirect taxes); *Springer v. U.S.* 102 U.S. 586 (1880) (specifically relying on *Hylton, supra*, the court held that income taxes fall within the category of excises or duties.)

It is interesting to note that the very paragraph out of Adam Smith's *Wealth of Nations* that the Supreme Court quoted authoritatively, "The impossibility of taxing the people in proportion to their revenue, by **any** capitation, seems to have given occasion to the invention of taxes upon consumable commodities," tells us that there are a variety of capitation taxes as the word **"any"** indicates a plurality of possibilities. Since capitation taxes are direct taxes, we can conclude that there are a variety of ways in which a direct tax in the form of a capitation tax can be levied.

In 1798 a direct tax was enacted on real property (houses and land), as well as a tax of 50 cents each on all slaves between the ages of twelve and fifty. Debate on this legislation started after Secretary of the Treasury Wollcott completed his report on direct taxation. These unpopular taxes contributed to Thomas Jefferson's presidential victory over John Adams in 1800. In 1802, President Jefferson, determined to reduce federal taxation, repealed all internal taxes, with the exception of a tax on salt.

On January 17, 1815, during the War of 1812, Secretary of the Treasury Dallas proposed a direct federal income tax to raise $3,000,000 which was never adopted because of the peace which immediately ensued. (*American State Papers*, Vol. II, pg. 887) This war, however, demonstrated the risk of Jefferson's policy of relying entirely on *tariffs* as the sole source of financing the federal government. Tariff rates were doubled in 1812, but the peacetime deluge of imports in 1815 led domestic manufacturers to support the Tariff Act of 1816, which raised import duties to a new high. Although Congress had raised some revenue from taxes on internal sources, trade tariffs remained the most significant single source of revenue for the federal government until 1894.[5]

The government's reliance on tariffs as its principal source of funding was favored by the manufacturers because it served to protect them from foreign competition while imposing little, if any, burden upon them. However, later we will see that the high tariffs of the late 1800s imposed enormous burdens upon the urban consumers and the farmers; both groups of whom began to voice discontent. This discontent would later provide the impetus for purported passage of the 16th Amendment and the adoption of the Corporate Excise Tax Act of 1909 in an effort to more evenly distribute the burden for the support of government. Those who were suffering under the high tariff would later seek to level the playing field by shifting some of the tax burden off of consumption and onto incomes.

# Federal Income Taxation

## Civil War Income Taxes

Federal income taxation made its modern appearance as a means of financing the Civil War. The first income tax act was "An act to provide increased revenue from imports, to pay interest on the public debt, and for other purposes," known as the Direct Property Tax Act of August 5, 1861 (*12 Statutes at Large* 292), which imposed a tax of three percent on incomes in excess of $800 "whether such income is derived from any kind of property, or from any profession, trade, employment, or vocation carried on in the United States or elsewhere, or from any other source whatever..." As a "direct tax," this tax was apportioned among the several States.

The 1861 law was hastily passed and then superseded by a subsequent act before it went into operation. It was not a separate and distinct law, but only a portion of a general revenue act. This tax, however, was never collected, but was replaced by "An act to provide internal revenue to support the government and to pay interest on the public debt" **July 1, 1862** (*12 Stat.* 432) which imposed a tax on "*every person residing in the United States*" at three percent of annual incomes between $600 and $10,000 and five percent over $10,000. (Section 90) *This law was, therefore, the first federal income tax law to go into actual operation.* Significantly, the word "tax" in the 1861 statute was changed to "duty" in the 1862 statute. Here the word "duty" was not being used in its "constitutional sense," that being a tax on imports or a duty created by a voluntary act of the Citizen.

These "duties on incomes" were to be payable for each year thereafter until and including the year 1866. Everyone was required to make a return of his income on a list or schedule and, in case of neglect or refusal, the assessor was permitted to assess the income at his discretion. He could then increase the amount if he considered the return understated, but if anyone declared under oath or affirmation that his income did not amount to $600, he was exempt. Deductions were allowed for payment of other national, state or local taxes. At the time, the average annual earnings of an American family was far less than $600.

In medieval times, the word "duty" was used to describe a tax on a common person payable to the local land owner or nobility in exchange for the protection afforded by him. Constitutionally, a duty on an imported article is an indirect tax as the payment of the tax is avoidable. (One can choose not to purchase the article, thus avoiding the tax.) In medieval times this duty on a person was a direct tax on the person. What do you think happened to the common people in medieval England who refused to pay their protection duty to the local nobility? This happened from time to time and Civil War ensued. If the tax had been indirect, it would have been avoidable. It's unlikely anyone would fight a Civil War over an avoidable tax.

Obviously, in 1861 Congress' first thought was that the tax about to be levied on the earned income of individuals was a direct tax. After rethinking the issue, Congress probably realized that such a direct tax would be a "pain in the neck" as intended by the framers of the Constitution, and decided to rename it a "duty" and see if they could get away with it. Having read hundreds of pages of the Congressional Record, I can tell you that such an approach is often argued for by members of Congress.

It must be interjected here that, on September 24, 1862, President Lincoln officially declared martial law "within the United States." He declared that "during the existing insurrection and as a necessary measure for suppressing the same, all rebels and insurgents, their aiders and abettors within the United States, and all person[s] discouraging volunteer enlistments, resisting militia drafts, or guilty of any disloyal practice, affording aid and comfort to rebels against the authority of the United States, shall be subject to martial law and liable to trial and punishment by court-martial or military commissions." *(13 Stat. 730)* On January 1, 1863. Lincoln issued his *Emancipation Proclama-*

*tion* which he claimed was by "military necessity." *(12 Stat. 1268-9)* On September 15, 1863, Lincoln issued a proclamation suspending the writ of *habeas corpus* "throughout the United States." *(13 Stat. 734)* In all of these actions, Lincoln pretended to act "by virtue of the power vested in me as commander-in-chief of the army." So, under the pretense of preserving the Union, Lincoln unconstitutionally destroyed the fundamental principles of the Union; destroying both individual and States' rights. When the war ended, proclamations were issued by both Lincoln and Johnson declaring that the "said insurrection is at an end." Every proclamation issued during the war was specifically mentioned as revoked; with one glaring exception: Lincoln's "martial law proclamation" was never mentioned or revoked. *(14 Stat. 812, 813), (April 2, 1866) 814, 817 (August 20, 1866)* This set of unusual circumstances ought to cause us to apply minimal authority to the legislative history of the Civil War era in our effort to determine what is "constitutional income."[6]

> **It is true that during the war for the maintenance of the Union, an income tax was one of the measures resorted to in order to provide means for carrying on the great contest. It was freely submitted to by the people in the same spirit of patriotism, which marked their toleration of many exactions and deprivations inseparable from a state of war. Robert Sewell, The Income Tax: Is it Constitutional? 28 American Law Review 808 (1894).**

Next came "An act to provide internal revenue to support the government, to pay interest on the public debt, and for other purposes", [*13 Stat.* 223] of June 30, 1864. This Act increased the tax rate to five percent on annual incomes between $600 and $5,000; seven and a half percent between $5,000 and $10,000; and 10 percent of the excess over $10,000. The act made numerous changes in the administration of the law and extended its operation "until and including the year 1870 and no longer." The justification for a graduated income tax was to "cause those men who have large fortunes and derive therefrom large incomes, to pay a little amount in addition to the rate paid by the small men who exhaust nearly all of their income in the support of their families." Sen. Grimes, Cong. Globe, 38th Congress, 1st Session, 1874 (1864).

Significantly, the act provided in Section 182 that "wherever the word "state" is used in this act, it shall be construed to include the territories and the District of Columbia, where such construction is necessary to carry out the provision of this act." Before this law went into operation, however, it was amended by the act of March 3, 1865, (*13 Stat.* 469) which abolished the seven and a half percent rate and provided for a tax of 10 percent on all incomes over $5,000.

The Joint Resolution of July 4, 1864, (*13 Stat.* 417) imposed a special tax of five percent on the excess of incomes over $600 for the preceding year only for the purpose of raising bounties to be assessed October 1, 1864. As an additional tax, it effectively raised the rate of tax for income received in 1863 to eight percent on incomes between $600 and $10,000 and 10 percent on incomes over $10,000. "During the year ending July, 1864, the income tax proper yielded about $23 million." Seligman, *The Income Tax, supra* at 447.

"An act to declare the meaning of certain parts of the internal revenue act, approved June 30, 1864, and for other purposes" [*14 Stat.* 4] was passed on **March 10, 1866**. Section 3 of this act stated that "it shall be the duty of all *persons* required to make returns...to declare in such returns whether the several rates and amounts therein contained are stated according to their *values in legal tender currency*." And, significantly, Section 4 provided:

> **"That whenever the rates and amounts contained in the lists or returns aforesaid shall be stated in coined money, it shall be the duty of each assessor receiving the same to reduce such rates and amounts to their equivalent in legal tender currency, *according to the value of such coined money* in said currency at the time when and place where said lists or returns are receivable, and which value the said assessment shall determine. And the lists required by law to be furnished to collectors by assessors shall in**

**all cases contain the several amounts of taxes or duties assessed, estimated, or *valued in legal tender currency only.*"**

While today we may have more knowledge, back then people were obviously wiser as they understood the difference in the value of gold and silver coin versus paper money. Since the inception of the Federal Reserve System and the accepted use of paper money, the difference between "legal tender currency" and "coined money" is dramatic. At this writing, an ounce of gold is worth about 400 Federal Reserve Notes, while constitutionally an ounce of gold is worth $20.

Next followed "An act to reduce internal taxation and to amend 'An act to provide internal revenue to support the government, to pay interest on the public debt, and for other purposes' approved June 30, 1864" [*14 Stat.* 98] on **July 13, 1866**. This act specifically continued the principle of determining "values in legal tender currency or according to their values in coined money..." "[T]he lists required by law to be furnished to collectors by assessors shall in all cases contain the several amounts of taxes assessed, estimated, or valued in legal tender currency only."

By the end of 1866, with the Civil War over it was evident that the finances of the government would permit a reduction in taxation so, on **March 2, 1867**, "An act to amend existing laws relating to internal revenue and for other purposes," [*14 Stat.* 471] was passed which raised the exemption to $1,000 and imposed a uniform rate of five percent on all incomes over that sum until 1870.

Then on **July 14, 1870**, "An act to reduce internal taxes and for other purposes" [*16 Stat.* 256] was passed which reduced the tax to two and a half percent on amounts over $2000 for 1870 and 1871. Under the provisions of Section 6 of this act, the enforcement of the tax was limited to the years 1870 and 1871 and no longer. Thus, the tax expired and was not reenacted. Collections continued, however, until the close of 1873.

> **"Objections to its renewal are long, loud, and general throughout the country. Those who pay are the exception, those who do not pay are millions; the whole moral force of the law is a dead letter. The honest man makes a true return; the dishonest hides and covers all he can to avoid this obnoxious tax. It has no moral force. This tax is unequal, perjury-provoking and crime encouraging, because it is at war with the right of a person to keep private and regulate his business affairs and financial matters. Deception, fraud, and falsehood mark its progress everywhere in the process of collection. It creates curiosity, jealousy, and prejudice among the people. It makes the tax-gatherer a spy...The people demand that it shall not be renewed, but left to die a natural death and pass away into the future as pass away all the evils growing out of the Civil War." *Congressional Globe*, 41st Congress, 2d. Session, 3993 (1870).**

So said Mr. McCarthy speaking in Congress against the continuance of the tax.

Administration of the Civil War taxes fell upon the assessors of Internal Revenue under the general supervision of the Commissioner of Internal Revenue. Although the Commissioner gave instructions that the returns should not be made public, there was no law preventing publicity, and newspapers began publishing the lists until forbidden by the law of 1870.

Remarkably, it appears that out of an entire population of nearly 40 million, in 1868 returns were filed by only 250,000 people! Indeed, it has been estimated that the number of persons who filed returns in 1866 was a little over one percent of the population, while in later years it varied from two-thirds of one percent to less than one-fifth of one percent. Evidently, the administration of the Civil War income taxes was quite ineffective and it seems probable that not more than 25 percent of the actual taxable income of the country was reached. In 1866, when the income tax yielded about $73 million, the total internal revenue was about $311 million. Purportedly, the then acting Secretary of the Treasury believed this income tax to be unconstitutional and did little to enforce the collection of it.[7]

It is interesting to note that over this period of time, Congress was forever tinkering with the tax. It is as if there was no fundamental basis for determining the fair and just way to levy an income tax. Instead, Congress was probably wanting to appear to be "working on the problem."

Overall, there were few court challenges made against the Civil War income tax acts. Because of the war environment, Americans simply submitted to them as unavoidable patriotic necessities. Keep in mind that all of these acts were instituted as "war-time" measures when the government was operating under a form of martial law. Compared to today's "peacetime" tax rates, they were modest in their percentages. Among those who did, however, challenge the Civil War income taxes was one William M. Springer of Illinois. Mr. Springer was a lawyer and had been a member of Congress.

In June of 1866, the deputy assessor of internal revenue for the district of Illinois delivered to Mr. Springer notice that he had 10 days to make a return listing his income, gains and profits for the year 1865. Springer delivered a statement dated July 21, 1866, to the deputy, together with a written protest against the deputy's authority to demand the statement, on the ground that the acts of Congress were unconstitutional and void. (Acts of June 30, 1864 and March 3, 1865) The statement showed that Mr. Springer had income of $50,798[8] (apparently as an attorney) of which $4,799.80 was to be assessed as taxes due. Payment being refused, the collector served notice on Springer that, unless payment was made within 10 days, the law authorized distraint and sale of his *real estate*, which had not produced the "income," and a penalty of 10 percent. The property was seized and sold by (and to) the United States. On December 2, 1874, an action of ejectment was brought against Springer.

Springer's argument was that the tax assessed upon his income, gains and profits was a direct tax which was not apportioned among the several States as required by the Constitution. He also insisted that the rates be reduced to reflect the difference in value between "coined money" and "legal tender currency." Relying very heavily on the questionable *dicta* in *Hylton*, the Court held "that *direct taxes*, within the meaning of the Constitution, are only capitation taxes, as expressed in that instrument, and *taxes on real estate*; and that the tax of which the plaintiff in error complains is within the category of an excise or duty." *(Springer v. U.S., 102 U.S. 586, 602 [1880])* Of course, they appropriated his *real estate*, not his law practice! Unfortunately, Springer did not raise the issue as to the source of his income.

Springer's brief was a mini treatise on direct taxation citing many historical sources. It appears he was exhaustive in his review of the political economists although the Court found fault with his brief because he did not cite any sources from the State Conventions that ratified the Constitution.

After citing twenty-six authorities on political economy and taxation, Springer makes the following statement at page 11 in his brief:

> **"We have cited above all the authorities on Political Economy that we have been able to procure and examine. If there be any author on the subject entertaining views different from the above, we have been unable to find his work. We assert, then, without fear of successful contradiction, that all authors and writers on Political Economy and Taxation agree that A TAX UPON INCOMES IS A DIRECT TAX!"**

Springer's timing was bad though as the tax he was objecting to had already been repealed and the issue was not judicially ripe. It seemed that the court had its mind made up as it ignored Springer's "elaborate brief" and instead relied on *Hylton* and the other so called "direct tax" cases. We saw earlier that the *Hylton Case* was a staged case and should not carry any judicial weight. Like it or not, the right political environment is sometimes necessary to get the Supreme Court to rule correctly.

It appears also that Springer was railroaded as his property was seized by a summary proceeding and without a court judgement. Later when he did go to court he was denied the opportunity to contribute to the jury instructions.[9,10] Springer also made a fatal error by failing to claim he was paid a wage or a salary. Instead he stipulated that he had "profits in any trade or vocation from which income is actually derived."

## Confederate Income Taxes

On August 19, 1861, a direct tax of one-half of one percent was levied upon all property by the Confederate Congress. This tax would later evolve into an income tax. Collection of these sums was left to the States, but instead of levying the tax, all the States, except Texas and South Carolina, borrowed the money by issuing bonds and treasury notes. Although the Confederate Constitution contained a provision as to direct taxes analogous to that found in the Constitution for the United States, President Davis ruled in 1861 that the provision regarding apportionment could be dispensed with until the war ended and a census taken. (See his message to Congress, December, 1863).

Because this direct tax was very unpopular, the Confederate Congress modified the law and allowed for payment of the taxes in kind. Thus farmers paid the tax in agriculture products, manufactures paid with products needed by the government and the army, and so on. As this was a tax on gross revenue, the Confederate Congress considered it a direct tax.

On April 24, 1863, the Confederate Congress passed a general taxing act which consisted of an eight percent tax on property; license taxes; an income tax payable in cash; and an income tax payable in kind. These taxes were to be collected for two years beginning in 1864. The income tax rates varied up to 15 percent. Every *person* was required to make a return and, if the assessor was dissatisfied, he was to select "one disinterested citizen in the vicinage as a referee," the taxpayer to select another, and these two to call a third. The findings of a majority of these referees were to be conclusive. Later the rates increased with the top rate being 25 percent.

In addition to this income tax proper, farmers were to pay one-tenth of their produce in kind. These "taxes in kind," expected to obtain large quantities of bacon, corn, fodder and other supplies needed by the army, were very unpopular, especially in North Carolina, where numerous public meetings were held to protest against the discrimination which imposed a heavy burden on the farmer while others were permitted to pay their taxes in depreciated currency. (The *Income Tax, supra*, 482 *et seq*.) Thus the Confederate Government considered an income tax to be a direct tax. Evidently the Confederacy was more honest on the issue of taxation than the Union.

## The Unconstitutional Tax Law:

### The Act of 1894

From 1872 to 1894 there was no federal income tax in America; the government was content to rely upon tariffs and excises during this time of peace. A great decline in prices on agricultural commodities during the beginning of the nineties and the steady growth of large fortunes in the Eastern industrial and financial centers, as well as the appearance of new concentrations, or combinations, of capital known as "trusts," (monopolies), led to increasing political unrest. Suspicion of these aggregations of capital engendered a movement which resulted in the Sherman Anti-Trust Act of 1890. It was a time of growing conflict between "capital" and "labor."

Farmers, who represented a large percentage of the population, became increasingly unhappy with the tariff laws. Falling agricultural prices were attributed to the appreciation of gold, which led to the "free-silver" movement. The farmers believed that without the protective tariffs, they could obtain their necessities more cheaply; and that it was the protected manufacturers of the East who were responsible for the falling prices of agricultural products. As a result, they began to disclaim the policy of protective tariffs and became more favorably inclined to the idea of an income tax. "Despite the existence of the income tax as an issue, most of the political fury of the southern and western populists was devoted to monetarist (free-silver, Greenback party) movements rather than to fiscal reforms such as the income tax."[11]

Throughout the country, the general property tax levied at the state and local level had become almost exclusively a real property tax. The rich urban investors, the wealthy businessmen and the professional classes were escaping taxation almost entirely as most of their wealth was in personal property, stocks, bonds and bank accounts. In general, such assets were difficult to find and assess by the taxman. Thus, the weight of state and local taxation was falling more and more upon the small farmer, who was unable to shift the tax burden to the community at large. Such a taxing system was unequal in its burdens for the support of government. On the contrary, it appeared to benefit the very classes responsible for falling agricultural prices. Thus, the complaints of the farmers became louder and more numerous. Any attempt at revenue reform was met with stiff resistance.

The inequality and injustice of the tariff system, and the movement toward "free-silver," led to President Cleveland's Democratic victory in 1892. Facing budget deficits, Cleveland sent a message to Congress in December, 1893, suggesting an income tax on the population at large and also on corporate incomes. In referring to the tariff bill he said: "The committee (House Ways and Means), after full consideration and to provide against the temporary deficiency which may exist, before the business of the country adjusts itself to the new tariff schedules, has wisely embraced in its plan a few additional internal revenue taxes, including a small tax upon incomes derived from certain corporate investments."

On January 24, 1894, Mr. McMillan of Tennessee introduced a bill (H.R. 5442), "to impose a tax on *corporate and individual incomes*, to increase the tax on distilled spirits and for other purposes." This bill closely followed the construction of the Civil War income tax statutes.

The new income tax law was passed by Congress on August 28, 1894. "An act to reduce taxation, to provide revenue for the government, and for other purposes" [*28 Stat.* 509]. This provided for an income tax of two percent on the annual "*gains, profits*, and income received in the preceding calendar year by *every citizen of the United States*, whether residing at home or abroad, and every person residing therein, whether said gains, profits, or income be derived from any kind of property, rents, interest, dividends, or salaries, or from any profession, trade, employment, or vocation carried on in the United States or elsewhere, or from any other source whatever..." in excess of $4,000, including the incomes of all *corporations, companies and associations other than partnerships*.

In fixing the exemption at $4,000, the tax applied only to a small number of comparatively wealthy people. Many thought this tax drew a dividing line at those earning $4,000, and, therefore, those earning that amount or more became a class apart from the rest of the nation. In addition, the $4,000 exemption did not apply to corporations.

Because the tax applied to all personal property acquired by gift or inheritance, other objections were raised immediately on the basis that (1) inheritances are otherwise taxed in many States, (2) gifts and inheritances are irregular and, therefore, not properly income, and (3) the man who inherited real estate at the value of $100,000 would be free of the tax, while the man who inherited the same amount in personal property would have to pay $2,000 in taxes.

In addition, the law provided no exemption for corporate stock which might be owned by a state or municipality; the law did not exempt the salaries of federal judges or the President; the tax on salaries of government officials was collected at the source for the current year, while all other persons were paying upon the income received in the preceding year; and, there was no distinction between earned and unearned income. "Earned income" is that income received on account of labor, it is the bi-weekly paycheck; "unearned income" is that income derived from investments-dividends, interest, winnings, capital gains, etc.

The Income Tax Act of 1894 was challenged by Charles Pollock, of Massachusetts, who brought an action against the Farmer's Loan and Trust Company. Mr. Pollock, holder of ten shares of the capital stock of said company with a value exceeding $5,000, alleged he had brought suit on his own behalf, and as a representative of the other stockholders. He complained that the company was about to pay a tax of two percent of its net profits and that said payment would diminish the assets of the company and, therefore, lessen the dividends on the shares. He further alleged that the law was unconstitutional for several reasons, including the fact that the income of the Trust company was, in part, from real estate and from stocks and bonds of the States, counties and municipalities. And, significantly, he argued that it was an unapportioned direct tax.

Two other cases were joined and argued with Pollock, *Moore v. Miller*, 5 App. D.C. 413 and *Hyde v. Continental Trust Co.*, (no cite). Because the United States was not a party to the suits, it was reduced to filing briefs *amicus curiae*, friend of the court. In its argument, the government relied on *Hylton* regarding the directness of the tax and focused on the question of uniformity. "The opponents of the tax were not content to limit direct taxes to taxes on land and capitation taxes. They considered a tax on personal property a direct tax and again, the taxation of income from personal property to be tantamount to taxing the personal property."[12] Stating the premise of his argument in his opening paragraph, Joseph H. Choate, counsel for the plaintiff-appellants, said "The act of Congress which we are impugning before you is communistic in its purpose and tendencies..." (*Pollock*, 157 U.S. at 532) The briefs in *Pollock* amounted to a treatise on taxation. The entire Transcript of Record in the bound records for both Pollock cases amounts to approximately 1,450 pages.

The Court's decision, delivered by Chief Justice Fuller on April 8, 1895, held that a tax on rents or income from real estate is a direct tax. In addition, a tax upon income derived from the interest on bonds issued by municipal corporations is a tax upon the power of the State and its instrumentalities to borrow money and is, therefore, unconstitutional. The Court remained evenly divided, however, "as to whether a tax upon income from personal property was direct; and as to whether any part of the tax, if not considered as a direct tax, was invalid for want of uniformity."[13] Significantly, the Court refused to comment "on so much of it [the tax] as bears on gains or profits from business, privileges, or employments, in view of the instances in which taxation on business, privileges, or employments has *assumed the guise of an excise tax* and had been sustained as such." (id. 635) *Pollock*, therefore, is no authority for a tax levied upon a wage earner, as this issue is without the scope of the *Pollock Case*.

Ten days later a petition for rehearing was filed. During the first hearing there was a vacancy on the bench and the parties argued that a rehearing by a full bench was appropriate on such an important issue. The petition was granted and, on May 20, 1895, by a bare majority of one (5-4), the Court ruled that the entire income tax law was unconstitutional. The Court held that:

> **"1. Taxes on real estate or the rents and income from real estate are direct taxes;**
>
> **2. Taxes on personal property or the income of personal property are also direct taxes;**

**3. The tax imposed by the Act of 1894, inasmuch as it falls upon the income of real and personal property, being a direct tax within the meaning of the Constitution, was unconstitutional and void because it was not apportioned according to representation among the several States, all these sections, constituting one entire scheme of taxation, are necessarily invalid." Pollock v. Farmers' Loan and Trust, 157 U.S. 429 (1894), reh. 158 U.S. 601, 637 (1895).**

**"The decision aroused strong feelings when it was announced. The opponents of the tax naturally believed that the country had been saved from socialism or worse, while the supporters of the tax were more resentful than ever of the wealth and power of the privileged few." The American Journal of Tax Policy, supra at Vol. 2, 240 (1983).**

On June 13, 1898, "An Act to provide ways and means to meet war expenditures, and for other purposes" was passed to raise funds for the Spanish-American War. [*30 Stat. 448*] "[S]pecial taxes" were "imposed annually" on bankers, brokers, tobacco, cigars, cigarettes, snuff, tobacco dealers and manufacturers, medicines, preparations, mixed flour and tea. In addition, "excise taxes" were imposed upon those engaged in refining petroleum and sugar; and, "stamp" taxes were imposed on "bonds, debentures, certificates of stock and indebtedness, documents [and] instruments..." Section 29 imposed an inheritance tax upon "legacies and distributive shares of personal property over $10,000." A landmark case regarding this tax was *Spreckels Sugar v. McClain.* We will quote from this case later.

## The Corporate Tax Act of 1909

In response to the increasing demands of the American people for an income tax, on August 5, 1909 Congress passed "An act to provide revenue, equalize duties, and encourage the industries of the

United States, and for other purposes" [*36 Stat.* 112] in response to the Supreme Court's *Pollock* decision. This act provided that certain corporations, joint stock companies and insurance companies would be "subject to pay annually a special *excise tax* with respect to the *carrying on or doing business*....equivalent to one per centum upon the entire net income over and above five thousand dollars received by it from all sources during the year." (Emphasis added.)

Religious, charitable and educational associations were exempt from the tax. So were mutual savings banks. Moreover, deductions were allowed for "ordinary and necessary expenses," all uncompensated losses, interest paid on indebtedness, national, state and foreign taxes paid and dividends received from other taxed companies. Provision was also made that the tax returns, corrected or not, "shall constitute public records and be open to inspection as such." Finally, jurisdiction was "conferred upon the circuit and district courts of the United States...to compel attendance, production of books, and testimony by appropriate process" for "any person summoned" "to appear."

This law was historic and unique in the annals of fiscal experiments. No other nation had before attempted to levy a similar tax wholly and exclusively on incorporated bodies. This is probably because the taxation authority of our Constitution is unique in the world in that it has divided all taxes into either direct or indirect taxes subject to regulating rules. In addition, the history of this law presents many peculiar features and curious anomalies.

It might be supposed that, being a revenue bill, it would necessarily originate in the House of Representatives as required by the Constitution. However, it not only did *not* originate in the House, but was never even before the House for consideration, discussion or vote! It was one of the last of numerous amendments tacked on to the voluminous Tariff Act. "...[T]he corporation excise was appended to the tariff bill by a large majority and the entire bill passed the Senate by a substantial majority."

> **"The bill was then returned to the Senate-House Conference Committee. There was considerable discussion of the fact that the corporation excise-a dramatic departure in taxation-had been added to the bill in the Senate and had never been discussed in the House. [The *Pollock* case] held that a tax imposed on property by reason of the taxpayer's ownership of it was unconstitutional unless apportioned among the several States, while the corporate excise tax was imposed only upon carrying on business in a corporate form, said to be a privilege. As Randolph Paul put it, 'Thus did a few words change a tax upon income into a tax on something else measured by income.'" The American Journal of Tax Policy, *supra* at 249.**

It is difficult to understand how an act which purports to "encourage the industries of the United States" would specifically single out corporations for special taxation. And, though it might be considered to be an "income tax," lawyers have most strenuously claimed that it is *not an income tax, but is an excise tax on the privilege of doing business in a corporate capacity, measured by income*. Indeed, it was President Taft, in his special message to Congress on June 16, 1909, who stated the following:

> **"The decision in the Pollock case left power in the National Government to levy an *excise tax* which accomplishes the same purpose, as a corporation income tax, but is free from certain objections urged to the proposed income tax measure. I, therefore, recommend an amendment to the tariff bill imposing upon all corporations and joint stock companies for profit, except National banks (otherwise taxed) savings banks and savings and loan associations, an excise tax measured by two per cent on the net income of such corporations. *This is an excise tax upon the privilege of doing business as an artificial entity* and of freedom from a general partnership liability enjoyed by those who own the stock." (Emphasis added) 44 Cong. Rec. 3344 (1909).**

The constitutionality of the law was immediately challenged in court when several cases were consolidated under the heading of *Flint v. Stone Tracy Company*. In this case, decided March 1, 1911, the Supreme Court held that:

> **"...the Corporation Tax, as imposed by Congress in the Tariff Act of 1909, *is not a direct tax but an excise*; it does not fall within the apportionment clause of the Constitution; but is within, and complies with, the provision for uniformity throughout the United States; *it is an excise on the privilege of doing business in the corporate capacity...*" (Emphasis added) Flint v. Stone Tracy Company, 220 U.S. 107, 108 (1911).**

## Problems with interpretation of the historical record

The current tax laws are based upon the Internal Revenue Act of 1954 as amended. Yet, to date, there is no statutory definition of the word "income" either in the Internal Revenue Code or the Courts. Neither the courts nor the executive branch have authority to define any word used in the Constitution. Only the People may define such a word. Even though there is a well-settled legal definition of "income" as net income from business, investment or corporate earnings, there remains doubt and confusion as to what is taxable. Clearly, there are many difficult problems associated with determining if you have any "income." Court decisions make it clear that, in order to have income, there must be an element of gain. The Code implies that taxable income is net income; that is, one must first deduct certain allowable expenses to end with net income. For the individual, those deductions are statutory; for the corporate taxpayer, there are business deductions and credits allowable in determining net income. Herein lies what appears to be a discriminatory nature of the modern tax system and the difficulty in determining if one has "taxable income."

In combining both individuals and corporations in the same tax code, there appears to be a built-in discrimination. The courts rule that a tax on business enterprises is an indirect excise on the privilege of doing business as an artificial entity. But, when ruling on cases involving individual wage earners, some courts are quick to rule that the tax is a direct tax, while other courts say it is an excise tax. It can't be both at the same time! And, while the wage earner exists by right and can exercise his 5th Amendment right in refusing to produce books or records; the corporate taxpayer exists by privilege and has no such rights and must, therefore, produce the corporate books or records. Evidently, a tax on a privilege is inherently an indirect tax, while a tax on a right is a direct tax.

In addition, a corporation is considered to be a legal "person," as the tax is imposed upon every "citizen of the United States" wherever located.[14] And, finally, there is the distinction between areas over which the Congress enjoys exclusive jurisdiction (where constitutional limitations do not apply) and the several States of the Union (where constitutional limitations of apportionment and uniformity continue to apply). But what about the "body politic" that exists in corporate form overlaying the several States of the Union? And why are the statutes and regulations so voluminous and confusing, needing many tens of thousands of pages of manuals, Treasury Decisions, and commentary to explain them? You'll know why by the end of this book.

Among the states which purportedly ratified the 16th Amendment, at least four of them have overturned state income taxation on the basis that earning a living is a fundamental right which cannot be taxed. In Washington state the Supreme Court held that "income is property" and, therefore, a tax on income is a tax upon property and is not an excise. The Washington Supreme Court further ruled, a graduated income tax is unconstitutional because it is not uniform.[15] In Oregon the Supreme Court also concluded that income is property and that the individual, unlike corporations, cannot be taxed for the mere privilege of existing and owning property, which are natural rights.[16] In Tennessee the Supreme Court held that the "right to receive income or earnings is a right belonging to every person, and realization and receipt of income isn't a "privilege" that can be taxed."[17] In Arkansas, the Supreme Court held that the State cannot tax occupations of a common right.[18] And in a Mississippi case the court ruled that a privilege tax did not apply to an unlicensed plumber.[19]

Apparently, these States hold the view that income, for purposes of taxation, is to be defined as it was in stock dividend case of *Eisner v. Macomber*; namely, profit or gain which is derived from capital, labor, or both combined. This understanding conforms to that of the United States Supreme Court in *Merchants' Loan and Trust Co. v. Smietanka* (255 U.S. 509, 519; pg 5, *supra)* where the Court stated that "there would seem to be no room to doubt that the word [income] must be given the same meaning in all of the Income Tax Acts of Congress that was given to it in the Corporation Excise Tax Act and what that meaning is has now become definitely settled by decisions of this court." The meaning of the word "income" in the Corporation Excise Tax Act was, as determined by *Eisner*, of course, profit or gain resulting from business or corporate activities.

It must be remembered that the same high Court has stated:

> **"that there is a clear distinction...between an individual and a corporation..." "The individual may stand upon his constitutional rights as a citizen. He is entitled to carry on his private business in his own way. His power to contract is unlimited. He owes no duty to the State or his neighbors to divulge his business, or to open his doors to investigation, so far as it may tend to incriminate him. He owes no such duty to the State, since he receives nothing therefrom, beyond the protection of his life and property. His rights are such as existed by the law of the land long antecedent to the organization of the State, and can only be taken from him by due process of law, in accordance with the Constitution." "He owes nothing to the public so long as he does not trespass upon their rights." Hale v. Henkel, 201 U.S. 43, 74 (1905).**

However, the Supreme Court has also ruled that he who accepts a benefit can not assert his rights.

As late as 1943, Representative Carlson, in discussing the Individual Income Tax Collection Act of 1943, stated that the "sole test of taxability under [the 1909] act was whether a corporation was engaged in business." He opined that the provisions of that act "with the approval of the Supreme Court *might have been* extended to individuals engaged in business. In that way investment income of most individuals as well as of corporations *could doubtless have been* brought under the terms of the act. And the field of income *could have been* completely covered by applying the principle that the ownership and management of investment property is an activity or privilege with respect to which Congress may impose an excise." He goes on to say that the 16th Amendment "made it possible to bring investment income within the scope of the general income-tax law, but *did not change the character of the tax*. It is still fundamentally an excise or duty with respect to the privilege of receiving passive income which is only possible under the protection of civil government.

> **"The income tax is, therefore, not a tax on income as such. It is an excise tax with respect to certain activities and privileges which is measured by reference to the income which they produce. The income is not the subject of the tax: it is the basis for determining the amount of tax" House Congressional Record, March 27, 1943, p. 2580.**

And, finally, we have the eloquent dissent of Mr. Justice J. Train in *Penn Mutual Indemnity Co. v. C.I.R.*, 32 T.C. 653 (1959) wherein he says the "principle of the [*Eisner v. Macomber*] case is still in effect...And, so long as such principle continues in force, it should be followed and applied by this Court." (at 675) "...[T]he 16th Amendment in some fashion prohibits Congress from levying an income tax on anything which is not income..." (at 677) "A tax imposed on that which is not income is nonetheless valid *unless it is an unapportioned direct tax*. Thus, the key question is whether the tax is direct or indirect." (at 678) "...[I]ncome within the meaning of the 16th Amendment means gain, and, conversely, that when there is no gain there is no income." (at 680) "That there cannot be 'income' without 'gain' accords with the common understanding of the term, a test of construction which is particularly appropriate in our system of a self-assessed Federal income tax." (at 681) "'The Amendment allows a tax 'on income' without apportionment, but an unapportioned direct tax on anything that is not income would still, under the rule of the *Pollock* case, be unconstitutional.' *Commissioner v. Obear-Nester Glass Co.*, 217 F.2d. 56 (1954)." (at 689) *"However, the 16th Amendment did not repeal the constitutional requirement as to direct taxes."* "Thus, the *Pollock* decision did not declare that *any* income tax would be a direct tax but limited its decision on this point to taxes on income from real estate and taxes on income from invested personal property."

> **"The Supreme Court of the United States has thus held that certain kinds of income taxes are indirect, and that still other kinds of income taxes are direct, and that still other kinds of income taxes are invalid, irrespective of whether they are direct or indirect. E.R.A. Seligman, The Income Tax Amendment, 25 Political Science Quarterly 193, 197 (1910).**

The Court in *Pollock* specifically declared, at page 635: "We...have not commented on so much of [the act] as bears on gains or profits from business, privileges, or employments, in view of the instances in which taxation on business, privileges, or employments has assumed the guise of an excise tax and then been sustained as such." Twenty one years later in the *Brushaber v. Union Pacific R.R. Co.*, the Supreme Court said at 16, "[T]axation on income was in its nature an excise entitled to be enforced as such unless and until it was concluded that to enforce it would amount to accomplishing the result which the requirement as to apportionment of direct taxation was adopted to prevent, in which case the duty would arise to disregard form and consider substance alone, and hence subject the tax to the regulation as to apportionment which otherwise as an excise would not apply to it..." Going back to *Pollock*, the court took a shot at *Hylton:* "it is not a logical argument to say that a particular tax cannot be construed to be direct simply because it may be impractical to impose it by apportionment." But we will see in Chapter 9 that though you do not have "constitutional income" you might unknowingly opt to have "statutory taxable income" and thereby a legal duty to pay an income tax on it. Of course this could only be true if you waived your constitutional rights.

A historical study of "income" taxation would not be complete without mention of the intimate relationships between it, money and war. Among the issues confronting the Nation during the Civil War, was that of banking and money. Lincoln's successor to the Presidency, Andrew Johnson, was impeached because of his refusal to allow the establishment of a central bank in America. Lincoln, himself, had issued "Greenback" dollars (U.S. Notes) rather than borrow "money" from the central bankers. Some people think this was why he was assassinated. President Kennedy was another president who attempted to issue a currency, silver certificates, not to the liking of the bankers.

Among Mr. Springer's arguments (*supra)* at court was the illegitimacy of the depreciating value of "legal tender" notes against "specie," gold and silver coin. Under the Constitution (Article I, Section 10), No State shall make any Thing but gold and silver coin a legal tender in the payment of debts. Mr. Springer did not appreciate being forced to accept depreciating "Greenbacks" and then expected to pay an "income" tax on his "good fortune!"

In concluding their examination of the "Origins of the Income Tax," Bernhard Grossfeldt and James D. Bryce, authors of the *American Journal of Tax Policy*, *supra*, found that an "examination of the history of the income tax in three of the leading nations of the world (England, Germany and America) shows a number of interesting parallels. For example, in all three nations, the income tax was first imposed during a major war in which the nation's survival was endangered. Perhaps war is the father of everything, as Heracleitas says." (pg. 250)

"In each case, the first income tax was repealed shortly after the end of the war that had caused its imposition. But the income tax, having shown its ability to raise enormous amounts of revenue during war times, was needed later in peace time by the increasing demands of *modern central governments*." (pg. 250) The authors then discreetly suggest that among the "lessons" of the history of the income tax, one might consider "the effect of social theorists who seek to use the income tax as a redistributive measure." (pg. 251)

The same year that the Federal Reserve System was established (1913), the first modern "Income Tax Act" was passed in America. And, immediately, World War I was declared. This war created more debt, increased taxation and culminated in the new League of Nations. But the effort to establish a League of Nations failed. Then along came World War II which overcame this opposition and established the New World Order's United Nations. War creates debt; debt creates "money"; "money" creates taxes; taxes finance war. It is a vicious circle. Here's the punch line: When the Federal Reserve System prints its "loan" to America, it does not print the "money" needed to pay the interest on the loan at the end of the "year." In agreeing to pay interest on the "national debt," the government has agreed to do something it *cannot* do! The "money" to pay the interest simply does not exist; hence, the need for refinancing year after year!

The mechanics of our fiat money system is such that money is created only when it is borrowed into existance. In other words, when a load agreement is signed (ie. the promissory note) the money to fund the loan is created out of thin air, subject only to certain ratios as to the amount of money that can be created.

Since all money is debt, and all debt needs to be serviced with an interest payment, where does the new money come from to service the interest payments on the old money? It comes from new debt. The level of debt for the entire system must therefore increase each year. Mathematically, there is no way out of this system.

The debt pyramid will increase until we all collectively reach our debt capacity. When the debt pyramid can no longer increase in size, it will implode quickly. In a tight economy, bankruptcy can be contagious. It creates a domino effect. Any asset based on debt will deflate in value. Much wealth will vaporize.

What the income tax ultimately does is harvest money out of the monetary system, which allows the debt machinery to operate at a faster speed without creating unbearable inflation. The long term effect is to smother our people, our economy and our country in an artificial debt using fiat money creating a form of hi-tech slavery unrecognized by the average person. But later in this book we will see that there is also a fitting place for an income tax that is balanced and useful for the legitimate support of government.

Read on.

*This cartoon, "Revenue Reform" by George Coffin, from the period 1880-1900, shows the nation stopped in any attempt to make changes in the funding of government.*

# Chapter 3
## Why Was an Income Tax Necessary?

**"We favor an income tax as part of our revenue system, and we urge the submission of a constitutional amendment specifically authorizing Congress to levy and collect a tax upon individual and corporate incomes, to the end that wealth may bear its proportionate share of the burdens of the Federal Government."**

***—Democrat Party Presidential Platform, 1908***

Have you ever noticed how some people seem to be born into their political party, not ever having questioned what they believe or where they belong? While the phenomenon occurs in both the Democrat and Republican camps, it is particularly true of the Democrats. I think the root cause of this propensity on the part of Democrats has to do with the issue of the protective tariffs around the turn of the last century. We will see in this chapter how the Republican Party was manipulating the American people into thinking that the high tariffs were healthy for our economy, when in fact what the tariffs really did was to pour money into the bank accounts of those who were able to monopolize American industry under tariff protection.

One hundred years ago it was the Republicans who were the big spenders and the Democrats were the defenders of the Constitution. Even though the roles are somewhat switched today, this deep rooted mistrust of the Republicans prevents many conservative people from leaving the Democrat party as they can't seem to stomach the idea of being a Republican. You will understand by the end of this chapter how this mistrust of the Republican Party was justified.

Prior to the income tax system of revenue generation for our national government, most of the monies collected in taxes for the support of government came from tariffs collected on imported goods. In the year 1910, the budget for the national government was $1,042,000,000. That's right, one billion dollars. You need to remember this was before the private Federal Reserve System (which isn't federal and has no reserves) when the dollar was backed by gold, and mortal man had yet to figure out how to inflate a gold-backed currency. Also at this time there had been little success in breaking up the business monopolies that controlled much of American industry and America was involved in a struggle between the super rich and those who toiled for a living. Others will remember this time as a struggle between capital and labor.

Labor thought it was going to level the playing field with an income tax which would tax only the nation's wealthy. That was the plan, but today we all know the income tax has not worked out this way. This is evidenced by the fact that the large corporations, family trusts and foundations pay little or no tax while the middle class is drowning in taxation. Nothing has changed. The reality was that in 1909 the very rich, with help of Republican Senator Aldrich of Rhode Island, gave in to this pressure, but did so in such a way that the entire income tax issue could later be manipulated to protect that which was supposed to be taxed—accumulated wealth—while re-imposing the tax burden on those who where already overtaxed under the tariff system and who were to get relief by the passage of the 16th Amendment. By the time you finish this book you will understand how this happened. You will also understand that the lion's share of the income taxes collected by the IRS is done so by usurpation and not by the authority of **We the People**.

The purpose of the "protective tariff" was to protect American jobs from cheap foreign imports. The theory was such that if we placed a tariff on imported goods, then American companies could more easily compete, would sell more domestically made goods, and thereby be able to employ more people and pay them a higher wage. This was the theory. But the reality was far different.

The following is a quote from the Congressional Record of the year 1909. The issue being debated in the United States Senate was the income tax.

> **Mr. HEFLIN. "The great body of consumers struggling for the "wherewith" to buy the simple necessities of life are taxed, and heavily taxed, by this Aldrich bill, not only to raise revenues to meet the extravagant expenditures of the Republican Party, but taxed for the benefit of those who profit by the Republican policy of high protection - those who furnish the Republicans with campaign funds with which to corrupt the ballot box and debauch American manhood. (Applause on Democratic side.)**
>
> **When you, by tariff taxation, lay heavy burdens upon the things that a man needs and must have to make his wife and children comfortable and happy, you are working injury to this man and his family - you are standing between them and a worthy existence, and you are committing a crime against the American home.**
>
> **Mr. Speaker, I want someone on that side of the House to tell me the difference between the bold robber who holds you up on the highway and robs you of your money, and the government that does the bidding of a band of robbers who prescribe the conditions by which**

> **you shall come and surrender your money? I will tell you the difference: One takes his chances and runs the risk of losing his own life in his efforts to rob others, while the other gang uses the governmental machinery to hold up and plunder the citizen and in the name of law commits its crime against humanity.**
>
> **Their patriotism is measured by the size of the fortunes that you permit them to filch from the American consumers. The stars on the flag resemble dollar marks to them, and the stripes represent the special favors that they enjoy at the hands of a government controlled by the Republican Party.**
>
> **The Republican Party regards the presence of a few money kings as evidence of American's prosperity; but not so. These are the product of governmental favoritism, the creatures of unjust tariff taxation. The laws that made them millionaires have robbed millions of people of the necessities of life." 44 Cong. Rec. 4421 (1909).**
>
> **Mr. SULZER. "Mr. Chairman, all legislation [the protective tariff] bestowing special benefits on the few is unjust and against the masses and for the classes. It has gone on until less than 8 per cent of the people won more than two-thirds of all wealth of our country. It has been truly said that monarchies are destroyed by poverty and republics by wealth. If the greatest Republic the world has ever seen is destroyed, it will fall by this vicious system of robbing the many for the benefit of the few." 44 Cong. Rec. 3761 (1909).**

What had happened with the protective tariff was that the tariffs were set much higher than what was needed to protect American jobs. Instead the tariffs were used to keep the cost of American and foreign goods high such that those who owned the manufacturing companies could receive a windfall profit. Those American businessmen who managed to benefit financially from the high tariff were positioned to buy up any smaller competitors within their industries, thus stifling domestic competition. Great business monopolies were being created and American society was being transformed into a class society of the super rich and everybody else. This sad state of affairs was no secret to anyone.

> **Mr. HEFLIN. "The Aldrich bill strikes hard the necessities of life all along the line, and if gentlemen here think that the people are ignorant of what you are doing you will find in the next election that you are mistaken.**
>
> **Mr. Speaker, the States wisely and justly provided that every taxpayer shall know the exact amount of taxes that he pays every year - taxes on money loaned or hoarded, so much on personal property and so much on real estate. The taxpayer knows, as he has a right to know, just how much [in] taxes he is required to pay to the city, county, and state government. But, Mr. Speaker, under your mysterious tariff-tax law, you tax the citizen, and you refuse to let him know just how much he is taxed by the Federal Government. The tariff tax is hid in the price of the things that he must buy, and at the end of the year he knows that the cost of living has increased; but he does not know how much you have taxed him under the system of a high protective tariff. This is wrong, and you should amend this tariff bill now,...so that the consumer may know as he buys the necessities of life what the tariff tax is, and at the end of the year he will know the amount of the tariff tax that you have compelled him to pay." 44 Cong. Rec. 4420 (1909).**

With monopolies in place and a high protective tariff to keep foreign competition out, the wealth class of businessmen who didn't work but lived off "incomes" were in effect placing a tax on the goods they sold. This "tax" was paid by the American people in the form of higher profits. The tax was on consumption. It was a tax on the necessities of life. But government didn't benefit from the tax; American businessmen did. Quoting again from the Congressional Record:

> **Mr. BYRD. "Its very name (protective tariff) means inequality of tax burden. It means a tax upon consumption and not upon wealth, upon what one eats and wears and not upon his property; it means that the citizen who can scarcely provide food and raiment for his wife and children contributes as much or more to the support of the Government as does the multimillionaire, and it means that the consumer is not only taxed for the support of his country, but is compelled to contribute five times more to swell the fortunes of millionaire manufacturers and trust manipulators." 44 Cong. Rec. 4415-6 (1909).**

The tariff was so high that the percentage of foreign goods sold in America represented only five percent, or one twentieth of the total goods sold. With such a low level of imports, the government would not be collecting much in the way of imposts (custom fees), and the tariff was, therefore, not maximizing the amount of revenue the government was collecting. The people realized the purpose of the tariff was not to raise revenue for the support of government, but was to make the friends of the Republican members of Congress rich. The founding fathers and **We the People** gave Congress the power of taxation to run the government and to protect life, liberty and the pursuit of happiness. Instead, Congress was using the tariff to insure that their businessmen friends got rich and had ample money left over to help them get re-elected. Sound familiar? Congress can do such things only because the People let them.

Today we have the same problem, yet the script is different. Instead Congress now has entrapped the poor and the unproductive in a web of government entitlements. Instead of depending on the rich to get reelected, they depend on the poor whose vote they have purchased by taxing everyone else. Taxes are again not collected for the running of government, but instead to buy votes and political power. Welfare, food stamps, medicare, social security, education, the National Endowment for the Arts, these expenditures are not for the essential functions of government. And just as the protective tariff was a hidden tax, today's income tax is hidden in the sense that the people never actually take possession of the money they pay in taxes. Instead it is taken from them after they earn it, but before they are paid. Government knows that government can maximize its revenue if it can take money from the citizen undetected. The same complaint was made of the tariff as the amount of the tax was hidden in the cost of goods sold.

At this time there were few barriers to the monopolization of American industry. The Sherman Anti-Trust Act was passed in 1890 but had yet to take its full effect. Great combinations of companies were organized into trusts or holding corporations. These represented the monopolization of individual industries. With high tariffs to keep out foreign competition and with the ability to control an entire industry, domestic prices could be set much higher than that necessary to return a reasonable profit. American businessmen, whose friends were the Republicans in Congress, were getting extremely rich and the American people knew it.

> **Mr. CUMMINS. "In the same way, our farmers found that the great creamery companies of the land were extorting from them unfair profits and paying them unfair prices for their products. So they organized mutual creamery companies; and all over the State such companies are to be found. Again, we discovered that the elevator companies, in combination with the railways, had monopolized the business of buying grain, and that our farmers were at the mercy of the companies which actually transported their product to the market. Therefore they organized mutual elevator companies." 44 Conc. Rec. 4039 (1909).**

Every time an American citizen bought a pound of sugar, a pair of shoes, or a wool sweater they paid what amounted to a punitive tax. Only five percent of the time the tax went to support of government because only five percent of the time it was a foreign article purchased on which a custom duty was collected. The other 95 percent of the time, the tariff surcharge was collected by the American businessman because of his ability to charge higher prices, thanks to the tariff and the monopolization of industries. In terms of dollars, it was estimated that 20% of the tariff premium went to the support of government and 80% of the tariff premium went into the pockets of American businessmen. The tariffs amounted to a tax placed on the American people not by government, but by business. I'd be mad, too.

According to Senator Borah of Idaho, himself a Republican:

> **"Mr. Carnegie told us time out of mind that he could not run his [steel] mills or manufacturing plants without the protection which he demanded. In view of the fact that he did run his mills after the protection was given, and accumulated wealth which he will not live long enough to distribute, it seems to me that the Republican Party did make Mr. Carnegie."**

> **Mr. JAMES. "Who is prepared to defend a system of taxation that requires a hod carrier, who for eight long hours each day winds his way to the dizzy heights of a lofty building with his load of mortar or brick, to pay as much to support this great Republic as John D. Rockefeller, whose fortune is so great that it staggers the imagination to contemplate it and whose property is in every city and state in the Republic and upon every sea protected by our flag...How men can defend a system of taxation in a republic which requires of the poor all of its taxes and exempts the rich absolutely I am totally unable to see. In the everyday walks of life we expect more for church, for charity, for the uplifting of society,**

and education from those who are more prosperous, most wealthy, most able to give. Yet the system of taxation advocated by the Republican Party drives the taxgatherer to the tenement house and makes him skip the mansion, drives him to the poorhouse and lets him pass the palace....

I have heard it urged by some gentlemen upon the Republican side that the passage of an income tax law would undermine and at last destroy the protective-tariff system. This Mr. Speaker, is the equivalent to saying that in order to give a few monopolists and manufacturers the right to reach into the pockets of all the people, you have kept the taxgatherer from reaching into the pockets of the few, the fortunate few, the intrenched few, the successful few; but you have driven the taxgatherer to the same pockets which monopolies pillaged under the protective tariff for taxes to sustain the Government. The protective-tariff system is vicious enough in itself without adding to it the iniquity of saying that in order to perpetuate it you must place the taxing burden of the Government upon the masses of the people, who must also bear the heavy burden the protective-tariff system inflicts upon them.

Mr. Speaker, no tax was ever more unjust, in my opinion, than a tax upon consumption, for all must eat to live, all must wear clothes, and when you place a tax upon what it takes to sustain one[self], you announce the doctrine that all men share alike in the blessings of government, that all men prosper equally. But we have only to look about us to see how false this doctrine of taxation is. A tax upon what some people eat and what they wear would deny them the necessities of life, while others, rolling in opulence and accumulation of their wealth into the millions, would not feel such a tax. Then, besides this, Mr. Speaker, the protective-tariff system has become so vicious in this Republic that the Republican Party's candidate, Mr. Taft, promised the country a revision, and a revision downward. But, like that party al-

> **ways does, it procrastinated this relief. It said it would come to the people after the election. The Democrat Party said the reason it wanted first to be entrenched in power and put off this promised relief until after the election was because the Republican Party intended to deceive the people. What a shameless violation of the promised revision downward do we now behold! The betrayal of the people by the Republican Party is written in this House and at the other end of the Capitol, for the revision has been upward and not downward. The reason the Republican Party would not reform the tariff before the election was they knew if they did reform it in the interest of the people, the corruption fund, which they were so used to receiving, would be denied them by the favored few with whom they were in partnership." 44 Cong. Rec. 4398 (1909).**

Because the protective tariff tax was a tax on consumption, most people in America paid about the same amount of tax each year. Whether you are rich or poor, you can only eat so much food and wear out so many clothes in a year's time. But those who labored for a living had a larger appetite than those who clipped interest coupons off their bonds and did nothing else productive during the day. In a sense, the working man paid as much or more for the support of government than the rich man.

> **Mr. DANIEL. "You consider the prices of the ordinary necessities of life, and you will find that the poor people pay more for what they consume than do any other people. It is because they have to buy "by the small," on account of their small capital, while the great can have large transactions and in wholesale ways get the lowest prices." 44 Cong. Rec. 4237 (1909).**

Nowhere in American society, in government nor in our Constitution, were one class of citizens given the right to place a tax on another class of citizens. But this is the effect of what was happening. This situation was similar to that of medieval England, where the king would grant an exclusive license to one of his friends to operate a particular business in a protected geographical area. Such an exclusive license allowed this friend of the king to charge an excessive price for his product or service and thereby earn excessive profits. In effect, the king's friend was taxing the subjects of the king with the king's permission. King Solomon said, "There is nothing new under the sun."

> **Mr. BORAH. "Mr. President, to illustrate further, our system of taxation had its origin in the period of feudalism, when the tax was laid upon those, and those only, who could not resist the payment of it. That was the first tax under our present taxing system. The plan then was, as stated by a noted writer - and it was earnestly argued in those days - that it was a proper distribution of the burdens of government that the clergy should pray for the government, the nobles fight for it, and the common people should pay the taxes. The first fruits of that system, and the first modification of that system, were had during that economic and moral convulsion which shook the moral universe from center to circumference - the French revolution. Historians dispute today as to the cause of the French revolution. If you would know the cause, you will not find it in the days transpiring with the fall of the Bastile; you will not find it in the days when Robespierre, drunk with human blood, leaned against the pillars of the assembly, as he listened to his own doom. It is back of that. It is in those immediate years preceding, when the burden of government had become intolerable, when the stipends paid to the miserable satellites of royalty had become criminal; when bureaucracy reached out into every part of the nation and bore down upon the energies and the industries of the common man; and when, Mr. President, 85 percent of that fearful burden was collected from the peasantry of France, which forced them from their little homes and farms into the sinks and dives of Paris, where the French revolution was born.**

> **The history of taxation is well worthy of the attention of those who believe that in order to maintain a republic, we must always have at the base of our civilization an intelligent, free, and, to some extent, an unburdened citizenship." 44 Cong. Rec. 3988-9 (1909).**

Today many Americans ought to be able to identify with the words of Senator Borah. Today there are factions within our law enforcement agencies that are increasingly viewing the American public as a resource from which they will extract the money they want to run their departments. Abuse of the civil forfeiture law by the bureaucracy is a case in point. People are being thrown in jail left and right for all sorts of petty offenses. America currently has the highest incarceration rate in the world, largely because many prosecutors don't give a hoot about justice, but only seek to win. It's as if governement prefers that we become "customers" of the criminal justice industry instead of us being productive members of a free republic.

## Election of Senators

During the time the income tax amendment was being debated, the American people had two constitutional remedies in mind to level the playing field. One was a constitutional amendment to overturn the obnoxious part of the Supreme Court's *Pollock Decision* regarding income taxes, and the other was direct election of U.S. Senators by the People. Both amendments were endorsed by the Democratic Party platform in 1908. The ultimate purpose of both amendments was to reduce the protective tariff and to place an income tax upon the built-up fortunes of America. The perception was the United States Senate was a club for millionaires and was responsible for the injustices of the high protective tariff.

*"The Bosses of the Senate" cartoon created by Joseph Keppler depicts the influence of the monopolists as they watch over the actions of the Senate. The cartoon appeared in Puck Magazine on January 23, 1889.*

If you remember your high school civics, you will recall that the framers of the Constitution had the states legislatures elect the members of the United States Senate. The idea was to have the states represented in the U.S. Senate as the national government was really just a federation of states with only 17 enumerated powers. Thus the People were represented in the lower house of Congress and the states were represented in the upper house of Congress. But please realize that those state legislators who chose the members of the U.S. Senate were also elected representatives and were closer to the people than the members of the national House of Representatives. Thus originally the U.S. Senators were selected by those elected representatives who should have had the closest contact with the people.

At the time of the income tax debates, the people did not think they were being represented in the U.S. Senate. Since wealth is always organized, and the rest of us generally mind our own business, individuals who represented powerful financial interests were regularly appointed to the U.S. Senate. The people of America had lost a measure of control of their own government. These powerful financial interests, most of whom were Republicans, while claiming to be protecting the American working man, would engineer the protective tariff in such a way that their businessmen friends would rake in the profits.

> **Mr. ADAIR. "The action of the Senate in dealing with the tariff emphasizes the fact that we have too many millionaires in that body and that a few high-priced funerals would be a good thing for the country. As I am informed, there are now in the United States Senate 38 millionaires representing over $140,000,000. What can the people expect at their hands but legislation designed to aid the special-privileged class. I surely hope, Mr. Speaker, that the day will soon come when Senators will be elected by a popular vote of the people, and that**

> **the United States Senate will no longer be the dumping ground for millionaires, who have nothing in common with the plain people.**
>
> **The power to rule men by intellectual and moral force, the test of statesmanship of a former day, is fast passing away, while the wealth, the uncrowning king, oftentimes lacking both and coveting neither, arrogantly seeks to rule in a domain where it is only fitted to serve...Patriotism has given place to material expediency, and the love of country is supplanted by the love of money. An aptness for percentages and the successful manipulation of railroads and stock boards are often regarded as the most essential of senatorial equipments.**
>
> **I hope the day will soon come when the United States Senate will be composed entirely of men who will represent more loyalty and less wealth, more patriotism and less plutocracy; men who love their country more than their money. When that body is so made up, such tariff bills as the one we are now considering will never emanate from that end of the Capitol." 44 Conc. Rec. 4435 (1909).**

There is a belief among those who are a part of the freedom movement in America that there was some sinister motive in the purposes of the 17th Amendment (direct election of U.S. Senators by the People). The allegation is that when the state legislatures selected the members of the Senate, this gave the states representation in Congress making us a constitutional republic. Now the fear is that we no longer have the states represented at the federal level, but instead we have degenerated from a constitutional republic into a democracy. Remember a democracy is two foxes and a chicken voting on what's for dinner.

I disagree. The purpose of the 17th Amendment was to remedy a problem. The Senate had become a plutocracy and was exploiting the people. It was a "House of Lords." It legalized plunder on behalf of the upper class of society through the protective tariff. What may have been a good design on the part of the framers had become perverted by the love of money. The 17th Amendment was the Peoples' attempt to bring fairness back into the running of government. In Chapter 10, I will present a way for the state legislatures to regain the influence over Congress that the framers of the Constitution originally intended them to have.

We are not a degenerative democracy as long as we have limited powers at the national level and we continue to make the rights of the individual paramount in our system of government. The right to life, liberty and property is antecedent, and superior, to all other rights. These are the primary ingredients of a constitutional republic. A constitution, in a constitutional republic, is meant to limit the power of government and to bar a majority (or anyone for that matter) from exploiting a minority. It is the limited nature of our national government, with all other powers reserved to the states or to the People, that makes us a constitutional republic and not a democracy. The election of senators by the People does not in and of itself change this.

But, even though our system of government is to be limited at the national level, and our individual rights are to be protected, at least in theory, where the heart of man is wicked no amount of laws can guarantee justice. Benjamin Franklin said, "Men will ultimately be governed by God or tyrants."

Today our government is still designed to be a constitutional republic, at least on paper, but has in fact been transformed into a democracy with a bureaucracy powerful enough to intimidate the individuals who occupy the constitutional offices of government. The servant has become the master. Today we are governed by what the mass media says the polls indicate as most politicians would rather violate the Constitution than have a bad day in the newspaper.

## The Protective Tariff

At the time the income tax amendment was being debated (1909), most of the wealth of the country was located in New York City and the New England states. Quoting again from the Congressional Record.

> **Mr. JAMES. "Mr Speaker...He [Mr. Hill, senator from Connecticut] tells us that Connecticut, which has been taxing all the rest of the people of the United States under the protective-tariff system until it has grown rich, if this taxation upon incomes is placed upon her wealth, would pay more than 30 other States in the Union. Yet the gentlemen is so patriotic that he is willing to state that when the poor man is willing to give his blood or his life when the Republic is in peril, when the battle is on, that not until then is he willing that his people shall make any contribution to sustain the Government out of the abundant fortunes they have piled up under the system of the protective tariff.**
>
> **Mr. HILL. I challenge any man to say that the New England States did not pour out their blood as well as their wealth in the war of the rebellion. [Applause on the Republican side.]**
>
> **Mr. JAMES. They may have been pouring out their blood upon the battlefields. And if they have, I deny that you speak for them when you say they are unwilling to bear their part of the burden of taxation to keep up this Government, which has blessed them so abundantly. [Applause on the Democratic side.] I would state to the gentleman that his party is not for the income tax even as a war measure. The history about this question has been written. No declaration of any man can affect it; and the record lives which tells us that when this Government was in the throes of war with Spain [1898], when from shop and field and factory brave men had left loved ones at home and were at the front, offering their lives**

> **upon their country's altar and in defense of its flag, the Democratic side offered an income-tax law as a part of the war-revenue measure, which placed a tax on the [unearned] income of the rich, asking that as the poor were standing in the front of the cannon on the fields of conflict the fortunes of the corporations and the rich, which in peace were exempt from taxation, might pay something to sustain the Government in the hour of its peril. But even in this great crisis you gentlemen upon the Republican side were unwilling to cast your votes in favor of the income tax, even as a war measure, and the whole Republican side voted no. [Applause on the Democratic side.] But, instead, you put the burden of taxation upon the poor, who were at home and at the front. You made them not only fight the battles, but pay the taxes too. [Applause on the Democratic side.]**
>
> **Mr. Speaker. "....the immense fortunes, which President Roosevelt called 'swollen fortunes,' but which might perhaps have been more appropriately called 'stolen fortunes,' must bear some part of the burden of taxation in this Republic." 44 <u>Cong. Rec.</u> 4396 (1909).**

Back then the Democrat Party stood for principle on this issue. When the Republicans would mouth their desire to protect the American worker with the protective tariff, the Democrats would call a spade a spade. In 1892, the Republican Party platform stated:

> **"We reaffirm the American doctrine of protection. We call attention to its growth abroad. We maintain that the prosperous condition of our country is largely due to the wise revenue legislation of the last Republican Congress. We believe that all articles which can not be produced in the United States, except luxuries, should be admitted free of duty, and that on all imports coming into competition with the products of American labor, there should be levied duties equal to the difference between wages abroad and at home."**

Also in 1892, the platform for the Democrat Party had this to say:

> **"We denounce Republican protection as a fraud - a robbery of the great majority of the American people for the benefit of the few. We declare it to be a fundamental principle of the Democratic Party that the Federal Government has no constitutional power to impose and collect tariff duties except for the purposes of revenue only, and we demand that the collection of such taxes shall be limited to the necessities of the Government when honestly and economically administered.**
>
> **We denounce the McKinley tariff law enacted by the Fifty-first Congress as the culminating atrocity of class legislation..."**

In 1896 the Democrat Party platform voiced a similar objection to the protective tariff. The 1900 Democrat Party platform was a little more blunt:

> **"We condemn the Dingley tariff law as a trust-breeding measure, skillfully devised to give the few favors which they do not deserve and to place upon the many burdens which they should not bear.**
>
> **Private monopolies are indefensible and intolerable. They destroy competition, control the price of all material and of the finished product, thus robbing both producer and consumer.... They are the most efficient means yet devised for appropriating the fruits of industry to the benefit of the few at the expense of the many, and unless their insatiate greed is checked, all wealth will be aggregated in a few hands and the Republic destroyed.**
>
> **The dishonest paltering with the trust evil by the Republican Party in state and national platforms is conclusive proof of the truth of the charge that trusts are the illegitimate product of Republican policies; that they are fos-**

**tered by Republican laws; and that they are protected by Republican administration for campaign subscriptions and political support."**

Just to drive home the point, let's look at another passage in the Congressional Record so that we understand how the protective tariff was being used by the Republican Party to benefit those who made campaign contributions to the Republicans. This quote discusses the American economy in aggregate and the amount of the excess profits enjoyed by American business.

**Mr. NEWLANDS. "In this connection I wish simply to state briefly that the [protective tariff] schedule presented by the Finance Committee of the production in this country of commodities covered by the tariff act shows that the total production amounted to about $13,000,000,000, and that the total imports of such commodities equaled about one-twentieth of the domestic production, and that the amount expended for wages in producing these commodities [totaling] over $13,000,000,000 amounted to about $2,500,000,000.**

**This act imposes a duty of about 45 percent upon the foreign commodities which come in competition with our domestic production. So that it is safe to say that the value of this $13,000,000,000 worth of domestic products would be counter balanced on the outside of our tariff wall by an equal amount of commodities valued at only $9,000,000,000. In other words, by the imposition of these duties we give to the American manufacturers the right to add to the foreign price of these commodities a total of over $4,000,000,000 annually - an amount more than sufficient to pay for the entire labor cost of all the commodities, aggregating, according to the statement of the Financial Committee, two billions and a half.**

**Of all the privileges enjoyed by corporations, the most valuable is this charter [protective tariff], given to the domestic corporations, which permits them to impose upon domestic consumers a charge of nearly $4,000,000,000 in excess of what they would pay if the competitive products on the outside were given free entry." 44 Cong. Rec. 4235 (1909).**

That was the big picture. Now let's look at the effect of the protective tariff on a specific industry. In this case it is the agricultural implements industry.

**Mr. BYRD. "Well, does my friend know that every time a dollar tax is voted upon any article imported into this country that the domestic producer of such article adds the same as an extra profit on his product? This was once denied by the advocates of protection, but it was conceded by the most stalwart Republican Senators in the recent great tariff debate. I would like for him to tell the country wherein is to be found equality of taxation under such a system. One man is not only taxed for the support of the Government, but for the benefit of his fellow-man. While he pays $1 to the Government, he is compelled to pay from five to seven times this amount to his neighbor who is engaged in a manufacturing enterprise. For instance, the American farmer consumes $25,000,000 worth of agricultural implements annually. The tax thereon is 20 percent. The Government in 1907 collected only $3,600 in revenue [tariff collected on imported agricultural implements], but according to admissions of Republican Senators the 20 percent Dingley rate was levied in favor of the manufacturer on the $25,000,000 consumed at home, amounting to a tax of $5,000,000. So the American farmer, while he paid $3,600 to his Government, was compelled to donate $5,000,000 to the agricultural-implement trust." 44 Cong. Rec. 4416 (1909).**

The protective tariff was used by the Republican Party as a form of legalized plunder. The effect was to confiscate money from the average American for the benefit of the upper classes who were the owners of the corporations and the great trusts which had monopolized much of American industry. Congressman Byrd testified on July 12, 1909, that if Congress cut the tariff in half, imports would increase fourfold thereby doubling the amount of money the government collected in tariff revenue. This would have resulted in an aggregate decrease of $7,000,000,000 in the cost of all consumer goods. Obviously the greater goal was not to generate revenue for the government, but to increase the wealth of those who supported the Republican Party.

> **Mr. BYRD. "If the rich are to be taxed by these measures to run the Government, and the poor are to be taxed by high protection to enrich the manufacturers and trusts, then, in the name of reason, what good can you expect from this legislation? The income tax is right, and it is the only fair means to raise revenue to run the Government, and when it is adopted, it is to be hoped that the American people will raise in rebellion against your infamous protective system which is designed for no other purpose than to enrich the rich." 44 Cong. Rec. 4417 (1909).**

> **"There is no occasion for surprise in the fact that Senator Daniel and Senator Bailey propose as a substitute for this [legislation] impost taxes that would not compel the people to pay $6.50 to the protected manufacturers for every dollar collected at the Custom House." Editorial, Mr. Aldrich's Surprise, N.Y. Times, page 8, April 21, 1909.**

The People of America sought to remedy this situation by adding to the revenue collection system of government an income tax. The argument was that since wealth benefitted from the existence of government, wealth should pay for this benefit. Remember that the Constitution only gives the federal government authority in 17 areas, and back then Congress and the executive branch largely respected this. Under a limited constitutional government, one of the primary benefits one received from government was protection. This is how it is supposed to be.

> **"The Taxation of incomes is a comparatively modern idea. Its introduction may be ascribed to two distinct causes: on the one hand the need of increased revenues, and on the other the professed desire to round out the existing tax system in the direction of greater justice....**
>
> **But the point to be emphasized here is that the income tax, whenever introduced into any American commonwealth, was enacted with the avowed purpose of removing inequalities in the tax system." Seligman, Edwin, R.A., The Income Tax, 9 Political Science Quarterly 610, 615 (1894).**

Anything within the exterior boundaries of a country, whether it be a person or property, benefits from the protection offered by civil government. The amount of protection property received was directly proportional to the value of the property. A rich man who owned $10,000,000 in real estate received a greater benefit than a poor man who owned none. Prior to the income tax, there was no national system of taxation that taxed the rich man for the benefit his property received from government.

At the time, the American people understood the word "income" to mean what we call today "unearned income" and profits from business. The common usage of the word "income" did not include the wages of a working man. It was the working man who needed tax relief as his consumption was heavily taxed. The goal was to shift some of the tax burden onto the income from accumulated wealth. **The purpose of the 16th Amendement was to bring tax relief to wage earners.**

> **"The poor man does not regard his wages or salary as 'an income.'" Governor A.E. Wilson (Kentucky) on the Income Tax Amendment, N.Y. Times, part 5, page 13, February 26, 1911.**

> **Mr. HEFLIN. "An income tax seeks to reach the unearned wealth of the country and to make it pay its share." 44 Cong. Rec. 4420 (1909).**

> **Mr. HEFLIN. "But sir, when you tax a man on his income, it is because his property is productive. He pays out of his abundance because he has got the abundance. If to pay his income tax is a misfortune, it is because he has the misfortune to have the income upon which it is paid." 44 Cong. Rec. 4423 (1909).**

When the cries of the people got so great to the point that some were talking of revolution, the Republicans finally yielded and entertained the idea of an income tax.

> **Mr. BYRD. "You are compelled, in order to save your political scalps, to make his [Dem. presidential candidate Bryan, 1898] favorite theory the law. It is indeed a bitter pill, but you know that something must be done to assuage the increasing wrath of the people on account of the grievous wrong that is now being perpetrated by the tariff...." 44 Cong. Rec. 4416 (1909).**

In theory, a protective tariff is a good concept. It protects American jobs and American industry. Patriotism and nationalism, in moderation, are good things. All things being equal, we benefit by keeping jobs and profits here. As with any law, no matter how well intentioned, the law will not have its desired effect unless administered by honest people. But beware of the politician who argues for a new law relying only on patriotism as his reason to support it; such a law probably has no other redeeming value.

## Attempted Pacification

Congress' first attempt to offer the people an alternative to the protective tariff was nothing but a sham. It was the first version of the Corporate Excise Tax Act of 1909 which was an amendment to the Payne-Aldrich Tariff Act. It was Congress' intent (more accurately the Republican Party's intent) to place an income tax on corporations measured by either gross receipts or net income. It didn't matter which was used to measure the tax, as this was not an income tax, but a tax on the privilege of doing business in a corporate capacity. Such a tax is more appropriately called an excise tax.

The *Pollock Decision* would not hamper Congress with this legislation as privileges are always taxed as an excise and are therefore not direct taxes within the constitutional meaning of the word "direct." The *Pollock Decision* only dealt with direct taxes, and under the doctrine of *stare decisis*, only those answered questions which are squarely before the court become "case law." An excise tax on a privilege would be outside of the precedent set by the *Pollock Decision.*

The people believed the large corporations in America had become a menace. There was a cry to weaken the power these corporations held. You'll remember that the Supreme Court said in *McCollum v. Maryland* that "The power to tax is the power to destroy." In the same way, **the power to create is the power to tax.** Since corporations are creatures created by statute, Congress has the right to tax their existence as a privilege. Government can tax what government creates. A corporation, which is an artificial entity, is considered a person in law. It is also considered a citizen. Its personhood and its citizenship are privileges. Under our constitutional system, the requirements for taxing those classes of citizens that are a creation of Congress are entirely different than the requirements for taxing the Citizens who enjoy their citizenship by right and are actually the creators of Congress. Those of us who enjoy our citizenship by right are the Posterity of **We the People**.

> **Mr. DAVIS. "We find that the corporations of the country are invading every avenue of business and trade. In my State we have trust companies formed for the purpose of transacting every kind and character of business. They administer upon your estate; they are guardians for your children; they absolutely carry their business to such an extent that it closes up the avenue of every individual effort. The individual is entirely destroyed and the law-made creature takes his place. Whenever an individual seeks an opportunity for employment or for business, he finds the door closed to him by the law-made creature, the corporation." 44 <u>Cong. Rec.</u> 4036 (1909).**

Congress has the right to levy an excise tax on whatever Congress creates, as the "creation" exists at the pleasure of the creator. It would be impossible to levy a direct tax on an entity that exists by privilege. Direct taxes are levied on things or persons that exist by right. Congress may extend to a natural person "United States Citizenship" as a privilege; i.e., the indigenous people of Puerto Rico. These people, while being U.S. citizens, are not the Posterity of **We the People** and do not enjoy their citizenship by right (More on this later).

In 1909, Congress first proposed to place a tax on corporations. This legislation would have exempted "holding companies" and trusts. These holding companies and trusts were the monopolies that controlled entire industries. While the people were demanding that something should be done about the power and control of American business interests, Congress was attempting to give the American people the legislation they were asking for while exempting the very entities the people sought to control. The American People didn't let Congress get away with this.

**Mr. NEWLANDS. "We now come to the monopolistic holding company, the great trust organizations like the steel trust, for the purpose of holding the stock of other constituent companies, with the view to controlling and monopolizing production in certain lines. Such an organization is not sustained by any moral consideration and is against public policy and the spirit of the interstate commerce law." 44 Cong. Rec. 4233 (1909).**

**Mr. COX. "The idea that men like Carnegie, now the holder of more than $300,000,000 worth of the bonds of the United States steel trust, escape federal taxation is indeed absurd." 44 Cong. Rec. 4424 (1909).**

**"You talk about the power of great aggregations of capital; you talk about the crushing out of the life of the rights and of the opportunities of the individual - the policy against which we have struggled for seven years...**

**But when the American people come to learn that this is simply a shifting of a tax in most cases upon the consumer, when they come to learn that millions of dollars can be invested in a corporation which will not pay one dollar of tax [a holding company], when they come to learn that this is a plain invitation to go on and enlarge a system which we have battled against these seven years, there is no danger of this or any other Congress taking the second step. The American people will attend to that in their own behalf...**

**Based upon the theory that it is an excise tax, it exempts from that excise the very corporations [the holding companies] that in all human probability are the best able to pay the tax. It exempts the great bondholders, the great accumulated fortunes of this country." 44 Cong. Rec. xxxx (4046) (1909).**

The argument made by the Republicans was that holding companies were corporations that held the stock of other corporations. Once the subsidiary corporations paid a tax, to tax the holding corporation was in effect double taxation. This would have been true had it been property that was being taxed. A tax on property, measured by the value of the property, is a direct tax.

But property wasn't being taxed, it was the privilege of doing business in a corporate capacity that was being taxed. Any corporation that exercised this privilege would have to pay the tax. The underlying corporation exercised its privilege of existing in a corporate form and would therefore be taxed on this privilege. Next, the holding company also exercised its unique and separate privilege of existing in corporate form and would have to pay its own tax for this privilege. The latter were more able to afford this tax as most of the holding companies were monopolistic in nature and earned profits beyond what was generally economically possible.

Commenting on the proposed legislation to tax corporations while exempting holding companies, Senator Cummins said:

> **Mr. CUMMINS. "Senators, I do not believe that such a law will stand. I do not mean that it will not stand the investigation of the courts. I mean that it will not stand the criticism of the people, who are above all the courts and all legislatures and all other authorities of the land." 44 Cong. Rec. 4041 (1909).**

This is a good example of how one can make a credible argument to do an evil thing. The goal was to make the small corporations pay the tax, while those corporations in the form of holding companies, that benefitted most from the protective tariff and would therefore be most able to pay this tax, would escape the tax. Organized wealth was again at work trying to escape its burden of taxation in an attempt to make the little guy, the small corporation, pay for the support of government.

> **Mr. NEWLANDS. "Now, what form of aggregations of capital have come under the just criticism of the country? The great combinations of capital. Has there been any complaint of the small corporations, of the commercial**

> **corporations, of business corporations, of the small manufacturing corporations? There is no complaint regarding them. The complaint is against the great combinations of capital in this country, and the abuses which exist today are the abuses which these great combinations of capital have originated and practiced.**
>
> **Inasmuch as this measure has in view not only revenue, but publicity with a view to ending such abuses, why put the light of publicity upon these numberless small corporations of the country, overburdening the records, and so confusing the inquiry that we may not be able to discern the abuses of the great combinations themselves?**
>
> **Our legislation, both with reference to revenue and publicity, should be concentrated upon those forms of wealth that have become most oppressive and upon those forms of wealth with reference to which the greatest abuses have existed; those forms of lawless wealth that have brought the law-abiding wealth of the country itself into discredit." 44 Cong. Rec. 4048 (1909).**

The plan to exempt holding companies and trusts was just too obnoxious and didn't sell within Congress. Instead we got the Corporate Excise Tax Act of 1909 which taxed all "for profit" corporations. Even though this legislation was ultimately of reasonable construction, its promotion was shady. Senator Aldrich, who was absolutely opposed to an income tax, managed to get the Congress to act first on the Corporate Tax Act of 1909 as a means to placate the people in an attempt to defeat the call for an income tax amendment to the Constitution. Aldrich thought that if Congress gave the people the Corporate Excise Tax Act they would no longer demand an income tax. Aldrich and his rich Republican friends were worried that an income tax would ultimately ruin their protective tariff arrangement.

The American people understood the purpose of any income tax amendment to the Constitution was to reach the gains, profits and unearned income of the country. The goal was to levy a tax on the accumulated wealth of the country. It was not the intention of the American people to tax the wages and salaries of the working man. The American people were frustrated by the Supreme Court's *Pollock Decision* where taxes on income from real estate and personal property (mostly stocks and bonds) were ruled to be direct taxes and required to be apportioned among the several States by the Constitution. This made it practically impossible to levy an income tax on the income from these sources since the wealth of the country had become so concentrated in New York and the New England states. Thus wealth escaped from national taxation and did not pay anything for the benefit it received from government.

## The Purpose of the Income Tax

**"The effect of the decision of the *Pollock Case* in 1895 was that taxes on income, if that income flowed from real or personal property, would be direct, and would, therefore, have to be apportioned among the states according to population. The necessity for apportionment seemed to render such taxes impracticable, and as there was an increasing public sentient calling for the collection of revenue from such a source, the Sixteenth Amendment was proposed...." W. C. J., Constitutional Law: Income Tax: Sixteenth Amendment, 4 California Law Journal 333, 334-5 (1915-6).**

**Mr. BARTLETT of Georgia. "Therefore the decision, [*Pollock*] in effect, puts the dollar of the millionaire beyond the pale of being equitably taxed according to his wealth, unless a constitutional amendment be invoked.... However, there should be some method by which the untold**

> **wealth and riches of this Republic may be compelled to bear their just burdens of government and contribute an equitable share of their incomes to supply the Treasury with needed taxes.**
>
> **As I see it, the fairest of all taxes is of this nature [a tax on gains, profits and unearned income], laid according to wealth, and its universal adoption would be a benign blessing to mankind. The door is shut against it, and the people must continue to groan beneath the burdens of tariff taxes and robbery under the guise of law." 44 Cong. Rec. 4414 (1909).**
>
> **"It will doubtless be argued that the adoption of this amendment will open a way to the curbing of swollen and ill-gotten fortunes, or at least will compel the owners to pay a larger share of the expenses of government than they now do, and that the poor will be relieved of taxes in the same proportion." Raleigh C. Minor, The Proposed Income Tax Amendment to the Federal Constitution, 15 Virginia Law Register 737, 751 (1910).**

Thus it is well settled that the purpose of the 16th Amendment was to overturn the *Pollock Decision* by way of a constitutional amendment. The purpose of this Amendment was not broader or narrower than that. The *Pollock Decision* dealt with **net income** from real estate and personal property. The *Pollock Decision* did not deal with taxes on the gross revenue of a natural person. Having read all the Congressional debates on the income tax amendment, I can say that the intent of the Congress in presenting the several States with the 16th Amendment was only to overturn *Pollock*. As the *Stanton Court* said, "we are here dealing solely with the restriction imposed by the 16th Amendment against the....taking the income tax out of the class of indirect (taxes), to which it generically belongs, and putting it in the class of direct, to which it would not otherwise belong...." Taxes on **net income** are inherently indirect; taxes on **gross income** are inherently direct. The *Stanton Case* was about taxes on his net income. Adam Smith would agree.

Apportionment among the states would require any income tax to be geared to what the average investor or businessman in Mississippi could afford, while the great incomes were actually located in New York. Under the apportionment rule, the tax collected from each state would be allocated according to the population of each state with each person being responsible for the same dollar amount of tax, on the average. If, in 1909, all that could be reasonably afforded by an investor or businessman of Mississippi was an income tax of $50 per person annually, then this is the same amount an investor or businessman in New York would pay, on the average. Such a condition made the levying and collection of such a tax impractical, especially since the tax sought to reach unearned income—gain and profit not wages. There were not many people in Mississippi who had the former.

Said another way, because the people of America understood the word "income" to mean unearned income, gain and profit, a tax on the income would inherently be an indirect tax subject only to the rule of uniformity. As an indirect tax, it would not have to be apportioned. But this was impossible because the Supreme Court had determined that there was a linkage between an income tax on net income and the source of the income. Unless this linkage could be severed, what was inherently an indirect income tax would have to be apportioned. The *Pollock Decision* needed to be overturned. A constitutional amendment was needed to accomplish this end. The 16th Amendment severed the linkage between net income and the source of the income upon which the *Pollock Decision* was based. At that time, only a minority of Americans had an "income" as most people worked for wages.

In other words, in apportioning a tax on income, as *Pollock* would have required, the quotient of total income tax paid by each state divided by the number of people who lived in the state would be the same in every one of the several States. Thus as a direct tax, a tax on the income of Mr. Carnegie and Mr. Rockefeller would be geared more to what the average investor or businessman in Mississippi could afford than to the amount of income the wealth of these men produced every year.

Gearing a national income tax to the lowest common denominator is impractical. There would have been three alternatives for Congress at this time. The first would be to do nothing, which is what the Republicans preferred, as they liked the high protective tariff system. The second would be to modify the direct taxation clauses of the Constitution to provide for a "direct" tax on incomes freed from apportionment. And the third would be to provide for an income tax of an "indirect" nature subject only to the rule of uniformity. What was done was the latter as the American People sought only to overturn the offensive parts of *Pollock* through the constitutional amendment process.

## Aldrich's Scheme

Senator Nelson Aldrich of Rhode Island, a Republican and the godson of Nelson A. Rockefeller, was considered the most powerful member of Congress. His daughter Abby married John D. Rockefeller, Jr. He was chairman of the Senate Finance Committee and had relationships with many of the central bankers of Europe. Although Senator Brown of Nebraska was the one who proposed the 16th Amendment, Aldrich definitely had his hand in the construction of it.

Stuck with the reality that the Republicans had to endorse an income tax amendment to the Constitution, Aldrich chose to manipulate the process. Reluctantly, he allowed the income tax amendment to be approved by the Senate Finance Committee. Later he acquiesced to its approval by Congress, and sent the amendment to the several States for ratification. His real motive, however, was to defeat it. The strategy employed was to write a defective amendment, ambiguous in its terms, allow it to go out to the States for ratification and defeat it there. Should it be defeated by the state legislatures, the issue of an income tax amendment to the Constitution would be dead for years.

If by chance the amendment was somehow ratified, by writing it with ambiguous terms, he could later manipulate it to the advantage of the wealth class who were currently benefitting from the protective tariff. Aldrich was very forward thinking and the Democrats were fools not to have proposed their own language years earlier as part of their party's presidential platform.

> **Mr. SULZER. "Sir, let me say, however, that I am not deceived by the unanimity in which this resolution is now being rushed through the Congress by the Republicans, its eleventh-hour friends. I can see through their scheme. I know they never expect to see this resolution [the 16th Amendment] become a part of the Constitution. It is offered now to placate the people. The ulterior purpose of many of these Republicans is to prevent this resolution from ever being ratified by three-fourths of the legislatures of the States, necessary for its final adoption, and thus nullify it most effectually...I have been here long enough to know, and I am wise enough to believe, that its passage now is only a sop to the people by the Republicans, and that their ulterior purpose is to defeat it in the Republican state legislatures." 44 Cong. Rec. 4418 (1909).**

> **Mr. BACON. "I particularly protest, however, that it is not proper parliamentary procedure to endeavor to force us to first vote on this amendment [the Corporate Tax Act of 1909] under a device which was given out to the public as intended for the purpose of preventing a vote on the income tax, which was given out as a great parliamen-**

*Entitled "Delivering the Goods," this 1908 cartoon by Herbert Johnson shows Senator Nelson Aldrich getting ready to slice up the consumer for the benefit of those who owned the trust monopolies. Aldrich was instrumental in creating the greatest trust of all; the money trust known today as the Federal Reserve Bank.*

> **tary achievement on the part of the Senator from Massachusetts [Lodge] and the Senator of Rhode Island [Aldrich], that they had so shaped matters that we would be compelled to vote upon the corporation-tax amendment [to the tariff bill] before we were allowed to vote first on the income-tax amendment [to the Constitution]. This amendment [the Corporate Tax Act of 1909] is avowed by the Senator from Rhode Island to be intended to defeat the income tax. If so, we should have the opportunity to vote first on the income tax amendment [to the Constitution]." 44 Cong. Rec. 4063 (1909).**

What Aldrich had done was to interject the Corporate Excise Tax Act of 1909, which was an amendment to the tariff bill, into the income tax debate. Through skillful parliamentary maneuvering Aldrich managed to have the corporate income tax bill heard by Congress before the constitutional income tax amendment. Aldrich was hoping that once the corporate income tax legislation was in place, the American people would be pacified and would not call for the taxation of individual wealth. Aldrich knew that any income tax on corporate profits could be passed to the consumer, and thus his rich friends would continue to escape taxation. This was Aldrich's plan "A" and he even admitted this on the floor of the Senate:

> **Mr. ALDRICH. "I do not expect the income tax to be adopted...And if it were adopted, I do not expect to destroy the protective system now...I think perhaps it would be destructive in time...I shall vote for the corporation tax as a means to defeat the income tax...I will be perfectly frank with the Senate in that respect...I am willing that the deficit shall be taken care of by a corporation tax. That corporation tax, however, at the end of two years, if my estimate should be correct, should be reduced to a nominal amount or repealed....at the end of two years." 44 Cong. Rec. 3929 (1909).**

It was through the Senate Finance Committee, chaired by Senator Aldrich, a Republican, that the final version of the Income Tax Amendment came to the floor of the Senate. *Sutherland on Statutory Construction* (sec. 48.14, 5th Edition) states that additional judicial authority may be given to the opinions of the chairman of a committee, "The committeeman in charge has the duty of defending the bill, has familiarized himself with the situation sought to be remedied by the bill and his statements may be taken as the opinion of the committee about the meaning of the bill." But our case here is a strange one as we have the committeeman in charge of the bill, Senator Aldrich, doing all he can to kill the amendment. Why is there so much scandal around a piece of legislation of such significance?

Aldrich was one unethical politician. The American people were demanding an income tax as a way to more fairly distribute the taxes that must be collected to support government. Aldrich schemed to maintain the feudalistic system of taxation that was presently in place. Aldrich was extremely successful in his scheming as what we have today is still a feudalistic system of taxation and not something that belongs in a constitutional republic of limited powers.

> **Mr. BYRD. "It is a well known fact that the tariff law will be the product of the brain of one Senator [Aldrich], and however infamous the measure may be, it will receive the unqualified support of enough Republicans to pass both Houses.**
>
> **It seems that the Republican Party has permanent control of the Government, and that Senator Aldrich absolutely dominates this party. As long as it triumphs, he will be czar of the Nation." 44 Cong. Rec. 4415 (1909).**
>
> **Mr. DANIEL. "Mr. President, if this was a class of competitive examination in order to show who was the most tired man of this debate, I would expect to win the first place in the competition. The Senator from Rhode Island [Aldrich] is a great actor, a great wizzard, and he is**

> **also a great ventriloquist. With an activity, eagerness, earnestness, and freshness which are unsurpassed in this body, he comes upon the stage and says we must adjourn right now; that he is tired out. That is only one phase of his diverse genius. He is very different from the rest of us plain and prolix people. He does by magic what we have to try to do by toil. He waves his wand and utters his incantations, and so-called "insurgents" march with the vigor and measured tread of Roman soldiers following Caesar to victory. More than that, Mr. President, we hear a murmur yonder; we hear a murmur here and a murmur there. Presently the Senator rises and flings his voice around the Senate and the next moment everybody is talking just like him, and Senators think that right which before they had murmured was wrong." 44 Cong. Rec. 4236 (1909).**

> **Mr. BORAH. "Take the....Senator from Rhode Island [Aldrich]. He has been perfectly frank. He has been open and candid. No friend of the income-tax law now dare go home and say to his constituents: 'The Senator from Rhode Island fooled me.' He has been open and above board. He has told you that he brought this measure [the Corporate Tax Act of 1909] here to kill the income tax, and he has told you furthermore that it is an enemy of protection. He has said unhesitatingly that if it is in his power he will throttle it for all time to come. Do you underestimate his influence?" 44 Cong. Rec. 3998 (1909).**

During the ratification process there was a great amount of debate over the 16th Amendment. The main point of concern was the Amendment's ambiguous terms. It was the Democrats' idea with the language drafted by specific Republicans who were strongly opposed to it. Aldrich wanted the Amendment to be highly criticized and defeated by the states. This is why it was so poorly written; it was Aldrich's plan "B." The debate was so intense that Senator Borah (Idaho) proposed Senate Resolution #175 authorizing a study to be done by the Judiciary Committee to answer the questions for which the amendment was being criticized (See the *New York Times* article The Rejected Amendment, at the end of Chapter 4).

## The Rejected Amendment

**The income tax amendment failed on Tuesday to get the necessary votes in the Assembly [New York Legislature], and that disposes of it for the present session. It may be brought before the Legislature at the next session, but it is not likely, in its present form, to be received with any more favor.**

**The chief objection to the amendment, we think, in the minds of the public, as well as its opponents in the Legislature, is that it was hastily drawn, involved a principle of mischievous effect on the interests of the states, and would give rise to indefinite contention as to its real meaning. There was, however, another objection relating not to the substance of the amendment, but to the manner in which it was brought into being. It was originally proposed to the Senate of the United States to save Mr. Aldrich and his associates from defeat on the revision of the tariff. To avoid this, the amendment, together with the corporation tax, was contrived. It was not a nice device - to use no stronger term - and in the exigency existing it was carried out in a bungling fashion. If we are to have the Constitution changed in this matter, it certainly would be better to have it done decently and in order." The Rejected Amendment, N.Y. Times, page 10, May 5, 1910.**

**"It is far from representing the considered opinion of Congress. No time was spent on it apart from that necessary for the formalities. There was no inquiry, and no discussion worthy of the name. It is a political dodge, adopted from the most questionable of motives. It is part of the**

**price paid for the enactment of a tariff law which was adopted under false pretenses." Editorial, The Income Tax, N.Y. Times, page 10, April 19, 1911.**

In my investigation of this subject matter, I looked for Congressional reports and Congressional hearings on the 16th Amendment and found little or none. A congressional report would have disclosed the purpose of the amendment and the reasons behind its wording. There was no report at all from the Senate Finance Committee when it voted the 16th Amendment out of committee. When the House Ways and Means Committee issued a report on the amendment it amounted to only a one paragraph report known as House Report #15 recommending approval of the 16th Amendment. I think this was scandalous.

One of the major issues of the War of Independence and of the Constitutional Convention was taxation. Had not the compromise been struck between the large states and the small states over apportionment and direct taxes, the country would have likely come apart after the Articles of Confederation proved to be a failure. Today over 80% of federal government revenue comes from income taxes. To have so much of our federal revenue dependent on such an ill-conceived amendment is at a minimum suspicious.

**Mr. McCALL. "Mr. Speaker, I imagine that nothing which I may be able to say will defeat the prearranged programme and prevent the passage of the joint resolution [on the income tax amendment], but for the House to perform its part in such a solemn transaction as amending the Constitution of the United States without having the form of the amendment seriously considered by one of its committees strikes me as a proceeding in extraordinary levity...I say this amendment should be more carefully considered...The amendment has not carefully been considered by a committee of this House or by anyone else in the United States that I know of." 44 Cong. Rec. 4391 (1909).**

I believe this also was by design. Certainly the fruit of this lack of committee review played to Aldrich's favor and to those of the wealth class who sought to control everything. For Aldrich also had a plan "C." This was in the event that this poorly worded and poorly constructed amendment were to somehow be ratified. Ambiguous in its terms, it could be manipulated later.

> **"Furthermore, the adoption of the sixteenth amendment, the 'crudest, most reckless bit of constitutional legislation known to our history,' removing the constitutional limitations on the power of Congress to levy taxes on incomes, and 'putting all property and all human effort at the mercy of the government' by authorizing it 'to take whatever it will and in any way it will,' appears to....be an act fraught with grave danger to the liberties of the people and, therefore, a step backward in our progress...." John W. Burgess, The Reconciliation of Government with Liberty, 369, New York, Charles Scribner's Sons, (1915); 31 Political Science Quarterly 143, 144 (1916).**

The People's intention in supporting the 16th Amendment was honorable and justified. Unfortunately, its ambiguous terms would have offended a man like Thomas Jefferson who believed that government should be "bound with the chains of the Constitution." We are blessed in that the Supreme Court did not construe the 16th Amendment in such a way as its critics had feared and as Senator Aldrich must have hoped. Both in the *Brushaber Case* and in the *Stanton Case* the Supreme Court held that the 16th Amendment created no new class of tax, and that income taxes (on unearned income, gain or profit from business activity) were inherently indirect taxes. Thus, the 16th Amendment did not give Congress any new power, nor did it create a new class of taxation, nor did it grant to Congress power to impose any type of direct tax without apportionment.

This last point will be addressed again in Chapter 6. No, the 16th Amendment did not give Congress any new power, but the IRS and the Tax Court conveniently ignore this and both are out of harmony with the Supreme Court. There are a large number of lower court decisions that falsely claim that the 16th Amendment provided for an exemption to the Constitution's apportionment rule for direct taxes. In a perfect world this would not be the case. But the world is not perfect.

In an editorial, *The New York Times* had this to say about the income tax amendment:

> **"Senator Root's argument only embarrasses the Republicans. Either they intended to do a bad thing, or else they designed to deceive the people into thinking they were voting to do that thing, but to avoid doing it by argument after enactment. It is bad for a party when people say after too many of their acts, 'stung again.' The tariff should be added to the above list, and then it may be asked how much of this can the people stand because the Republican Party was once the party of great ideas and acts." Editorial, Perfectly Plain and Bad Laws, N.Y. Times, page 8, March 2, 1910.**

Well, the average man and woman have been "stung again." Just as the working man paid for the support of government under the protective tariff, while the wealth of the Nation went untaxed, so now the working man is paying for the support of government under our current income tax system. But not only does he support government, he also supports a myriad of "entitlement programs." It is a system so complicated that those in Congress who wrote the statutes and approved their regulations cannot even understand them.

Why? Because the average American has forgotten the words of Wendell Phillips who said, **"Eternal vigilance is the price of liberty."**

## Purpose of Government

According to the Bible, the purpose of government is to reward good and punish evil. Our response to godly government is found in the same passage as God's purpose for government. "Submit yourself to every ordinance of man for the Lord's sake, whether it be to the king, as supreme, or unto governors, as unto them that are sent by him for the punishment of evildoers, and for the praise of them that do well." I Peter 2:13-14, Authorized King James Version. Our duty to submit to godly authority has a qualifier attached to it, and that is that the authority be godly, that it "praises good and punishes evil." When authority ceases to be godly, then we cease to have a duty to submit to it. Those people who founded America found themselves in the position where they could not please both God and government.

If God is who he says he is, then He is the ultimate designer of all that exists in the universe. The scriptures identify four types of government: personal government, family government, church government and civil government. If God is God then only He has the authority to set the jurisdictional boundaries between each type of government. For example, it is our duty as individuals and churches to be charitable, and not that of governement.

A civil government limited in jurisdiction to only the purposes identified in scripture would need very little money to operate. There would be no need to tax a man's right to exist. No need to tax his wages or salary.

As of 1909, when the income tax amendment was proposed, the federal government had yet to become the great nanny in the sky (the political corporation) solving everybody's problems from cradle to grave. Instead, our government largely followed the Biblical mandate just mentioned. Government's fundamental duty to protect life and property can also be found at Romans 13:3-4.

The Geneva Bible, which is the Bible the Pilgrims used, states:

**"For princes are not to be feared for good works, but for evil. Wilt you then be without fear of the power? Do well. For shalt thou have praise of the same. For he is the minister of God for thy wealth. But if thou do evil, fear: for he beareth not the sword for nought: for he is the minister of God to take vengeance on him that doeth evil." Romans 13:3-4 (Geneva Bible, 1st Edition, 1560).**

When government takes one third or more of a man's yearly earnings, using as its authority to do so a law that is many thousands of pages long and so complicated that virtually no one can understand it, is government doing good? Or is government doing evil?

The way to make people respect the law is to make the law respectable.

Adam Smith, in his famous book entitled *"Wealth of Nations,"* upon which our founders heavily relied when they wrote our Constitution, espoused this same general concept of government.

**"The first duty of the sovereign is, that of protecting the society from the violence and invasion of other independent societies...The second duty of the sovereign is, that of protecting, as far as possible, every member of the society from the injustice or oppression of every other member of it...The third duty and last duty of the sovereign or commonwealth is that of erecting and maintaining those public institutions and those public works, which, though they may be in the highest degree advantageous to a great society..." Adam Smith, Wealth of Nations, book V, 468-73, (1776) (Prometheus Books, Amherst, New York, 1991).**

At this time in history, our government's primary function was just that, the protection of life, wealth and property. Senator Dick of Ohio said:

**"The largest expenditures of government are for the protection of life and property." 44 Cong. Rec. 4960 (1909).**

In talking about whether or not the American People would give the Congress the power to tax incomes, Congressman Cox, from Indiana said:

> **"But the people, if treated fairly, with uniform taxation, readily yield this power to the Government for the protection which the Government gives in return to the people." 44 Cong. Rec. 4421 (1909).**

When Jesus said "Render unto Ceasar the things that are Ceasar's and to God the things that are God's," (Matthew 22:21) notice that He did not say, "Give Ceasar everything he asks you for." Inherent in the former statement is the idea that there are limits on what belongs to Ceasar. In God's world view, civil government has limited jurisdiction. If government asks you to render to it the mind of your child, will you obey or object?

Since those Americans who had accumulated great wealth benefitted more from government that those who had little, it was logical to assume that the wealthy should pay more for government than the poor as the former enjoyed a greater benefit. It is the "no free lunch" principle.

> **Mr. COX. "It is not my intention to belittle wealth, but, on the other hand, I believe it should be the duty of all to uphold it where it is honestly procured. The idea that men like Carnegie, now the holder of more that $300,000,000 worth of the bonds of the United States steel trust, escape federal taxation is indeed absurd....and then, to realize that all of these enormous fortunes are escaping their just and proportionate share of taxation while the people themselves are staggering under our present system of indirect taxation, it is no wonder to me they cry for relief. If it be the determination of the so-called "business interests" in this country to maintain an enormous navy at a cost of hundreds of millions of dollars annually, as well as an army, to protect and defend their various business interests, I insist that this part of the wealth of the country ought to**

> **stand its proportionate share of taxation, and I know of no way to compel them to do it as justly and equitably as an income tax. [Loud applause]" 44 Cong. Rec. 4424 (1909).**

If you give it some thought, you'll realize that it would be impossible to accumulate a lot of wealth if it were not for the institution of civil government. What if we lived in anarchy? How much would your stocks and bonds be worth? How much would your vacation home be worth that was hundreds of miles away from where you live? These things would be worth nothing. And what about your overseas investments in oil wells in Africa? If there were no United States navy, air force, or army to protect them, these investments would be worthless, too.

So those who have accumulated a level of wealth beyond what they can personally protect have received an extra benefit from civil government. In this case, the amount of benefit can be measured by the amount of property that has been accumulated. A tax on the income of this property could fairly accurately coincide with the degree of the benefit received. This was the purpose of the income tax, to tax income of property so that the property paid for the support of government in proportion to the benefit the property received from the existence of civil government. Sounds reasonable to me!

> **"Taxation is the equivalent for the protection which the government affords to the persons and property of its citizens; and as all are alike protected, so all alike should bear the burden, in proportion to the interests secured. [Cooley's Constitutional Limitations, 6th ed., 598, 607, 608, 615.]" Rehearing, Brief for Appellants at 79, Pollock v. Farmer's Loan and Trust Co., 158 U.S. 601 (1895).**

There is also an element of charity inherent in an income tax system that seeks to make property pay for the support of government. The charity involves property that is not productive and not producing an income. This would be the family farm that was just inherited by beneficiaries who where unable to work it for whatever reason. The farm would pay no income tax as it earned no income, thus allowing the new owners to keep the farm and not lose it to the tax man as they might under a direct tax.

> **Mr. HENRY of Texas. "From that day to this we have urged and pleaded for its [an income tax] adoption. The Republican Party has scoffed at it and scorned to believe in it until lashed by public conscience. In 1908 the Democracy [Democratic Party platform] pronounced in favor of such law and amendment. We said:**
>
> **We favor an income tax as part of our revenue system, and we urge the submission of a constitutional amendment specifically authorizing Congress to levy and collect tax upon individual and corporate incomes, to the end that wealth may bear its proportionate share of the burdens of the Federal Government.**
>
> **We have now reached a point where an income tax seems an inevitable necessity. The appropriations of the Federal government have become so great that the internal-revenue taxes and import duties no longer suffice...There is a shortage in that regard of more than $150,000,000 annually. In accordance with my judgement that amount should be laid upon the incomes of the country by the enactment of a genuine income-tax law." 44 Cong. Rec. 4412 (1909).**

Another argument advanced in support of the income tax amendment was the necessity for the government to generate greater revenue in time of emergency and war. When a country is challenged by war, it can take all of the resources of the entire country to prevail. Countries that lose wars will expend all of their resources only to lose. At the beginning of World War II, Germany was spending up to 70 percent of its gross national product on the war effort.

During the 1909 income tax debate, many Congressmen argued that we needed the income tax amendment as a tool available to Congress in the event of war or emergency.

> **Mr. PAYNE. "But if this Nation should ever be under the stress of a great war, exhausting her resources, and the question of war now being a question as to which nation has the longest pocketbook, the greatest material resource in a great degree, I do not wish to be left, I do not wish this Nation to be left, without an opportunity to avail itself of every resource to provide an income adequate to the carrying on of that war.**
>
> **I hope that if the Constitution is amended in this way the time will not come when the American people will ever want to enact an income tax except in time of war." 44 Cong. Rec. 4390 (1909).**
>
> **"To deny to a great empire like the United States the possibility of utilizing so powerful a fiscal engine in times of national stress would be almost equivalent to advocating national suicide." Edwin R.A. Seligman, The Income Tax Amendment, 25 Political Science Quarterly 193, 218 (1910).**

Government's duty to protect the borders of a nation from invasion falls within the biblical mandate of government to "Be a terror to those who do evil and praise those who do well."

The income tax amendment as originally intended, that being a tax on unearned income, gain and profit, was a reasonable way to solve the taxing inequities of the time. However, the ink was hardly dry on the ratification process when Congress was proposing an income tax statute, only seven months after the purported ratification of the 16th Amendment. Plus, Congress made the tax retroactive almost to the day the amendment was ratified. In a few short years the tax rates increased far beyond what anyone anticipated they would have been during the ratification process. Never trust the words of a politician unless you have first judged their character over a period of years.

Today it is the conservative Republicans that champion the idea of a limited form of government. But one hundred years ago the Republicians were the big spenders who wanted a central bank and easy credit. Back then it was the Democrat Party that stood for the Constitution and for limited government. It was the Democrat Party whose word you could trust. Today many people think we really have just one party joined at the head with two branches that only appear to be different.

> **"Let us not be unmindful that liberty is power, that the nation blessed with the largest portion of liberty must in proportion to its members be the most powerful nation upon the earth. Our Constitution professedly rests upon the good sense and attachment of the people. This basis, weak as it may appear, has not yet been found to fail. Always vote for a principle, though you vote alone, and you may cherish the sweet reflection that your vote is never lost. America, in the assembly of nations, has uniformly spoken among them the language of equal liberty, equal justice, and equal rights."**
>
> ***—John Quincy Adams, 6th President of the United States of America.***

*Photo: Library of Congress*

***Senator Norris Brown (1884-1963)***

*Republican Senator Norris Brown from Nebraska drafted the 16th Amendment and wrote a nine-page position paper on the subject. Senator Brown argued rather clearly the intent of the 16th Amendment: that being the taxing of income from investments and business profits as a means to bring tax relief to wage earners.*

*Photo: Library of Congress*

***Justice Edward Douglas White (1845-1921)***

*U.S. Supreme Court Justice White wrote the dissenting opinion in the Pollock Case of 1898. As chief justice of the U.S. Supreme Court he wrote the Court's opinion for the Brushaber Case of 1916.*

*Photo: Library of Congress*

***Senator William E. Borah (1869-1940)***
*Idaho Senator Borah was one of the so-called progressive Republicans in Congress and a strong supporter of the 16th Amendment. The highest mountain peak in Idaho is named after him and he was a candidate for president in 1936.*

*Photo: Library of Congress*

***Senator Joseph W. Bailey (1863-1929)***
*A Democrat from Texas, Senator Bailey was the most outspoken proponent of the 16th Amendment and was considered one of the best orators in the Senate.*

*Photo: Library of Congress*

***Senator Nelson Aldrich (1841-1915)***

*As Chairman of the Senate Finance Committee in 1909, Senator Aldrich was considered one of the most powerful members of Congress . He was also married to the daughter of John D. Rockefeller and openly represented the interests of America's wealthiest families in the U.S. Senate.*

# Chapter 4
## Pigeon Holes for Taxpayers

**"So that, perhaps, the true question is this: is income property, in the sense of the constitution, and must it be taxed at the same rate as other property? ....The fact is, property is a tree; income is the fruit; labor is a tree; income, the fruit; capital, the tree; income, the fruit. The fruit if not consumed as fast as it ripens, will germinate from the seed which it encloses, and will produce other trees, and grow into more property; but so long as it is fruit merely, and plucked to eat, and consumed in the eating, it is no tree, and will produce itself no fruit."**

***Waring v. The Mayor and Alderman of the City of Savannah*, 60 Ga. 93, 100 (1878).**

In the next two chapters we will segregate taxpayers and income taxes into their appropriate pigeon holes. It is necessary to understand why such things should be classified differently in order to know where you fit into this picture. For example, income taxes on the wages of one person may be an indirect tax while the same tax on another person may be a direct tax. In this case the status of the taxpayer is controlling. In other cases, the nature of the income tax could determine whether the tax is direct or indirect. First we'll briefly discuss what the word "income" means.

An examination of any law dictionary or law encyclopedia will show that there are many different types of income. In the latest version of *Black's Law Dictionary* there are thirteen species of income listed. Among these are earned income, fixed income, gross income, imputed income, operating income, and so on. The 1906 edition of *Cyclopedia of Law and Procedure* lists seven different types of income. In the case of Equitable Trust Co. v. Prentice, 240 N.Y. 1, 164 N.E. 723, 725 (1928) the court said, income is "A word having different meanings, dependent upon the connection in which it is used and the result intended to be accomplished."

Whenever any legal professional tries to put all income taxes into a single pigeon hole, confusion results. This is because there are many purported "income taxes" which are not income taxes at all. For example, a tax on a person's gross receipts, what Adam Smith called the "revenue of a person," is not a tax on income, it is a tax on the person, a capitation tax, it is the "tree" referred to in the *Waring Case* cited above. According to *Waring,* property = labor = capital. Any tax which diminishes these three items is a direct tax. Any tax that diminishes only the fruit of these three is an income tax. The income tax issue is complex. The only way to avoid confusion and clearly understand the subject of income taxes is to break the subject down into parts. Each part must be analyzed independently of the other parts. Only when we understand each part of the income tax puzzle, are we ready to assemble the parts back together and understand the whole of the income tax issue. In so doing, we will end up with a lot of pigeon holes for income taxes by the end of this chapter.

> **"The Supreme Court of the United States has thus held that certain kinds of income taxes are indirect, that certain other kinds of income taxes are direct, and that still other kinds of income taxes are invalid, irrespective of whether they are direct or indirect." Edwin R.A. Seligman, The Income-Tax Amendment, 25 Political Science Quarterly 193, 197 (1910).**

The word "income" occurs only once in the Constitution. It was added to the Constitution when the Income Tax amendment was purportedly ratified on February 3, 1913. It is the term "constitutional income" for which this book seeks to discover the meaning. What we will discover is that the meaning of "constitutional income" is more narrow than that of the generic word "income."

So why is it that our task is to "discover" what the word income means? Why don't we do as the court does; why don't we "determine" what the word income means? The legal community used to view the law as something that was to be discovered just as science viewed the physical world as something to be discovered, i.e., the law of gravity. In the legal realm, the law must make sense. It must have a foundation. There must be "authority" for every law. As a culture, we used to believe the law originated with God's law. Thomas Jefferson wrote of this in the Declaration of Independence when he penned the words, "the laws of Nature and of Nature's God."

Our legal foundation was based on the common law, which had its roots in Scripture. The great legal minds of Jefferson's time would study the Scripture in order to "discover" what the law already was. About the time scientists decided they would determine what the origin of man was, instead of relying on both the scientific and scriptural evidence, so did the legal community begin to determine what the law ought to be, in their opinion, instead of discovering what the law already was. Mortal man was never given standing by the ultimate Jurist of the universe to make such a determination.[1]

Even when God gave Moses the Ten Commandments, there were circumstances that arose among the people—"fact patterns"—for the legal community, that needed to be adjudicated. Since real life presents many shades of gray, Moses was overwhelmed with the task of resolving all the conflicts among the people. He soon had to delegate his judicial authority to a network of judges. So we had the first court system, which out of necessity, would have to establish a system of jurisprudence.[2] The question for any civilized people is "On what foundation will any system of jurisprudence be based?"

Will it be based on a foundation of absolutes, or will it be relative where even the words lose their meaning as it seems fitting for those in power to redefine them?"

Now who is it that has established what the constitutional meaning of the word "income" is? The answer is self-evident to students of American history, but for the average American today it is a total mystery. It is the Sovereigns of our country, at the time the word "income" was added to the Constitution, who established the meaning of the word. Put more directly, it is the **We the People**, in our sovereign capacity, at the time of the ratification of the 16th Amendment, who have forever established the meaning of the word "income." Now it is up to us to discover what the People understood this word to mean during the time period between July 27, 1909, when the 16th Amendment was sent out to the states by Congress for ratification, and February 3, 1913, when the 35th state purportedly ratified it.

James B. McDonough stated:

> **"The people are the source of all political power. No limit can be imposed on them in their sovereign capacity as to their absolute right to amend their own constitution in such manner as they please, unless that limit is imposed by the people themselves." McDonough, Amending the Constitution of the United States, 76 Central Law Journal 335, 337 (1913).**

Similarly, on the issue of what were the meaning of the terms "direct tax," "tax," and "indirect tax" we read in the *Harvard Law Review:*

> **"The task of interpretation must therefore be to discover what was the meaning common to each of these terms at the time the Constitution was adopted." Francis W. Bird, Constitutional Aspects of the Federal Tax on the Income of Corporations, 24 Harvard Law Review 31, 32 (1911).**

In attempting to resolve what the word "income" meant within the context of the 16th Amendment, the Supreme Court said in the *Eisner v. Macomber Case:*

> **"Congress cannot by any definition it may adopt conclude the matter, since it cannot by legislation alter the Constitution, from which alone it derives its power to legislate, and within whose limitations alone that power can be lawfully exercised." Eisner v. Macomber, 252 U.S. 189, 206 (1919).**

> **Mr. CUMMINS (Iowa). "It does not; it can not. The character of a tax, the validity of a tax, must be determined by its essential characteristics. It must be determined by the circumstances under which it is laid and the thing or things upon which it is laid. Congress cannot make an income tax a special excise tax by so denominating it. We must look further into the subject than the language used by the committee." 45 Cong. Rec. 3976 (1909).**

> **"If it be true that by varying the form the substance may be changed, it is not easy to see that anything would remain of the limitations of the Constitution, or of the rule of taxation and representation, so carefully recognized and guarded in favor of the citizens of each State. But constitutional provisions cannot be thus evaded. It is the substance and not the form which controls, as has indeed been established by repeated decisions of this court." Pollock v. Farmers' Loan & Trust Co., 157 U.S. 429, 581 (1895).**

This book will not attempt to be a treatise on the issue of "constitutional income." That some sources can be taxed under the authority of the 16th Amendment is well settled. Sources like interest income, net income from rents, and essentially any income we know today as "unearned income" or "passive income" is taxable under the 16th Amendment. There are a few exceptions, like interest from government bonds, but we will leave this topic for others.

This book seeks to resolve the controversy as to whether or not the 16th Amendment provides the authority to tax wages and salaries as "income" within the meaning of the word "income" as it is used in the 16th Amendment. The Supreme Court said in *U.S. v. Sprague*:

> **The Constitution was written to be understood by the voters; its words and phrases were used in their normal and ordinary [meaning] as distinguished from [their] technical meaning; where the intention is clear there is no room for construction and no excuse for interpolation or addition. United States v. Sprague, 282 U.S. 716, 731 (1930).**

Consequently, we will look at the newspapers of the day, the Congressional debates, law journal articles, economic journal articles and court cases from the time period when the 16th Amendment was ratified.

## Classes of Taxpayers

Before we get into the meat of this issue, we need to lay some groundwork. The first issue the reader needs to be aware of is the legal concept of "classes." If you were a veterinarian, you would divide the animal world into two classes; those being "small animals" and "large animals." If you were a school administrator, you would divide your student body into different classes according to age and the number of years of school experience. If you were going to join efforts with a group of people to pursue a lawsuit, there would be something you held in common with your fellow plaintiffs, i.e., you were all wronged by the same party and each of you have a similar "fact pattern." This commonality among you would constitute a class and you would pursue a "class action lawsuit." Since we are interested in "constitutional income," we need to look to the

Constitution for our division into classes of those things or persons which the government may tax. We will need to divide people into classes, and we will need to divide "artificial entities" into classes as they come under the authority of the government to levy taxes.

Now our government is one of limited powers. Its powers are written down in the Constitution. We say it is a government of limited powers, or a "limited constitutional government." If the powers were not limited, then what would be the purpose of a written constitution? None.

## Geographical Classification

Geographically, there are two systems of government provided by the Constitution. Each of these systems of government is regulated to a specific geographical area. One geographical area constitutes the several States. Today there are fifty of them. We call them the "several States of the Union." The other geographical area consists of all other areas which are part of the United States but are not themselves States of the Union. These are possessions, territories, enclaves and insular possessions, or federal states. They include such places as Puerto Rico, the U.S. Virgin Islands, Guam, American Samoa, military bases, enclaves, etc. In the case of a military base within the exterior boundaries of one of the several States (i.e., the military base down the road from your community if you live in one of the 50 states), the federal government can not lawfully exercise its exclusive authority on the military base unless the legislature of that state ceded the real estate to the federal government. It is not enough for the federal government to just buy the property; the physical real estate must be ceded to the federal government by an act of the legislature of the state in order for the federal government to have exclusive jurisdiction. In this example, the federal government is known as the "United States." This is not the same as the "United States of America."

The power of our government to govern the areas under its jurisdiction which are outside, "without," the several States is given at Article I, section 8, clause 17, and Article IV, section 3, clause 2 of the Constitution. The first reads, "[The congress shall have power] To exercise exclusive legislation in all cases whatsoever, over such district (not exceeding ten Miles square) as may, by cession of particular States, and the Acceptance of Congress, become the Seat of the Government of the United States, and to exercise like Authority over all Places purchased by the Consent of the Legislature of the State in which the Same shall be, for the Erection of Forts, Magazines, Arsenals, dock-Yards, and other Needful buildings." The latter clause reads, "The Congress shall have Power to dispose of and make all needful Rules and Regulations respecting the Territory or other Property belonging to the United States...."

The power to "exercise exclusive legislation" does not constitute a government of limited powers. It is an all powerful government, but limited to specific geographical areas. We must remember that the Constitution was written by the states for the states. It was not written for any other purpose. This means the federal government is not restricted by the limitations of the Constitution in areas like Puerto Rico, unless Congress decides to limit itself, by statute, in these areas. For example, Congress could choose to adopt the Constitution as a statute for these federal areas if Congress wanted to do so. When Congress does this, Congress can make minute changes or huge omissions in the "statute" form of the Constitution. Then Congress could make all sorts of noise about "constitutional this" and "constitutional that" when all they are really talking about is a statute.

> **"6. That where the Constitution has been once formally extended by Congress to territories, neither Congress nor the territorial legislature can enact laws inconsistent therewith." Downes v. Bidwell, 182 U.S. 244, 271 (1901).**

What is significant about this is that Congress may pass laws which pertain only to the possessions and territories, and these laws may show up in the United States Code books. Consequently, just because you read a law in the United States Code books doesn't mean that law applies to you. You must first check the law's geographical and personam jurisdiction to see if the law applies to you. With hundreds of different definitions of the term "United States," it is likely it doesn't.

Furthermore, because Congress can create "words of art" and "terms of art" for any statute it passes, Congress may choose to define the term "United States" as only the possessions and the territories. When Congress does this, a simple reading of the statute will cause the reader to think the statute applies to the "United States" as the conversational meaning of the term implies, i.e., the 50 states; when in fact the statute may only apply to the possessions and territories. Within the entire body of federal and state law, there are some 450 different definitions of the term "United States." This should raise a red flag in your mind.

Those who seek to return the federal government to its constitutional boundaries like to quote the Supreme Court case of Downes v. Bidwell, 182 U.S. 244, 267 (1901), as follows:

> **"The power of Congress over the territories of the United States is general and plenary, arising from and incidental to the right to acquire the territory itself, and from the power given by the constitution to make all needful rules and regulations respecting the territory or other property belonging to the United States. It would be absurd to hold that the United States has power to acquire territory, and not power to govern it when acquired."**

What the Supreme Court is saying is what we read earlier, that the Constitution was written by the states and for the states; it was not written for the territories and possessions. Consequently, those people who live in the territories and possessions do not enjoy the same constitutional protections that we who live in the 50 states enjoy. In the territories and possessions, Congress is not bound "by the chains of the Constitution," as Thomas Jefferson put it.

For our subject matter of taxation, there are two other cases which are more on point. The first case is an income tax case from Hawaii in the year 1903. Hawaii was a territory at this time and did not become a state until 1959. In pertinent part, the opinion of the court was:

> **"The provision that the legislative power shall extend to 'all rightful subjects of legislation' includes, therefore, full and comprehensive power to legislate in the matter of taxation. Article I, sections 8, of the Constitution, requiring 'that all duties, imposts, and excises shall be uniform throughout the United States,' can have no application to the powers of taxation of a state or territorial legislature. It is a rule only for taxation by the United States. The decisions of the Supreme Court construing and applying that provision of the Constitution and most of the discussion thereof found in the opinions filed in Pollock v. Farmers' Loan & Trust Co., 157 U.S. 429, 15 S. Ct. 673, 39 L.Ed. 759, and on rehearing, 158 U.S. 607, 15 S. Ct. 912, 39 L.Ed. 1108, so freely quoted from and earnestly relied upon by the appellants, can have no bearing, therefore, upon the present discussion." W. C. Peacock & Co. v. Pratt, 121 F. 772, 776 (1903).**

Because Hawaii was a territory in 1903, the court said that the power of taxation possessed by the government within the territory of Hawaii is not restricted by the Constitution. Therefore, in territories Congress may tax whatever Congress wants to and however Congress wants to. Any tax law either Congress or the territorial legislature passes for the Territory of Hawaii would therefore be constitutional. As we saw earlier, the power of Congress to govern in the territories is unlimited, unless Congress chooses to limit itself. Too bad for you if you live in a territory or possession.

The second case is from the Philippines and takes place after the 16th Amendment was ratified. The controversy was over income taxes paid in the year 1918 and concerns one of the first income tax statutes passed by Congress only five years after the 16th Amendment was purportedly ratified. Quoting from the case:

> **"The power of Congress, in the imposition of taxes and providing for the collection thereof in the possessions of the United States, is not restricted by constitutional provision (section 8, article 1), which may limit its general power of taxation as to uniformity and apportionment when legislating for the mainland or United States proper, for it acts in the premises under the authority of clause 2, section 3, article 4, of the Constitution, which clothes Congress with power to make all needful rules and regulations respecting the territory or other property belonging to the United States, Binns v. United States, 194 U.S. 486, 24 S. Ct. 816, 48 L.Ed. 1087; Downes v. Bidwell, 182 U.S. 244, 21 S. Ct. 770, 45 L.Ed. 1088." Lawrence v. Wardell, 273 F. 405, 408 (9th Cir. 1921).**

It cannot be said more plainly. The two rules which limit Congress' authority to levy taxes, namely the rule of apportionment and the rule of uniformity, do not apply outside of the several States.[3] In legalese, we would describe this geographical area as "within the exterior boundaries of the United States and without the exterior boundaries of the several States." Put another way, this describes the possessions, territories, enclaves, insular possessions, and Washington D.C. In these areas, Congress is not bound by the Constitution, and therefore, there is no such thing as "constitutional income" as the word "income" is used in the Constitution. How can you have "constitutional income" when the Constitution doesn't apply? "Income" is whatever Congress says it is.

> **"It is conceded by the court that Congress may lawfully impose direct taxes in the District for District purposes, without regard to the rule of apportionment, and that Congress is under no constitutional necessity to impose direct taxes by the rule of apportionment upon the District of Columbia, or upon the territories, even though such a direct tax is laid upon the States." William Bradford Bosley, The Constitutional Requirements of Uniformity in Duties, Imposts and Excises, 9 Yale Law Journal 164, 169 (1900).**

Now ask yourself a question, "Is it possible that Congress passed an income tax law, uninhibited by the Constitution, which applies only in the territories and possessions, and then defined the territories and possessions to mean "United States?" If Congress did this, would you find this law in Title 26, the Internal Revenue Code? Yes, you would! Would the law be unconstitutional? Well, if the law only applied to the territories and possessions, the law is constitutional regardless of what the law taxes or how the taxes are applied. So be careful when you state a particular income tax statute is "unconstitutional." If that statute only applies to the territories and possessions of the United States, you would be incorrect.

> **"We are of the opinion that the island of Porto Rico is a territory appurtenant and belonging to the United States, but not a part of the United States within the revenue clauses of the Constitution. Downes v. Bidwell, 182 U.S. 244, 287 (1901).**

So here are our first two classes of persons: (1) Those who live within the exterior boundaries of the several States (they live in a state as we commonly think of a state) and enjoy the protections of a limited constitutional government and; (2) a separate class of persons who live in the United States but without the exterior boundaries of the several States and do not enjoy the protections of a limited constitutional government. As we will see later, it is very important to be careful with the words we use. The word "state" is one of those suspect words with multiple definitions. We will see in Chapter 9 that the word "state" can actually apply within the several States while not designating one of the several States of the Union. Don't feel badly if this is confusing to you; it was designed to be that way.

Lastly, there are some things that the government has no right to tax regardless of whether the tax is direct or indirect. This would have to do with one sovereignty placing a tax on another sovereignty, i.e., a state taxing the federal government, or *visa versa*. Since the "power to tax is the power to destroy," different sovereignties within our governmental system cannot tax each other nor can they tax the instrumentalities of each other.

> **"Justice Harlan, who concurred with the views expressed by Justice White, added: 'In such a case it is immaterial to inquire whether the tax (on the income of municipal bonds) is, in its nature or by its operation, a direct or an indirect tax; for the instrumentalities of the states are not subjects of national taxation in any form or for any purpose.' And Justice Brown stated that a tax upon the income of municipal bonds was, in his opinion, a 'tax upon something which Congress has no right to tax at all, and hence is invalid.' Here is a question, not of the method of taxation, but of the power to subject the property to taxation in any form. Pollock v. Farmer's Loan and Trust Co., 157 U.S. 429, 654 (1895); 158 U.S. 601, 693, (1895)." Edwin R.A. Seligman, The Income Tax Amendment, 25 Political Science Quarterly 193, 199 (1910).**

## Government Employees

The next class we will look at has to do with the place of employment of a natural person. For the purposes of federal income taxation, there are three classes of persons with regard to the place of employment. There are those who work in the private sector, those who work for state government or instrumentalities of state government, i.e., counties, cities, other governmental districts; and those who work for the federal government and its instrumentalities.

Very early in American jurisprudence the doctrine of "The power to tax is the power to destroy" was established. This was a quote from Supreme Court Chief Justice Marshall in the 1803 case of *McCulloch v. Maryland*. In this case, the state of Maryland was attempting to tax a bank which was an instrumentality of the federal government. In ruling on this case, the court had to address the issue of our dual system of government whereby we have enumerated and limited powers granted to the federal government and other powers granted to our state governments. Each government is completely sovereign within its sphere of enumerated powers.

That our system of government is one of dual sovereignty is not expressly defined in any of our constitutions, although it is alluded to in the 10th Amendment. In reality, we actually have a governmental system based on a triple sovereignty where the People represent the third sovereignty of government. In resolving the issue as to whether or not the state of Maryland could tax an instrumentality of the national government, the Supreme Court said:

> **"There is no express provision [of the constitution] for the case, but the claim has been sustained on a principle which so entirely pervades the Constitution, is so intermixed with the materials which compose it, so interwoven with its web, so blended with its texture as to be incapable of being separated from it without rendering it to shreds." <u>McCulloch v. Maryland</u>, 17 U.S. 316, 426 (1819).**

In debating the income tax amendment, Senator Borah of Idaho commented on this passage of *McCulloch v. Maryland* when he said:

> **"Upon what principle, stated a little more fully, but never more comprehensively, did the Chief Justice argue that you could not tax the instrumentalities of Government?**

> **Upon the theory that the Constitution as a whole created two separate and distinct sovereignties independent of each other in their specific and reserved powers, and that however full the grant of power of taxation might be in the Constitution, there must always be subtracted from that power the right of the different sovereignties to perform their functions as such. In other words, said the Chief Justice, to construe it otherwise would be to rend the whole fabric to shreds." 45 Cong. Rec. 1,696 (1910).**

What the court was saying in practical terms was that if one sovereignty taxes another sovereignty, that the former will be in a position to destroy the latter, as the power to tax is the power to destroy. Consequently, there would not be two sovereigns in this case but only one. That being repugnant to our form of government, the court ruled the state of Maryland could not impose a tax on a bank which was an instrumentality of the national government. Likewise the People, being the third sovereignty, imposed limitations on the taxation power of Congress, that being the rule of apportionment and the rule of uniformity.

Immediately the question begs to be asked: "Well how come state employees pay an income tax to the federal government, and federal government employees pay an income tax to state governments?" Because the two sovereignties agreed to do so. It was not always this way, and there is a large body of court cases that say such an agreement is unconstitutional. In the case of *Collector v. Day* (later overturned), the income tax of the Civil War period was held to be unconstitutional in so far as it applied to the salaries of state judges. The court said:

> **The general government, and the States, although both exist within the same territorial limits, are separate and distinct sovereignties, acting separately and independently of each other, within their respective spheres. The former in its appropriate sphere is supreme; but the States within the limits of their powers not granted, or, in the**

**language of the tenth amendment, 'reserved,' are as independent of the general government as that government within its sphere is independent of the States." Collector v. Day, 11 Wall. 113, 124 (1870).**

In the first *Pollock Decision,* Justice Field wrote on page 602:

**"The taxing power of the Federal government does not therefore extend to the means or agencies through or by the employment of which the States perform their essential functions, since, if these were within its reach, they might be embarrassed, and perhaps wholly paralyzed, by the burdens it should impose. 'That the power to tax involves the power to destroy; that the power to destroy may defeat and render useless the power to create; that there is a plain repugnance in conferring on one government a power to control the constitutional measures of another...It is true that taxation does not necessarily and unavoidably destroy, and that to carry it to the excess of destruction would be an abuse not to be anticipated; but the very power would take from the States a portion of their intended liberty of independent action within the sphere of their powers, and would constitute to the State a perpetual danger of embarrassment and possible annihilation. The Constitution contemplates no such shackles upon state powers, and by implication forbids them." Pollock v. Farmer's Loan & Trust, 157 U.S. 429, 602 (1895).**

And finally in the case of *Dobbins v. Commissioners,* 16 Pet. 435, it was held by the court that the salary of a governmental official could not be taxed if the office itself was exempt from taxation.

This relationship between the state and federal governments, or I should say lack of a relationship, was done away with in 1939 when the federal government and the state governments entered into an agreement whereby each government could tax the employees of the other. It is my belief that this relationship is illegal, the Constitution being the supreme law of the land and the law that is violated in this case, agreement or no agreement. The practice of one government taxing the employees of another government enmeshes together what was intended to be kept separate. It is a violation of the very essence of our system of checks and balances. More on this problem in Chapter 9.

Our founding fathers recognized that man had a sinful nature, and that some men would use every opportunity to take advantage of their fellow citizens. We have all heard the saying, "Power corrupts, and absolute power corrupts absolutely." This being the reality of the human species, an elaborate system of checks and balances was built into our governmental system. The dual system of sovereignties (or triple system of sovereignties if you include the People) is one of them. By allowing the federal government to tax state government employees and *vice versa*, our system of checks and balances has been eroded. It is not just for the benefit of a particular government employee to guard against taxation of him by a sovereign other than the one they are employed by, but it is for the protection of the People. How can the state defend the People against an encroaching federal bureaucracy when the employees of the state can at any time find themselves under the microscope of the federal government's tax collector? Statutory agreement or no statutory agreement, this relationship is illegal.

On the issue of income taxes and taxes on employment, the federal government's relationship with its employees is a unique one within the country. No one has a right to work for the federal government. Employment with the federal government is, in law, considered a privilege.

There are common elements to any employer/employee relationship regardless of who the parties are. This being the case, the relationship between the federal government and its employees is unique and entirely different from the relationship between our national government and a citizen of one of the several States. When an employee sells his time to an employer, the employer owns the hours that the employee offered for sale. During the hours of employment, the employer can make all kinds of demands on the employee. Burger King, as an employer, might choose to demand of its employees that they wear clean clothes to work, that they wash their hands after going to the bathroom, that they receive their pay at certain specified intervals, and so on.

The federal government can make similar demands of its employees since the relationship is a voluntary one and one of privilege. Just like a retail clothing store can mark up its merchandise so that when it's put on sale and marked down, the savings appear to be dramatic. So can the federal government artificially raise the pay of all its employees only to "mark them down" by extracting a tax on the employee's pay. The deduction on the pay can be called anything Congress wants to call it. Congress can pass a statute that named this diminution of pay by any name under the sun. Congress could call it a contribution, a gift, a present, a walk in the park if it wanted to. They could even call it an "income tax" as there is no constitutional or other legal restraint on the federal government's taking deductions out of their own employee's pay checks, except those restrictions that Congress chooses to impose on itself by statute. Such statutes would be "nonconstitutional" or "extraconstitutional" as they are not restricted by any constitutional provision.

The same is true for state governments taxing the pay of their own employees. And in practice, but not constitutionally, the same situation prevails in the relationship of state government employees to the federal government and *vice versa*.

Related to the issue of taxing government employees is the issue of taxing government debt instruments. According to professor Seligman and the Supreme Court, such taxes are unconstitutional.

> **"The Supreme Court of the United States has thus held that certain kinds of income taxes are indirect, that certain other kinds of income taxes are direct, and that still other kinds of income taxes are invalid, irrespective of**

> **whether they are direct or indirect." Edwin R.A. Seligman, The Income-Tax Amendment, 25 Political Science Quarterly 193, 197 (1910).**

And finally, there are some things that are completely outside Congress' authority to tax:

> **Mr. CUMMINS. "But Congress can not touch by a tax, the equivalent of a power to destroy....We have observed them already in the discussion of this question. Everybody concedes that the United States can not tax the bonds of a state government or of a municipal government organized by state law. No more can the State tax the bonds of the United States or any other instrumentality of the Nation." 44 Cong. Rec. 3977 (1910).**

The concept here is that our system of dual sovereignties, state and federal, precludes one of the sovereignties from taxing the other sovereignty as the power to tax each other would convey the power to destroy each other. This is the tax that Seligman referred to above as being invalid regardless of whether it was direct or indirect. The same concept ought to hold true among our three departments of government. The executive department of government should not have the power to directly tax the personnel who make up either the legislative department or the judicial department of government. The fact this is no longer true is evidence that our fundamental structure of government has been corrupted.

## Federal Judges

There is one other class of persons as it relates to "constitutional income" taxation at the federal level. This has to do with the taxation of federal judges. Initially, one might think this is a minuscule issue as it only affects about 1,500 people, but it really affects all of us. Unfortunately, this effect is a negative one.

The national Constitution provides that "The judges, both of the Supreme and inferior courts, shall hold their offices during good behavior, and shall, at stated times, receive for their services, a compensation, which shall not be diminished during their continuance in office." U.S. Const., art. 3, sec. 1.

One of the major issues that motivated the Revolutionary War generation to reject King George's government and to form a new one was the control the king had over the colonial judges. In listing the grievances of the American colonists against the king, the Declaration of Independence states, "He has made judges dependent on his will alone, for the tenure of their offices, and the amount and payment of their salaries."

Our Constitution guards against the control of others over our judges by the creation of an independent judiciary. As with so much of our constitutional system, this protection provided by our Constitution has been violated. There is a long history of cases on this issue, all affirming the constitutional independence of the judiciary. The controlling case on this topic is the Supreme Court case of *Evans v. Gore*, decision June 1, 1920. Judge Walter Evans was a United States District Judge for the Western District of Kentucky. His salary was being taxed under the income tax act called "Act of February 24, 1919," and he sued to recover income taxes paid under protest. In the decision the court stated:

> **"The Constitution was framed on the fundamental theory that a larger measure of liberty and justice would be assured by vesting the three great powers, the legislative, the executive, and the judicial, in separate departments, each relatively independent of the others; and it was recognized that without this independence, if it was not made both real and enduring, the separation would fail of its purpose. All agreed that restraints and checks must be imposed to secure the requisite measure of independence; for otherwise the legislative department,**

**inherently the strongest, might encroach on or even come to dominate the others, and the judicial, naturally the weakest, might be dwarfed or swayed by the other two...." Evans v. Gore, 253 U.S. 245, 249 (1920).**

**"Is it not, to the last degree important, that he should be rendered perfectly and completely independent, with nothing to influence or control him but God and his conscience? ...I have always thought, from my earliest youth till now, that the greatest scourge an angry Heaven ever inflicted upon an ungrateful and a sinning people, was an ignorant, a corrupt, or a dependant Judiciary." id., 251.**

**"In the general course of human nature, a power over a man's subsistence amounts to a power over his will." id., 252.**

**"For the articles which limit the power of the legislative and the executive branches of the government, and those which provide safeguards for the protections of the citizen in his person and property, would be of little value without a judiciary to uphold and maintain them, which was free from every influence, direct or indirect, that might by possibility in times of political excitement warp their judgements.**

**"Upon these grounds I regard an act of congress retaining in the Treasury a portion of the compensation of the judges, as unconstitutional and void." id., 258.**

**"After further consideration, we adhere to that view and accordingly hold that the Sixteenth Amendment does not authorize or support the tax in question." id., 263.**

Today, all members of the federal judiciary pay income taxes. As we have seen before, such a relationship between departments of government, which are to be independent, is unconstitutional. The authority that provides for the imposition of this tax on federal judges is the Public Salary Tax Act of 1939. Sections 209 and 210 of this act state:

> **"Sec. 209 In the case of the judges of the Supreme Court and of the inferior courts of the United States created under article III of the Constitution, who took office on or before June 6, 1932, the compensation received as such shall not be subject to income tax under the Revenue Act of 1938 or any prior Revenue Act.**
>
> **Sec. 210 For the purpose of this Act, the term "officer or employee" includes a member of a legislative body and a judge or officer of a court."**

How can a judge, who is under the jurisdiction of the IRS, possibly act with independence on an income tax issue? The answer is he can not. It doesn't take a rocket scientist to realize the huge contribution this situation provides to the power of the taxman.

> **"Let me tell you how it will be. Here's one for you, nineteen for me.**
>
> **'Cause I'm the taxman, yeah I'm the taxman.**
>
> **Should five percent appear too small, be thankful I don't take it all.**
>
> **'Cause I'm the taxman, yeah I'm the taxman.**
>
> **If you drive a car, I'll tax the street. If you try to sit, I'll tax the seat.**
>
> **If you get too cold, I'll tax the heat. If you take a walk, I'll tax your feet.**
>
> **Taxman. 'Cause I'm the taxman, yeah I'm the taxman."**
>
> ***~The Beatles, Revolver, Apple Records 1 (1966).***

Does the Treasury or the Nation really benefit from this minuscule amount of additional revenue taken from the paycheck of a federal judge at the expense of the independence of the judiciary? And what about Congress? Should Congress be under the jurisdiction of an agency of the executive branch? Why don't we just pay the employees of the legislative and judicial branches of government 20 percent less and free them from the jurisdiction of the IRS so that we can maintain our system of checks and balances and separation of powers among the three departments of government? Federal judges and members of Congress should not be paying income taxes on their earned income.

There is an unseen hand behind the erosion of our system of constitutional government. In 1787, when Benjamin Franklin walked out of Independence Hall where the Constitutional Convention was being held, a woman asked him "What kind of system of government have you given us?" He replied, "A constitutional republic, if you can keep it."

To whom this unseen hand belongs and its purpose is beyond the scope of this book. But let me offer the following quote out of the Congressional Record, July 5, 1909, volume 44, page 4115. The subject matter being debated was the income tax amendment.

> **Mr. MONEY. "Mr. President, I am one of those who believe that there never will be another amendment to the Constitution of the United States. Already, I understand, about 13 States have called for a convention of all the States. If that convention should be called, as it will ultimately be, I have no doubt the first resolution that will be offered will be to abolish the Constitution of the United States for the very reason that we have been for some time acting under a suspension of it, and those who are in authority are heartily tired of it." 44 Cong. Rec. 4115 (1909).**

Now let's test what we have learned about classes of taxpayers under the federal income tax system by asking a series of questions.

When imposing an income tax on United States citizens living in a territory, possession, district or enclave, can Congress define what the word income means? Yes.

When imposing an income tax on employees of the federal government (except for federal judges) regardless of where they live and work, can Congress define what the word income means? Yes.

When imposing an income tax under the authority of the 16th Amendment on a Citizen of the United States living and working in a private enterprise in one of the several States of the Union, can Congress define what the word income means? No, Congress can't. Any income tax levied under the authority of the 16th Amendment, must apply the "constitutional meaning" of the word "income."

Now if Congress were to levy an income tax on the gross revenue of a person (a human being), which is a species of a capitation tax, then Congress can call it anything it wants to call it, but the tax must be apportioned among the several States. Remember the framers of the Constitution relied on Adam Smith's definition of a direct tax as being, among other things, a tax on the revenue of a person.

> **"Capitation taxes, so far as they are levied upon the lower ranks of people, are direct taxes upon the wages of labour." Adam Smith, Wealth of Nations, book V, 540 (Prometheus Books, Amherst, New York, 1991) (1776).**

The point of this chapter is to show that there are many classes of taxpayers upon which the tax laws will apply differently. Just because you read in the income tax statutes that "Thou shalt pay an income tax" doesn't mean that you owe the tax. You must first determine upon which class of taxpayers and in which geographical area the tax is imposed.

Then ask yourself, "Am I within this class?" "Am I within this geographical area?

| Class | Subclass | Can Congress define the word "income?" |
|---|---|---|
| United States Citizens living in a federal area aka United States | President, Article III judge | No |
| | All other Citizens | Yes |
| Citizen of the United States living in the several States aka The United States of America | Government employee | Yes |
| | Federal judge | No |
| | Citizen working in the private sector | No |
| | Citizen working in a federal area i.e. a military base | Yes |
| Alien | Resident alien | Yes |
| | Non-resident alien | Yes |
| Artificial person | None | Yes |

*Figure 4.1—Classes of taxpayers*

*New York Times*, **page 1, August 3, 1909**

# INCOME TAX VOTED IN ALABAMA HOUSE

## By Unanimous Vote Proposed Constitutional Amendment Is Authorized.

## SENATE TO ACT TO-MORROW

### Assurances from Governor Show That There Will Be No Opposition.

*Special to The New York Times.*

MONTGOMERY, Ala., Aug. 2.—Unanimously voting in support of the measure, the House of Representatives of Alabama authorized to-day the amendment to the United States Constitution proposed by Congress several weeks ago. Upon special request the measure was taken up under the head of "special orders." Col. Thomas L. Bulger of Dadeville spoke in favor of the amendment, and it was rushed through at once and into the Senate. That body is expected to take action by Wednesday, and Gov. B. B. Comer will affix his signature to the measure on the same afternoon.

Action on the question has been one of the quickest in the history of the State. Last week, on the second day's session of the Legislature, in special session, a resolution was introduced favoring the amendment. That afternoon the resolution was placed in the hands of the Judiciary Committee of both houses, and on the next day was reported back to the houses favorably. On Saturday the Legislature was adjourned, and to-day an especial dispensation of the Chair permitted the question to come up for final vote. By the end of this week Alabama's Representatives in Congress will be apprised of this State's vote, and the income amendment will be as good as in the Constitution so far as this State is concerned. That there will be no objection to the measure whatever is assured in the office of Gov. B. B. Comer. "You may state," is the announcement from that source, "that Alabama has no objection whatever to the amendment. It is a very good way to keep the country away from greater infidelity."

Continued next page

In introducing the measure to the House, Col. Bulger, who is one of the State's political leaders, stated that he was "Anxious to see Alabama the first State in the Union to give her indorsement to the Sixteenth Amendment to the United States Constitution." The only interruption to his speech was a query by Representative J. T. Glover of Birmingham, who wanted to know if the amendment would affect salaries. Col. Sam Will John, also of Birmingham, responded that it would not, unless Congress passed a law including salaries.

Then the vote was called for.

In his speech favoring the amendment Col. Bulger reviewed the conditions necessitating the Constitutional change.

continued from previous page

***New York Times*, page 1, June 30, 1909**

# ALDRICH TRICK PUTS INCOME TAX ASIDE

## Uses Senate Rule to Force a Vote First on the Corporation Tax Plan.

## HAS A CLASH WITH BAILEY

## Admits He Hopes to Kill Income Assessment by Corporation Scheme and Then Repeal That.

*Special to The New York Times.*

WASHINGTON, June 29.—Senator Aldrich's well-known ability to get out of tight legislative places was again revealed to-day, when the question of an income or corporation tax came before the Senate. By his move the insurgent Republicans and the Democrats who had been united on the Bailey-Cummins plan for a direct tax on incomes were completely routed. As one of the insurgents said to-night, they are all "up in the air."

The Republican "regulars" generally understood before the Senate convened to-day that the Senator from Rhode Island had decided upon some new move to circumvent his opponents. To-day's tariff discussion began with Senator Tillman's amendment to put a tax on tea, and although the South Carolina Senator fought hard for his measure on the ground that it would bring in several millions of dollars revenue to the Government, it was lost by a vote of 55 to 18.

**Continued next page**

Continued from previous page

**How the Trick Was Played.**

It was on the conclusion of the dutiable and free paragraphs shortly after 2 o'clock this afternoon that the corporation tax was called up. Then by a clever parliamentary manoeuvre that took the insurgents unawares, the proposed Administration substitute for the income levy was so handled that the income tax was indefinitely sidetracked and the corporation tax was left before the Senate in such a tactical position that under the rules of that body any amendment to it will be out of order.

Senator Bailey of Texas was out of the chamber when this move was executed. He returned shortly afterward and had a little talk with Mr. Aldrich and Mr. Lodge, smiling sheepishly at what had happened. Under the rules of the Senate an amendment in the third degree is out of order. Mr. Aldrich and Mr. Lodge hit upon the expedient of so introducing the corporation tax as to put it in the second degree, and all further amendment would therefore be out of order.

No sooner was Senator Tillman's tea tax voted down than Mr. Lodge offered a long general countervailing clause covering all the schedules as a substitute for the Bailey-Cummins income tax. This countervailing clause provides simply that in the case of imports on which the country of origin has paid a bounty there shall be levied additional duties equal to the bounty. It had nothing whatever to do with the income tax, but served the purpose of constituting an amendment in the first degree.

Continued next page

Continued from previous page

**Even Senator Lodge Winked.**

Mr. Aldrich then presented the corporation tax as an amendment to Mr. Lodge's amendment. That made the chain somewhat complete, and no further amendments were in order. Debate then proceeded, while most of the committee members, sure of the situation, left the chamber, smiling contentedly. Even Senator Lodge, whose eyes are ordinarily fixed deprecatingly on space, looked up to his friends in the gallery and actually winked.

The result of the Aldrich manoeuvre is practically to foreclose all chances of anything like a direct vote on the income tax. This vote Mr. Bailey had assured his Democratic colleagues he would secure for them on the floor. The first vote will be to include the corporation tax amendment into Mr. Lodge's substitute.

When that motion is carried the next vote will be to accept the substitute as amended—that is, the corporation tax and the countervailing duty provisions together in place of the Cummins-Bailey income tax. Only in the improbable event of the corporation and countervailing provisions being voted down will the income tax be reached at all. Supporters of the Administration say that it is now certain that the corporation tax will pass the Senate amended.

So sure are the organization leaders of the situation that Mr. Aldrich expects to go away to-morrow for a day or two of rest. He laughingly declined this afternoon to divulge his proposed place of retreat, but said he would return soon.

Continued next page

## From previous page

**Aldrich Explains His Stand.**

The debate on the tax did not get very far to-day, though important explanations were made. In reply to taunts from Senator Clay of Georgia, Mr. Aldrich, stating his position with reference to the corporation tax, said bluntly:

"I shall vote for the corporation tax as a means of defeating the income tax. I shall be perfectly frank in that respect. I shall vote for it for another reason. The income of the Government this year will show a deficit of $60,600,000. Next year this will be a deficit of $45,000,000. I am willing that that deficit shall be taken care of by a corporation tax, but at the end of two years it should either be reduced to a nominal amount or repealed."

Mr. Aldrich said that he did not favor as a permanent form of taxation a "tax which is sure in the end to destroy the protective system."

Thereupon Mr. Bailey entered the debate.

"Under the statement made by the Senator from Rhode Island," said Mr. Bailey, "those who have said they favor an income tax, and now join him in this subterfuge to defeat it may see clearly what they are doing. We now are told that this corporation tax is to be entirely repealed, or at least emasculated within the next two years, and see that, after all, it is simply a contest between an income tax as part of our fiscal system or a corporation tax as a subterfuge to be continued two years."

"My support of the corporation tax," replied Mr. Aldrich promptly, "is not a subterfuge. The corporation tax is a tax clearly within the right of Congress to impose, and those Senators who are honestly in favor of an income tax that is constitutional and that can be operated will support the income tax proposition of the Administration as against the proposition of the Senator from Texas, which is certainly, in the minds of the most thoughtful people, unconstitutional."

Editorial, *New York Times*, page 10, May 5, 1910

## THE REJECTED AMENDMENT.

The income tax amendment failed on Tuesday to get the necessary votes in the Assembly, and that disposes of it for the present session. It may be brought before the Legislature at the next session, but it is not likely, in its present form, to be received with any more favor.

The chief objection to the amendment, we think, in the minds of the public, as well as its opponents in the Legislature, is that it was hastily drawn, involved a principle of mischievous effect on the interests of the States, and would give rise to indefinite contention as to its real meaning. There was, however, another objection relating not to the substance of the amendment, but to the manner in which it was brought into being. It was originally proposed to the Senate of the United States to save Mr. ALDRICH and his associates from defeat on the revision of the tariff. To avoid this the amendment, together with the corporation tax, was contrived. It was not a nice device—to use no stronger term—and in the exigency existing it was carried out in a bungling fashion. If we are to have the Constitution changed in this matter, it certainly would be better to have it done decently and in order.

*New York Times*, **page 10, May 30, 1911**

# DRAMA FOR WAGE EARNERS.

## Director of Theatre Leagues Explains Their "Democracy."

*To the Editor of The New York Times:*

Referring to the letter signed by Leila V. Scott of the Hartley House, in relation to the Wage Earners' Theatre movement, permit me to make a reply so as to inform not merely Miss Scott of the situation but also the general public and all those interested in enabling the people of small means, those who work and do not make a living, to have access to the better things in life, the theatre, opera, music, &c. The Wage Earners' Theatre Leagues, organized this year, but in reality a development of efforts of many years, have become so large that now practically every group interested in the advancement of public life is affiliated with the leagues. The leagues are organized on a democratic basis, but there is no violation of democracy in the control of the distribution of tickets by the leagues themselves. The Department of Drama and Music of the People's Institute, prior to its dissolution, (and affiliation of its membership with the Wage Earners' Theatre Leagues) has called upon its head the severe criticism of letting anybody have reduced rate tickets with the result that theatrical people and managers of concerts objected to the "democratic" spirit prevailing when people luxuriously dressed and riding in taxicabs availed themselves of the opportunity of obtaining tickets at lower rates through being members of the movement.

Public school teachers are at present not as yet accepted to membership to the leagues because Mr. Maxwell has under consideration a plan of possibly permitting the formation of School Theatre Leagues.

Continued next page

## Continued from previous page

The purpose of our movement is not to sell tickets at half rate or less, but to *assist the people who, because of their* economic conditions (the people who work being usually poor) are deprived of the opportunities which people of means enjoy, namely, to go to good theatres, listen to good music and operas, &c. If our purpose is not emphasized, then people will flock to our distribution centres for tickets instead of going to the box offices for theatre tickets, and no one would be served, the people of limited means would be excluded, and the theatres would merely lose money. As it is, by observing positive rules, we serve the people, bring to the theatres a new clientele, and bring joys to those who never or seldom have an opportunity to go to the theatres today, if it were not for our movement.

Unlimited numbers of people would attempt and do attempt even now to get a dollar ticket for 50 cents, but this is not our purpose. We may be reduced to a cut-rate ticket office. We are a movement of the people organized to bring art to the toilers. The details will have to be worked out by the settlement houses and other affiliated branches themselves. They are the ones to distribute the tickets, not I or the people in my office.

JULIUS HOPP.

61st Congress, 1st Session. | SENATE. | Document No. 98.

TAX ON NET INCOME OF CORPORATIONS.

---

# MESSAGE

FROM THE

# PRESIDENT OF THE UNITED STATES,

RECOMMENDING

AN AMENDMENT TO THE TARIFF BILL IMPOSING UPON ALL CORPORATIONS AND JOINT STOCK COMPANIES FOR PROFIT, EXCEPT NATIONAL BANKS (OTHERWISE TAXED), SAVINGS BANKS, AND BUILDING AND LOAN ASSOCIATIONS, AN EXCISE TAX MEASURED BY 2 PER CENT ON THE NET INCOME OF SUCH CORPORATIONS; ALSO PROVIDING FOR A CONSTITUTIONAL AMENDMENT GIVING POWER TO IMPOSE TAXES ON INCOMES.

---

June 16, 1909.—Read; referred to the Committee on Finance and ordered to be printed.

---

*To the Senate and House of Representatives:*

It is the constitutional duty of the President from time to time to recommend to the consideration of Congress such measures as he shall judge necessary and expedient. In my inaugural address, immediately preceding this present extraordinary session of Congress, I invited attention to the necessity for a revision of the tariff at this session, and stated the principles upon which I thought the revision should be effected. I referred to the then rapidly increasing deficit, and pointed out the obligation on the part of the framers of the tariff bill to arrange the duty so as to secure an adequate income, and suggested that if it was not possible to do so by import duties, new kinds of taxation must be adopted, and among them I recommended a graduated inheritance tax as correct in principle and as certain and easy of collection. The House of Representatives has adopted the suggestion and has provided in the bill it passed for the collection of such a tax. In the Senate the action of its Finance Committee and the course of the debate indicate that it may not agree to this provision, and it is now proposed to make up the deficit by the imposition of a general income tax, in form and substance of almost exactly the same character as that which in the case of Pollock v. Farmers' Loan and Trust Company (157 U. S., 429) was held by the Supreme

**Continued next page**

from previous page



Court to be a direct tax, and therefore not within the power of the Federal Government to impose unless apportioned among the several States according to population. This new proposal, which I did not discuss in my inaugural address or in my message at the opening of the present session, makes it appropriate for me to submit to the Congress certain additional recommendations.

The decision of the Supreme Court in the income-tax cases deprived the National Government of a power which, by reason of previous decisions of the court, it was generally supposed that Government had. It is undoubtedly a power the National Government ought to have. It might be indispensable to the nation's life in great crises. Although I have not considered a constitutional amendment as necessary to the exercise of certain phases of this power, a mature consideration has satisfied me that an amendment is the only proper course for its establishment to its full extent. I therefore recommend to the Congress that both Houses, by a two-thirds vote, shall propose an amendment to the Constitution conferring the power to levy an income tax upon the National Government without apportionment among the States in proportion to population.

This course is much to be preferred to the one proposed of reenacting a law once judicially declared to be unconstitutional. For the Congress to assume that the court will reverse itself, and to enact legislation on such an assumption, will not strengthen popular confidence in the stability of judicial construction of the Constitution. It is much wiser policy to accept the decision and remedy the defect by amendment in due and regular course.

Again, it is clear that by the enactment of the proposed law, the Congress will not be bringing money into the Treasury to meet the present deficiency, but by putting on the statute book a law already there and never repealed, will simply be suggesting to the executive officers of the Government their possible duty to invoke litigation. If the court should maintain its former view, no tax would be collected at all. If it should ultimately reverse itself, still no taxes would have been collected until after protracted delay.

It is said the difficulty and delay in securing the approval of three-fourths of the States will destroy all chance of adopting the amendment. Of course, no one can speak with certainty upon this point, but I have become convinced that a great majority of the people of this country are in favor of vesting the National Government with power to levy an income tax, and that they will secure the adoption of the amendment in the States, if proposed to them.

Second, the decision in the Pollock case left power in the National Government to levy an excise tax which accomplishes the same purpose as a corporation income tax, and is free from certain objections urged to the proposed income-tax measure.

I therefore recommend an amendment to the tariff bill imposing upon all corporations and joint stock companies for profit, except national banks (otherwise taxed), savings banks, and building and loan associations, an excise tax measured by 2 per cent on the net income of such corporations. This is an excise tax upon the privilege of doing business as an artificial entity and of freedom from a general partnership liability enjoyed by those who own the stock.

I am informed that a 2 per cent tax of this character would bring into the Treasury of the United States not less than $25,000,000.

Continued next page

## Continued from previous page



The decision of the Supreme Court in the case of Spreckels Sugar Refining Company against McClain (192 U. S., 397) seems clearly to establish the principle that such a tax as this is an excise tax upon privilege and not a direct tax on property, and is within the federal power without apportionment according to population. The tax on net income is preferable to one proportionate to a percentage of the gross receipts, because it is a tax upon success and not failure. It imposes a burden at the source of the income at a time when the corporation is well able to pay and when collection is easy.

Another merit of this tax is the federal supervision which must be exercised in order to make the law effective over the annual accounts and business transactions of all corporations. While the faculty of assuming a corporate form has been of the utmost utility in the business world, it is also true that substantially all of the abuses and all of the evils which have aroused the public to the necessity of reform were made possible by the use of this very faculty. If now, by a perfectly legitimate and effective system of taxation, we are incidentally able to possess the Government and the stockholders and the public of the knowledge of the real business transactions and the gains and profits of every corporation in the country, we have made a long step toward that supervisory control of corporations which may prevent a further abuse of power.

I recommend, then, first, the adoption of a joint resolution by two-thirds of both Houses proposing to the States an amendment to the Constitution granting to the Federal Government the right to levy and collect an income tax without apportionment among the States according to population, and, second, the enactment, as part of the pending revenue measure, either as a substitute for, or in addition to, the inheritance tax, of an excise tax upon all corporations, measured by 2 per cent of their net income.

WM. H. TAFT.

THE WHITE HOUSE, *June 16, 1909.*

O

# Chapter 5
## Pigeon Holes for Taxes

**Mr. ALDRICH. "What is the use of playing on words? I want to know whether an income tax is not a tax of the same kind, paying out of the same fund upon the profits. It makes no difference what you call it. It is only a question of words. The Senator for Iowa may say this is an income tax. I may say it is a corporation tax. Another may say that it is a tax upon earnings. Another may say that it is an excise tax. You may characterize it as you please; it is a precise duplication."**

***—45 Cong. Rec. 4232 (1910).***

**"'The name of the tax is unimportant' that 'it is the substance and not the form which controls'; that the limitations of the Constitution cannot be 'frittered away' by calling a tax indirect when it is in fact direct."**

***—Pollock v. Farmers' Loan and Trust Co., 157 U.S. 429, 580-1, 583 (1895).***

A limited constitutional government can never have an unlimited power of taxation. After all, isn't the very essence and purpose of any free government to protect life, liberty and property? Protect it from what? Predators, of course. Any government, no matter how well meaning at its inception, will become a predator itself if given unlimited power, especially unlimited power over taxation. Remember the "power to tax is the power to destroy." In the *Pollock Decision,* Supreme Court Justice Field wrote:

> **"As stated by counsel: 'There is no such thing in the theory of our national government as unlimited power of taxation in Congress. There are limitations,' as he justly observes, 'of its powers arising out of the essential nature of all free governments; there are reservations of individual rights, without which society could not exist, and which are respected by every government. The right of taxation is subject to these limitations.' (citations omitted)." Pollock v. Farmers' Loan & Trust, 157 U.S. 429, 599 (1895).**

## Direct Taxes v. Indirect Taxes

Our national Constitution gives the national government the power to levy taxes. The Constitution divides the universe of all possible taxes into two parts, that of direct taxes and indirect taxes. We use the word "universe" the way a statistician would use the word as we want this universe of all possible taxes to include every conceivable tax known to man. As such, our Constitution gives the national government the authority to levy any and every conceivable tax.

> **"Everything to which the legislative power extends may be the subject of taxation, whether it be person or property, or possession, franchise or privilege, or occupation or right. Nothing but express constitutional limitation upon legislative authority can exclude anything to which the authority extends from the grasp of the taxing power, if the legislature in its discretion shall at any time select it for revenue purposes; and not only is the**

> **power unlimited in its reach as to subjects, but in its very nature it acknowledges no limits, and may be carried even to the extent of exhaustion and destruction, thus becoming in its exercise a power to destroy." Thomas M. Cooley, LL. D., A Treatise on the Law of Taxation, vol. 1, 9 (1903).**

Even though Congress has the power to levy any and every possible kind of tax, there are limitations on this power. These limitations come in the form of rules. As we saw in chapter 1, there are three rules that Congress must obey when imposing a tax. One is a rule of exception, and the other two are rules of limitation. The rule of exception prohibits Congress from taxing exports. The first rule of limitation provides that when levying a direct tax, the tax must be apportioned among the several States. This rule in the Constitution reads, "Representatives and direct taxes shall be apportioned among the several States which may be included within this Union." U. S. Const., art. I, sec. 2, cl. 3. The rule appears a second time in the Constitution as follows, "No capitation, or other direct tax, shall be laid, unless in proportion to the census or enumeration hereinbefore directed to be taken." U. S. Const., art. I, sec. 9, cl. 4. This is the only constitutional provision found twice in the document. One of the battle cries of the War of Independence was, "No taxation without representation!" "Taxation and representation go together."

Because direct taxes, when levied, are mandatory and unavoidable, the framers of the Constitution saw fit to tie direct taxation directly to representation. The issue of tying taxation to representation was so important, especially to the smaller states, it is likely the United States of America would have not survived the Articles of Confederation had the direct taxation rule not been tied to apportionment.

The other rule of taxation is a limitation on the levying of an indirect tax. This rule provides that "The Congress shall have power to lay and collect taxes, duties, imports and excises, to pay the debts and provide for the common defense and general welfare of the

United States; but all duties, imposts and excises shall be uniform throughout the United States." U.S. Const., art. I, sec. 8, cl. 1. Understanding the difference between a direct tax and an indirect tax is key to answering the question, "*Constitutional Income: Do You Have Any?*"

The national Constitution consists of only 4,440 words. It is a short yet an incredibly thorough document. It was written in the common language of the day, so that the common man could understand it. There were no "words of art" or "terms of art" used in its text. Appropriately, only a regular dictionary is necessary to define the words used in our Constitution.

You might say that "words of art" and "terms of art" are secret or disguised words. They are usually common words used in a statute with an uncommon and special meaning for that particular statute. We noted before that within the corpus of federal and state law there are some 450 plus meanings of the term "United States." As we shall see later on, anytime you see the term "United States" in any legal document, don't assume you know what this term means. The effect of "words of art" and "terms of art" is that the common man is unable to comprehend the meaning of a law as he doesn't understand the secret language of the legal community. It is my observation that when these terms have been used for many decades, even the legal community forgets the purpose of such "words of art" and "terms of art." Statues are written in code books. The meaning of the word "code" designates a "secret language." Get the picture?

Why do we care what a direct tax is? We care, because a tax on a man's wage or salary is a direct tax. We'll also want to know if the 16th Amendment provides an exception to the apportionment rule found in the Constitution such that a direct tax may be levied without apportionment. If each of us is subject to the income tax imposed on us by the IRS, and supposedly we work from January until about May each year to pay this tax, shouldn't we make an effort to understand this tax we pay? And shouldn't we also understand the constitutional rule Congress must follow in levying this tax? Of course we should! After all, wouldn't you say that a man who worked for four to five months each year to pay for something he didn't understand was either a slave or a fool?

We don't need to play any games to discover what the terms "direct taxes" and "indirect taxes" meant to the people of America in the latter part of the 18th century. Those who wrote our Constitution were generally of a pure motive. Otherwise they could not have said so much in so few words. In the first *Pollock Decision* at page 573, Chief Justice Fuller wrote, "From the forgoing it is apparent: 1. That the distinction between direct and indirect taxation was well understood by the framers of the Constitution and those who adopted it."

But later in this book, when we discuss the Internal Revenue Code, we will be playing word games and we'll need to remember what "words of art" and "terms of art" mean.

A direct tax includes all taxes that are not indirect. And an indirect tax includes all taxes that are not direct. In the case of *Pollock v. Farmers' Loan & Trust Co.*, the court said at page 557:

> **"And although there have been from time to time intimations that there might be some tax which was not a direct tax nor included under the words 'duties, imposts and excises,' such a tax for more than one hundred years of national existence has as yet remained undiscovered, notwithstanding the stress of particular circumstances has invited through investigation into sources of revenue."**

Under the American system of constitutional government, there are only two types of taxes, direct and indirect. And to each type of tax, one of two constitutional rules applies when any tax is levied. We must remember it is immaterial what the tax is called. The courts must look past the name of the tax and analyze any tax based on its practical application, based on its substance. The issue of what constitutes a direct tax and what constitutes an indirect tax was exhaustively debated by Congress in the summer of 1909. Congress well understood the difference. Let's first look at what constitutes an indirect tax.

An indirect tax is either a tax that does not fall directly on the ultimate payer of the tax, is a tax on a privilege, or is a tax which can be avoided. The term indirect does not actually appear in the Constitution. An indirect tax includes "duties, imposts and excises." U.S. Const. art I, sec. 8 cl. 1. The federal excise tax on gasoline is a good example. The burden of the tax can be shifted by any commercial enterprise that buys gasoline. The trucking company can add the cost of the excise tax on gasoline to the amount it charges for shipping the goods carried by the truck. The bus company adds the same cost to the price of a bus ticket. And the private person, who is not in commerce, can avoid the tax altogether by choosing to ride his bicycle. The federal excise tax on gasoline is a constitutional tax.

The tax on the sale and manufacture of alcohol, tobacco and firearms is an excise tax. Frequently an excise tax is a tax on the happening of an event, i.e., the sale of a pack of cigarettes; or a tax on a privilege, such as the manufacture of alcohol; or a tax on an activity, like air travel. According to Curtis Bradshaw, the federal government could levy an excise tax on "pickup trucks, pianos and brassieres if need be."

> **"Excises are a species of tax consisting generally of duties laid upon the manufacture, sale, or consumption of commodities within the country, or upon certain callings or occupations, often taking the form of exactions for licenses to pursue them. "The taxes created by the law under considerations as applied to savings banks, insurance companies, whether of fire, life, or marine, to building or other associations, or to the conduct of any other kind of business, are excise taxes, and fall within the requirement, so far as they are laid by Congress, that**

**they must be uniform throughout the United States."Pollock v. Farmers' Loan & Trust Co., 157 U.S. 429, 592 (1895).**

**"An excise is a charge laid on articles produced or consumed in a country, and also on licenses to deal in certain commodities or carry on or do business." Allen Ripley Foote,[2] The Power of Taxation Should be Regulated, State and Local Taxation, Second International Conference, International Tax Association, 203 (1909).**

A duty is a "thing due." It is a tax on imports. It is a tariff. It is synonymous with the word "impost," also found in the Constitution. It was the primary form of taxation that ran the country prior to the income tax amendment. It can also be a tax on the happening of an event like recording a document and paying a "stamp duty" for that document.

**Mr. SUTHERLAND (Utah). "The citizen may pay or not, according as he determines to use or not to use the article upon which the particular duty is imposed." 44 Cong. Rec. 2083 (1909).**

Whether to categorize an income tax as a direct tax or an indirect tax has been the subject of much controversy. As we saw earlier, Congress can give any tax it comes up with any name Congress wants to give it. What matters is the **substance** of the tax, and how the tax is applied, not its **form**.

In America a mandatory tax on our right to exist can never be an excise tax as Congress exists at the privilege of the American People, not the other way around.

**"That decision affirms the great principle that what cannot be done directly because of constitutional restriction cannot be accomplished indirectly by legislation which accomplishes the same result." Fairbank v. U.S., 181 U.S. 283, 294 (1901).**

**"If it be true by varying the form the substance may be changed, it is not easy to see that anything would remain of the limitations of the Constitution, or of the rule of taxation and representation, so carefully recognized and guarded in favor of the citizens of each state. But constitutional provisions cannot be thus evaded. It is the substance, and not the form, which controls, as has been established by repeated decisions of this court." id., 296.**

Just as our job is to discover what the word "income" means, so it is with the terms "direct taxes" and "indirect taxes." The answer lies with what the People understood these terms to mean at the time the Constitution was either ratified or amended. Since the terms "direct taxes" and "other direct tax" are part of the original Constitution, we must look to the period of the founding of our nation for their definitions. Any tax not believed by the founders to be a direct tax will be an indirect tax.

## Taxes on Wages and Salaries are Direct

There were two authors read by English speaking people who wrote during the late 1700s and used the terms "direct" and "indirect" taxes. These were Adam Smith, who wrote the *Wealth of Nations*, and Jacques Turgot from France. From 1774 to 1776, Turgot held a position in France that would have been similar to our Secretary of the Treasury.

**Mr. CUMMINS. "I had referred to the fact that at the time of the Constitutional Convention, so far as I can now recall, this term had been mentioned by but two economic writers - one, Adam Smith, in the Wealth of Nations, and the other a French writer by the name of Turgot. Their general idea was that a direct tax was a tax upon property or [gross] revenue and an indirect tax was a tax upon consumption or expense. But later eco-**

> **nomic writers have amplified that general idea by supplying the fundamental thought, namely, that an indirect tax was one which could be shifted from the person who was called upon to pay it to another who was to buy the thing upon which the tax was imposed." 44 Cong. Rec. 3972 (1909).**

Although Turgot was from France, he did not fully accept the older taxation doctrines of the French Physiocrats. In Turgot's work, Plan d'un mémoire sur les impositions, 1764, he wrote:

> **"The tax which the proprietor pays immediately on his revenue is called direct tax. The tax which is not assessed directly on the revenue of the proprietor, but which falls on the cost of production of the revenue, or on the expenditure of the revenue, is called indirect tax." Teachings of Political Economists defining Direct and Indirect Taxes, at 3, by Max West, Pollock v. Farmers' Loan and Trust Co., 157 U.S. 629 (1894).**

> **"From an economic point of view such a tax, as has been before shown, is and always has been regarded as a direct tax...of almost every acknowledged authority on political economy or finance in the English language—Adam Smith, Ricardo, Mill, Wayland, Brande, Say, Perry, as well as the Encyclopedia Britannica and almost every other cyclopaedia or dictionary of English or American origin. In all the debates in the British Parliament it is doubtful that any British statesman can be named who has ever spoken of an income tax as other than a direct tax. The same may also be affirmed of French authors and statesmen." David Ames Wells, The Theory and Practice of Taxation 363 (D. Appleton and Company, New York) (1907).**

The following quote from the *Wealth of Nations*, appears in the Supreme Court's decision for the Hylton case. Adam Smith wrote:

> **"The impossibility of taxing people in proportion to their revenue, by any capitation, seems to have given occasion to the invention of taxes upon consumable commodities; the State, not knowing how to tax directly and proportionably the revenue of its subjects, endeavors to tax it indirectly by taxing their expense, which it is supposed, in most cases, will be nearly in proportion to their revenue. Their expense is taxed by taxing the consumable commodities upon which it is laid out." Adam Smith, Wealth of Nations, book V, 541 (Prometheus Books, Amherst, New York, 1991) (1776).**

In the Senate debate over the income tax issue, Senator Sutherland from Utah made the following statement:

> **"A tax upon incomes is not a tax upon expense. A tax upon income is a tax upon revenue, which the Supreme Court in that case [Hylton], quoting with approval Adam Smith, says is a direct tax. They distinguish and place in sharp contrast with one another a tax upon revenue and a tax upon expense." 44 Cong. Rec. 2094 (1909).**

If we back up two paragraphs from the paragraph of Adam Smith's quoted authoritatively by the Supreme Court in the *Hylton Case* we read:

> **"Capitation taxes, so far as they are levied upon the lower ranks of people, are direct taxes upon the wages of labour, and are attended with all the inconveniences of such taxes." id. at 540. (This quoted sentence is taken out of the section of Adam Smith's Wealth of Nations entitled "Capitation Taxes.")**

In Book V of Adam Smith's *Wealth of Nations*, Smith has a four-page section entitled "Taxes upon the Wages of Labour." Five times in this section Smith states that a tax on wages is a direct tax and, as we saw above, Smith says it is a species of a capitation tax (id. at 534-38). Smith goes on to describe at great length how both England and France had graduated capitation taxes based on a person's rank or wealth. There is no doubt that today's graduated income tax on wages and salaries is a capitation tax and, therefore, must be apportioned among the several States.

A tax on the existence of a person, i.e., a tax on his head, is a capitation tax. A tax on the right of a person to exist, i.e., a tax on his wage or salary, is also a capitation tax as one cannot exist without working. Labor is property. A tax on labor is a tax on property. A tax on property is a direct tax.

In the 1909 Congressional debates over the 16th Amendment, Adam Smith was quoted far more than any other authority and was always quoted with approval. Adam Smith was quoted 18 times, Albert Gallatin,[2] four times and Jacques Turgot, three times. There were numerous other political economists quoted, but these three dominated the debate.

Albert Gallatin was appointed Secretary of the Treasury under Thomas Jefferson. He held that position for 14 years, longer than any other American. As a member of Congress, Gallatin was chairman of the Ways and Means Committee. He engineered the Louisiana Purchase for President Jefferson. In Montana, Gallatin Gateway, Gallatin County and the Gallatin River are named after him.

Just as Adam Smith greatly influenced the framers of the Constitution, he was also the respected and undisputed authority on taxation among those members of Congress who debated the 16th Amendment.[3]

> **"There is every reason to believe that the framers of the Constitution followed the usage of Adam Smith, who eleven years before the convention met had refuted the Physiocratic doctrine as to the incidence of taxes, whose work had gone through several editions before 1787, and who is known to have exerted a very decided influence upon the American leaders of that time. Albert Gallatin, writing in 1796, stated emphatically his belief that the distinction in the minds of the framers of the Constitution was that of Adam Smith. Gallatin was born and bred a Frenchman, and would have been as likely as any American of the time to accept the Physiocratic**

> **view; and in the absence of any evidence to the contrary the testimony of such an authority as Gallatin should be considered conclusive in any question of finance. Now Adam Smith gave no formal definitions of direct and indirect taxes, but it is impossible to mistake his meaning. He called taxes on receipts or incomings direct, and taxes on consumption or expenditure indirect." Max West, The Income Tax and National Revenues, 8 The Journal of Political Economy 433, 435 (1900).**[4]

Albert Gallatin in his *Sketch of the Finances of the United States* wrote:

> **"The most generally received opinion, however, is that by direct taxes in the Constitution, those are meant which are raised on the capital or revenue of the people; by indirect, such as are raised on their expense.**
>
> **The taxes which it is intended should fall indifferently upon every different species of revenue are capitation taxes....These must be paid indifferently from whatever revenue the contributors may possess." Rehearing Brief of Appellant at 112, Pollock v. Farmers' Loan and Trust Co., 158 U.S. 601 (1895).**

Capitation taxes are required by the Constitution to be apportioned among the several States. Capitation taxes are outside the scope of the 16th Amendment. The constitutional requirement that capitation taxes must be apportioned has never been modified by any constitutional amendment.

Just as we saw that an indirect tax is avoidable, i.e., you can choose to ride a bicycle instead of pay the excise tax on gasoline, a direct tax is unavoidable. Similarly, whereas an indirect tax could be passed on to another party, i.e., the bus company adds the cost of the excise tax on gasoline to the price of a bus ticket, the cost of a direct tax cannot be passed on. How are you going to pass on the cost of the taxes that are taken out of your paycheck? How are you going to avoid these "payroll taxes?" Are you not going to work and starve to death? The income tax on wages and salaries is a direct tax. Now let's double check to make sure we are right about this.

Quoting further from the Congressional Record as the Senate continued to debate the issue of an income tax, Mr. Sutherland said:

> **"This view is confirmed by the comments of Albert Gallatin in his Sketch of the Finances of the United States, written a year or two after the decision [of the Hylton case]. He says:**
>
> **'The most generally received opinion, however, is that by direct taxes in the Constitution are those meant which are raised on the capital or revenue of the people; by indirect, such as are raised on their expense. As that opinion is in itself rational and conformable to the decision which has taken place on the subject of the carriage tax, and as it appears important, for the sake of preventing future controversies,....that a fixed interpretation should be generally adopted, it will not be improper to corroborate it by quoting the author from whom the idea seems to have been borrowed.' [Naming Doctor Smith's Wealth of Nations.]"**

Senator Sutherland then quotes from Smith the same statements contained in Justice Paterson's opinion, and continues:

> **"The remarkable coincidence of the clause of the Constitution with this passage in using the word 'capitation' as a generic expression, including the different species of direct taxes, an acceptation of the word peculiar, it is believed, to Doctor Smith, leaves little doubt that the framers of the one had the other in view at the time, and that they, as well as he, by direct taxes meant those paid directly from and falling immediately on the revenue; and by indirect, those [falling] upon the expense. It has indeed been held by some that 'direct taxes' meant solely that tax which is laid upon the whole property or revenue of persons.... instead of admitting only one kind of direct tax [in the Constitution], expressly recognizes several species by using the words 'capitation' or 'other direct tax' and 'direct taxes.'**

> **'Should those considerations be thought correct, it results that all taxes laid upon property which commonly affords a revenue to the owner [whether such property be, in itself, productive or not] in proportion to its value are direct; a class which will include taxes upon lands, houses, stock, and labor. All of which, therefore, must, when laid, be apportioned among the States according to the rule prescribed by the Constitution.'" 44 Cong. Rec. 2094-5 (1909).**

This same quote appears in the *Pollock Decision* at pages 569-70. We need to belabor this point as it is precisely on point for the purposes of this book. We will see that any direct tax levied on wages, salaries, land, property, persons or whatever must be apportioned among the several States. More accurately, it must be apportioned among the several States if it is going to apply within the several States. Remember there is no constitutional restriction preventing Congress from levying an unapportioned direct tax in the territories and possessions.

In debate over the income tax amendment in the Senate, Mr. Sutherland has again quoted from the Hylton case and said:

> **"He [Mr. Justice Chase] then says he will close his 'discourse'- he does not call it an opinion or decision - by reading a passage or two from Smith's Wealth of Nations. Let me read one quotation:**
>
> **'The impossibility of taxing people in proportion to their revenue, by any capitation, seems to have given occasion to the invention of taxes upon consumable commodities; the State, not knowing how to tax directly and proportionably the revenue of its subjects, endeavors to tax it indirectly by taxing their expense, which it is supposed, in most cases, will be nearly in proportion to their revenue. Their expense is taxed by taxing the consumable commodities upon which it is laid out.'**

**"Clearly, in the opinion of Adam Smith, which the Supreme Court in this earliest case cited with approval, a direct tax is upon the revenue of the taxpayer, while an indirect tax is a tax upon his expense...." 44 Cong. Rec. 2093 (1909).**

**"Mr. SUTHERLAND. A tax upon incomes is not a tax upon expense. A tax upon income is a tax upon revenue, which the Supreme Court in that case [Hylton], quoting with approval Adam Smith says is a direct tax. They distinguish and place in sharp contrast with one another a tax upon the revenue and a tax upon expense.**

**Certainly the Senator will not contend that an income is not revenue." 44 Cong. Rec. 2094 (1909).**

In this debate, when Senator Sutherland and Adam Smith use the word "income" and "revenue," they mean the gross receipts of a person. This is altogether a different animal than what is meant by the term "net income."

The previous statements were from the Senate debates of May 17, 1909 on the income tax issue. Yes, we did quote this before. So here we have the words of Adam Smith quoted in the *Hylton* decision from 1796, quoted again in Gallatin's work of 1796, quoted again in the *Pollock Decision*, and quoted in the Congressional Record during the debates on the 16th Amendment. If the 16th Amendment did not create a new type of tax, then the tax on the revenue of a person is still a **direct tax.**

Six weeks later on June 30, 1909, the Senate was again debating the income tax issue. Senator Heyburn of Idaho said:

**"I should like to submit this definition among the others for consideration:**

**'It is also said that the tax is direct because it cannot be added to the price of the thing sold, and therefore ultimately paid by the consumer.'**

> **I think that is the best definition I have ever heard. That is by Mr. Justice Peckham [of the Hylton Court]." 44 Cong. Rec. 3971 (1909).**

Prior to the *Pollock Case* the Supreme Court, in its *dicta*, appeared to have narrowed the definition of "direct tax" from that of Adam Smith's definition of "direct taxes." The *dicta* says that a direct tax includes only taxes on land and taxes on the person, or capitation taxes. But this was based on Alexander Hamilton's argument. Hamilton was known for his bias toward federalism and expanded federal powers.

In *Veazie Bank v. Fenno*, a tax on the notes of a State Bank was attacked as a direct tax and as being unconstitutional because it was not apportioned. Mr. Hoar, the Attorney-General of the United States, relied again upon the *Hylton* case and upon Hamilton's brief, which had then been recently published. Chief Justice Chase says:

> **"Much diversity of opinion has always prevailed upon the question, what are direct taxes? Attempts to answer it by reference to the definitions of political economists have been frequently made, but without satisfactory results.**
>
> **"It may be rightly affirmed, therefore, that in the practical construction of the Constitution by Congress, direct taxes have been limited to taxes on land and appurtenances, and taxes on polls, or capitation taxes."**
>
> **"Our conclusions are, that direct taxes, within the meaning of the Constitution, are only capitation taxes, as expressed in that instrument, and taxes on real estate." Pacific Insurance Co. v. Soule, 74 U.S. 95 (1868). Dwight W. Morrow, The Income Tax Amendment, 10 Columbia Law Review 379, 404-5 (1910).**

In relying on any case we always need to separate the *dicta* from the opinion. *Dicta* does not carry the authority of *stare deci-*

*sis*. "Case law" is only that which is actually ruled on by the court and relates only to the question directly before the court.

> **"The only thing decided on in the Hylton case was the carriage tax was not a direct tax within the meaning of the Constitution. Both Patterson and Chase express doubt whether anything but capitation taxes and taxes on land are 'direct taxes.'" Dwight W. Morrow, <u>The Income Tax Amendment</u>, 10 Columbia Law Review 379, 403 (1910).**

If this is all true, then an income tax falling on the revenue of a person (gross receipts) is a species of a capitation tax as defined by Adam Smith and is therefore still a direct tax. Remember Smith wrote in his *Wealth of Nations:* "Capitation taxes, so far as they are levied upon the lower ranks of people, are direct taxes upon the wages of labour." Furthermore, according to *Pollock,* a tax on any form of property because of its ownership is a direct tax.

Point two in the *Pollock Decision* states:

> **"Second. We are of the opinion that taxes on personal property or on the income of personal property are likewise direct."**

The purpose of the 16th Amendment was to overturn *Pollock.* It was to strike down the *Pollock Rule*. The *Pollock Rule* allowed the source of the income to be considered when determining whether an income tax was direct or indirect regardless of whether the tax was on net income or gross income. Under the *Pollock Rule*, an income tax on the net income from real estate was a direct tax because taxes on real estate were direct taxes. But the logic behind the *Pollock Decision* was defective because the *Pollock* tax was on net income severed from the source. These taxes did not diminish the source of the income and are, therefore, inherently indirect.

In writing about the income tax of 1894, which was the subject of the *Pollock Case*, Professor Seligman said: "The first point that arrests our attention is that the tax is really an income tax—i.e. a tax on net gains or profits, and not, as in some other countries, on gross income with or without certain deductions." Seligman, Edwin, R.A., The Income Tax, 9 *Political Science Quarterly* 610, 620 (1894). Direct taxes on real estate and personal property, which diminish the source of the income, i.e., taxes on gross receipts, were outside the scope of the *Pollock Case*. Wages and salaries are considered to be personal property and the question of taxes on these was not squarely addressed by the *Pollock Court*.

> **"It has been well said that, 'The property which every man has in his own labor, as it is the original foundation of all other property, so it is the most sacred and inviolable. The patrimony of the poor man lies in the strength and dexterity of his own hands, and to hinder his employing this strength and dexterity in what manner he thinks proper, without injury to his neighbor, is a plain violation of this most sacred property.'" Adam Smith, Wealth of Nations, Book I, Chapter 10. Butchers' Union Co. v. Crescent City Co., 111 U.S. 746, 757 (1883).**

The Supreme Court chose not to define "direct tax" as it had prior to *Pollock*, as doing so would violate the original intent of the framers. Remember, the Constitution includes the phrase "or other direct tax" in the plural. Today, I believe what remains of *Pollock*, combined with the original intent of the 16th Amendment, sets the pendulum right in the middle—where it belongs. Our job as the Citizens of this Nation is to see to it that the government stays within the boundaries imposed by the Constitution, including the 16th Amendment. If we fail at this task who will do it for us?

The general rule is that whenever a tax is on gross receipts, or as Adam Smith said "on the revenue" of something, the tax is direct. This is because a gross receipts tax diminishes the value of the thing taxed. The tax falls directly on the thing taxed. Whereas an income tax, which taxes only the gains and profits (net income) of a source of income, does not diminish the underlying source of the income. Income is that which can be severed from the source without diminishing the source. An income tax diminishes only the income flowing from the source. An income tax does not diminish the value of the source of the income, as the source of the income remains whole.

> **"A tax levied on property that produces no income can be paid only through the confiscation of a part of the property." Allen Ripley Foote, The Power of Taxation Should be Regulated, State and Local Taxation, Second International Conference, International Tax Association 203, 206 (1909).**

For example, suppose Al has $50,000 in the bank earning interest at five percent for an annual yield of $2,500. Al's $2,500 of income is "passive." The tax rate on income is 35 percent and Al pays $875 in income tax. Generally, what is being taxed is what is diminished by the tax. The underlying principal of $50,000 remains whole, and in fact grew to $51,625 ($50,000 + $2,500 - $875 = $51,625). The $2,500 of interest payments that flowed from the underlying source of capital is the income. This is an indirect tax. Indirect taxes can be avoided. Al can keep the $50,000 at home in his mattress and avoid the tax, or place the funds in a non-interest bearing account and avoid the tax. Direct taxes cannot be avoided.

Now let's say Bill makes $50,000 per year working in the private sector in one of the several States. Bill's $50,000 in remuneration is "earned income." Bill takes the standard deduction for himself and his dependents and has a taxable income of $43,500. The tax rate is 35 percent and Bill pays $15,225 in taxes. Did the underlying source of the income remain whole? Was the tax on "income" or was it on gross revenue? Was the tax indirect and avoidable, or was it unavoidable and direct? Maybe we should ask Bill if he thought he was diminished by the tax? Of course he was! This latter example is a species of a capitation tax and is a direct tax and must therefore be apportioned among the several States insofar as no privilege enters into the picture.

In a brilliant article on the 16th Amendment appearing in the *Yale Law Journal*, Arthur Graves had this to say:

**"Practically, it is not every kind of income tax which is a direct tax. The term "income tax" has been too generally and broadly used to cover a variety of taxes imposed on persons and property which may ultimately be payable out of income....Some of the taxes imposed under the internal revenue provisions of our Civil War, while payable out of income or revenue, were not properly income taxes, as, for instance, the tax on premium receipts of insurance companies, and possibly that on bank profits and undivided surplus. But the income tax levied against the general income of the citizen is of a very different nature. It is distinctly a personal tax and undoubtedly a direct tax; in fact, it is difficult to conceive of a tax more direct or personal in its nature than the general income tax.**

**"It may be said in defense of the earlier decisions of the Supreme Court, regarding income taxes, that as the question is not at all a simple one, but surrounded with a great many economic perplexities, the failure to distinguish between the general income tax levied against the person and an excise tax levied against specific sources of revenue, or against property of business, but payable out of income, is not surprising. Very likely it required just an important case, involving the imposition of a general income tax, fraught with great consequences and freed from the influences and emotions of the Civil War, as was presented in Pollock v. Farmers' Loan and Trust Co., with its learned and exhaustive arguments and opinions, to give to the country the eminently just decision that the personal income tax is a direct tax.**

**"It is very interesting to notice in this connection that George Ticknor Curtis, who became one of our foremost American jurists, writing in 1866, many years prior even to the institution of the Springer suit, declared that the personal income tax was undoubtedly a direct tax and ought to be levied by apportionment among the several**

> **States. He had the courage to suggest that "the personal income tax of the Civil War was unconstitutional and the revenue therefrom illegally collected." Arthur C. Graves, Inherent Improprieties on the Income Tax Amendment to the Federal Constitution, 19 Yale Law Journal 505, 508-9 (1910).**

> **"Certainly it would be difficult to conceive of any tax, or legislative assessment, more direct in its operation and nature than a tax on a man's income." George Ticknor Curtis, An Inquiry into one of the Constitutional Restrictions on the Revenue Powers on the United States, 33 Harper's New Monthly Magazine 354, 355 (1866).**

A gross receipts tax **is not** an income tax, notwithstanding the fact that the government calls it one. Imagine you're at a New Year's Eve party and someone asks you "How did your year go?" If you answer "I barely kept the wolves away," then you didn't "get ahead" for the year. If you didn't "get ahead," you probably didn't have a "gain or profit". You therefore didn't have any income for the year as the word "income" is used within the context of the 16th Amendment. When you didn't "get ahead," i.e., there was no "gain or profit", any tax on your personal gross receipts would be a direct tax and would constitutionally be required to be apportioned among the several States.

> **"To speak of a poll tax (or other direct tax on a natural person) as a tax on property requires resort to the legal theory that a freeman is owner of himself and his labor force in a sense analogous to a master's ownership of his slave." Prof. Isaac A. Loos, Allen Ripley Foote, The Division Between State and Local Taxation, State and Local Taxation, Second International Conference, International Tax Association, 203, 206 (1909).**

> **"Direct taxes are those that are levied 'upon the very person who it is supposed as a general thing will bear their burden.' The general property, the income tax, the**

> **poll tax, may be classed as direct taxes for the reason that when a person pays one of these taxes, he is likely to bear the burden himself and is not likely to shift it to another." Israel Freeman, Constitutionality of Federal Corporation Tax Law, 72 Central Law Journal 59 (1911).**

> **Mr. BAILEY. None of us, except the simple Democrat of the old-fashioned school, have all we want, but many of us have all we need. After we have satisfied our needs, then the Government has a right to take its toll." 44 Cong. Rec. 1702 (1909).**

There were several times in the early history of America when direct taxes were imposed. These included taxes on slaves. Now what is it that gives a slave value such that he can be a thing taxed? The value of a slave is determined by the present worth of the expected future value of the slave's labor. Just as the historical taxes on slaves were direct taxes, so is today's tax on labor.

But our sieve needs one more layer to it. Before calling a gross receipts tax a direct tax, we need to determine if the thing taxed (the underlying investment or source) exists by right or by privilege. If it exists by right, then Adam Smith's criteria—as embraced by the framers of the Constitution—applies—the tax is direct. If the underlying thing taxed exists by privilege, then Congress may write a taxing statute measuring the amount of the tax due by the gross receipts of the thing taxed, but at the same time actually levying the tax on the privilege exercised by the subject of the tax, not on the subject itself.

Do you exist by right, or is your existence a privilege? Did government grant you the right to exist? Who made you? Is government the one who designed your DNA chain, who put breath into your lungs, who created the reproductive systems of your mother and father that created you?

However, if your citizenship is not one of right, but of privilege, then government may place a tax on your existence. Such a tax would be an indirect tax.

The prophet Jeremiah quoted his God to say,

**"Before I formed thee in the womb, I knew thee." *Jeremiah* 1:5 (Authorized King James Bible).**

And King David said:

**"For Thou didst form my inward parts; Thou didst weave me in my mother's womb. I will give thanks to Thee, for I am fearfully and wonderfully made." *Psalm* 139:13-14 (New American Standard Bible).**

But what if there is no god? Then I believe it is reasonable for government to assert that the people exist by the good graces of government. Government could then tax our right to exist every day of the week. After all, if we all came from monkeys, then we owe the existence of our civilized society to the government, as without government, it would be a jungle out there.

The reality is that legitimate government is a creation of the People. Government's right to exist derives "from the consent of the governed." Whenever government power exceeds the boundaries granted to it by the People, that government becomes illegitimate, at least in the areas where it operates without the concent of the people. An illegitimate government will remain in power as long as the People tolerate it.

## Taxes on Privileges are Indirect

Corporations are creatures created by government. Any creator may place any demand on his creation he wants to. He may even destroy his creation should he choose to do so. And since the "power to tax is the power to destroy," therefore the power to create includes the power to tax. Government may tax what government created.

**MR. BAILEY (Texas) "...Or suppose I had concurred with him, and had levied a tax on the individual and exempted all corporations...that I was trying to exempt the great corporations and to lay the burden of government upon the man of flesh and blood, made in the image of his God." 44 Cong. Rec. 2447 (1909).**

The case of *Flint v. Stone Tracy Co.* is on point here. This case was about the constitutionality of what was known as the Corporation Excise Tax, which was imposed by the Payne-ALDRICH Tariff Act of 1909. This case was tried by the Supreme Court in 1911, prior to the ratification of the Income Tax Amendment. So there was no authority provided by the 16th Amendment for the statue that imposed the tax. We were still under the *Pollock Decision*.

The tax was called a "special excise tax" and imposed a one percent tax on net income (after a $5,000 exemption). The statute said the tax was levied "with respect to the carrying on or doing business by such corporation...." Congress had levied the tax on the privilege to do business in a corporate capacity.

The plaintiff argued:

**"Any tax when placed on the right of the man or of the corporation to live is a capitation tax and as direct as any tax can be." Flint v. Stone Tracy Co., 220 U.S. 107, 119 (1911).**

**"If the tax is construed as an income tax it is unconstitutional because it is imposed upon income from real estate and personal property, and therefore a direct tax not apportioned among the States according to population...." id. 120.**

**The separate provision taxing the income of foreign corporations derived from "capital invested within the United States" is clearly unconstitutional within the ruling in the Pollock Case. On such capital invested in real**

> **or personal property the tax is direct and not an excise...the tax is partly an excise tax on business transacted and partly a direct tax on capital invested." id. 132.**

There were actually multiple plaintiffs in this case, and their argument was essentially that the tax was a tax on the right of a corporation to exist. They also argued corporations were creatures of state government and that the federal government had no right to tax the creation of the states. The key to the case was whether the thing taxed existed by right or by privilege. A human being exists by right; a corporation exists by privilege. The court said:

> **"The act now under consideration does not impose direct taxation upon property solely because of its ownership, but the tax is within the class [indirect taxes] which Congress is authorized to lay and collect under Art. I, Sec. 8, cl. 1 of the Constitution, and described generally as taxes, duties imposts and excises, upon which the limitation is that they shall be uniform throughout the United States."**

> **"Within the category of indirect taxation, as we shall have further occasion to show, is embraced a tax upon business done in a corporate capacity, which is the subject-matter of the tax imposed in the act under consideration. The Pollock Case construed the tax there levied as direct, because it was imposed upon property simply because of its ownership. In the present case the tax is not payable unless there be a carrying on or doing business in the designated capacity, and this is made the occasion for the tax. Measured by the standard prescribed. The difference between the acts is not merely nominal, but rests upon substantial differences between the mere ownership of property and the actual doing of business in a certain way." id. 150.**

**"Excises are "taxes laid upon the manufacturer, sale or consumption of commodities within the country, upon licenses to pursue certain occupations, and upon corporate privileges." Cooley, Constitutional Limitations, 7th ed., 680 (1903).**

**"The tax under consideration, as we have construed the statute, may be described as an excise upon the particular privilege of doing business in a corporate capacity, i.e., with the advantages which arise from corporate or quasi-corporate organization...." Flint v. Stone Tracy Co., *supra* at 151.**

With regard to the Corporate Excise Tax of 1909, the issues was not how the tax was measured, nor did it have anything to do with the underlying asset that was taxed. The fundamental issue had to do with the "corporate privilege" that was the subject of the tax. Any time a privilege is taxed, the tax is an excise tax and the rule of apportionment does not apply. The tax is therefore levied subject to the rule of uniformity. The plaintiff was wrong; Congress had the authority to levy the tax. See President Taft's letter to Congress dated June 16, 1909 found at the end of Chapter 4. President Taft must have also been a good lawyer as he went on to be Chief Justice of the Supreme Court. This letter contains an excellent explanation on the argument of taxing privileges.

Under this legal concept, the government may even tax the income from some underlying asset which itself is not taxable, such as government bonds. This is because the income of the untaxable asset flows to the privileged entity and the government has levied the tax on the privilege, not on the asset.

**"It was held, after a review of some of the previous cases in this court, that, where the tax was within the legitimate authority of the Federal government, it might be measured, in part, by the income from property not in itself taxable, and the distinction was undertaken to be pointed out between an attempt to tax property beyond**

> **the reach of the taxing power, and to measure a legitimate tax by income derived, in part, at least, from the use of such property." Flint v. Stone Tracy Co. *supra*, 162-165. United States Exp. Co. v. State of Minn., 223 U.S. 335, 344 (1912).**

> **Mr. CLAPP. "...that when you come to levy an excise tax for the privilege of doing business, you cannot trace to the antecedents or the genealogy of the funds which come into the possession of that corporation." 44 Cong. Rec. 4229 (1909).**

Senator Daniel of Virginia, in debating the 16th Amendment, offered an excellent analysis of the legal criteria of taxing a corporation. He said:

> **"There are many things—settled personal views—about this excise tax which we ought to remember, and I propose to state, just as I have stated the difference between corporations and partnerships, what are some of the marked and settled opinions which have had judicial exposition and indorsement as to the power to tax corporations. I will state some of them. I think it will be found settled in the judicial reports of this country, and so well settled that no lawyer familiar with the decisions could hope to disturb the decisions, as follows:**

> **(1) That a corporate franchise is a distinct subject of taxation, and not as property, but as the exercise of a privilege.**

> **(2) That it may be taxed by a State or Country which creates it.**

> **(3) It may be taxed by a State or Territory in which it is exercised, although created by a foreign country.**

> **(4) It may be taxed by the United States, whether created by the United States or a foreign country or by a State, Territory, or district of the United States.**
>
> **(5) The franchise of the corporation may also be taxed by a State, although created by the United States, unless created as a part of the governmental machinery of the United States.**
>
> **"The same or rather the like limitation applies upon corporations created by the States. You may tax any private corporation of a State, but a corporation of the State, that is chartered by the State to perform some function of its government, partakes of a governmental nature, just as one so formed by the United States; and as the one cannot be taxed by the Federal Government, so the other cannot be taxed by the State." 44 Cong. Rec. 4237-8 (1909).**

Moving back in time to 1904 we will next look at the *Spreckels Sugar Case.* The tax in controversy here was a gross receipts tax. The tax was imposed by legislation entitled "An Act to Provide Ways and Means to Meet War Expenditures, and for Other Purposes" of 1898. The statute imposed a tax of one quarter of one percent on the gross revenue of businesses that refined sugar and oil. Because the tax fell on the gross receipts of the business, whether or not there was any profit (income) realized, the tax had the effect of diminishing the thing (the source) taxed. Consequently, the plaintiff argued:

> **"that the tax was a direct tax, which had not been apportioned among the several states as required by the Constitution...." Spreckels Sugar Refining Co. v. McClain, 192 U.S. 397, 399 [1904].**

The *Spreckels Court* said:

> **"The contention of the government is that the tax is not a direct tax, but only an excise imposed by Congress under its power to lay and collect excises which shall be uniform throughout the United States. Art. 1, sec. 8. Clearly the tax is not imposed upon gross receipts as property, but only in respect of the carrying on or doing the business of refining sugar [or oil]. It cannot be otherwise regarded because of the fact that the amount of the tax is measured by the amount of the gross annual receipts. The tax is defined in the act as 'a special excise tax' and, therefore, it must be assumed, for what it is worth, that Congress had no purpose to exceed its powers under the Constitution, but only to exercise the authority granted to it of laying and collecting excises." id. 411.**

> **"The difference in effect between a tax measured by gross receipts and one measured by net income, recognized by our decisions, is manifest and substantial, and it affords a convenient and workable basis of distinction between a direct and immediate burden upon the business affected and a charge that is only indirect and incidental. A tax upon gross receipts affects each transaction in proportion to its magnitude and irrespective of whether it is profitable or otherwise. Conceivably it may be sufficient to make the difference between profit and loss, or so to diminish the profit as to impede or discourage the conduct of the commerce. A tax upon the net profits has not the same deterrent effect, since it does not arise at all unless a gain is shown over and above expenses and losses, and the tax cannot be heavy unless the profits are large." United States Glue Co. v. Town of Oak Creek, 247 U.S. 321, 329-30 (1918).**

Here we learned that when a tax is levied on the gross revenue of the thing taxed or is levied on the underlying asset, the tax is a direct tax, unless the thing taxed exists by privilege. If you are a wine maker, and the government imposes a tax on your gross revenue, the tax is an excise tax because the sale and manufacture of alcohol is thought to be controlled by government in its role of protecting the general welfare of the people. You have, therefore, been granted a privilege to be a wine maker and to sell your product in commerce. The tax is levied on the privilege you exercise as a producer of an alcoholic product; the amount of the tax is measured by either the gross receipts or the net income of the activity. When levying an excise tax, Congress may choose whatever measuring device it wants to use to determine the amount of the tax due.

> **"In affirming the constitutionality of this act the court said, in Spreckels Sugar Refining Co. v. McClain, that the tax was an excise on the ground that it was imposed, 'not upon gross annual receipts as property, but only in respect of the carrying on or doing the business of refining sugar.' The court further said that the amount of the tax is measured by the amount of the gross annual receipts. It will be observed that the language used by the court here is precisely that of the Corporation Tax amendment."**
>
> **"The brief filed by the late Solicitor General Powers very naturally emphasized this point, and cited a list of decisions of the court in accord with that in the Spreckels Case. There the government felt that it was on safe ground. As was to be expected, the court accepts this view of the law, so carefully framed to secure its approval. The counsel for those who sought to overturn the law appeared to place much reliance upon their argument that this was a direct tax, and therefore unconstitutional, not being apportioned among the States. That argument is swept away by Justice Day, when he points out that the tax is not imposed upon property or even upon income, but only upon "the carrying on or doing of business" in the designated capacity. The tax is not, therefore, direct, and it is not an income tax, but only what the act describes it to be, a special excise tax." Editorial, The Corporate Tax Sustained, N.Y. Times, pg. 10, March 14, 1911.**

In debating the income tax amendment, Senator Root (New York) said:

> **"That the language has been carried along through a series of decisions of the court, where it has held various provisions of taxation not to impose direct taxes, and therefore not to be subject to the constitutional provision for apportionment. It has spoken of them in slightly varying forms of language, as being with respect to the use or the privilege or the business or the facility or carrying on business; thus attaching the tax not to the thing, not to the property, but to the incorporeal, intangible privilege or power or process. These words are designed to accomplish that; and I think they are taken from the very words of the court in the Spreckels case." 44 Cong. Rec. 4013 (1909).**

Remember that the tax in the *Spreckels* case was measured by the gross receipts of the business. Senator Root points out that the tax was not on the gross receipts, but on the privilege of the "carrying on or doing the business of refining sugar." So the tax was on the privilege of refining sugar and/or oil.[5] The amount of tax due was measured by the amount of gross income. But what happens if you remove the element of privilege? Then the thing taxed shifts to the business and the tax is on the gross receipts instead of being measured by the gross receipts. Such a tax diminishes the source of the tax, as the tax must be paid whether or not there is a gain or profit. According to Senator Root's argument, absent a privilege to lay the tax on, the tax would then be a direct tax and would have to be apportioned. If this is still unclear, reread President Taft's letter to Congress at the end of Chapter 4.

In debating the Corporate Excise Tax of 1909, Senator Rayner said:

> **"It is a tax laid upon the business and privileges of a corporation, and the measure of the tax is the net profits of the corporation." 44 Cong. Rec. 4028 (1909).**

But what if you make $15 an hour as a garbage man? Is it a privilege to be a garbage man? You're still paying a tax on your gross revenue. It's called an income tax, but the term is misapplied. It's really a gross receipts tax. Adam Smith called it a tax on the revenue of a person. The framers of the Constitution would call it a direct tax in the form of a capitation tax. As such, a person's revenue (gross receipts) is taxable as a direct tax and the tax needs to be apportioned among the several States. The good news is that the Internal Revenue Code (IRC) also recognizes this and does not tax the garbage man's wage. At least not if he is collecting garbage in one of the 50 states. The bad news is that Congress wrote the IRC in such a deceptive way that the garbage man could never figure it out, nor could a triple Ph.D. More on this later.

> **Mr. CUMMINS (Iowa). "Our people are separated into three classes: The men who work, who are laying up out of their earnings provision for the future, and on whom the hand of the taxgatherer should be laid most lightly; the owners of land, the farmers and other landowners, whom it is universally acknowledged that it was the intention of the fathers of the Constitution to protect by the provisions regarding the apportionment of direct taxes; and the possessors of the stored-up wealth of the country, which is being invested in the corporations that are doing the business of the country. And by the simple course of dropping out from this income-tax measure the parts that are unconstitutional under the decision of the Supreme Court, that are unjust according to the acknowledged judgement of all students of the income tax, that are incapable of enforcement within such a time as to relieve the deficiency that may be before us and by saving the tax upon the stored-up wealth of the country invested in corporations, called an "excise," we shall have accomplished the great object of the income tax." 44 Cong. Rec. 4006 (1909).**

The founding fathers deliberately made it difficult to levy a direct tax. But they understood there could be times when a direct tax would be necessary. Having just lived through the War of Independence, the framers well understood that when the very existence of the nation was at risk, it would be entirely appropriate for the government of a free people to place a tax on the existence of the people. Such a tax would be a tax on land, as one can not exist apart from the land; or a tax on the head of a person (head = cap, hence the term "capitation"), which is a tax on the person's right to exist. This tax could also be structured as a tax on the person's labor. In times of emergency, it is reasonable for government to levy heavy rates of taxation. In a war situation, the choice might be between paying a heavy tax or perishing. According to Adam Smith and to the reading of the Constitution itself, there can be many species of direct taxes.

The intention of the framers was that under normal peacetime circumstances, the national government would not tax a person's right to exist, as the feudal system did, but would fund itself by taxes on privileges, imports, consumption and other avoidable indirect taxes.[6] The reason American colonists died on the battlefield, and the signers of the Declaration of Independence risked their "lives, fortunes and their sacred honor" was to throw off the feudal system. The feudal system has crept back onto our land, but only because of the ignorance of our people. If enough Americans are willing to study the law and take action, we could defeat this feudal system using only paper bullets. Karl Granse, a contemporary common law lawyer from Minnesota said, "The only law that exists today is the law you are willing to enforce with your own life, liberty and property."

In the early stages of World War II, Germany was spending 70 percent of its national income on their military effort. England was spending 50 percent of her national income on her military. Just prior to losing the war, Germany must have been spending several hundred percent of its national income on the war effort. If you know anything about the history of World War II you will remember at the end of the war Germany was cannibalizing itself in an effort to defend its own borders. When a country is in a desperate condition, it may be necessary for national survival to tax the capital of the nation. This was the framers' intention when they provided for the rule of apportionment when levying a direct tax; that all citizens should contribute equally to the extraordinary needs of the nation. Quoting Representative Hill from the Congressional Record:

> **"I agree with the chairman of the Ways and Means Committee (Mr. Payne), who made the opening remarks in this discussion, that we ought to have the power to lay an income tax in time of war, but I am not in favor of giving this Government the power to lay an income tax in time of peace. With an amendment limiting it to time of war or other extraordinary emergencies, I would gladly vote for it; yes, I would vote to take every dollar of the property of every citizen of the United States, if need be, to defend the honor, dignity, or life of this Nation in the stress of war; but when it comes to a question of current expenses in time of peace, I would cut the expenses of the Government so as to keep them within our natural income." 44 Cong. Rec. 4393 (1909).**

Debating the ratification of the Constitution at the Massachusetts convention (1787) Judge Dana, after urging the necessity of Congress being vested with the power to levy direct taxes, said:

> **"It was not to be supposed that they would levy such unless the impost and excise should be found insufficient in case of war."**

Mr. Sedgwick, commenting upon the same subject, said:

> **"Congress would necessarily take that which was easiest to the people; the first would be impost, the next excise, and a direct tax will be the last; for, ...drawing money from the people by direct taxes being difficult**

> **and uncertain, it would be the last source of revenue applied to by a wise legislature." 44 Cong. Rec. 2086 (1909).**
>
> **Mr. Nelson. "... In time of emergency, such as war, this tax may be required to save the life of the Nation; and we should assert now the right of the Nation to this form of taxation, or it may be forever lost." 44 Cong. Rec. 2457 (1909).**

Lastly, another authority on taxation quoted in the 1909 congressional income tax debates was economist John Stuart Mill who wrote:

> **"A direct tax is one which is demanded from the very person who, it is intended or desired, should pay it. Indirect taxes are those which are demanded from one person in the expectation and intention that he shall indemnify himself at the expense of another." Charles J. Bullock, Direct and Indirect Taxes in Economic Literature, 13 Political Science Quarterly 442, 461 (1898).**

## Summary

Summarizing what we have learned from this chapter, we can establish the following test: When any tax includes all these elements, it is a direct tax:

1. Either it places a tax on the whole of something because of ownership and falls on the owner of the thing taxed, or it is a tax on a species of property or on a natural person, a tax on the existence of the thing taxed.
2. The thing or the person taxed is diminished by the tax.
3. The tax cannot be shifted.

4. It is not a tax on consumption, nor a tax on an identified activity, nor a tax on a privilege, nor a tax on the happening of an event.

Any tax that does not satisfy these elements is not a direct tax and is therefore an indirect tax. Consequently, the Supreme Court went too far in the *Pollock Decision* as a tax on the net income of real estate is not a tax on the ownership of real estate. Income from real estate is the fruit of the invested capital; it is the net. It may be severed from the capital leaving the underlying investment whole. When only income is taxed, the underlying investment is not diminished. The tax on the income from real estate may be shifted to those who pay the rents. The tax on the income from real estate may not even be payable by the owner of the real estate if there were some kind of management arrangement in place where the owner does not receive the income stream. Nor is it a tax on the existence of the real estate, as the amount of the tax is measured by the degree to which the property is successfully managed. It does not fall on the ownership of the real estate. A successfully managed building may pay a lot of tax while an identical building next door, that is poorly managed, might not pay any tax at all. Clearly the *Pollock* tax was not levied on the ownership nor the value of the building. Tax in the *Pollock Case* was an indirect tax and the Supreme Court went too far in linking an inherently indirect income tax with the source of the income. The boundary line between the two being that point where the underlying asset is diminished by the tax as opposed to only the (net) income being diminished by the tax. The purpose of the 16th Amendment was to overturn *Pollock*.

To my knowledge, the question of whether or not a tax on a man's wage or salary is an indirect tax or a direct tax has never been squarely before the Supreme Court, except in the case of *Evans v. Gore*. *Evans v. Gore* was a 1920 case about a federal judge who was having his salary diminished by an income tax and the Supreme Court ruled the tax was unconstitutional. But the question in this case related to a constitutional provision affecting only federal judges. Since most of us reading this book are not federal judges, *Evans v. Gore* does not affect us. But the Court has discussed the issue three times in it's *dicta.*

The first time was in the *Hylton Case*, 1796, where they quoted with approval Adam Smith in stating that a tax on a man's revenue is a direct tax. The second time was in the *Springer v. United States*, 1880, where Springer failed to put this question directly in front of the court. It is unfortunate that Springer made numerous strategic errors in prosecuting his case. The third time was in *Pollock*, 1895, where the court said, quoting with approval *Springer*:

> **"While this language is broad enough to cover interest as well as the professional earnings, the case would have been more significant as a precedent if the distinction had been brought out in the report and commented on in arriving at judgement, for a tax on professional receipts might be treated as an excise or duty, and therefore indirect, when a tax on the income of personalty might be held to be direct." Pollock v. Farmers' Loan & Trust, 157 U.S. 429, 579 (1895).**

The reality of a tax on a man's labor was very well described by Senator Bailey of Texas as he debated the income tax amendment. Senator Bailey had one of the more vocal voices in this debate. As a Democrat, he was an avid supporter of the 16th Amendment. Here is his statement:

> **"I believe in earning an income by personal service every man consumes a part of his principal, and that fact ought always to be taken into consideration. The man who has his fortune invested in securities may find in a hundred years, if he spent his income, that the fortune still intact, but the lawyer or the physician or the man engaged in other personal employment is spending his principal in earning his income. That fact ought under every just system of income taxation to be recognized and provided against. 44 Cong. Rec. 4007 (1909).**

A tax on the labor of a man, whether or not he is a construction worker or a rocket scientist, is a tax on the man. It is a species of a capitation tax. Adam Smith described it as a capitation tax and a direct tax. It diminishes the man as the man consumes part of his capital in earning his wage or salary. It is a direct tax. Such a tax in the post 16th Amendment era must be apportioned among the 50 states before it can be collected from those who, absent a privilege, work and live within the several States of the Union.

A tax on a privilege, although measured by income, is not an income tax either. It is an excise tax. The tax of the *Spreckels Sugar Case* from the Spanish-American War and the Corporate Excise Tax of 1909 are such taxes. The 16th Amendment provides no authority for such a tax. These taxes are levied under the authority of the original Constitution, not the 16th Amendment.

An income tax within the meaning of the 16th Amendment is a tax on net income. It is not a tax on a privilege nor is it a tax on a source.

There are many species of income taxes. As Professor Seligman said, "An income tax can be direct or it can be indirect." It would be a whole lot less confusing if we would stop calling a gross receipts tax an income tax. It is not, as the tax does not fall on income, but instead falls on the source of the income. Don't worry, we will tie the apparent loose ends of this contradiction together by the end of the book.

**Species of Income Taxes, after the *"Pollack Case"* (1895) and before the 16th Amendment (1913)**

| Tax is on gross receipts, underlying investment/source is diminished by the tax. | | Tax is on net income, underlying investment/source remains whole. | |
|---|---|---|---|
| Property or person taxed exists by right | Property or person taxed exists by privilege | Property or person taxed exists by right | Property or person taxed exists by privilege |
| Direct tax | Indirect tax | Direct tax | Indirect tax |

*Figure 5.1—Species of Income Taxes After the Pollack Case*

**Species of Income Taxes, after the 16th Amendment (1913 to the present)**

| Tax is on gross receipts, underlying investment/source is diminished by the tax. | | Tax is on net income, underlying investment/source remains whole. | |
|---|---|---|---|
| Property or person taxed exists by right | Property or person taxed exists by privilege | Property or person taxed exists by right | Property or person taxed exists by privilege |
| Direct tax | Indirect tax | Indirect tax | Indirect tax |

*Figure 5.2—Species of Income Taxes After the 16th Amendment.*

# Chapter 6
## The 16th Amendment

**Harmony. Preserving a statute or part of a statute against repeal by another statute or part of a statute by construction which reconciles the statutes and parts with one another so that effect may be given to all provisions.**

***—50 American Jurisprudence, 1st Statutes § 363.***

Lawyers and legislators are artisans who use words as their medium. Just as a carpenter will construct a house out of wood, metal, stone and glass; so the lawyer/legislator constructs a statute out of words and phrases. We might call the latter "wordsmiths."

There are only three possible constructions for the 16th Amendment. For clarity, these three are shown in the figures that follow. The position of the government and the lower courts is that the 16th Amendment provides for the levying of an income tax uninhibited by either of the two constitutional rules that limit government's taxing power. If this were true, then the 16th Amendment would have given Congress a new power of taxation.

The position of the author and of the Supreme Court is that the 16th Amendment created no new taxing power or authority but only clarified the classification of a tax on net income as an indirect tax.

The figures on the following page use the term, "universe of all possible taxes." This is a term from statistics. It means that all possible known taxes are included in our example. Our Constitution gave Congress plenary taxing authority. In other words, Congress can levy any possible tax known to man. The question Congress must resolve prior to levying any tax is, "what constitutional rule applies to the tax—the rule of uniformity, or the rule of apportionment?" The IRS would have us believe that no rule applies to the income tax. Following are the three possible constructions of the 16th Amendment:

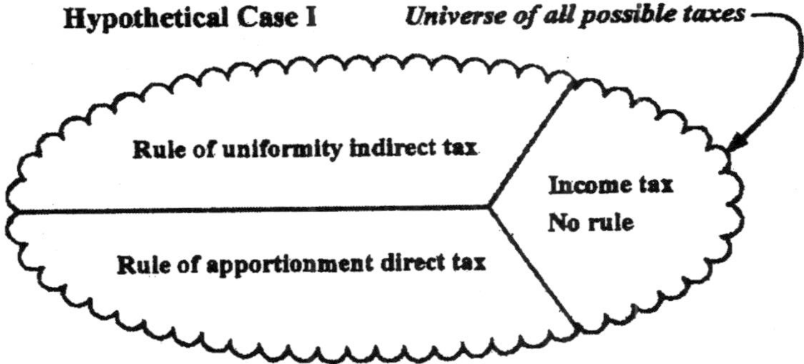


*Figure 6.1 Income tax creates a new category of taxation*

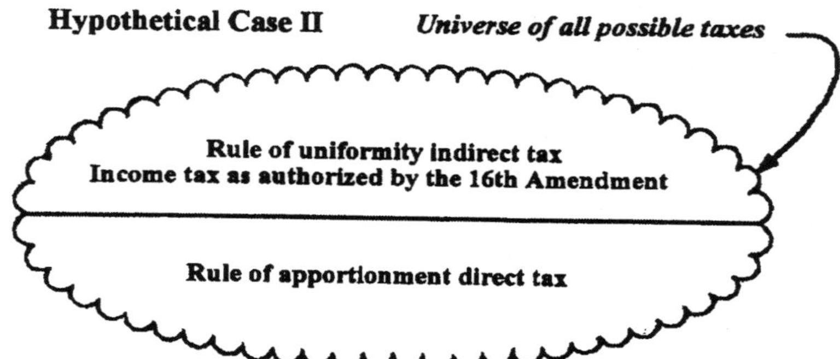

*Figure 6.2 Income taxes restricted to indirect taxes*

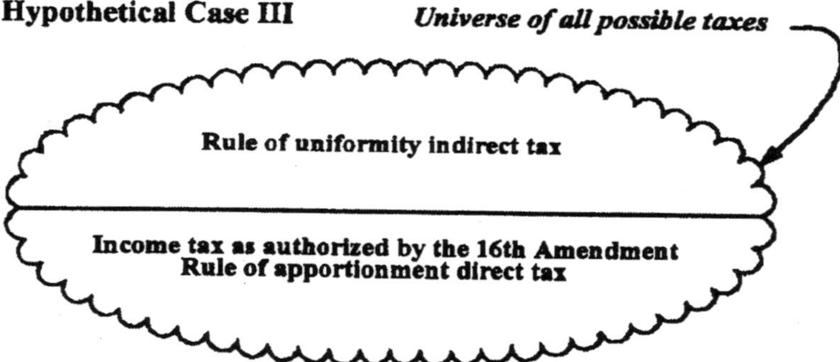

*Figure 6.3 Income taxes restricted to direct taxes*

If our form of government was not a constitutional republic with limited enumerated powers, we could have Monte Hall from the TV game show *Let's Make a Deal* help us choose which of the three cases apply. Is it door #1, #2 or #3? Instead we have a method of legal analysis available to us whereby sticking to the rules of our system of American jurisprudence, we will arrive at the correct answer.

## Harmony

Because every law must have authority and because the law must "make sense," the law cannot be in conflict with itself. The law must be in Harmony. What is Harmony?

Suppose you are a building contractor and you're building a house. The floor plan (bird's eye view) show three windows on the north side of the house. Then you look at the plans for the north elevation (this is the drawing of the north side of the house) and this drawing shows no windows at all. Well, there is a problem isn't there? Does the contractor order the windows and install them? What if it was not the intent of the owner or the architect to have the windows on the north wall? The contractor must resolve the apparent discrepancy in the plans. He must ask the owner or architect to correct the drawings so that every sheet of the drawings is in "Harmony" with every other sheet.

Now suppose the parents of a 15-year-old girl prohibit their daughter from smoking cigarettes. The rule is laid down whereby if she is caught smoking cigarettes she is grounded for two weeks. Now the girl gets caught and is grounded by dad. Not wanting to miss an important social event, daughter asks mom if she can go. Mom's a softy and says yes, but dad says no. What's the problem? The problem is mom and dad are not in "Harmony." They are in conflict.

In order for a constitutional system of government to work, all the written laws of the land must be in Harmony with each other. If the laws of the land were in conflict with one another, what would be the use of having any laws at all? We would return to the rule of the jungle or a warlord type of power system, and the law would be determined by whoever has the most power, not by the written word.

On the issue of national taxation, we have four locations in the Constitution where the power of Congress to lay and collect taxes is defined. Each of these sections must be in agreement, in Harmony, with each other section. Otherwise the result will be confusion and chaos. Where there is a conflict of law, we look to the greater legal authority for clarification. In this case, our authority is the U.S. Constitution. Where there appears to be a conflict within the Constitution, we look to the intent of the Framers, or in the case of an Amendment to the Constitution, we look to those who debated and voted on the Amendment and to the understanding of the People as they expressed to their elected representatives their will on the issue. There is a reason why the Constitution mandates at article 1, section 5, clause 3 that Congress keep a journal of its proceedings:

> **"Rejection by the legislature of certain terms in a statute has been regarded as conclusively showing an intent that the act as passed should not embrace the matter referred to. There is no doubt that where the language of a statute or constitutional provision is not plain, and different meanings may plausibly be attributed thereto, one of the most satisfactory methods of ascertaining the intention of the framers of the instrument is by resort to the amendments and changes thereof, as shown by the official records; and consideration of such extrinsic material is not open to the objections, subsequently discussed, to resort to debates or explanatory statements of a measure in the course of its passage through a legislature or constitutional convention. The rejection of proposed amendments may be the most significant in determining the meaning of an uncertain statutory or constitutional provision." Annotation, Resort to Constitutional or Legislative Debates, Committee Reports, Journals, etc., as aid in Construction of Constitution or Statute., 70 American Law Reports 5, 22-25.**

On the issue of the meaning of the various provisions of the Constitution, the Supreme Court said:

> **"We are bound to interpret the Constitution in the light of the law as it existed at the time it was adopted." Mattox v. U.S., 156 U.S. 237, 243 (1895).**

It is obvious the construction of the 16th Amendment leaves much to be desired. The effect of the amendment was debated at the time it was drafted, debated during the ratification process, and is still unnecessarily being debated today. This book would not need to be written had its construction been more clear, and had the terms of that amendment been qualified by the amendment itself.

> **"As the case stands the proposal [the 16th Amendment] ought to be negatived [sic] even by those who favor an income tax pure and simple. No law should be enacted whose meaning is disputed before enactment, for whatever construction comes to be placed upon it, there is ground for disappointment and ill feeling." Editorial, The Income Tax, N.Y. Times, pg. 8, April 15, 1910.**

> **"[It] is not whether the principle of an income tax is sound, but whether, even if the soundness of that principle be wholly assumed, the amendment actually proposed will secure its applications. Until that question is definitely answered, it is pure nonsense to argue the merits of an income tax. The more thoroughly we may believe in an income tax, the more absurd it would be for us to give the assent of the State of New York to an amendment that may be declared void as soon as it reaches the Supreme Court. The amendment that has been sent to our Legislature by Congress is clearly open to that objection." Editorial, The Gist of the Question, N.Y. Times, pg. 12, May 3, 1910.**

The legal profession also understood at the time of the debate over ratification of the 16th Amendment that the construction of the amendment was poor. Quoting from the *Yale Law Journal*:

> **"It would seem as if the Supreme Court, in construing the United States Constitution as it shall be after the adoption of the proposed amendment, will find itself in the**

midst of inconsistent and contradictory provisions which cannot be construed in Harmony with each other. It will be presented with contradictory alternatives, one of which it will have to adopt. Fortunate, indeed, will be this country if the Supreme Court, under these circumstances, shall boldly override the unqualified language of the proposed amendment and exclude from its operations an income tax levied on the instrumentalities of the States. Yet to do this will be a violent stretch of its judicial authority. But what are we to say of an instrument whose provisions and grants are so inharmonious and inconsistent that the Supreme Court cannot construe one part thereof without the contradicting and doing violence to the other, nor can it uphold the other without boldly overriding and nullifying the first?

"Constitutional, indeed, the imposition of an income tax will be, yet, nevertheless, this amendment is inherently improper under the limitations which ought to guard the concessions of authority to our federal government. In that matchless code, called by one of England's greatest statesmen "the most wonderful work ever struck off at a given time by the brain of man," this amendment will be an anomaly. In an otherwise harmonious instrument which speaks of a government of enumerated powers, seeking to preserve the dignity and vitality of sovereign States, this provision will stand out as the one discordant note, inconsistent with all that has gone before, unexplained, uncalled for, unnecessary, the only grant to the federal government of unrestrained and arbitrary power in respect of taxation over every State and every citizen within those States." Arthur C. Graves, Inherent Improprieties in the Income Tax Amendment to the Federal Constitution, 19 Yale Law Journal 505, 532 (1910).

"A proper regard for its genesis, as well as its very clear language, requires also that this Amendment shall not be extended by loose construction, so as to repeal or

> **modify, except as applied to [net] income, those provisions of the Constitution that require an apportionment according to population for direct taxes upon property, real and personal. This limitation still has an appropriate and important function, and is not to be overridden by Congress or disregarded by the courts." Eisner v. Macomber, 252 U.S. 189, 206 (1920).**

From its beginning, Senate Joint Resolution #40, a.k.a. the 16th Amendment, had questionable construction. The primary issue was its unqualified language and in particular the meaning of the phrase "from whatever source derived." Was it the intention of the People, the state legislatures, and the Congress to include all things within this meaning?

> **"If it is desired to safeguard the rights of the States, and protect them with regard to their own securities and those of their municipalities, it is a very simple matter to frame an amendment which will be unambiguous...and appreciating the supreme importance of an amendment to the Federal Constitution, we ought to be able to express ourselves without doubt in respect to a matter of fundamental concern to the States." Gov. A.E. Wilson on the Income Tax Amendment, N.Y. Times, pg. 13, Feb. 26, 1911.**

In support of the 16th Amendment, Republican Congressman Picket of Iowa, who was obviously full of baloney said:

> **"The resolution [S.J.R. 40] is simple in construction and covers but one subject and one purpose. It is formulated in clear and unambiguous terms, leaving no possibility for doubtful construction. It involves only the power to impose an income tax." 44 Cong. Rec. 4395 (1909).**

What was clear in Congressman Picket's mind is not so clear in the minds of others generations later.

> **"As repeatedly held, this did not extend the taxing power to new subjects, but merely removed the necessity which otherwise might exist for an apportionment among the States of taxes laid on income. *Brushaber v. Union Pac. RR. Co.*, 240 U.S. 1, 17-19; *Stanton v. Baltic Mining Co.*, 240 U.S. 103, 112 - 113; Peck & Co. v. Lowe, 247 U.S. 165, 172-173 (1918).**

On its face, the 16th Amendment could have multiple interpretations. We are fortunate in that the Supreme Court settled the question in the cases of Brushaber v. Union Pac. R.R. Co., 240 U.S. 1 (1917), Tyee Realty Co. v. Anderson, 240 U.S. 115 (1916), Thorne v. Anderson, October Term 1915, No. 394 (24,613); Dodge v. Osborn, 240 U.S. 118 (1916); and Stanton v. Baltic Mining Co., 240 U.S. 103 (1916) cases such that the effect of the 16th Amendment is to nullify the theory, relied on in *Pollock,* that a tax on net income is a tax on the source of the income. Since an income tax, when the word "income" is used properly, leaves the source of the income undiminished, an income tax is inherently an indirect tax and is subject to the rule of uniformity and not the rule of apportionment.

Before we move on it is worth noting that during the ratification process there was very little debate over the meaning of the word "income." This was so because everyone knew what this word meant; it meant what we call today "unearned income," and/or profit severed from the source.

> **"Apparently the Commissioner confuses the term 'profit' with the term 'income.' 'Income' may necessarily be 'profits,' but 'profits' are not necessarily 'income.' The Commissioner uses the term 'sale of *capital* assets,' both in sections 100 and 105, from which it appears that the 'profit' of which he speaks is in fact converted capital and not 'income.'" Brief for Stratton's Independent Limited at 14, Stratton's Independence v. Howbert Ltd., 231 U.S. 399 (1913).**

The average man who labored for a living earned a wage, or if he was lucky, a salary. He did not have "an income." "The poor man does not regard his wages or salary as 'an income.'" Gov. A.E. Wilson on the Income Tax Amendment, N.Y. Times, pg. 13, Feb. 26, 1911. Only those who were idle during the work week, yet still made money had an "income." Unfortunately, it appears since everyone knew what income meant, there was little concern that the word income would later be redefined.

Suppose it was of interest to you to determine what percentage of Americans living during the period 1909 to 1913 thought that humans lived on Mars? If you looked in newspapers, magazines, and scientific journals of the time, how much evidence would you uncover? Probably none, and the reason for the lack of evidence is obvious—humans had no way of getting to Mars, so the whole notion was preposterous. So it is with the idea that wages are income. There is little evidence to say that it isn't, because no one in their wildest dreams ever thought wages would be taxable under the 16th Amendment. It was not an issue that was debated as the literature of the time is nearly void of any discussion on the topic.

## Hypothetical Case I: No Rule

We will address the Figure 6.1 scenario first, being that no Constitutional rule applies to the levying of an income tax. If the 16th Amendment relieved income taxes from the rule of apportionment but did not make them subject to the rule of uniformity, then no rule applies. The idea that a government of a free people can have an unlimited power to levy any kind of tax is unthinkable. The idea is rejectable on its face. Such a condition would render to shreds the fabric on which our Constitution is written.

> **"Liberty, it has been well said, depends, not so much upon the absence of actual oppression, as on the existence of Constitutional checks upon the power to oppress. These checks should not be destroyed or impaired by judicial decisions." Maxwell v. Dow, 176 U.S. 581, 617 (1900).**

> **"Unrestricted power of taxation is the greatest power over accumulated wealth, manufacturers, industry, and personal freedom which any government can have; for liberty, as Hampden found out, cannot be worth much to a man who may be taxed in any way some other man pleases." Congress and the Constitution, The Nation, page 214, March 21, 1895.**

For Hypothetical Case I to be correct, the 16th Amendment would have had to create a new class of taxes—a new creature of tax if you will.

> **"Thus, in the matter of taxation, the Constitution recognizes the two great classes of direct and indirect taxes, and lays down two rules by which their imposition must be governed, namely: The rule of apportionment as to direct taxes, and the rule of uniformity as to duties, imposts and excises.**
>
> **And although there have been, from time to time, intimations that there might be some tax which was not a direct tax nor included under the words "duties, imposts and excises," such a tax for more than one hundred years of national existence has as yet remained undiscovered, notwithstanding the stress of particular circumstances has invited a thorough investigation into sources of revenue" Pollock v. Farmers' Loan & Trust Co., 157 U.S. 429, 557 (1895).**

In an article entitled "The Income Tax and the Constitution" appearing in the *Harvard Law Review* in 1907, Edward Whitney wrote:

> **"Apportioned taxes have turned out a failure. They are difficult enough to assess within the limits of a state, and under control of a state board of equalization. They have been tried by the nation and each trial was a failure. The last direct tax was paid back again. There will probably never be another. Whatever taxes are levied in the future will be levied under the rule of uniformity. If we are to amend the Constitution, a matter now so often discussed, we should not try to tinker (with) it by introducing a specific exception to a broken down general rule. Amendments to the Constitution should conform to its main plan. They should be drawn on broad lines, and not introduce a multitude of special cases." Edward Whitney, The Income Tax and the Constitution, 20 Harvard Law Review 280, 292 (1907).**

The rule of apportionment is not a broken down rule, but instead is a rule meant to keep our government a government of limited scope, without the funding to provide "a Multitude of New Offices, and sent hither Swarms of Officers to harass our People, and eat out their Substance" (The Declaration of Independence).

At the time the Constitution was written, we had just fought the War of Independence. One of the primary grievances against King George was a heavy tax burden. The framers of the Constitution set up a national government with limited powers and limited duties. It was not going to cost a lot of money to run a government of limited duties. The previous national government organized under the Articles of Confederation had no power of taxation. Most of the responsibility of governing was to be the domain of the states, not the national government. The states were free to raise revenue through direct taxation if they chose to do so. The rule of apportionment has worked as it was intended to work. It has the effect of what Thomas Jefferson so aptly stated, it "binds the government with the chains of the Constitution."

> **"Here we find the propositions of either Morris or Rutledge the same fundamental principle of American government, whose justice, it seems, was never objected to by a single member of the conventions - that the power to impose taxes ought not to be committed to a majority of mere members with no safeguards for its exercise, making possible the imposition of burdens on a certain portion of the community to the exclusion of the remainder. The discussion which took place during those days in July in the convention shows that 'those patriotic men well knew that the unrestrained and unregulated power of taxation had been, in all the experience of the world, the chief instrument of oppression and tyranny, and while the power was indispensable to the existence of the nation, it was not the less necessary that it should be kept with definite bounds.' Sen. George F. Edmunds, *Salutary Results of the Income Tax Decision,* 19 The Forum 513, 516 (1895)." Arthur C. Graves, Inherent Improprieties in the Income Tax Amendment to the Federal Constitution, 19 Yale Law Journal 505, 513 (1910).**

The essence of a constitutional form of government is one of limited powers delegated to government. All gains in the freedoms of man in western civilization have been at the expense of much toil, blood and treasure. In all cases, beginning with the Magna Carta in 1215, the significant gains have been evidenced by written documents which delineated, and were meant to secure, the freedoms and liberties of those who fought for them. It is unthinkable that a people, who secured their freedom by spilling their own blood on the battlefield, would hand over to any government an unlimited power to tax the gross receipts of their labor. In our time, our freedoms and liberties are secured by our Constitution. In pertinent part, *Black's Law Dictionary* defines a "Constitution" as:

> **"The organic and fundamental law of a nation or state, which may be written or unwritten. Establishing the character and conception of its government, laying the basic principles to which its internal life is to be conformed,**

> **organizing the government, and regulation, distributing, and *limiting* [emphasis mine] the functions of its different departments, and prescribing the extent and manner of the exercise of sovereign powers." Black's Law Dictionary, 311, (6th ed. 1990).**

In Ballentine's we find the definition of "constitutional liberty" to be:

> **"The liberty guaranteed under the American system of constitutional government; a very broad and extensive concept, embracing not only freedom from physical restraint, but the right of man to be free in the enjoyment of the faculties with which he is endowed by the Creator, subject only to such restraints as are necessary for the common welfare." 16 American Jurisprudence, 2nd Series, Constitutional Law § 358, 359. Ballentine's Law Dictionary, 253 (3rd ed. 1969).**

How can a man be free and secure to enjoy anything, if over half of his earnings are taxed away; if there is no limitation on government's ability to tax him? When a man pays a tax on his right to exist, his "right" has been reduced to a privilege granted to him by government.

> **"It must be conceded that there are rights in every free government beyond the control of the State. A government which recognized no such rights, which held the lives, liberty and property of its citizens, subject at all times to the disposition and unlimited control of even the most democratic depository of power, is after all a despotism. It is true that it is a despotism of the many - of the majority, if you chose to call it so - but it is not the less a despotism." Loan Ass'n v. Topeka, 87 U.S. (20 Wall.) 655, 665 (1874).**

If the People, when they ratified the 16th Amendment, delegated to the Congress an unlimited and unrestricted power to tax income and to tax the sources of income, how can such power be consistent with a constitutional form of government? Such a delegation of power would constitute a voluntary acceptance of the status of slavery wholly inconsistent with the American system of constitutional government. It is also arguable that such a conveyance of power would be unconstitutional as the purpose of the constitution, as stated in its preamble, is to "secure the Blessings of Liberty to ourselves and our Posterity." Is it constitutional for one generation to give an unrestricted power to tax income and to tax the sources of income to the government and thereby make the next generation destitute? When one entity has the power to potentially take 100 percent of the gross receipts of another entity, isn't the latter in slavery to the former?

The idea that the American People granted to government an unlimited and unrestricted power to tax income is inconsistent with our form of government and is rejectable on its face, and was rejected by the Supreme Court in the *Brushaber Case*.

> **"But it is clearly the result that the proposition and the contentions under it, if acceded to, would cause one provision of the Constitution to destroy another; that is, they would result in bringing the provisions of the Amendment exempting a direct tax from apportionment into irreconcilable conflict with the general requirement that all direct taxes be apportioned. Moreover, the tax authorized by the Amendment, being direct, would not come under the rule of uniformity applicable under the Constitution to other than direct taxes, and thus it would come to pass that the result of the Amendment would be to *authorize a particular direct tax not subject either to apportionment or to the rule of geographical uniformity,* thus giving power to impose a different tax in one state or states than was levied in another state or states. This result, instead of simplifying the situation and making clear the limitations on the taxing power, which obviously the Amendment must have been intended to ac-**

> **complish, would create radical and destructive changes in our constitutional system and multiply confusion. <u>Brushaber v. Union Pac. R.R. Co.</u>, 240 U.S. 1, 11-12 (1916).**

Analyzing this passage out of the Supreme Court's *Brushaber Opinion* we see that the Court addressed the issue of Harmony by the statement that they could not sanction "one provision of the Constitution to destroy another." If the 16th Amendment provided an exception to the Constitution's direct taxation clauses, then the Constitution would not be a harmonious document. The Constitution would have clauses in conflict with each other as the direct taxation clauses would have been in conflict with the 16th Amendment.

Next let's analyze the statement, "authorizing a particular direct tax not subject either to apportionment or to the rule of geographical uniformity..." Such a tax freed from any constitutional limitation would constitute an expansion of congressional taxing authority. It would be a new species of constitutional tax.

During the ratification process, the 16th Amendment came under much criticism. The chief complaint was the unqualified language of "from whatever source derived." Governor Hughes of New York, who later became a Justice of the Supreme Court, saw this phrase as a threat to the sovereignty of the several States. Gov. Hughes feared the 16th Amendment would give the national government the power to tax state debt instruments and the instrumentalities of the states. In order to address this criticism of Gov. Hughes', Senator Borah of Idaho presented Senate Resolution #175 to the Senate which would authorize the Senate Judiciary Committee to study the issue raised by Gov. Hughes and to render a report to the Senate. This was done on February 10, 1910, fully 7 months after the 16th Amendment was sent out to the states for ratification, yet still three years before it was finally ratified. In presenting his request for S.R. #175 to the Senate, Senator Borah explained the purposes of and the power of the 16th Amendment. The following are some of Senator Borah's remarks he read from a prepared speech given on the Senate floor:

**"I submit for the consideration of the Senate, first, that this amendment, if adopted, will add nothing to the power of the National Government to lay and collect taxes in the way of power; that the power of the National Government at the present time, as I have said, is full, complete, unlimited, and unfettered, save as to exports from the States, which has nothing to do with the argument here.**

**"It is true that there are two rules with reference to the manner in which the Congress shall exercise the power - that of uniformity and that of apportionment - but as to the power itself, putting aside for the moment the manner of its exercise, I submit that the power is at the present time vested in Congress without any limitation, unfettered in every sense of the term." 45 Cong. Rec. 1695 (1910).**

Senator Borah continued:

**"Third, the amendment did not deal, does not purport to deal, and was not intended to deal with the question of power. It intended to deal, and does deal, alone with the manner of exercising that power which is already complete, that which is already without any limit. The sole obstacle to be removed by those who sought to change the Constitution was that of apportionment. No one has ever contended that it was not within the power of Congress to lay a tax upon incomes. That power has belonged to Congress from its organization, under the original taxing power of Congress." id. at 1695.**

**"Thus the whole power of taxation rests with Congress. When you exclude exports from States and conform to the rule of uniformity and of apportionment, there is no limitation upon the taxing power of the National Government as it exists at the present time. I submit that it would be difficult to find language which would convey more than the full and complete power which is now conferred by the Constitution." 45 Cong. Rec. 1696 (1910).**

Borah again:

**"In conclusion, on this phase of the subject, I submit:**

**"First. That the proposed amendment adds nothing to the taxing power of the National Government. This power was complete, unfettered, plenary before. It can be no more than that should this proposed amendment be adopted.**

**" Second. The proposed amendment does not deal or purport to deal with the question of power which is already complete, but simply with the manner and method of exercising and using that power.**

**"Third. No one has ever questioned the power of the National Government to lay an income tax, for, as was said by Justice White, the question has always been "whether an admittedly unlimited power to tax has been established according to the instruction as to the method," and it was to remedy the method alone [to overturn Pollock] that the amendment was submitted.**

**"Fourth. The words 'from whatever source derived' add nothing to the force of the amendment. It would, in constitutional parlance, be just the same if it said 'to lay and collect taxes on incomes without apportionment,' for who could then say that you would not have the right to lay taxes upon all incomes? The present taxing power would not be a particle stronger if it stated 'to lay and collect taxes upon all property from whatever source.'**

**"Fifth. To construe the proposed amendment so as to enable us to tax the instrumentalities of the State would do violence to the rules laid down by the Supreme Court for a hundred years, wrench the whole Constitution from its *harmonious* (emphasis mine) proportions and destroy the object and purpose for which the whole instrument was framed.**

> **"Sixth. To construe it to cover those incomes from sources within the jurisdiction and control of the sovereignty laying the tax is to construe it in *Harmony* [emphasis mine] with the principles given us by Marshall and followed from that hour to this." 45 Cong. Rec. 1698 (1910).**

Senator Borah was one of the principal proponents of the 16th Amendment. He was very vocal in the debates in Congress over the issue. Senator Borah even wrote a book about income taxes. Could he have stated any more clearly that the 16th Amendment did not create a new power of taxation? I don't believe he could have. He also made it clear that even though the Amendment used the language "from whatever source," there were still sources that were outside the authority of the Amendment. In fact, the language the Supreme Court used in stating its opinion on this point, in the *Stanton v. Baltic Mining Co.* case, seems to have been taken from Senator Borah's speech to the Senate on February 10, 1910.

> **"By the previous ruling (*Brushaber Case*) it was settled that the 16th Amendment conferred no new power of taxation but simply prohibited the previous complete and plenary power of income taxation possessed by Congress from the beginning from being taken out of the category of indirect taxation to which it inherently belonged..." Stanton v. Baltic Mining Co., 240 U.S. 103, 112 (1916).**

The *Pollock Court* had taken income taxes out of the class of indirect taxes (excises, duties and imposts) and had placed income taxes in the class of direct taxes. Now remember the *Pollock Case* **only** dealt with income taxes on the net income from real estate and personal property. Because the *Pollock Decision* was obnoxious to the American People, the American People sought to overturn the *Pollock Decision* by way of a constitutional amendment.

With the Congress and the Supreme Court now in agreement, we can therefore conclude the following to be true after the purported ratification of the 16th Amendment:

1. Under our form of constitutional government, there remain two great classes of taxes; that of direct taxes and that of indirect taxes otherwise known as excises, duties and imposts.

2. Capitation, and other direct taxes, must be apportioned among the several States.

3. Indirect taxes must be uniform throughout the United States.

4. Taxes on incomes, when the word "income" is used in its "constitutional sense," regardless of their source, are indirect taxes of a species known as excises.

5. Constitutional income taxation does not tax the source of the income as the tax is only on net income, leaving the source of the income undiminished by the tax.

6. The purpose of the 16th Amendment was to negate the theory upon which *Pollock* was decided, the theory being that a tax on net income was also a tax on the source of the income.

## Hypothetical Case III: Income Tax is a Direct Tax

We shall now look at Hypothetical Case III where it is alleged the 16th Amendment provides authority for a direct tax while being relieved of the requirement of apportionment. The starting point is to determine whether or not the income tax provided for by the 16th Amendment is a direct tax, keeping in mind that a tax "on incomes" and a tax "on sources" are two different types of tax. A tax "on incomes" diminishes the income severed from the source. A tax "on sources" diminishes the source.

The 16th Amendment was called Senate Joint Resolution #40 as it moved through Congress for Congress' approval. It had a predecessor known as Senate Joint Resolution #39 which read:

> **"The Congress shall have power to lay and collect *direct* [emphasis mine] taxes on incomes without apportionment among the several States according to population." 44 Cong. Rec. 3377 (1909).[1]**

The immediate response to S.J.R. #39 was criticism from Senator Mr. Laurin who stated:

> **"I think if the Senator from Nebraska will change his amendment to the Constitution so as to strike out the words "and direct taxes" in clause 3, section 2, of the Constitution, and also to strike out the words "or other direct" in clause 4 of section 9 of the Constitution, he will accomplish all that his amendment proposes to accomplish and not make a constitutional amendment for the enacting of a single act of legislation. id. at 3377.**

Senator Brown's response was:

> **"That may be true, Mr. President, but my purpose is to confine it to income taxes alone, and to forever settle the dispute by referring the subject to the several States." id. at 3377.**

It is clear that if Congress intended to provide constitutional authority for the levying of an indirect tax on income and a direct tax on the source of income, such authority would have been enumerated within the income tax amendment. When S.J.R. #39 was replaced by S.J.R. #40, which ultimately became the 16th Amendment, the term "direct taxes" was replaced with only "taxes."

There is more. S.J.R. #39 had its own predecessor known at S.J.R. #25 which proposed to amend the Constitution and read as follows: "The Congress shall have power to lay and collect taxes on incomes and inheritances." (id. at 1568) This proposed amendment was also introduced by Senator Brown from Nebraska who made a speech at the time of its introduction. As in S.J.R. #39, the very next statement made after the introduction of S.J.R. #25 was from Senator Rayner of Maryland who raised the issue of harmony with the direct taxation clauses of the Constitution. Senator Rayner stated:

**"In looking at the joint resolution I see that it reads 'The Congress shall have power to lay and collect taxes on incomes.' It has that power now. Congress has the power now to lay and collect taxes on incomes and on inheritances.**

**I will call the Senator's attention to the fact that unless you change the clause of the Constitution which provides for apportionment [of direct taxes] the joint resolution would not repeal that clause. The two clauses would stand *in pari materia* together and you would still have an apportionment." 44 Cong. Rec. 1568-9 (1909).**

The definition of *"in pari materia"* is:

**"Statutes which relate to the same subject or object are *in pari materia*, although they were enacted at different times and it is a fundamental rule of statutory construction that such statutes should be construed together for the purpose of learning and giving effect to the legislative intention." (citation omitted) Ballentine's Law Dictionary, 632 (3rd ed. 1969).**

It is clear with S.J.R. #39 and S.J.R. #25 that any income tax amendment that was going to provide for a direct tax on the source of income, in the constitutional meaning of the term "direct tax," would have to conform to constitutional clauses requiring apportionment of direct taxes. Either that or the direct taxation clauses would need to be struck from the original document. The principle of "Harmony" was at work here.

It is also clear in both cases, when the very next statement in the debate of both resolutions concerns the Harmony of the proposed amendment with the direct taxation clauses of the Constitution, that Congress was well aware whether or not they were contemplating the income tax amendment to provide for a direct tax or an indirect tax. Furthermore, the issue of what was a direct tax versus an indirect tax was exhaustively evaluated by Congress the summer of 1909 as they considered the 16th Amendment and the Corporate Tax Act of 1909. This debate consumes 352 pages of the Congressional Record of which 34 pages relate to the issue of direct taxes vs. indirect taxes. Now the pages of the Congressional Record are large and the print is small. You would have to multiply the above numbers by four to get something equivalent to the number of pages in a book such as this one.

When Congress debated the direct tax vs. indirect issue, the debate wasn't over what constituted one type of tax versus the other, but only as to which was more appropriate. Adam Smith's criteria for categorizing direct taxes and indirect taxes appeared to have been accepted by all, and as we pointed out earlier, Adam Smith is the most quoted authority on this issue.

It is abundantly clear that Congress realized if it was going to propose an amendment to the Constitution that was going to provide for the levying and collection of a direct tax on incomes, then Congress was going to have to modify the "direct taxation" clauses in the original Constitution. Not once, but twice, other members of Congress had rejected, on this very point, a proposed Constitutional amendment that sought to provide authority for the collection of a direct tax without apportionment without having modified these clauses. We can therefore conclude, as the Supreme Court did in *Brushaber*, that the 16th Amendment only dealt with indirect taxes, i.e., taxes on incomes and not taxes on sources of incomes (absent a privilege).

We keep revisiting this point because the IRS and the lower courts claim that the 16th Amendment provides authority for a direct tax on income exempted from the apportionment rule. Income taxes on net income from business or unearned income from accumulated wealth are indirect taxes. Income taxes on wages and salaries are direct taxes.

Continuing on, Senator Brown from Nebraska wrote all three versions of the income tax amendment, S.J.R. #25, S.J.R. #39, and S.J.R. #40. You would think that after getting shot down twice on the same point, by the third attempt, i.e., S.J.R. #40, he would have gotten it right.

There is more. Our evidence on this point is overwhelmingly compelling. The Senate voted on the 16th Amendment (S.J.R. #40) at 1 o'clock on July 5, 1909. Senator Aldrich had earlier tried to ram it through the Senate on Saturday, July 3rd, a holiday weekend, for an immediate vote without debate when only 52 senators were present. A few senators protested and the vote was set for the following Monday. As a result of the minimal debate that did take place on July 3rd, several amendments were proposed to S.J.R. #40 that came up for a vote at the appointed hour of 1 PM Monday, July 5th.

The first of these was an amendment to S.J.R. #40 by Senator Bailey of Texas to provide that conventions of each of the several States be required to ratify the constitutional amendment as opposed to the state legislatures.

This was voted down. Next was another amendment by Bailey to add the language "and may grade the same" to modify the term "income tax" as a way to provide that the tax may be graduated. Bailey proposed this language on Saturday, July 3rd. By Monday, July 5th, when this came up for a vote, Bailey realized it would fail and tried to have it withdrawn. Bailey wanted it withdrawn because, according to Bailey:

> **"Mr. President, I am satisfied that this amendment will be voted down; and voting it down would warrant the Supreme Court in hereafter saying that a proposition to authorize Congress to levy a graduated income tax was rejected." 44 Cong. Rec. 4120 (1909).**

In other words, Senator Bailey understood that once Congress rejected a particular provision while amending the Constitution, Congress would be forever bared from implementing that provision by way of statute in the future.

Bailey was told by the Senate's Vice President that he could not withdraw the amendment and that it must be voted on. The rules required it. Senator Aldrich intervened and somehow the rules were suspended and the amendment was withdrawn without a vote.

Next was an amendment by Senator McLaurin of Mississippi. His proposed amendment to S.J.R. #40 was as follows:

> **The SECRETARY. "Amend the joint resolution by striking out all after line 7 and inserting the following: 'The words 'and direct taxes' in clause 3, section 2, Article I, and the words 'or other direct,' in clause 4, section 9, Article I. of the Constitution of the United States are hereby stricken out.'" 44 Cong. Rec. 4109 (1909).**

The Senate rejected this, as this amendment failed by voice vote. Had this amendment passed, it would have provided authority for an income tax that was inherently a direct tax to be levied without apportionment. It would have changed the original wording of the Constitution. Except for capitation taxes, it would have done away with all other direct taxes.

Lastly there was an amendment by Senator Bristow of Kansas to replace S.J.R. #40 with S.J.R. #39. S.J.R. #39 read:

> **"The Congress shall have the power to lay and collect *direct* [emphasis mine] taxes on incomes without apportionment among the several States according to population."**

This substitute amendment also included a provision to elect senators by popular vote. After some debate this was also rejected by voice vote.

Next, S.J.R. #40 was voted on and passed 77 to 15. So what can we conclude from all of this? Well, first of all we can conclude that the Senate understood it was the practice of the Supreme Court to look at the proceedings of Congress to see what the intent of Congress was. If Congress voted on a measure and rejected it, then the Supreme Court would interpret that vote as a clarification of the intent and purposes of Congress.

> **"One of the most readily available extrinsic aids to the interpretation of statutes is the action of the legislature on amendments which are proposed to be made during the course of consideration in the legislature. Both the state and federal courts will refer to proposed changes in a bill in order to interpret the statute as finally enacted. The journals of the legislature are the usual sources for this information. Generally the rejection of an amendment indicates that the legislature does not intend the bill to include the provisions embodied in the rejected amendment." Sutherland on Statutory Construction, sec. 48.18 (5th Edition).**

We also learned that twice the Senate was offered the opportunity to vote on a measure to provide that the income tax being considered by the 16th Amendment would provide for a direct tax within the constitutional meaning of the term "direct tax." Twice in the hour or so prior to the final Senate vote on the income tax amendment, the Senate rejected the opportunity to bring direct taxes within the scope of the 16th Amendment. This issue was squarely before Congress, and Congress rejected it.

> **"It is plain, then, that Congress had this question presented to its attention in a most precise form. It has the issue clearly drawn. The first alternative was rejected. All difficulties of construction vanish if we are willing to give to the words, deliberately adopted, their natural meaning. U.S. v. Pfitsch, 256 U.S. 547, 552 (1921).**

> **"When a court reviews an agency's construction of the statute which it administers, it is confronted with two questions. First, always, is the question whether Congress has directly spoken to the precise question at issue. If the intent of Congress is clear, that is the end of the matter; for the court, as well as the agency, must give effect to the unambiguously expressed intent of Congress." Chevron U.S.A. v. Natural Resources Defense Council, Inc., 467 U.S. 837 (1984).**

Now of these two opportunities to include direct taxes within the authority of the 16th Amendment, the second of the two also included a provision on the election of Senators by popular vote. But the same issue of the election of Senators was later approved by the Senate and sent out to the several States as the 17th Amendment to the Constitution. This Amendment was purportedly ratified and is now part of our Constitution. Therefore, the reason the second Bristow amendment failed was due to the term "direct taxes" and not because of the election of senators issue.

It can't be any more clear. The 16th Amendment does not provide authority for a direct tax on incomes, but only authority for an indirect tax on incomes. A direct tax on incomes is a tax that diminishes the source of the income. An indirect tax on income is a tax on unearned income or profit; such a tax leaves the source of the income undiminished. Twice during the debates on the 16th Amendment (SJR #25 and SJR #39), Congress rejected the idea of bringing direct taxes within the authority of the 16th Amendment. Then twice more, on July 5, 1909, Congress rejected the idea by direct vote of the Senate. Despite this congressional hostility to the idea, the IRS and the lower courts admit they are collecting a direct tax. The executive branch can not do that which was rejected by the legislative branch.

> **"Acts of Congress are to be construed and applied in Harmony with and not to thwart the purpose of the Constitution." Phelps v. U.S., 274 U.S. 341, 344 (1927).**

> **"Courts should construe laws in Harmony with the legislative intent and seek to carry out legislative purpose. With respect to the tax provisions under consideration, there is no uncertainty as to the legislative purpose to tax post-1913 corporate earnings. We must not give effect to any contrivance which would defeat a tax Congress plainly intended to impose." Foster v. U.S., 303 U.S. 118, 120-1, (1938).**

Today, the government's story is that the 16th Amendment provides authority for an unapportioned direct tax. But in 1916 the Attorney General of the United States' office understood this differently. In the case of *Peck & Co. v. Lowe* the attorney general for the United States stated:

> **"It is, however, equally clear that a general income tax is an excise tax laid upon persons or corporations with respect to their income: that is, a person or a corporation is selected out from the mass of the community by reason of the income possessed by him or it....**
>
> **This is brought out clearly by the decisions of this court in *Brushaber v. Union Pacific Railroad Co.*, 240 U.S. 1, and *Stanton v. Baltic Mining Co.*, 240 U.S. 103. In the former case it was pointed out that the all-embracing power of taxation conferred upon Congress by the Constitution included two great classes, one indirect taxes or excises, and the other direct taxes, and that of apportionment with regard to direct taxes. It was held that the income tax in its nature is an excise; that is, it is a tax upon a person measured by his income...It was further held that the effect of the Sixteenth Amendment was not to change the nature of this tax or to take it out of the class of excises to which it belonged, but merely to make it impossible by any sort of reasoning thereafter to treat it as a direct tax because of the sources from which the income was derived." Brief for the United States at 14-15, Peck & Co. v. Lowe, 247 U.S. 165 (1917).**

This argument by the United States was in response to the question put to the court by Peck & Co. as to whether the 16th Amendment created any new taxing power. The argument by the Attorney General's office, that the income tax authorized by the 16th Amendment is an excise tax, is correct. Excise taxes are indirect taxes.

> **"The Sixteenth Amendment to the Constitution has not enlarged the taxing power of Congress or affected the prohibition against its burdening exports." Brief for Appellant at 11, Peck & Co. v. Lowe, 247 U.S. 165 (1917).**

Had the 16th Amendment provided for an unapportioned direct tax this would have been an enlargement of the taxing power of Congress. At least on the issue of whether there was an exemption to the apportionment rule for direct taxes, all parties to the *Peck & Co. v. Lowe* case agreed there wasn't. The issue of the case dealt with the taxation of exports, not direct taxes. We'll see later in this chapter that the Supreme Court ruled that there was no enlargement to the taxation authority of Congress. Therefore it is settled; the 16th Amendment did not grant to Congress an exception to the apportionment rule for direct taxes required by the Constitution.

Just as the intent of Congress should be followed when construing a statute, so must the intent of the People, in their sovereign capacity, be followed when construing an amendment to the Constitution.

The construction of the 21st Amendment to the U.S. Constitution absolutely proves our argument. It was necessary for the 21st Amendment to repeal the 18th Amendment before the 21st Amendment could have any effect. Both Amendments related to "intoxicating liquors." The 18th Amendment prohibited the manufacture, sale, or transportation of them; whereas the 21st Amendment provided for the transportation or importation and use of them. Section 1 of the 21st Amendment reads "The eighteenth article of amendment to the Constitution of the United States is hereby repealed." The 21st Amendment would not have been in Harmony with the totality of the Constitution unless the 18th Amendment was first repealed. Similarly, had it been the intention of Congress to offer to the people an income tax amendment which would give Congress the power to impose a direct tax on the sources of income without apportionment, the 16th Amendment would have provided for such power only by modifying the direct taxing clauses of the Constitution found at Article I section 2 clause 3 and Article I section 9 clause 4. The 16th Amendment did not do this.

Section 2 of the 18th Amendment included an enforcement clause which read "The Congress and the several States shall have the concurrent power to enforce this article by appropriate legislation." The 21st Amendment did not include such an enforcement clause as the 21st Amendment was not conveying a new power to Congress, but in fact was adding a limitation on the power of Congress. Nor does the 16th Amendment have an enforcement clause, as it does not convey a new power to Congress, but only clarifies a theory of taxation. That theory was the basis for the *Pollock Rule*. The *Pollock Decision* was overturned by the 16th Amendment.

Congress did not modify the direct taxation clauses of the Constitution by the construction of the 16th Amendment. Therefore, the 16th Amendment does not provide authority for a direct tax on sources of income which enjoy constitutional protection. (Some sources of income do not enjoy constitutional protection, like income derived from sources in without (outside) the several States of the Union.) Therefore, there is no authority for Congress to tax the wages and salaries of an American Citizen living and working in one of the several States of the Union, unless that tax is apportioned.[2]

All the 16th Amendment did was to prevent an income tax, which was constructed to be inherently an indirect tax, from being declared a direct tax due to a consideration of the source from which the income came. The 16th Amendment struck down the theory upon which the *Pollock Case* was decided. After ratification of the 16th Amendment, taxes which diminish the source of income absent a privilege are inherently direct taxes, whereas those that diminish only the income flowing from a source are inherently indirect. Only the latter may be levied under the authority of the 16th Amendment.

Whenever Congress has the power to define the word "income," those geographical areas, those persons, or those things for which the word "income" can be defined by Congress do not enjoy protection from the constitutional limitations placed on Congress as it relates to the imposition of an income tax. In order to really understand the Internal Revenue Code, you need to resolve whether or not you are a person or a thing, or whether you live in a geographical area for which Congress has the power to define the word "income" uninhibited by the 16th Amendment. If you don't understand this last paragraph, reread Chapter 4.

## Hypothetical Case II: Income Tax is an Indirect Tax

This is the case where the author camps. This is also where the Supreme Court camps. This is the case where the 16th Amendment reversed the *Pollock Decision* and forever placed taxes on incomes within the classification of indirect taxes. But the 16th Amendment has only done so for income taxes that are inherently indirect. Income taxes that are inherently direct remain outside the scope of the 16th Amendment. In the case of *Brushaber v. Union Pacific Railroad Co.*, the first question Brushaber brought before the Court was:

> **"The evident purpose of this amendment [16th] was not to abandon the former policy of safeguarding the several sections of he Union against disproportionate taxation, but merely to substitute an apportionment accord-**

> **ing to "incomes for whatever source derived," in lieu of a *per capita* apportionment. Brief for Appellant at 10-11, Brushaber v. Union Pac. R.R. Co., 240 U.S. 1 (1916).**

In other words, Brushaber was asserting that the 16th Amendment provided for a constitutionally direct income tax still subject to the rule of apportionment, although now apportionment would be measured by the incomes of the several States and not measured by their population. In the brief for the government, the government also asserted that the 16th Amendment provided authority for a constitutionally direct income tax.

> **"1. Income taxes, at least when laid on income derived from real or personal property, are direct taxes, and therefore not subject to the uniformity rule, EXPRESSLY prescribed by the Constitution.**
>
> **"(a) It is settled that the uniformity requirement of clause 1 of section 8 of Article I of the Constitution, is limited to duties, imposts, and excises, and does not apply to *direct* taxes. *Pollock v. F.L. & T. Co.,* 157 U.S. 557; *Spreckels Sugar Refining Co., v. McClain,* 192 U.S. 397, 413; *License Tax Cases,* 5 Wall. 462, 471. And the *Pollock* case (158 U.S. 601, 637), finally determines that a tax on income derived from either real or personal property is a *direct* tax.**
>
> **"(b) Apportionment being restricted to *direct* taxes *only (Flint v. Stone Tracy Co., supra 152)*, the Sixteenth Amendment, in removing that restriction, recognized *any* tax upon income 'from whatever source derived' as a *direct* tax, and as such subject to the apportionment rule unless specifically exempted." Brief for the United States at 11-12, Brushaber v. Union Pac. R.R. Co., 240 U.S. 1 (1916).**

So, both Brushaber and the government argued that the 16th Amendment provided for a species of direct tax, i.e., an income tax, to be levied as a direct tax without the normal rule of apportionment as required by the Constitution. The Supreme Court stated they were both wrong! Commenting on the briefs, and the question brought before the Court, the Court said:

> **"The various propositions are so intermingled as to cause it to be difficult to classify them. We are of opinion, however, that the confusion is not inherent, but rather arises from the conclusion that the 16th Amendment provides for a hitherto unknown power of taxation; that is, a power to levy an income tax which, although direct, should not be subject to the regulation of apportionment applicable to all other direct taxes. And the far-reaching effect of this *erroneous assumption* [emphasis mine] will be made clear by generalizing the many contentions advanced in argument to support it, as follows: (a) The Amendment authorizes only a particular character of direct tax without apportionment, and therefore if a tax is levied under its assumed authority which does not partake of the characteristic exacted by the Amendment, it is outside of the Amendment, and is void as a direct tax in the general constitutional sense because not apportioned. (b) As the Amendment authorizes a tax only upon incomes 'from whatever source derived,' the exclusion from taxation of some income of designated persons and classes is not authorized, and hence the constitutionality of the law must be tested by the general provisions of the Constitution as to taxation, and thus again the tax is void for want of apportionment." Brushaber v. Union Pac. R.R. Co., 240 U.S. 1, 10-11 (1916).**

Unfortunately, the above quote from the *Brushaber Opinion* is written with run-on sentences and unnecessarily complex sentence structure. *Cornell Law Quarterly* reported on the *Brushaber Case* using easier to understand language. According to *Cornell Law Quarterly*, the question put to the Supreme Court was:

> **"The contention of the appellant was as follows:**

**(I) The sixteenth amendment provided for a new kind of a direct tax, a tax on incomes "from whatever source derived." Ramon Siaca, The Federal Income Tax Law of 1913: Construction of the Sixteenth Amendment, 1 Cornell Law Review 298, 299 (1916).**

The Court's answer to this question was that income taxes are not direct taxes, but are inherently indirect taxes. Now this holds when it is net income that is being taxed and the underlying source remains untaxed. Here the Supreme Court was using the word "income" as the American people understood the word to mean, that being unearned income or severed profit. *The Brushaber Case* was about the payment of a tax upon corporate dividends. It had nothing to do with wages or salaries.

To determine what it is that is actually being taxed, examine what is being diminished by the tax. Is the source being diminished by the tax? Or is it only the income stream that flows from the source that is being diminished by the tax, thus allowing the underlying source of the income to remain whole? When only the income that flows from the source is diminished by the tax, the tax is inherently indirect and the 16th Amendment provides that the nature of the source, i.e., land or personal property, shall not be considered when attempting to classify the tax as direct or indirect. The theory upon which the *Pollock Case* was decided had no effect once the 16th Amendment was purportedly ratified. The *Pollock Rule* was, therefore, struck down.

The Supreme Court's answer to the question brought forward by *Brushaber* was:

**"It is clear on the face of this text that it does not purport to confer power to levy income taxes in a generic sense, - an authority already possessed and never questioned, - or to limit and distinguish between one kind of income taxes and another, but that the whole purpose of the Amendment was to relieve all income taxes when im-**

> **posed from apportionment from a consideration of the source whence the income was derived." Brushaber v. Union Pac. R.R. Co., 240 U.S. 1, 17-18 (1916).**
>
> **"Second, that the contention that the Amendment treats a tax on income as a direct tax, although it is relieved from apportionment and is necessarily therefore not subject to the rule of uniformity as such rule only applies to taxes which are not direct, thus destroying the two great classifications which have been recognized and enforced from the beginning, is also *wholly without foundation* [emphasis mine] since the comment of the Amendment that all income taxes shall not be subject to apportionment by a consideration of the sources from which the taxed income may be derived forbids the application to such taxes of the rule applied in the Pollock Case by which alone such taxes were removed from the great class of excises, duties, and imposts subject to the rule of uniformity, and were placed under the other or direct class." id. at 18-19.**
>
> **"Indeed, from another point of view, the Amendment demonstrates that no such purpose was intended, and on the contrary shows that it was drawn with the object of maintaining the limitations of the Constitution and *harmonizing* [emphasis mine] their operation." id. at 19.**

Again, the *Cornell Law Quarterly* simplifies what the Court said:

> **"The court through Chief Justice White held that the tax was constitutional. The major proposition of the appellant's argument is not true. Hence, the conclusion does not follow. The sixteenth amendment does not permit a new class of direct tax, (in fact as it will be later shown, the court does not think that the amendment treated the tax as a direct tax at all), carrying with it the distinguishing characteristic of a hitherto unrecognized uniformity."**

> **"The amendment, the court said, judged by the purpose for which it was passed, does not treat income taxes as direct taxes but simply removed the ground which led to their being considered as such in the Pollock case, namely, the source of the income. Therefore, they are again to be classified in the class of indirect taxes to which they by nature belong." Ramon Siaca, The Federal Income Tax Law of 1913: Construction of the Sixteenth Amendment, 1 Cornell Law Quarterly 298, 299 and 301 (1916).**

Said another way, the theory upon which the *Pollock Case* was decided, i.e., the *Pollock Rule*, was overturned by the 16th Amendment.

*Harvard Law Review* had this commentary on the *Brushaber Case*:

> **"In *Brushaber v. Union Pacific Railroad Co.*, Mr. Chief Justice White, upholding the income tax imposed by the Tariff Act of 1913, construed the Amendment as a declaration that an income tax is "indirect," rather than as making an exception to the rule that direct taxes must be apportioned." The Income Tax and the Sixteenth Amendment, 29 Harvard Law Review 536 (1915-6).**

Also, commenting on *Brushaber, California Law Review* said:

> **"The constitutionality of this act and the construction of the 16th Amendment have been passed by the Supreme Court in the case of Brushaber v. Union Pacific Railroad Co. The construction which Mr. Chief Justice White....lays upon the 16th Amendment, as declaring that income taxes are to be regarded as indirect rather than as excepting them from the rule of uniformity...the one [construction] adopted by the court has the merit of harmonizing all of the provisions of the Constitution, and of subjecting income taxes to the requirement of uniformity." Constitutional Law: Income Tax: Sixteenth Amendment, 4 California Law Review 333, 335-6 (1915-6).**

And finally from the field of economics we have the following report from *The Journal of Political Economy*:

> **"Finally it holds the purpose of the amendment was not to change the existing interpretation of the term 'direct tax', except to the extent necessary to accomplish the result intended - that is, the prevention of any resort to the sources from which a taxed income is derived in order to cause such a direct tax on the income to be held to be a direct tax on the source itself and thereby to take an income tax out of the class of excises, duties, and imposts and place it in the class of direct taxes." Washington Notes, The Income Tax Decision, 24 The Journal of Political Economy 299, 300 (1916).**

This point is being belabored because it is precisely this point on which the government is in error. The government claims that the 16th Amendment provides an exception to the direct taxation clause of the Constitution whereby a direct tax can be levied on the wages and salaries of the American People without apportionment. As you can see the Supreme Court has already ruled on the question. The Supreme Court, by way of sound reasoning and good logic, has stated that such an exception does not exist. That ruling is today being ignored by the IRS and by the lower courts. For example, the Ninth Circuit Court of Appeals stated:

> **"Notwithstanding Becraft's insistence that...his position can fairly be reduced to one elemental proposition: The Sixteenth Amendment does not authorize a direct non-apportioned income tax on resident United States citizens and thus such citizens are not subject to the federal income tax laws. [2] We hardly need comment on the patent absurdity and frivolity of such a proposition. For over 75 years, the Supreme Court and the lower federal courts have both implicitly and explicitly recognized the Sixteenth Amendment's authorization of a non-apportioned direct income tax on United States citizens**

> **residing in the United States..." See, e.g., Brushaber v. Union Pacific Railroad Co., 240 U.S. 1, 12-19" In Re Becraft, 885 F.2d 547, 548 (9th Cir. 1989).**

By now you should realize that Becraft was right and the Ninth Circuit was wrong. The Ninth Circuit utterly misquotes the *Brushaber Case*. In its *Brushaber Ruling*, the Supreme Court harmonized the 16th Amendment with the original Constitution when it rejected the claim by both Brushaber and the government that the 16th Amendment authorized a "non-apportioned direct income tax."

Most of the other circuits have similar rulings. Compounding the problem are the commentaries on the law itself. If one looks up the Constitution in Volume 1 of the United States Code Annotated published by West Publishing Co., you will see in the footnotes that West Publishing Co. claims that the 16th Amendment provides this exemption to the apportionment rule required by the Constitution for direct taxes. West Publishing Co. is simply wrong as the Supreme Court has ruled otherwise.

Taking the "belt and suspenders" approach and doubling checking our conclusion, we will look at three other cases. The first of these is *Tyee Realty Co. v. Anderson*. One of the questions brought before the Supreme Court was as follows:

> **"Every contention relied upon for reversal in the two cases is embraced within the following propositions: (a) that the tax imposed by the statute was not sanctioned by the 16th Amendment because the statute exceeded the exceptional and limited power of direct income taxation for the first time conferred upon Congress by that Amendment, and, being outside of the Amendment, and governed solely therefore, by the general taxing authority conferred upon Congress by the Constitution, the tax was void as an attempt to levy a direct tax without apportionment." Tyee Realty Co. v. Anderson, 240 U.S. 115, 117 (1916).**

The Tyee question was the same question as in Brushaber. Tyee was arguing that the tax being collected was a direct tax, but not an income tax. The Supreme Court's answer said it was an indirect income tax and that it was constitutional:

> **"But we need not now enter into an original consideration of the merits of these contentions because each and all of them were considered and adversely disposed of in *Brushaber v. Union Pac. RR. Co.* That case, therefore, is here absolutely controlling and decisive." id. at 117-8.**

Bundled with the Brushaber case was another case called *Edward Thorne v. Charles W. Anderson, Collector of Internal Revenue*. In this case the plaintiff, Thorne, also argued that the 16th Amendment provided new taxation power for Congress. Thorne said that the 16th Amendment allowed for an exemption to the apportionment rule for direct taxes. As we saw in the *Brushaber Opinion,* such an assertion is "wholly without foundation."[3]

Furthermore, in the case of *Stanton v. Baltic Mining Co.*, again this question was presented to the Supreme court:

> **"Class B: (1) That as the 16th Amendment authorizes only an exceptional direct income tax without apportionment...." Stanton v. Baltic Mining Co., 240 U.S. 103, 112 (1916).**

The Supreme Court ruled:

> **"But, aside from the obvious error of the proposition, intrinsically considered, it manifestly disregards the fact that by the previous ruling [*Brushaber*] it was settled that the provisions of the 16th Amendment conferred no new power of taxation, but simply *prohibited* [emphasis mine] the previously complete and plenary power of income taxation possessed by Congress from the beginning from being taken out of the category of indirect taxation to which they *inherently* [emphasis mine] belonged and be-**

**ing placed in the category of direct taxation subject to apportionment." Stanton v. Baltic Mining Co., 240 U.S. 103, 112-3 (1916).**

By the Supreme Court's statement: "conferred no new power of taxation" in the *Stanton v. Baltic Mining Co. Case*, what the court was saying was the two constitutional classes of taxation remained intact upon ratification of the 16th Amendment. Any constitutional provision allowing for an unapportioned direct tax on incomes would constitute a new class of taxes. This didn't happen, so there is therefore no new class of taxes under the Constitution.

**"Thus, in the matter of taxation, the Constitution recognizes the two great classes of direct and indirect taxes, and lays down two rules by which their imposition must be governed, namely: The rule of apportionment as to direct taxes, and the rule of uniformity as to duties, imposts and excises." Pollock v. Farmers' Loan & Trust Co., 157 U.S. 429, 557 (1895).**

## Transcript of Record:
## Stanton v. Baltic Mining Co.

Although *Brushaber* was the precedent setting case for the first income tax cases that went up to the Supreme Court after the purported ratification of the 16th Amendment, the *Stanton Case* is more interesting to our point. The *Stanton Case* was about:

**"In No. 140 (Brushaber) and No. 359 (Stanton) a stockholder seeks to restrain the corporation taxpayer from voluntarily paying its tax." Brief for the United States at 3, Brushaber v. Union Pacific R.R. Co., 240 U.S. 1 (1916).**

We saw earlier that an income tax on the wages or salary of an American Citizen living and working in one of the several States of the Union is a direct tax. This is the position of the IRS and most of the lower courts. Only by claiming that the 16th Amendment has provided an exception to the apportionment rule of the Constitution can the IRS collect this tax on wages and salaries with a straight face. The government regularly claims they have this exemption authority by falsely claiming these early cases settled the question in the government's favor.

A review of the Supreme Court's Transcript of Record for the *Stanton Case* shows that 12 times Stanton claimed that the 16th Amendment provided this "apportionment rule exception" for direct taxes when the tax was an income tax in the nature of a direct tax. Then another 10 times Stanton alluded to this perceived exception. In addition, so did a Mr. John R. Van Derlip who filed an *amicus curiae* brief in the *Stanton Case*. The government and Mr. Van Derlip made the same claim 15 times. A sampling of Stanton's assertions is as follows:

> **"The Sixteenth Amendment authorizes direct taxes upon 'incomes,' but not upon capital or property. Income taxes may now be imposed without regard to apportionment among the States, according to their population."**
>
> **"All forms of direct taxation other than taxes on 'incomes,' clearly remain subject to the same constitutional limits as formerly." Brief for Appellant at 24, Stanton v. Baltic Mining Co., 240 U.S. 103 (1916).**
>
> **"This is a direct tax on 'net income,' and nothing else can constitutionally be taxed directly, without apportionment." id. at 36.**
>
> **"The Sixteenth Amendment only authorizes direct taxes on 'incomes.'" id. at 60.**
>
> **"It must, however, constantly be borne in mind that here we are dealing with a direct tax on 'net income,' and not an excise, such as the decisions of this Court have frequently dealt with." id. at 74.**

> **"All forms of direct taxation of real and personal property, other than income taxes, still require apportionment; otherwise they are unconstitutional." id. at 139.**

In Mr. Van Derlip's *amicus curiae* brief, he made the following claims:

> **"The growing needs of the Government for revenue in these latter days have been deemed by the people a sufficient reason for relaxing, in a degree, the strict regulations in relation to the laying of direct taxes which prevailed prior to the promulgation of the 16th Amendment..."**
>
> **"The effect of that amendment is to be considered in the light of these historical facts which disclose most clearly that, while the amendment lets down the bars in some degree, the extent of their lowering was carefully measured and must be fully respected..."**
>
> **"The 16th Amendment was designed to accomplish, and in distinct terms did accomplish, the simplifying of the process of taxing incomes from whatever source derived, by relieving it from the hampering conditions theretofore attaching to a direct tax."**
>
> **"By the [16th] Amendment, §2 of Article I of the Constitution had been modified as respects the persons to be included in any enumeration which should be the basis for the laying of a direct tax. This same section has now been modified for a second time by the 16th Amendment with the result that the first sentence of the section, in effect, now stands as if enacted in the following words: 'Representatives and direct taxes shall be apportioned among the several states which may be included within this Union, according to their respective numbers, counting the whole number of persons in each state, excluding Indians not taxed; provided, however, that the Congress shall have power to lay and collect direct taxes upon incomes, from whatever source derived, without**

apportionment among the several states, and without regard to any census or enumeration.'" *Amicus Curiae* Brief by Van Derlip at 24-25. Stanton v. Baltic Mining Co., 240 U.S. 103 (1916).

"The single purpose and sole effect of the 16th Amendment are to disencumber the federal taxing power as theretofore existing in respect of incomes, so as to allow the laying of a direct tax upon incomes without apportionment, and without regard to any census or enumeration." id. at 30.

"The nature of an income tax is not changed by the amendment, but it still remains a direct tax." id. at 31.

"The situation presented by the 16th Amendment may be thus summed up:

1.) Income is the gain or profit derived from labor, or from property, or from both, and, if from property, it can only be that which is produced by its use without impairing the capital investment and which leaves such investment intact.

2.) Gains, profits and income are property which, before the adoption of the 16th Amendment, could not be taxed except in accordance with the rule of apportionment, because an income tax is a direct tax.

3.) The 16th Amendment does not change the nature of the income tax; it still remains a direct tax.

4.) By the 16th Amendment, however, a new rule introduced into the Constitution where by a direct tax may now be assessed upon incomes without apportionment. id. at 71-72.

> **5.) No other change was affected by the Amendment, and, as to taxation of all classes of property other than incomes, the original constitutional limitations still obtained."**

Every quote you just read from the *Stanton* Transcript of Record was rejected by the Supreme Court. In every way, shape and form the claim was made that the 16th Amendment provided an exception to the apportionment rule. If true, this would have been the "new rule" spoken of in *Stanton*. It would have created a "new tax," a new category of constitutional taxation. The claim was made that Congress was now "disencumbered" from the apportionment rule; as such Congress would have had "new power." All this was rejected by the Supreme Court. In the Court's Opinion on the *Stanton Case*, the Supreme Court said:

> **"But aside from the obvious error of the proposition intrinsically considered, it manifestly disregards the fact that by the previous ruling [Brushaber] it was settled that the provisions of the Sixteenth Amendment conferred no new power of taxation but simply prohibited the previously complete and plenary power of income taxation possessed by Congress from the beginning from being taken out of the category of indirect taxation to which it inherently belonged and being placed in the category of direct taxation subject to apportionment by a consideration of the sources from which the income derived.... We are here dealing solely with the restriction imposed by the Sixteenth Amendment to the right to resort to the source whence an income is derived in a case where there is power to tax for the purpose of taking the income tax out of the class of indirect to which it generically belongs and putting it in the class of direct to which it would not otherwise belong in order to subject it to the regulation of apportionment." Stanton v. Baltic Mining Co., 240 U.S. 103, 112-3 (1916).**

The question as to whether there is authority for the government to collect an unapportioned direct tax was settled *in the negative* by the Supreme Court. It was settled in the *Brushaber Case*. Then the Court affirmed their *Brushaber* ruling in the *Tyee Case*, in *Dodge v. Osborn*, and lastly in *Stanton*. An income tax on the severable net income from business or accumulated wealth is an indirect tax. An income tax on the earned income from wages and salaries is a direct tax. The government is wholly without power to collect the latter without apportionment among the several States.

Just in case this wasn't enough, my research caused me to look into the period of World War II. The number of persons filing income tax returns approximately doubled as wars are often looked at by governments as opportunities to grab power. Reporting on "The Revenue Bill of 1941" the House's Committee on Ways and Means prepared House Report No. 1040 dated July 24, 1941. On page 17 of this report, in the section called *Constitutionality of Proposal*, the Committee on Ways and Means stated:

> **"It seems clear that Congress has the constitutional power to enact this proposed amendment. Generically an income tax is classed as an <u>*excise*</u> [emphasis mine] (*Brushaber v. Union Pac. R.R. Co.,* 240 U.S. 1). The only express constitutional limitation upon such taxes is that they be geographically uniform." H. Rep. No. 1040, at 17 (1941).**

Twenty-eight years after the purported ratification of the 16th Amendment, we have the House of Representatives' Committee on Ways and Means asserting that the income tax is an ***excise tax*** (emphasis mine), which is a species of an ***indirect tax*** (emphasis mine). The 16th Amendment does not provide authority for a "direct tax" on the American Citizen.

> **"There is no excise here, for appellees exercise no taxable privilege which can be the subject of an excise, or of any tax other than one in the nature of a property tax [direct tax]. The things mentioned below to show that**

> **appellants "engage in business" are simple acts of ownership, not taxable as privileges, and a tax because of them is a tax on property-ownership and not an excise. Hale v. State Board, 302 U.S. 95, 97 (1937).**

What the Supreme Court is saying in the *Hale Case* is that when there is no privilege being exercised, there is no excise tax which can be linked to the privilege. In this case, absent a privilege, when the tax falls directly on the property because of ownership, it is therefore a **direct tax**.

The purpose of the income tax was to bring tax relief to wage earners. All of us have a common law right to make a living and support ourselves.

> **Mr. McCUMBER. "I appreciate that there is a good deal of complexity about this slight differentiation between a tax upon property and a tax upon the right to do business; and there is a good deal of rather delicate refinement, it seems to me between the two." 44 Cong. Rec. 3976 (1909).**

The 16th Amendment provides Constitutional authority for an indirect tax on incomes within the several States. This is settled by the Supreme Court and by the debates in Congress. The income tax of the 16th Amendment is a tax that diminishes the income that flows from the source, leaving the source of the income undiminished. Such must be the case for the tax to be an indirect tax. When the "capital producing the income remains" the tax was only on the income and not on the source of the income. The taxable income may be severed from the source without diminishing the source. Only the income is diminished by the tax, the source is not diminished by the tax as the source "remains." Any tax that diminishes the source, absent a privilege, is not a tax on incomes; it is a tax on the source of the income, and therefore would be a direct tax levied outside of the authority of the 16th Amendment.

*This cartoon called "The New Man on the Job" was created by John Scott Clubb in 1913. Clubb shows how the idle rich will bring tax relief to the working man by way of the income tax. This cartoon perfectly captures the original intent of the 16th Amendment and the central thesis of this book.*

> **"A tax on income may be oppressive and unwise, but it is not destructive. The capital producing the income remains.... The humble workers are not helped by the taxes which the rich evade. The evasions of the rich are in fact the burdens of the poor." Editorial, Bad Tax Laws, N.Y. Times, pg. 10, March 24, 1911.**

If Congress desires to tax the source of income, and the source exists by right, Congress must apply the apportionment rule in levying this tax as the source is diminished by the tax. If the source of income exists by privilege, Congress may elect to levy the tax either with the rule of apportionment or the rule of uniformity, but not both and not neither. Congress will have to be careful to identify exactly what is being taxed so as to survive a judicial challenge to the statute.[4]

## A picture speaks a thousand words

As I wrote earlier, it is my opinion that the *Pollock Decision* had a major flaw in it. The court in *Pollock* ruled that a tax on the net income from investments in real estate and investments in personal property was actually a tax on the real estate or on personal property itself and was therefore a direct tax. This is known as the *Pollock Rule.* Since the taxing statute that was the subject of the *Pollock Case* did not apportion the tax among the several States, the court ruled the statute to be unconstitutional.[5]

Income from real estate is in and of itself property, but it is not property in the form of real estate; it is property in the form of money. It is personal property. Real estate and money should not be lumped together when the issue is "income taxes," at least not at the federal level. Real estate is a source of income. Money can be a source of income, too, when it is in the form of principal. But for the purposes of the 16th Amendment, only "constitutional income" may be taxed under its authority.

Furthermore, when government is acting in its constitutional roll of protecting property, the tax levied on the income from real estate can be thought of as an insurance premium. It is a legitimate exaction paid for the protection government extends to the property. As such, it makes perfect sense to classify such a tax as an excise. However, when government goes beyond its constitutional boundaries and steals from the rich to buy votes from those who have their hands out, this is altogether a different matter. A graduated income tax is a tax to redistribute wealth. It is communistic.

Now let's look at a hypothetical case of an income tax on real estate. Suppose we have an office building complex with building A and building B. These two buildings were built at the same time by the same developer, using the same contractor. The design and size of the buildings are identical, and the construction of the buildings was just completed. Each building is on opposite sides of the same street intersection. Upon completion of construction, the buildings were sold to different owners. Being identical, located on the same street corner and in the same real estate market, both buildings rent for $18 per square foot per year. Assume the developer provided the long-term financing for both buildings.

In our example we have tried in every way to make the buildings the same. The only difference between the two is in how the owner, i.e. the taxpayer, manages his building. Owner A is a good businessman and building A is well managed; owner B is not such a good businessman and his building is not well managed. The financial performance of each building is as follows:

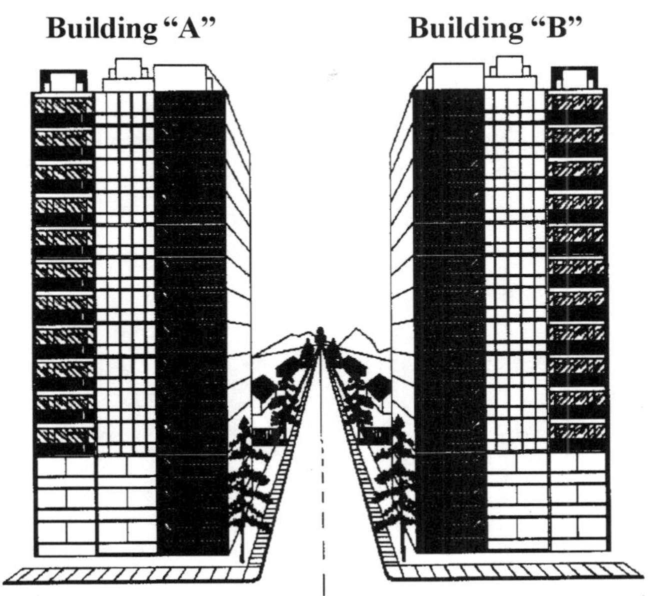


| **Gross Revenue Building A** | |
|---|---|
| 25,000 sq. ft. x $18/sq./ft. x 90% = | $405,000 |
| **Expenses Building A** | |
| Operating Expenses | $140,000 |
| Annual Debt Service | 220,000 |
| Net Income | 45,000 |
| Income Tax Due (40%) | $ 18,000 |

| **Gross Revenue Building B** | |
|---|---|
| 25,000 sq. ft. x $18/sq./ft. x 80% = | $360,000 |
| **Expenses Building B** | |
| Operating Expenses | $160,000 |
| Annual Debt Service | 220,000 |
| Net Income | - $ 20,000 |
| Income Tax Due (40%) | No tax due |

*Figure 6.4 Net Income Tax vs. Gross Receipts Tax*

Let us assume that out of the operating expense are paid the cost of maintaining the building and an allowance for depreciation. Let us further assume that, less normal wear and tear, both buildings are well maintained and there is no deferred maintenance causing the buildings to be worth less at the end of the year than they were at the beginning of the year.

Assume our hypothetical owner of building B has a vacancy rate of 20 percent whereas owner A's vacancy rate is only 10 percent. Owner B operates an unorganized business and is not as profitable as most others in the real estate field. Owner A is a good businessman and is well liked by his tenants; his building is profitable. Owner B pays no income tax on the building he manages as he has no gain or profit. Yet owner A pays $18,000 in income tax.

Is the income tax paid by owner A an indirect tax or a direct tax? What is diminished by the tax? Is it a tax on the ownership of the building? Does the market value of the building determine the amount of tax due? Or is it the income that flows from the building that is diminished by the tax? In our example, only the income is diminished by the tax, as only owner A pays the tax. Therefore the tax is not on the source of the income, the building itself, but only on the income. In our example, both buildings were well maintained, there was no deferred maintenance, and the buildings "remained whole." The tax is an income tax, because it does not diminish the value of the source of the income. It is an indirect tax. A direct tax is a tax on ownership of the thing taxed and is normally measured by the value of the thing owned. In this example, the value of the building has nothing to do with the amount of the tax due.

Now suppose there was a 15 percent tax on the gross revenue of the buildings without any allowance for any deductions. Owner A would owe $60,750 and owner B would owe $54,000. In this scenario, both owners would have a difficult time covering their operating expenses and would probably allow for some deferred maintenance. Since the taxes would be paid ahead of this deferred maintenance expense, the value of the building—the source of the income—

would be diminished by the tax as both owners pay the tax. With a backlog of deferred maintenance, the value of each building would be less at the end of the year. This tax would be a gross receipts tax, and would therefore be a tax on the source known as a direct tax.

There has been some debate among the state courts of our 50 States as to whether or not "income" is property. This may be a controlling issue for individual states as each of the states has its own Constitution with its own rules of taxation. But at the national level, it is a moot issue. Whether or not income, as defined by the Supreme Court to be gain or profit severed from capital, is property makes no difference as to whether or not the tax is direct or indirect. The issue is what is the tax on? Is it on the source? Or is it on only the income that flows from the source?

I believe that since the tax in question in the *Pollock Case* was only on net income, the tax was inherently an indirect tax and it was error on the part of the court to call it a direct tax. By declaring the income tax on the net income of real estate a direct tax, the Supreme Court caused the pendulum to swing too far in the direction of limiting the power of the national government to tax. The purpose of the 16th Amendment was to bring the pendulum back to the middle. Unfortunately, the flawed and ambiguous language of this amendment has facilitated the abuse of the 16th Amendment we experience today.

Having read the entire transcript of record for both the *Pollock Cases*, I can understand why the Supreme Court ruled in favor of Pollock. Counsel for Pollock nearly wrote a treatise on income taxation. They employed the best experts and appeared to have been exhaustive in their research.

On the other hand, the brief written by Richard Olney, Attorney General for the United States, was poorly researched. Additionally, his brief and oral argument contained many half truths and outright lies. Anyone remotely familiar with the income tax issue should have been easily able to see through his baloney. Speaking for myself, I couldn't stomach a second reading of his work.

> **"Clearly the word 'uniform' means something and was inserted [in the Constitution] for some definite purpose. But the learned Attorney General [Mr. Olney] says that the word 'uniform' is surplusage. Surplusage! Those men whose names I have mentioned [Washington, Hamilton, Madison and Franklin] and their illustrious peers throwing in a word for mere surplusage!" Closing Argument by Mr. Choate at 42, Pollock v. Farmers' Loan and Trust Co., 157 U.S. 429 (1894).**

I might add that at the same time we got the income tax amendment, it was the Republican party and Senator Aldrich that gave us the Federal Reserve Act and the Federal Reserve Bank, a private banking system that is not federal and has no reserves. The IRS has worked hand in glove with the Federal Reserve Bank to bankrupt our Nation during the years 1929 to 1933, steal our gold in the year 1933 and enslave us with a feudal system that taxes our right to exist.

Thomas Jefferson said, "If the American people ever allow private banking interests to take control of their money, they will one day wake up and realize they are slaves on the continent their forefathers conquered."

# Chapter 7
## Income: The Meaning of the Word

**"Why not assume that the framers of the Constitution, and the people who voted it into existence, meant exactly what it says?"**

***~ Lake County v. Rollins, 130 U.S. 662, 670 (1889).***

Black's *Dictionary of Law*, first and second editions (1891 and 1910), defines the term "income tax." The first edition, published in 1891, would have been the edition applicable to the income tax debates that surrounded the 16th Amendment.

**INCOME TAX: A tax on the yearly profits arising from property, professions, trades, and offices." Henry Campbell Black, A Law Dictionary 612 (1910).**

West Publishing Co.'s popular *Judicial and Statutory **Definitions of Words and Phrases***, 1904 edition, defines at page 3507, an income tax to be:

> **"INCOME TAX: An 'income tax' is a tax which relates to the product or income from property or from business pursuits. Levi v. City of Louisville, 30 S.W. 973, 974, 97 Ky. 394, 28 L.R.A. 480.**
>
> **"The term 'income tax' includes a tax on the gross receipts of a corporation or business. Parker v. North British Ins. Co. 7 South. 599, 600, 42 La. Ann. 428."**

We will see that all parties in the debate understood that the definitions of "income tax" provided by Black and West were the ones which applied to the proposed income tax amendment, that being a tax on "net income" or "profits" from investments, property or businesses. What was to be taxed under the proposed 16th Amendment did not include the wages or salary of a Citizen.

The definition of "CAPITATION tax" taken from the first edition of *A Law Dictionary* by Henry Campbell Black (now *Black's Law Dictionary*) published in 1891 is in perfect harmony with the argument put forth in this book.

> **"CAPITATION TAX. One which is levied upon the person simply, without any reference to his property, real or personal, or to any business in which he may be engaged or to any employment which he may follow." Henry Campbell Black, A Law Dictionary, 171 (1891).**

The second edition of *Black's* contained the same definition. *Bouvier's* 1856 6th Edition which says:

> **"CAPITATION. A poll tax; an imposition which is yearly laid on each person according to his estate and ability."**

What the Congress, the state Legislatures and the People thought they were adding to the Constitution by way of the income tax amendment would have been better written as: *"The Congress shall have power to lay and collect indirect taxes on unearned incomes and annual profits, from whatever source derived, without apportionment among the several States, and without regard to any census or enumeration."*

> **Mr. HEFLIN. "An income tax seeks to reach the unearned wealth of the country and to make it pay its share." 45 Cong. Rec. 4420 (1909).**

The word "income," when used in the 16th Amendment, means "unearned income or profit," and "severed profit." It is the annuity check you get in the mail from your investments, it's your passive income. It is not the money you worked for. It is the net income, the profit left over from your "income property" after you have paid all your expenses and taxes on the property. It is the interest income that accrues to your savings account even while you sleep.

The government would have us believe that every time a dollar passes hands someone has received "taxable income." Through the case law of the lower courts there has been an overt evolution of the meaning of the word "income" from that of "gain and profit" to mean "economic benefit." The *Eisner Case,* the stock dividend case, is the one that, although its decision is sound and correct, has been interpreted incorrectly by the lower courts. *Eisner* says that "income may be defined as the gain derived from capital, from labor, or from both combined." The government would have us believe the *Eisner Case* says that labor equals income. The government is taxing our gross earnings where the word "income" in the *Eisner Case* only pertained to net income. If your employer gives all his employees a turkey for Thanksgiving, the taxman has his hand out for his cut of the gift. Is this what **We the People** said they wanted when they lobbied Congress for an income tax amendment to the Constitution? Where is the government vested with the authority to change a meaning of a word within the Constitution? Speaking about the very word "income" the Supreme Court said:

**"[I]t becomes essential to distinguish between what is and what is not 'income,' as the term is there used, and to apply the distinction, as cases arise, according to truth and substance, without regard to form. Congress cannot by any definition it may adopt conclude the matter, since it cannot by legislation alter the Constitution, from which alone it derives its power to legislate, and within whose limitations alone that power can be lawfully exercised." Eisner v. Macomber, 252 U.S. 189, 206 (1920).**

Congress' authority is derived from the Constitution. It was the intent of the framers that the legislative branch of government be the most powerful of the three branches, as it is the representative of the People in government. The root of all power is in the People in their sovereign capacity.

Unfortunately, Congress has erred in allowing the executive branch of government to gradually, but steadily, increase in power until the bureaucracy has become a predator wielding raw power over everyone including the members of Congress and the members of the Judiciary. With this raw power, the bureaucracy ignores the limitations on its authority and instead claims the word "income" is an all encompassing word and includes every dollar that changes hands. We will see that it was intended that the constitutional meaning of the word "income" be limited in scope.

## Judicial Meaning of the Word "Income"

**Sec. 30 Judicial definitions of income. By the rule of construction, *noscitur a sociis,* however, the words in this statute must be construed in connection with those to which it is joined, namely, gains and profits; and it is evidently the intention, as a general rule, to tax only the profit of the taxpayer, not his whole revenue. Roger Foster, A Treatise on the Federal Income Tax Under The Act of 1913, 143 (Lawyers Co-operative Publishing Co., 1914).**

For the purposes of this book, we will assume the 16th Amendment was ratified, notwithstanding Bill Benson's work *The Law That Never Was*. In realty, I believe Benson is correct that the 16th Amendment was never properly ratified. However, in the bigger picture, it makes little difference as Congress' authority to tax is plenary, i.e. total. Congress can tax income with or without the 16th Amendment. What the 16th Amendment did was to overturn the *Pollock Decision* by way of constitutional amendment allowing income taxes on net incomes from real estate and personal property to be levied according to the rule of uniformity instead of the rule of apportionment.

> **"Indeed, in light of the history which we have given and of the decision in the *Pollock Case*, and the ground upon which the ruling in that case was based, there is no escape from the conclusion that the Amendment was drawn for the purpose of doing away for the future with the principle upon which the Pollock Case was decided." Brushaber v. Union Pac. R.R. Co., 240 U.S. 1, 18 (1916).**

*Pollock* dealt with a net income tax on the proceeds from real estate and from personal property. All other issues were without the scope of *Pollock* and not incorporated within its questions before that court. Any mention of other issues within the printed case are only dicta and not a part of the decision of the *Pollock Court*. Therefore, the scope of the 16th Amendment, which was intended to overturn *Pollock*, is limited only to the issues before the *Pollock Court*. That being whether or not a tax on net income from real estate and personal property is a direct tax subject to the rule of apportionment, or an indirect tax subject to the rule of uniformity. The *Pollock Case* had nothing to do with taxes on wages or salaries.

We can call the theory upon which the *Pollock Case* was decided the *Pollock Rule*. The *Pollock Rule* said that a tax on income was the same as a tax on the income's source. All the 16th Amendment did was prevent this theory from being used again in the future. The 16th Amendment struck down the *Pollock Rule*.

Speaking on the issue of dicta, Senator Hughes said:

> **"Chief Justice Marshall said in a noted case that the court would not be bound, and was not bound, by every expression it used in argument or by every statement of law it made, but only by its direct decision upon some question immediately before it for determination. He advised in that opinion that the bar, the country, and the courts before who its decisions might be read should not be bound, for the court itself was not, and others ought not to be bound, by language thus used." 44 Cong. Rec. 4044 (1909).**

> **Mr. BARTLETT. "...Surely when the members of this high court itself thus express their dissent for the decision [*Pollock*], members of the bar and the people should not be expected to have confidence in the decision [*Pollock*] or to believe that it correctly decides the question, and they are justified in believing and asserting that Congress has been deprived by this decision of the power to levy taxes for the support of the Government in the way and manner intended by the Constitution. Therefore, if it requires a constitutional amendment to restore to Congress this power [to overturn *Pollock*] of levying a tax upon the wealth of the country, in order that it may bear its just proportion of the burdens of government, and to restore [to overturn *Pollock*] to the people and to Congress their right to levy and collect taxes for the support of the Government in the way it had been done for a hundred years prior to this decision [of *Pollock*], I must vote for the amendment." 44 Cong. Rec. 4409 (1909).**

The Supreme Court has told us how we determine the intent of a portion of the Constitution and the meaning of the words used within it. We opened this chapter with a quote from the Supreme Court that asks us the obvious. If the People are sovereign and the government derives its just powers from the consent of the governed, then the meaning of the term "constitutional income" has already been determined by **We the People**.

> **"...the Constitution obtains its force from the people, and not the convention.... But where the proceedings show the positive and unmistakable intent of the framers of the instrument that the particular phraseology shall not be extended beyond its plain meaning, corroborative force is given to the conclusion that the people acted on this construction, and ratified the instrument in the belief that the words were used in a sense obvious to the common understanding." Annotation, Resort to constitutional or legislative debates., supra at 13.**

When the American people encouraged their state legislators to ratify the 16th Amendment, was it the understanding of the People that the word "income" as used in the Amendment meant "net income?" Remember a tax on net income does not diminish the income's source.

Let's revisit the *Brushaber Case*. In oral argument before the Supreme Court, Brushaber's attorney, Mr. Davies, made the assertion:

> **"And further, when the word "income" was used, it was meant income that was net. It was not gross income, that could be taxed in the case of some corporations or individuals, but it was in every case the income from whatever source derived, the income as a whole of the taxpayer, and that necessarily must be net income, because the ordinary meaning of the word "income" is not gross income or gross receipts, but net income, after making the deductions which diminish a man's income**

> **and diminish the ultimate profit to him as a result of his entire activities. Opening Argument for Appellant at 6, Brushaber v. Union Pac. R.R. Co., 240 U.S. 1 (1916).**

Because the case was argued in 1916, Mr. Davies would have been well aware of the debates that surrounded the ratification processes of the 16th Amendment. He was therefore speaking from a position of first hand knowledge. None of the parties to the case, nor the court, rebutted this position of Mr. Davies.

Adding force to Mr. Davies assertion is the fact that Congress sent the 16th Amendment out to the States for ratification during the same session in which Congress passed the Corporation Excise Tax Act of 1909. The Supreme Court has ruled that the word "income," as used in the 16th Amendment, has the same meaning as the word "income" as used in the Corporate Excise Act. What follows are the words of the Supreme Court:

> **"The use of this definition of "income" in the decision of cases arising under the Corporation Excise Tax Act of 1909, and under the Income Tax Act (1913) is, we think, decisive of the case before us. ... It is obvious that these decisions in principle rule the case at bar if the word 'income' has the same meaning in the Income Tax Act of 1913 that it had in the Corp. Excise Tax Act of 1909, and that it has the same scope of meaning that was in effect decided in *Southern Pac. Co. v. Lowe*, where it was assumed ...there was no difference in its meaning as used in the Act of 1909 and the Income Tax Act of 1913. There can be no doubt that the word must be given the same meaning and content in the Income Tax Acts of 1916 & 1917 that it had in the Act of 1913. When to this we add that in *Eisner v. Macomber* a case arising under the same Income Tax Act of 1916 which is here involved, the definition of "income" which was applied was adopted from *Stratton's Independence v. Howbert* ...there would seem to be no room to doubt that the word must be given the same meaning in all of the Income Tax**

**Acts of Congress that was given to in the Corporation Excise Tax Act and that what that meaning is has now become definitely settled by decisions of this court.**

**"In determining the definition of the word "income" thus arrived at, this court has consistently refused to enter into the refinements of lexicographers or economists and has approved, in the definitions quoted, what it believed to be the commonly understood meaning of the term *which must have been in the minds of the people* [emphasis mine] when they adopted the 16th Amendment." Merchants' L. & T. Co. v. Smietanka, 255 U.S. 509, 518-9 (1921).**

One of the rules of construction for determining the meaning of a law is that there must be a purpose for the law. There are some who say that the meaning of the word income in the 16th Amendment means corporate income. But if corporate income was already being taxed under the Corporate Excise Tax of 1909, what need would we have for the 16th Amendment? None.

When the *Merchants' L. & T. Co. v. Smietanka* court stated "...the word [income] must be given the same meaning in all Income Tax Acts of Congress that was given to [it] in the Corporation Excise Tax Act...." I believe what the court meant was that whatever accounting procedures accountants used to determine "income" for corporations, those same procedures would be used to determine what "income" was for unincorporated businesses.

Many of the early income tax cases involved complex accounting issues. The *Eisner* case was about stock dividends. The *Stanton* case was about depreciating mining properties. The *Peck v. Lowe* case was about taxing a company that earned part of its "income" from exports. All of these cases involved complex accounting questions.

I beleive that the Court wisely left the accounting to the accountants and dealt with the issue of "income" only in a generic way as it related to the Constitution.

Furthermore, when the Court used the phrase "which must have been in the minds of people," that is our clue to look where this book looks for our answer. And that is in Congressional Records, in law journals, political journals, newspapers, magazines, letters, etc. And when we look in these places, we find that the target of the income tax amendment was income from unincorporated businesses and income from investments.

> **"The British income tax decisions are interpretations of statutes so wholly different in their wording from the acts of Congress which we are considering that they are quite without value in arriving at the construction of the laws here involved." id. at 521-2.**

The British, unlike Americans, considered "labour" to be in and of itself "income." This is why the British meaning of the word "income" does not apply in all cases. But the British also made a distinction between earned income and unearned income. The tax rate on the former was lower than that of the latter. The British also did not have to contend with the constitutional classification of taxes into direct and indirect. In *Eisner v. Macomber*, the court, in defining the meaning of the word "income" said:

> **"The fundamental relation of 'capital' to 'income' has been much discussed by economists, the former being likened to the *tree* or the *land*, the latter to the *fruit* or the *crop*;.... For the present purpose we require only a clear definition of the term 'income,' as used in common speech, in order to determine its meaning in the Amendment. After examining dictionaries in common use... we find little to add to the succinct definition adopted in 2 cases arising under the Corporation Tax Act of 1909 (*Stratton's Indep. v. Howbert,* 231 U.S. 399, 415; *Doyle v. Mitchell Bros. Co.*, 247 U.S. 179, 185)- 'Income may be defined as the gain derived from capital, from labour, or from both combined.'" Eisner v. Macomber, 252 U.S. 189, 206-7 (1920).**

The *Doyle Case* at page 185 relies entirely on the *Stratton Case*, as does *Eisner. Stratton* is a Supreme Court case. These are two of the primary cases the government relies on to claim that "wages are income." The *Stratton Case* is thorough in its analysis of the meaning of the word "income." *Stratton* was argued and decided late in 1913, just as the 16th Amendment was purportedly being ratified and the first income taxing statute, based on the 16th Amendment, was being written. The *Stratton Case* states "For a correct definition of income, see,...." then there is a list of 12 cases. We will review those cases of the 12 which are germane to our question. The first of these cites is *Cornell Univ. v. Davenport,* 30 Hun, 177, 184 (N.Y. 1883): "The income from an investment is that which it earns, remaining itself [the investment] **intact**." Stratton also cites *Wilcox v. County Commissioners:*

> **"The income meant by the statute is the income for the year, and is the result of the year's business. It is the net result of many combined influences: the use of capital invested; the personal *labour* and *services* [emphasis mine] of the members of the firm; the skill and ability with which they lay in, or from time to time renew their stock; the carefulness and good judgement with which they sell and give credit; and the foresight and address with which they hold themselves prepared for the fluctuations and contingencies affecting the general commerce and business of the country. To express it in a more summary and comprehensive form, it is the creation of capital, industry and skill." Wilcox v. Co. Commissioners, 103 Mass. 544, 546 (1870).**

In other words, labour, services and capital are only components of a greater machinery. If that machinery is operated with skill, then income will result. Labour in and of itself is not income, nor is capital in and of itself income. If there's a tax on houses and an assessor visits a property only to find a pile of 2 x 4s and no house, can the assessor levy a tax on the 2 x 4s? No, the tax is on houses not 2 x 4s. The 2 x 4s are only a component of the house, just as labour is only a component of the machinery necessary to yield income. In *Eisner*, the court gave us even more to work with:

> **"Brief as it is, it indicates the characteristics and distinguishing attributes of income essential for a correct so lution of the present controversy. The Government, ... placed chief emphasis upon the word 'gain,' which was extended to include a variety of meanings; while the significance of the next 3 words was either overlooked or misconceived. 'Derived-from-capital';-'the gain-derived-from-capital,' etc. Here we have the essential matter: not a gain accruing to capital, not a growth or increment of value in the investment; but a gain, a profit, something of exchangeable value proceeding from the property, severed from the capital however invested or employed, and coming in, being 'derived,' that is, received or drawn by the recipient (the taxpayer) for his separate use, benefit and disposal; -that is income derived from property. Nothing else answers the description." Eisner v. Macomber, 189 U.S. 189, 207 (1920).**

In other words, according to the Supreme Court capital gains which are the result of monetary inflation are **not** to be considered "constitutional income." Remember the pivotal claim asserted by Mrs. Macomber was that the 16th Amendment did not convey to Congress the power to levy an unapportioned direct tax on stock dividends. The Suprene Court found in favor of Mrs. Macomber reinforcing their earlier rulings that an income tax is an excise tax. *Stratton* also cites *Smith v. Hooper* which states:

> **"The word 'income' has a broader meaning, but hardly broad enough to include things not separated in some way from the principle. It is not synonymous with 'increase.' The value of stock may be increased by good management, prospects of business, and the like, but such increase is not income. It may also be increased by**

> **an accumulation of surplus retained by the corporation, either as surplus or increase in stock, it can, in no propersense be called 'income.' It may become producing, but it is not income." Spooner v. Phillips, 62 Conn. 62, 24 Atl. 524, 16 L.R.A. 461. Surplus and accumulated reserve funds, until set apart and appropriated by the corporation for the payment of dividends, are capital, and, whatever their magnitude may be, they are not, as between life tenant and remainder-man, treated as income until they are distributed." Gibbons v. Mahon, 136 U.S. 549, 10 Sup. Ct. 1057, 34 L.Ed. 525. <u>Smith v. Hooper</u>, 51 A . 844, 846 (1902).**

The emphasis in *Stratton V. Hooper* was on the necessity of "severability" to exist before there was "income." In other words, having a gain is not enough to have income. One must first sever the gain from the source before there is income. Also cited by *Stratton* is *In re Armitage,* which states:

> **"When you have replaced the capital, I think it is perfectly clear that the balance which remains over and above is profit. But the question that we have to determine is this, whether that excess is to go as income to the tenant for life or is to be regarded as capital enuring for the benefits, not of the tenant for life only, but also for the benefit of those interested in the capital. Now the company is voluntarily winding up, and previously to the winding up there had been no dividends declared in respect of the excess, nor had the funds which producing this excess been in anyway capitalized; but I come to the conclusion beyond any doubt that this excess is to be regarded as capital and not as income and is not to go to the tenant for life." <u>In re Armitage</u>, 3 Ch. Div. 337, 347 (1893).**

*Stratton* cites *Sargent Land Co. v. Von Baumbach* which went to the Supreme Court of the United States. The *Stratton Case* cite comes from the court's opinion at the district court level which states:

> **"What does the word 'income' mean? In ordinary speech people recognize a difference between capital and income. ...it is something produced by capital without impairing that capital, and which leaves the property intact, and that nothing can be called income, for the purpose of this act, which takes away from the property itself. That necessarily means that the property itself remains in the business and continues to be used in the business, and that income was something that was derived from the use of it, leaving the property intact." 207 F. 423, 430 (1913).**

In the *Cornell v. Davenport Case*, also cited in *Stratton*, the court said:

> **"The income from an investment is that which it earns, remaining itself intact." Cornell v. Davenport, 30 Hun. 177 (1883).**

The question is, "Are wages income?" If all earnings from labour are income, and all income was severed from the man who earned it, the man would die. He could not feed, cloth or care for himself. He would not remain "intact" as in the *Cornell Case* et. al. cited earlier. Whether it be labour or capital the underlying source of the income must remain whole before there is income to be severed. Severability is a necessary element of income. Without severability there is no income. To say that "severability" is a necessary element of income in one case but not in another is to butcher the meaning of the word. If we can change the meanings of words to suit our whim, then the law has no meaning and we are no longer a society based on law.

> **"Humpty Dumpty said that words mean whatever you want them to mean. In the world of nonsense he may have been right. But in the world of sense he was wrong." Henry M. Hart, Jr., Albert M. Sacks, The Legal Process, 1188 (Foundation Press, 1994).**

> **"Mr. BAILEY. I believe that in earning an income by personal service every man consumes a part of his principal. And that fact ought always to be taken into consideration. The man who has his fortune invested in securities may find in a 100 years, if he spent his income, that fortune still intact, but the lawyer or the physician or the man engaged in other personal employment is spending his principal in earning his income. That fact ought under every just system of income taxation to be recognized and provided against." 44 Cong. Rec. 4007 (1909).**

Mr. Bailey, the senator from Texas quoted above, was a strong advocate for the 16th Amendment. According to *Sutherland on Statutory Construction*, the opinions of those Congressman who support a measure carry additional authority in judicial analysis.

And finally the *Eisner Opinion* states, "Income may be defined as the gain derived from capital, from labour, or from both combined."

The government and the lower courts want us to accept that in the *Stratton* and *Eisner Opinions*, the courts ruled that not only can income be **derived** from labour, but that income **equals** labour. This is not the same, nor is it what the court intended. Lets suppose that you have a friend who derives happiness from fishing. Does that mean that fishing equals happiness? Maybe for your friend it does. But maybe your friend's wife hates fishing. Or maybe this woman is happy when her husband goes fishing because he is out of her hair. Or it could be for her that fishing equals jealousy, as she would prefer her husband spent time with her rather than the fish. Yes, it is possible to derive income from labour unaided from capital, but that doesn't mean labour, in all cases, equals income.

As we noted earlier, the *Eisner Case* was a stock dividend case, and the *Stratton Case* dealt with a mining company. Both these firms were corporations. The question in the *Stratton Case* was whether a tax on the statutorily defined profit on a mining company was a direct tax as the mining company consumed its capital in the form of raw ore in the course of business.

A review of the Supreme Court's Transcript of Record for both the *Eisner Case* and the *Stratton Case* reveals that neither of these cases had anything to do with income taxes on wages or salaries. There is no question that virtually all corporations derive income from labor. Even today there are more humans that work for corporations than there are robots. As long as there is at least one human working for one corporation, corporations will derive income from labor. But the issue of whether wages equals income or whether salaries equals income had nothing to do with these cases. They offer no precedent on this question.

Congress addressed this very issue in the income tax amendment debates. The *Stratton Case* states at page 415, "But the same is true of the earnings of the human brain and hand when unaided by capital, yet such earnings are commonly dealt with in legislation as income." The debates in Congress shed light to what the court meant by "earnings of the brain **and** hand." It was the large earnings of a genius inventor or an unusually successful artist or professional. I call it "Elton John" income. It was not wages earned by the hand only unaided by the brain.

> **"Mr. President, there is one addition to the property tax that I would make. I would compel a man whose earning power from brain exercised in one of the professions or from inventive genius is great, to pay on his income beyond a certain point. When a lawyer like the Senator from New York can earn at the bar, of which I am glad to say he is the honored head, $150,000 every year, I think he ought to be made to pay the Government a tax on that earning power, because in taking from him the small tribute which the law exacts we subtract no comfort from his home. I believe that any man in law or medicine or any other employment in life who exhibits an earning**

> **capacity far beyond the necessities of his home ought to be compelled to pay the Government which protects him in the exercise of his talents and in the accumulation of this wealth. He ought to be willing to pay, and I am willing that he should be made to pay. But save and except only this earning capacity of talent or of genius, I would lay every dollar's worth of the Government tax upon the property of men and not on the wants of men." 44 Cong. Rec. 1702 (1909).**

Here, Congress differentiated between the basic labour of a man who was a wage earner, who "toiled" for a living, as opposed to the large income of a genius or artist who enjoyed a royalty. So did many of the state courts.

> **"All persons are born equally free, and have certain natural, essential and inalienable rights, among which may be reckoned the right of enjoying and defending their lives and liberties, of acquiring, possessing, and protecting property, and of seeking and obtaining their safety and happiness in all lawful ways." People may be required to pay taxes for the support of the government which secures to them these inalienable rights. But there can be no tax upon a man's right to live and earn his bread by the sweat of his brow." O'Connell v. State Bd. of Equalization, 25 P.2d 114, 125 (Mont. 1933).**

> **"The individual, unlike the corporation, cannot be taxed for the mere privilege of existing. The corporation is an artificial entity which owes its existence and charter powers to the state; but the individual's right to live and own property are natural rights for the enjoyment of which an excise cannot be imposed." Redfield v. Fisher, 292 P. 813, 819 (Or. 1930).**

The two proceeding cases are state cases, and there are more where they came from. Under the national Constitution, the sweat of a man's brow may be taxed, but not with an excise tax. It would be a tax on the man's right to exist. As we have seen, such a tax would be a direct tax and would have to be apportioned among the several States.

If I were in the business of marketing contract labour services, I could derive income from labour. Suppose I arranged groups of farm laborers for farmers, and I charged the farmer more for my laborers than I paid the labourers. I wouldn't need to employ any capital for this business. An office, telephone and a few office supplies would be enough to operate the business. If at the end of the year after paying myself a reasonable wage and all the other expenses, the remaining money left over, if I severed it from the business, would be "income derived from labour unaided by capital."

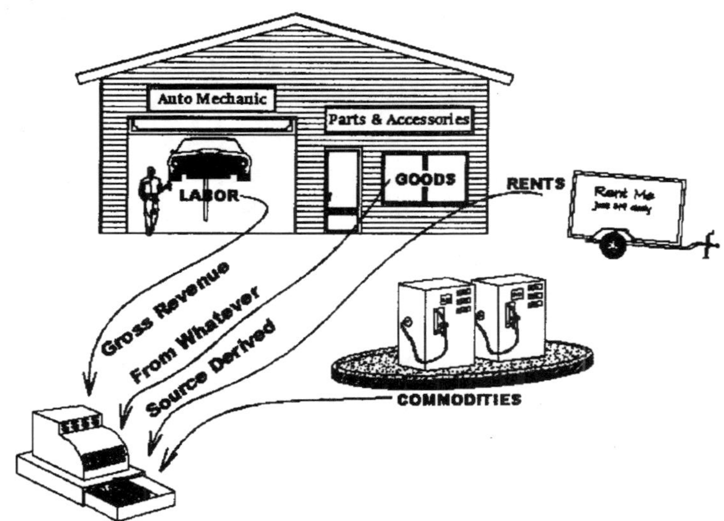


*Figure 7.1 Income derived from various sources*

Suppose you are a businessman and you own a gas station. This gas station has three sources of revenue: sales of gasoline, sales of automobile parts and accessories, and sales of auto repair services. The businessman sells the gasoline, accessories and auto parts for more than what he paid. He also charges his customers more per hour for the auto mechanic's time than he pays the auto mechanic. If the gas station is well managed, we can expect that the businessman has derived income from the sale of gasoline, accessories, parts and labor. This is what the Supreme Court meant when it said:

> **"Income may be derived from capital or labor or from both combined." Eisner v. Macomber supra at 207.**

For the auto mechanic it is necessary for his very survival that he earn a wage. No wage, no food, shelter or clothing. Not so for the businessman. The businessman's survival is not dependant on realizing a profit off the labor of his employees. Furthermore, the cost of any tax on the businessman's profit may be passed on to the gas station's customers. The income tax on the net income of the businessman is therefore an indirect tax whereas the income tax on the gross wages of the auto mechanic is a direct tax.

And finally, when the *Eisner Court* makes reference to its tree-land, fruit-crops analogy. This analogy draws from the *Waring v. City of Savannah Case* upon which the *Stratton Case* relied:

> **"The fact is, property is a tree; income is the fruit; labour is a tree; income the fruit; capital, the tree; income the fruit. The fruit, if not consumed [severed] as fast as it ripens, will germinate from the seed...and will produce other trees, and grow into more property; but so long as it is fruit merely, and plucked [severed] to eat....it is no tree, and will produce itself no fruit." Waring v. City of Savannah, 60 Ga. 93, 100 (1878).**

The *Waring Case* has gotten mixed reviews at the state level. The main complaint against *Waring* is that it seems to imply that income is not property. This criticism misses the whole point. The issue isn't "is income property?", at least not at the national level; the issue is, "When is an income tax a direct tax, and when is it an indirect tax?" A truckload of cigarettes is the property of the owner of the cigarettes. Yet there is an excise tax on the sale of these cigarettes, which one can argue is a tax on property, yet the tax is completely constitutional as an excise tax. The tax on the cigarettes is a tax on the purchase (consumption) of them. There is no source that is diminished by the tax and the tax is avoidable. Whereas a tax on a man's labour diminishes the man and is unavoidable. The criticism of *Waring* is not applicable for the question posed by the title of this book.

Relying on the *Waring Case*, it is obvious the *Eisner Court* referred to labour not as income in and of itself, but in the same class of things as capital and property. A tax that diminishes the value of capital or property, absent a privilege, is a direct tax. A tax that diminishes the value of labour is a direct tax within the constitutional meaning of the word "direct". This author agrees with previous rulings of the Tax Court that a tax on labour is a direct tax. Yet I disagree with the Tax Court that this direct tax is authorized by the 16th Amendment.

Take for example the direct tax levied on slaves in 1798. At the time, slaves were considered to be property. But what is it that gives the slave value? It is the expected value (present worth) of the future labor to be done by the slave.

A tax on a slave is a tax on labor, both are direct taxes.

## The Legislative Debates

The Congressional Record is rich with debate on this issue. For the year of 1909, the Congressional Record contains 352 pages of debate on the income tax issue alone. Also that year, Congress passed a revision to the tariff bill and the Corporate Excise Tax Act of 1909. It also considered a tax on inheritances. The debate on all of these issues was often interrelated, making the total amount of debate on taxation that year to be much more than those 352 pages represent. Having read and reread this debate, I can say the issue was exhaustively debated, including the issue of direct taxation vs. indirect taxation.

On the food chain of legal authorities, congressional debates are considered secondary authority and rank toward the bottom of this category. Ranked above congressional debates, yet still secondary authority, are congressional committee reports. While debating a measure in Congress, statements by supporters of the legislation carry additional weight as do prepared speeches read on the floor of Congress. Statements made by the author of the legislation also carry greater weight. But when there are dozens upon dozens of statements made by members on Congress, all pointing to the same conclusion, as to the intent of a piece of legislation, the sum effect carries great weight. The appendix of this book includes dozens of statements as to the intent of Congress in sending the 16th Amendment out to the state legislatures for ratification. Read through these myriad of statements and there will be no doubt as to the intent of the income tax amendment. And remember, our government, as an agent of the People, does not have the authority to go beyond what is the clear intent of the People.

> **"The United States Supreme Court has declared even the most basic general principles of statutory construction must yield to clear contrary evidence of legislative intent." Sutherland on Statutory Construction, sec. 48.01 (5th Edition).**

> **"It is true, at least generally, that statements made in debate cannot be used as aids in the construction of a statute. But the fact that throughout the consideration of this legislation there was common agreement in the debate as to the great purpose of the act may properly be considered in determining what the purpose was and what were the evils sought to be remedied." Federal Trade Commission v. Raladam, 283 U.S. 643, 650 (1931).**

In reference to the same issue being repeatedly mentioned by members of Congress, the Supreme Court had this to say:

> **"The frequency of these references and the attention directed to their subject matter are compelling circumstances. We agree that they indicate that Congress, in passing the Act, did not intend to permit the United States to continue to intervene by injunction in purely private labor disputes." U.S. v. United Mine Workers of America, 330 U.S. 258, 277-8 (1947).**

Although the latter cite relates to a labor dispute, what we have here is a rule of construction whereby when the congressional debate is overwhelmingly uniform, that this debate will be used in determining the intent of a statute. Read the quotes in the appendix of this book and you won't need to wait for the Supreme Court to tell you what the intent of Congress was.

There is an additional issue we must consider on the subject of the hierarchy of legal authority. The highest legal authority in our Nation is the Constitution, being considered "primary authority." But where do we go when we need to determine the intent of the framers of that great document? We go to the Federalist Papers and to Elliot's Debates (Madison's notes) for evidence as to the intent of the framers. In a sense, when the issue is clouded, the Federalist Papers and Elliot's Debates are elevated to a level nearly equal to the Constitution as they become the commentary on that document, for they document the arguments of the authors of the instrument itself.

In the case of an amendment to the organic law, the Congressional Record then becomes the commentary to the organic law in so far as that amendment is concerned. We then don't look to the judicial history for the meaning of the amendment as we normally would do on most other issues where "case law" is authoritative. Instead we look to either the judicial history or political history only to determine what the problem was that created the need for the constitutional amendment, i.e. "the evils sought to be remedied."

> **"These extrinsic aids may show the circumstances under which the statute was passed, the mischief at which it was aimed and the object it was supposed to achieve. Although a court may make and pronounce findings about the purpose of a statute, or the mischief it was to remedy, without referring to its historical background, knowledge of circumstances and events which comprise the relevant background of a statute is a natural basis for making such findings." Sutherland on Statutory Construction, sec. 48.03 (5th Edition 1992).**

Senator Brown of Nebraska proposed the income tax amendment. He actually proposed three of them. The first two versions were rejected as these were out of *harmony* and in conflict with the direct taxation clauses of the original Constitution. When Senator Brown, on April 28, 1909, proposed the first of his three income tax amendments known as Senate Joint Resolution (S.J.R.) #25, he had this to say about the *Pollock Case*, about Supreme Court Justice Harlan's opinion on *Pollock,* and the purpose of his proposed amendment:

> **Mr. BROWN. "Now listen to the justice-**
>
> **"'When, therefore, this court adjudges, as it does now adjudge, that Congress can not impose a duty or tax upon *personal property, or upon incomes arising either from rents of real estate or for personal property, including in-***

***vested personal property, bonds, stocks, and investments of all kinds*** **[emphasis mine], except by apportioning the sum to be so raised among the States according to population, it practically decides that, without an amendment of the Constitution—two thirds of both Houses of Congress and three-fourths of the States concurring—such property and incomes can never be made to contribute to the support of the National Government.**

**"'This is the trouble that confronts the Nation. Unless we have a Constitution about which the courts will not disagree, giving Congress the power to pass this legislation which we favor, Congress is without power to levy the taxes on this vast volume of property, even though Congress might desire to pass such a law. Mr. President, it ought to make the blood run to our faces when we stop to think that there is not another enlightened nation on the face of the earth that does not have and exercises the power to levy taxes on this kind of property except ourselves....'**

**"Mr. President, I come now for a moment to the proposition raised by the Senator from Maryland. Upon that question I simply want to demonstrate to him, as well as to the Senate, that as construed now the power of Congress to levy taxes on incomes by apportioning them according to population amounts practically to a denial of the power of Congress to levy such taxes. In the dissenting opinion of Mr. Justice Brown this was shown conclusively. Similar illustrations were made in the arguments to the court. There was shown mathematically the practical impossibility, tested by any measure of approximate justice, to apportion those taxes, and this illustration of the learned justice has never been impeached by word or intimation by anybody disagreeing with him in his general conclusions. On page 688, (second Pollock) the justice makes an application of the law according to population. He says:**

**"'By the census of 1890, the population of the United States was 62,622,250. Suppose Congress desired to raise by an income tax the same number of dollars, or the equivalent of $1 from each inhabitant. Under the system of apportionment, Massachusetts would pay $2,238,943. South Carolina would pay $1,151,149. Massachusetts has, however, $2,803,645,447 of property, with which to pay it, or $1,252 per capita, while South Carolina has but $400,911,303 of property, or $348 to each inhabitant. Assuming the same amount of property in each State represents a corresponding amount of income, each inhabitant of South Carolina would pay in proportion to his means three and one-half times as much as each inhabitant of Massachusetts. By the same course of reasoning, Mississippi, with a valuation of $352 per capita, would pay four times as much as Rhode Island, with a valuation of $1,459 per capita.'**

**"Mr. President, no man in this Chamber need have any doubt about how the apportionment proposition would work. All we need to do to be satisfied is to recall what would happen in our own States if the tax were to be distributed between the counties according to population. It is the theory of the friends of the income-tax proposition that property should be taxed and not individuals [emphasis mine]. I do not believe the fathers ever contemplated that income taxes must be apportioned according to population, but the courts have said that they did. I am here today presenting an amendment to the Constitution which will compel the courts to announce the contrary doctrine." 44 Cong. Rec. 1570 (1909).**

Earlier that day, Senator Brown said in reference to the *Pollock Decision:*

**"It is sufficient for the purpose that I have in mind this morning to say on that subject that I am in full accord with the proposition of laying some of the burdens of taxation upon the incomes of the country, but I raise this morning for the purpose of challenging the attention of**

> **the Senate to the fact that the Constitution of our country stands to-day in need of an amendment upon this subject if we are to have an income-tax law at all about the validity of which there can be no question.**
>
> **"....Our courts [as in *Pollock*] have demonstrated a faculty to change their opinions on this question, for they have decided it at different times different ways, and while we might hope and believe that that decision would be permanent, no man can justify a conclusion with any certainty that it would be permanent.**
>
> **"It is for that reason, Senators, that I present to you today the imperative and commanding necessity for an amendment to the Constitution which will give the court a Constitution that can not be interpreted two ways. I undertake to say that the people of the United States have a right to have an opportunity to amend the Constitution and to make it so definite and so certain that no question can ever be raised again of the power of Congress to legislate on the subject." 44 Cong. Rec. 1568 (1909).**

We see from the very beginning, it was the purpose of Congress to offer to the People the opportunity to overturn the *Pollock Decision* so that, as this quote states, incomes from rents of real estate and personal property including bonds, stocks and investments could be taxed. If Senator Brown wanted his income tax amendment to be "so definite and so certain that no question can ever be raised again," he shouldn't have let Senator Aldrich get his hand in the process. Senator Brown also affirmed that it was not the intent of his amendment to tax individuals. Nor could any such amendment without alternative language tax the wage or salary of a man. As we know from Adam Smith's *Wealth of Nations,* a tax on the wage or salary of person is a CAPITATION tax. CAPITATION taxes are outside the scope of the 16th Amendment. Nowhere in any of the congressional debates on the 16th Amendment did anyone ever challenge the authority of Adam Smith, who was by far the most quoted of all authorities.

Senator Brown also published a paper as to the purpose of the 16th Amendment. This paper can be found in the appendix of this book and at Senate Document No. 705, 61 Congress, 1910 and is entitled, Shall the Income-Tax Amendment be Ratified. *Sutherland on Statutory Construction* tells us at section 48.12, 5th Edition: "Commentaries of persons intimately involved with drafting of legislation are entitled to weight in interpretation of a statute." Senator Brown wrote in this document:

> **"It would not be necessary to eliminate this rule of apportionment except for the decision of the Supreme Court of the United States, in what is known as the Pollock case, decided in 1895, which held that a tax on incomes was a direct tax.**
>
> **"The effect, therefore, of the proposed amendment, if ratified, will be to restore to the people and to the Government a power for many years exercised by them in national emergencies to tax income without apportionment.**
>
> **"The sole question, therefore, presented by the amendment, and the sole consideration involved in its ratification or rejection, is whether of not the United States, the foremost nation of the world, shall be clothed with this prerogative of national sovereignty - the power to tax incomes according to their value and without regard to apportionment among the several States according to population."**

Notice in the previous paragraph, Senator Brown said the amendment would allow Congress to "tax incomes." If the purpose of the Amendment was to "tax people" don't you think he would have said so? Brown goes on to list those things that would be taxed.

> **"The growing objection to the tax on consumption [the protective tariff] is vitalized by the fact that such a tax discriminates against those least able to pay the tax and in favor of those whose ability to pay the tax is unquestioned and whose protection from the Government is so much greater because of their larger property requires and receives a larger measure of protection. When the government seeks to lay a tax for its defense or support on the incomes of the country, it should reach all incomes. If the income arises form an investment in lands, it should be taxed; if it arises from investments in manufacturing enterprises, in railroads, in banks, in newspapers, in the mercantile business, or in steamship lines, it should be taxed. Why should an income arising from an investment in State or municipal bonds not be taxed? Why should the holder of these securities enjoy his income free from any contribution to assist this Government, which protects him and his property no less than it protects other people owning another class of property? Why should he escape and other people be compelled to pay?" id. at 7.**

Senator Brown didn't say a word about taxing wages or salaries. His entire argument was dealt with taxing income from property, either real or personal. The totality of Senator Brown's argument focused on the very items that were at issue in the *Pollock Case.* The entire purpose of the income tax amendment was to bring tax relief to those who earned wages and paid a greater proportion of their earning in taxes under the tariff system (tax on consumption) and to place a greater tax burden on the accumulated wealth and investments of the country.

At this time in our history, most people from the wage-earning class kept what little savings they had in mutual savings banks and building associations. These were banks that were generally owned by their depositors and focused on providing mortgages to the lower classes.

These banks were very popular and very profitable. Yet in the 1894 income tax statute, in the Corporate Excise Tax of 1909, and in the first income taxing statute from 1913 passed under the authority of the 16th Amendment these banks were exempt from each of these taxing statutes. In 1894, 1909 and 1913 there was great public outcry directed at Congress to exempt these banks because an income tax on the profits of these banks would indirectly be an income tax on the depositors who were "wage-earners." (See the many quotes from the Congressional Record at the end of this chapter and in the appendix.) This public outcry and the resulting statutory exemptions granted over this 19 year period provides conclusive evidence that it was not the intent that income taxes were to be paid (not even indirectly) by those who only earned a wage or salary.[1]

The American people were well aware that any income tax amendment to the Constitution was a Democratic party proposition, as the Republican party had fought the income tax tooth and nail. There was a presidential election the year before the income tax amendment was sent out to the states for ratification. Harry Truman said "Platforms are contracts with the People." We all should remember the "Contract with America" of the Republican party that resulted with the so-called "Republican Revolution of 1994." Contracts are the basis of all human relations and even our relationship with our Creator. When contracts become meaningless, organized society ceases to exist. Now in the case of contracts, should our political leaders set the example for us, or do we expect them to be the worst offenders?

In the presidential election of 1908, the Republican party platform was silent on the income tax issue. The Democratic party platform had this to say:

> **"We favor an income tax as part of our revenue system, and we urge the submission of a constitutional amendment specifically authorizing Congress to levy and collect a tax upon individual and corporate incomes, to the**

**end that wealth may bear its proportionate share of the burdens of the Federal Government. 44 Cong. Rec." 3309 (1909). [This text from the Democrat Party platform of 1908 was quoted in the Congressional Record at least a dozen times during the income tax debates.]**

It is not the intent of this book to create a class warfare and to beat up on the wealthy. Most of us aspire to be wealthy someday. On the other hand, some of the wealthy, both today and in 1909, accuse those who support an income tax as being socialistic. There is balance in the middle, and this is what the majority of the American people and those members in Congress who supported the income tax amendment were trying to achieve. The latter's argument and purpose was to have wealth pay for its share of the expense of supporting government in proportion to the benefit wealth received from government. That is not socialistic. What becomes socialistic is to graduate the rate of the income tax. By graduating the income tax, some will pay more for government than they receive in benefits.

Our world has changed dramatically in our lifetimes. But back in 1909, their world was only just beginning to change. In 1909, the horse and buggy was everywhere and the automobile was a novelty. Back then the thoughts of Indian warriors, bank robbers who hid out in the wilderness and pirates on the seas were not only old stories in one's memory, but were contemporary with the people of that time. The American People understood the primary function of government was to provide protection for life, liberty and property. Government served to protect the citizenry from these predators.

What the citizen paid to government in taxes was actually more of an insurance premium for the protection the citizen received from government. Today we pay "protection money" to government to keep government away from us as government is now the predator.

All property therefore benefitted from the protection of government. Think of a fire district. Does a 100 unit apartment building receive a larger or smaller benefit from the existence of a well equipped and well funded fire district than that of, say, a single family dwelling? Of course the apartment building receives a greater benefit and the owner of which should therefore pay a greater amount for the support of the fire district than the owner of the single family dwelling. The thinking of Congress was that those who possessed wealth in the millions should pay more for the greater benefit they received from government than those whose net worth was only a few hundred dollars. Remember at the time nearly all the revenue collected by the federal government was from taxes on consumption.

**Mr. DIXON. "...In 1872 Senator Sherman said in the Senate:**

**'A few years of further experience will convince the whole body of our people that a system of national taxes which rests the whole burden of taxation on consumption and not one cent on property or income is intrinsically unjust. While the expense of the National Government is largely caused by the protection afforded to property, it is but right to require property to contribute to the payment of those expenses. It will not do to say that each person consumes in proportion to his means. This is not true. Everyone must see that the consumption of the rich does not bear the same relation to the consumption of the poor as the income of the one compares with the wages of the other. As wealth accumulates this injustice in the fundamental basis or our system will be felt and forced upon the attention of Congress.**

**'The income tax is a measure of justice. The people will pay in proportion to their financial ability to pay. It will tax wealth in proportion to its abundance rather than poverty according to its necessities. Federal taxation is**

not levied upon the wealthy of the country. It is imposed by way of taxes, internal-revenue duties levied upon liquors and tobacco used, and the import duties levied upon the clothing used and articles necessary for their comfort. The millionaires pay only on what they eat, drink, wear, and on what they use, and this is true of the poorer citizens likewise.

'The wealthy man makes no other contribution to the support of the Government; nothing for the army which protects his wealth; nothing for the judiciary which settles his property rights; nothing to the support of the administrative department of the Government which executes the law that insures the safety of his property. They pay upon the necessities of life as the poor man does, and contribute more only as their necessities are larger. ....Our party [Democrat] has ever contended that the burdens of the Government should be at least partially shifted from the backs of the poor to those who can bear it; to divide these burdens between wealth and consumption; to divide them between the man who has nothing but his labor and the man who has incomes many times greater, derived from fortunes made by others; to compel the men who are wealthy by reason of tariff legislation to divide the burdens of the Government with the people whose earnings are compelled to flow by legislation to increase the wealth of the favored beneficiaries....

'The position of the Democrat party is that Government has not the right to levy taxes of any kind except for the support of the Government honestly and economically administered. That not a cent should be taken from the people but enough to pay the expenses of the Government, and especially should the burdens of taxation not be placed upon the many for the especial benefit of a favored few. Under the pernicious system of taxation provided in our Republican tariff laws, the wealth of the country has gradually accumulated in the hands of the favored few.'" 44 Cong. Rec. 4433 (1909).

It is too bad the Democrat party no longer stands for those things they rightly fought for 90 years ago. Milton Freidman is right when he says, "There is no such thing as a free lunch." Instead of government giving each person protection in return for the support that person contributes to government, government is now Santa Claus and Robin Hood, stealing from one voter to offer a bribe to another.

> **Mr. SABATH. "I repeat, Mr. Speaker, that the income as well as the inheritance tax is a just tax. *It is a tax upon property and wealth and not upon the man* [emphasis mine]. Why should we tax as we are now doing every man, woman, and child equally, irrespective of the protection they require; whether their earnings are a dollar a day or a dollar a minute; whether they earn $900 a year or manage to squeeze from the proceeds of special legislation hundreds of thousands, yea, millions, of dollars a year? The cotton mills of the East require battle ships of the *Dreadnought* class to keep open the door of cotton consuming China. The bankers of Wall Street are ready to force a fight in the far East to secure a share in the swag of Chinese railroad exploitation while the masses are required to pay the bills of these vast armaments from their petty needs, ground from them by indirect taxation, and yet the accumulated wealth for whom all this military and naval expenditure is made refuse to pay their share of the country's expenses."44 Cong. Rec. 4666 (1909).**

In a speech to Congress on December 4, 1906, President Roosevelt said:

> **"There is every reason why, when our next system of taxation is revised, the National Government should impose a graduated inheritance tax, and, if possible, a graduated income tax. The man of great wealth owes a peculiar obligation to the State, because he derives special advantages from the mere existence of government." 44 Cong. Rec. 3945 (1909).**

Then in 1909, President Taft delivered a message to Congress on the issue of the income tax. This letter contains an excellent argument on the concept of taxing a privilege with an excise tax as opposed to taxing a right as a direct tax. If this point is not clear to you, reread President Taft's letter, found at the end of Chapter 4.

> **Mr. CUMMINS. "In the amendment I propose if the total income of the shareholder does not reach $5,000, he is not taxed. *It preserves the central fundamental idea of an income tax* [emphasis mine]. In the case proposed by the committee, if a poor devil has 1 share of stock in a corporation, and it is all the income he has, he is nevertheless taxed. My desire is to relieve the incomes of men to the extent necessary to maintain their families, to support and educate their children, because I believe that they owe a higher duty to their families than they owe to the Government." 44 Cong. Rec. 3975 (1909).**

And what was this "fundamental idea of an income tax?" It was that accumulated wealth and property was to be taxed, but only property and wealth that produced an income. It was not a **direct** tax on a person nor was it a **direct** tax on property. Nor was it even a tax on property of any sort, as neither the underlying property that produced the income nor the person that owned the property was diminished by the tax. And not only that, but only income, that is unearned income or severed profit, above a certain level, would be taxed. For example, if a man had a family, was wheelchair bound and could not earn a wage, yet owned bonds that paid him an interest income, this income would be exempt from taxation to the degree necessary for the man to support his family. This was the intent of Congress and the understanding of the People when they supported the income tax amendment.

> **Mr. BORAH. "I favor an income tax not for the purpose of putting all the burdens of government upon property or all the burdens of government upon wealth, but that it may bear its just and fair proportion of the burdens of this Government.**
>
> **We believe that every tax system based upon consumption should be supplemented by a system which taxes property and the wealth of the country; not for the purpose of inciting class feeling, but simply calling upon the great interests of the Nation to share that part of the burden of government for which they receive an unquestioned benefit." 44 Cong. Rec. 4682 (1909).**

And lastly, before we leave this issue, here is a quote from Senator Dick of Ohio:

> **"A fair and just income tax would transfer from the shoulders of those least able to bear it to the shoulders of the well-to-do and the rich, who can better bear it, the burden of raising annually many million dollars. An income tax has long been a well-established mode of raising revenue in most of the leading nations of the world, and is universally accepted as one of the most just and equitable methods of taxation. Writers on economic subjects and all authorities on taxation agree that a man should be taxed according to his ability to pay. Adam Smith says:**
>
> **"'The subjects of every State ought to contribute toward the support of the government as nearly as possible in proportion to their respective abilities; that is , in proportion to the revenue which they respectively enjoy under the protection of the State. In the observation or neglect of this maximum consists what is called the "equality or inequality of taxation."**
>
> **"M. Thiers, the great French statesman, says, 'a tax paid by a citizen to his government is like a premium paid by the insured to the insurance company, and should be in**

**proportion to the amount of property insured in one case and in the other to the amount of property protected and defended by the government.'**

**"Thorold Rodgers, the English economist, says: 'Taxation in proportion to benefits received is sufficiently near the truth for the practical operations of government.'**

**"Sismondi declares: 'Every tax should fall on revenue, not on capital, and taxation should never touch what is necessary for the existence of the contributor.'**

**"Robert Ellis Thompson in his work on 'Political Economy,' says: 'The most modern and theoretically the fairest form of taxation is the income tax. It seems to make every one contribute to the wants of the State in proportion to the revenue he enjoys under its protection."**

Senator Borah continued:

**"While the expenses of national government are largely caused by the protection of property, it is but right to require property to contribute to their payment. It will not do to say that each person consumes in proportion to his means. That is not true. Everyone can see that the consumption of the rich does not bear the same relation to the consumption of the poor that the income of the one does to the wages of the other." 44 Cong. Rec. 4959 (1909).**

**Mr. KEIFER. "That is admitted; but it is truthful history. Now, Mr. Speaker, there is something said about the necessity of an income tax to reach the idle rich; but if we had only the idle rich, I think I would rather like the programme; but there are in this country thousands and tens of thousands of enterprising spirits who have gone forth with energy, industry, and by displaying economy have acquired fortunes, and they are the persons who**

**are to be reached by an income tax; and I am willing they shall be when the trying times come." 44 Cong. Rec. 4399 (1909).**

Representative Keifer said there were "tens of thousands" of people who would be reached by this income tax. Yet the population of the country at the time was 90,000,000. How many of the 90,000,000 worked for wages? Certainly more than a few tens of thousands. Here again we see that the understanding of this Congressman was that wages and salaries were something without (outside) the scope of an income tax. Similarly, in a New York Times editorial on April 29, 1910 entitled "The Income Tax Amendment" the Times said, "Both parties are in favor of it. Every voter who has no income is in favor of taxing everybody - man, woman, or child - who has an income. And every legislator who is afraid of his constituents is in favor of the most popular proposal in sight."

At this time, women were not voters. One can gather from this statement by the New York Times, that most men did not have an income as this was "the most popular proposal in sight." Otherwise, instead of tens of thousands being taxed by the Amendment, tens of millions would have been taxed. Again, there is no way this statement could have been made if it was the understanding of the New York Times, of the People and of the state legislatures that wages and salaries were within the scope of the 16th Amendment. Our government has no authority to change the meaning of words found within the Constitution.

## The People

The following is from the most quoted case in American history, that of *Marbury v. Madison:*

**"That the people have an original right to establish, for their future government, such principles as, in their opinion, shall most conduce to their own happiness, is the basis on which the whole American fabric has been**

erected. The exercise of this original right is a very great exertion; nor can it nor ought it to be frequently repeated. The principles, therefore, so established are deemed fundamental. And as the authority, from which they proceed, is supreme, and can seldom act, they are designed to be permanent.

"This original and supreme will organizes the government, and assigns to different departments their respective powers. It may either stop here; or establish certain limits not to be transcended by those departments.

"The government of the United States is of the latter description. The powers of the legislature are defined and limited; and that those limits may not be mistaken or forgotten, the Constitution is written. To what purpose are the powers limited, and to what purpose is that limitation committed to writing; if these limits may, at any time, be passed by those intended to be restrained? The distinction between a government with limited and unlimited powers is abolished, if those limits do not confine the persons on whom they are imposed, and if acts prohibited and acts allowed are of equal obligation. It is a proposition too plain to be contested, that the Constitution controls any legislative act repugnant to it; or, that the legislature may alter the Constitution by an ordinary act.

"Between these alternatives there is no middle ground. The Constitution is either a superior, paramount law, unchangeable by ordinary means, or it is on a level with ordinary legislative acts, and like other acts, is alterable when the legislature shall please to alter it.

"If the former part of the alternative be true, then a legislative act contrary to the Constitution is not law: if the latter part be true, then written constitutions are absurd

**attempts, on the part of the people, to limit a power in its own nature illimitable." Marbury v. Madison, 5 U.S. (1 Cranch) 137 (1803).**

The People of America who ratified the 16th Amendment understood the population to be divided into three classes, that of wage-earners, farmers and those who lived off of incomes. They understood the purpose of the 16th Amendment to do exactly what the 1908 Democratic Party Platform said it would.

**"We favour an income tax as a part of our revenue system, and we urge the submission of a constitutional amendment specifically authorizing Congress to levy and collect a tax upon individual and corporate incomes, to the end that wealth may bear its proportionate share of the burdens of Federal Govt." 44 Cong. Rec. 3309 (1909).**

Alabama was the first state to ratify the 16th Amendment. We can therefore say that Alabama set a precedent as to what the state legislatures understood the scope of the amendment to be. The following appeared in the New York Times the day after the Alabama House voted on the Amendment. We need to realize that The New York Times is a "newspaper of record" and attempts to print all the significant news from across the country. Even back then the New York Times was read throughout the nation.

**"In introducing the measure [16th Amendment] to the House [of Representatives], Col. Bulger, who is one of the State's political leaders, stated that he was 'anxious to see Alabama, the first state in the Union, to give her indorsement to the Sixteenth Amendment to the United States Constitution.' The only interruption to his speech was a query by Representative J. T. Glover of Birmingham, who wanted to know if the amendment would affect salaries. Col. Sam Will John, also of Birmingham, responded that *it would not* [emphasis mine]...." Income Tax Voted in Alabama House, N.Y. Times, page 1, August 3, 1909.**

The Alabama Senate later approved the 16th Amendment on August 7, 1909 and Alabama became the first state in the Union to ratify the 16th Amendment. The fact that *The New York Times*, a newspaper of record, reported facts of the deliberations of the Alabama nationwide, and because Alabama was the first state to ratify the amendment, Alabama therefore set a precedent for other states to follow as to the meaning of the word "income" and the intent of the amendment when they ratified it. The construction given to the 16th Amendment by the Alabama House of Representatives is consistent with that of the Supreme Court of the United States in the *Brushaber Case*, the *Tyee Case* and the *Stanton Case*. The word "income" means "unearned income" and "severed profits."

On February 26, 1911, *The New York Times* published an interview with the Governor of Kentucky, Gov. Augustus E. Wilson. The subject of the interview was the 16th Amendment. Highlights of this interview with the Governor are as follows:

> **"The poor man does not regard his wages or salary as 'an income'....**
>
> **"But the point to be made is that most of the people who favor this Federal income tax believe that under it it will be the Carnegies and Rockefellers and other multimillionaires who [will] pay for the running of the government. The fellow out West thinks that the rich man in New York is the one who is going to pay this income tax; the man away from the rich centres thinks that the burden will fall exclusively upon the rich centres.... The poor man or the man in moderate circumstances does not regard his wages or salary as an income that would have to pay its proportionate tax under the new system." Gov. A. E. Wilson on the Income Tax Amendment, N.Y. Times, part 5, page 13, February 26, 1911.**

Repeatedly, the Supreme Court has stated that it is the People of America who are the ultimate sovereignty in this country. If **We the People** did not think the meaning of the word "income" as used in the 16th Amendment included "wages and salaries" than that settles it. Either the People are sovereign or they are not.

Senator Dick of Ohio, from whom we heard earlier and who was a supporter of the income tax amendment, submitted to the Congressional Record a number of letters of his constituents who wrote him on this issue. These letters express what the understanding of the American People was relating to what was proposed to be taxed under this legislation and what wasn't to be taxed. You will see that those who were "wage earners" did not consider themselves to have "an income," just as today people who have children consider themselves to be parents, and people who do not have children do not consider themselves to be parents.

The letters to Senator Dick had to do with the taxing of corporations which was to include Building and Loan Associations with whom many working people had savings and mortgages. While this tax was only to be applied to corporations, a tax on these banks would ultimately come out of the pocket of their depositors, most of whom were wage earners. The tax bite would, therefore, be felt indirectly by the wage-earning homeowner. Feeling that they should be exempt from any income tax legislation, as the object of any income tax should be to tax accumulated wealth, they wrote letters of objection. The following letters and telegrams come from the Congressional Record, volume 44, pages 4054 through 4059 (1909).

***Delaware, Ohio, June 29, 1909***

***Hon. Charles Dick, United States Senate***

On behalf of members of building and loan associations of Delaware County, Ohio, we respectfully urge that you use your best efforts to exempt these savings institutions of the wage-earners from proposed corporation tax, as was the case in the old income-tax law and the Spanish-American war stamp act.

*The Fidelity Building Association and Loan Company, D. H. Battenfield, President*
*People's Building and Loan Company, C.C. Riddle, President.*

---

*Youngstown, Ohio, June 29, 1909*
*Hon. Charles Dick, United States Senate*

Proposed tax on corporations will be disastrous to building associations. Ten thousand working people in this city would suffer. Exempt the associations.

*The Home Savings and Loan Company*

---

*Youngstown, Ohio June 28, 1909*
*Hon. Charles Dick, United States Senate*

Building and loan associations should be exempt from proposed corporation tax. Similar acts in the past have always exempted them. Such exemption would benefit 400,000 wage-earners in Ohio alone.

*James M. McKay.*
*Vice President Ohio Building Association League*

---

*Dayton, Ohio, June 27, 1909*
*Hon. Charles Dick, United States Senate*

We urge to use your efforts to exempt mutual building and loan associations from income tax. Seven thousand wage-earners and small savers in this association alone would thus be taxed.

*American Loan and Savings Association*

---

*Bellaire, Ohio, June 28, 1909*
*Hon. Charles Dick, Senate Chamber*

Over 5,000 working people ask you to oppose bill to tax incomes of building associations.

*The Buckeye Savings and Loan Co.,*
*By, W. G McClain , Secretary*

---

*Dayton, Ohio, June 27, 1909*
*Hon. Charles Dick*

On behalf of 50,000 wage-earners who have their savings in the Dayton building associations you are urged to consider the justice of having building associations exempted from the operation of the proposed tax on corporations.

*Montgomery County Building Association League,*
*S. Rufus Jones, President.*

---

*Troy, Ohio, June 29, 1909*
*Hon. Charles Dick*

Dear Sir: At the regular meeting of the People's Building and Savings Association Company last evening I was directed by the unanimous vote of the directors to write you to use your influence and vote to secure for building associations the exemptions in the proposed corporation tax suggested by President Taft.

Our own deposits represent almost entirely the savings of the wage-earners of this city, and speaking for the directors, who, with one exception, are Republicans, and for myself, a member of the same party and an office-holder by virtue of my membership in it, I do not believe that the Republican party can afford to place a tax upon the thrift of this class of people, while ignoring the opportunities presented by the income tax to lay the burden upon those best able to bear it, and who for the most part escape their just proportion of the Nation's taxes.

Whether it is just or not, there is a feeling that our party has not kept faith in revising the tariff upward, and to impose a direct tax, like that proposed by the corporation tax, would appear to the people only as another evidence of our party's and our representations' indifference to that great majority - the common people.

I am writing this because I believe that not only natural justice but party expedience, demands that for the balance of the session of Congress the Republican party should father only such legislation as will remove the feeling that I speak of and make the wage-earner feel that his voice has penetrated Washington and that the party will protect his modest savings from the excise man.

*Very truly yours,*
*J. C. Fullerton, Jr.*

---

It is obvious from these letters and telegrams that the American People did not believe it was appropriate to levy any species of income tax that was going to tax, even indirectly, the wage-earning class. The perception was that much of the accumulated wealth of the country was created by the protective tariff system and had up to that time escaped taxation. This was to be the target of the income tax.

On February 8, 1910 *The New York Times* reported on a message sent by the Governor of New Jersey to the New Jersey state legislature. The headline of this article read: **GOV. FORT UPHOLDS THE INCOME TAX, RELIEVING BURDEN ON POOR.**

The article provides an excellent view as to the scope and purpose of the income tax amendment. Much of this article is quoted below:

> **TRENTON, N.J., Feb. 7, -Gov. John Franklin Fort of New Jersey urgently endorses the proposed Sixteenth Amendment to the Federal Constitution which was passed by Congress last March (sic), and which provides for the levying of an income tax. In a special message sent to the New Jersey Legislature today, he strongly recommends that the amendment be approved, and says that "it is vital to the safety and security of the republic in time of need, and is without danger in the power conferred."**
>
> **In submitting the proposed amendment to the Legislature for action, the Governor says that he does so with a firm conviction that its approval will be in the interests**

of a just and equitable method of taxation. He expresses the belief that the failure to impose an income tax, if the necessities of the Government require it, would amount to a national calamity.

"An income tax is the most just and equitable tax that can be levied," he says in his message. "It imposes the exactions of Government upon the citizen in proportion to his ability to bear it, and upon the basis of the wealth which, under the laws of the country, he has been able to accumulate. Men should contribute to the needs of the State as God has prospered them."

### Tax Burdens Not Equal Now

It is evident that the burden of general taxes is not proportionately borne by all upon whom the burden rests. The citizen of moderate holdings, whether real or personal, usually does not escape, or attempt to escape, the prompt discharge of this obligation. The property of which he is possessed, by reason of its very meagerness, is easily found by the assessor, and when the tax is levied it is satisfied. This can not be said, however, of those who are essentially rich. It has been stated, with some semblance of certainty, that over 80 per cent of all the vested wealth of this country is owned and controlled by 3,000 estates, corporations, and individuals. It is obvious that 80 percent of the annual taxes levied is not borne by the group just mentioned.

"The taxes laid upon real estate are out of all proportion to its relative value to all the other property owned by our citizens. This results in the man with the small home bearing his full share of tax exactions, while the man of many times as great wealth escapes a large share of just taxation. The taxation of personal property is limited because of the difficulty to discover it, while real

> **estate, which is always discoverable, is fully taxed. An income tax is a tax which is sure to reach all classes of property, real and personal.**

Was there any mention of a tax on wages and salaries in this article? No! But the Governor did talk about taxing the income from real estate and personal property, bonds and securities. The article said the tax would be on the basis of wealth. Did this mean on the wage-earner, or on the basis of the amount of a man's wage? No, of course not. We read, **"An income tax is a tax which is sure to reach all classes of property, real and personal."**

On it's front page of July 23, 1909 the *Wall Street Journal* carried a guest editorial from Justice Brewer on the income tax. Justice Brewer was a member of the Supreme Court Bench. He said:

> **"If there is one tax in the world that has proved itself to be fair, flexible, cheap to collect, and easy to adjust, it is the income tax. It is, moreover, sound in principle, because public expenses are paid for out of income and not out of private capital, as they would be and are with inheritance taxes." Justice Brewer on Income Tax, The Wall St. Journal, July 23, 1909.**

Taxes paid **"out of income and not out of private capital"** are taxes on the unearned income and profit from an underlying investment. When this income is taxed, the underlying investment, or business remains whole. When the wages or salary of a person are taxed, this is diminishing his personal capital and is obviously outside the scope of Justice Brewers understanding of what an income tax was.

In another editorial by *The New York Times* entitled Bad Tax Laws, March 24, 1911 the Times had this to say:

> **"A tax on income may be oppressive and unwise, but it is not destructive. The capital producing the income remains. Destruction of capital by taking it over and using**

> **it is an unpardonable economic sin...The humble workers are not helped by the taxes which the rich evade. The evasions of the rich are in fact the burdens of the poor."**

The evidence can be piled higher and deeper, but by now you should be convinced. Wages and salaries are not "income" within the taxing authority of the 16th Amendment. Furthermore, I believe the construction of Title 26 recognizes this fact. Read on in Chapter 9 to see how Congress has most likely entrapped you into having a legal duty to pay a tax you don't have a constitutional duty to pay.

# Chapter 8
## Where's the Foundation?

**"For nothing is hidden, except to be revealed; nor has anything been secret, but that it should come to light."**

**~Mark 4:22**

In an earlier chapter we spoke of "primary authority" and "secondary authority." These are legal terms and have to do with the hierarchy of authority utilized by the courts. The Constitution is considered "primary authority." The Congressional Record is considered "secondary authority." There is another dimension to this categorization of authority known as "delegation of authority." In the American political system, there is no authority unless it has been delegated by **We The People**.

The delegation of authority begins with the Constitution as authorized by **We The People.** Every department of government is bound by this document. Congress may pass only those laws for which authority has been delegated to it by the Constitution. The government has no power except that expressly authorized by **We The People**.

So where did the government get the authority to place an unapportioned direct tax on the wages and salaries of the American People? Are we being **taxed without our consent**?

There is no doubt that the American People desired to allow Congress to tax incomes. But are there limits to this power? Can Congress call the air I breathe "income" and tax it? And what about the question of direct taxes vs. indirect taxes?

In defense of this unapportioned direct tax, the government claims that the Supreme Court determined:

> **Income may be defined as the gain derived from capital, from labor, or from both combined." Eisner v. Macomber, 252 U.S. 189, 207 (1919).**

The origin of this quote was from the *Stratton's Independence v. Howbert Case* at page 415. This quote also appears in the *Doyle v. Mitchell Brothers Co. Case* at page 185. But we saw earlier that deriving income from labor does not mean that labor equals income. In the gas station example in Chapter 7, we saw how labor may be applied in an effort to generate "income," but is not in and of itself income within the Constitutional meaning of the word.

Each of these three cases, *Stratton's Independence v. Howbert, Doyle v. Mitchell Brothers Co.* and *Eisner v. Macomber* involved corporations either suing or being sued by the Collector of Internal Revenue. *Stratton* and *Doyle* were about corporate profits. *Eisner* was about stock dividends. None of them had anything to do with the "are wages income" question.

In order for the government to buttress its claim that "wages are income" the government will also quote the Supreme Court in the *Stratton Case* where the court said:

> **"As to the alleged inequality of operation between mining corporations and others, it is of course true that the revenue derived from the working of mines results to some extent in the exhaustion of the capital. But the**

> **same is true of the earnings of the human brain and hand when unaided by capital, yet such earnings are commonly dealt with in legislation as income." *supra* at 415.**

We have to remember that Stratton was a mining corporation. In Stratton's briefs they argued that all a mining company ever did was to convert capital in the form of raw ore into capital in the form of money. If you accepted Stratton's logic, no mining company ever in the history of the world nor in the future until the end of eternity would have ever generated a profit. Appropriately the Supreme Court rejected their argument. Furthermore, there were several entries in the Congressional Record which addressed the issue of "earnings of the human brain and hand unaided by capital."

> **"Mr. BAILEY. There is one addition to the property tax [income tax] that I would like to make. I would compel a man whose earning power from brain exercised in one of the professions or from inventive genius is great to pay on his income beyond a certain point [sic]. When a lawyer like the Senator from New York can earn at the bar, of which I am glad to say he is the honored head, $150,000 every year, I think he ought to be made to pay the Government a tax on that earning power, because in taking from him the small tribute which the law exacts we subtract no comfort from his home. I believe that any man in law or medicine or any other employment in life who exhibits an earning capacity far beyond the necessities of his home ought to be compelled to pay the Government which protects him in the exercise of his talents and in the accumulation of this wealth... But save and except only this earning capacity of talent or of genius, I would lay every dollar's worth of the Government tax upon the property of men and not upon the wants of men." 44 <u>Cong. Rec.</u> 1702 (1909).**

At the time, 1909, the average American family earned $436 per year. So in Senator Bailey's example, he was using a man whose earnings was more than 340 times that of the average American.

Senator Bailey, a democrat from Texas, was a passionate and outspoken supporter of the 16th Amendment. At one point in the income tax debate Senator Bailey was misquoted by a newspaper reporter. When the Senator saw this reporter in the halls of Congress he punched him out! (See Senator Bailey Assaults Reporter, *New York Times*, May 28, 1909, page 1.)

So that we might be absolutely clear what construction we should place on the Stratton quote about "earnings from the human brain unaided by capital" and the Bailey quote about lawyers making $150,000 per year, let's back up a few paragraphs in the Congressional Record and listen to Senator Bailey again.

> **"I have no hesitation in declaring that a tax on any useful occupation cannot be defended in any forum of conscience or of common sense. To tax a man for trying to make a living for his family is such a patent and gross injustice that it should deter any legislature from perpetrating it." 44 Cong. Rec., 1702 (1909).**

So if the *Stratton, Doyle* and *Eisner v. Macomber* cases, all dealing with corporations, had nothing to do with the "wages are income" question, where else can we look to determine what construction should be placed on the Supreme Court's famous and infamous quote, which states:

> **"Income may be defined as the gain derived from capital, or labor, or from both combined."**

The Supreme Court has said themselves that Congress is without power to make income something that is not income within the meaning of the Constitution. Quoting again from *Eisner v. Macomber:*

> **"A proper regard for its genesis, as well as its very clear language, requires also that this Amendment [Sixteenth] shall not be extended by loose construction, so as to repeal or modify, except as applied to income, those provisions of the Constitution that require an apportionment**

> **according to population for direct taxes upon *property, real and personal* [emphasis mine]. This limitation still has an appropriate and important function, and is not to be overridden by Congress or disregarded by the courts....**
>
> **"It becomes essential to distinguish between what is and what is not 'income,' as the term is there used; and to apply the distinction, as cases arise, according to truth and substance, without regard to form. Congress cannot by any definition it may adopt conclude the matter, since it cannot by legislation alter the Constitution, from which alone it derives its power to legislate, and within whose limitations alone that power can be lawfully exercised." id. at 206.**

Remember that these three cases dealt with corporations. The question of "are wages income?" was not an issue in these cases. Since there is nothing in the *Transcript of Record* for any of these three cases that supports the government's contention that the Supreme Court ruled "wages are income," we need to look elsewhere.

Maybe we can find this authority in the *Springer Case*? The *Springer Case* arose over the Civil War income tax. But we read earlier of how this tax was a war time measure collected under martial law. We also noted that Springer never claimed he had wages, but instead, Springer claimed he had "profits in any trade or vocation from which income is actually derived."[1] Springer admitted he made over $50,000 in net income as a lawyer. This was over 100 times of what the average wage earner made at the time. Therefore, the *Springer Case* provides no authority for the government's "wages are income" contention.

Sometimes the government claims that the case of *Lucas v. Earl*, 281 U.S. 111 (1930) provides authority for their "wages are income" contention. This case was about a man named Earl who in 1901 entered into a contract with his wife to allocate half his future earnings and property to her. The case arose over the fees Mr. Earl earned as an attorney for the years 1920 and 1921, that being

$24,839 and $22,946 respectively. Mr. Earl must have been a successful attorney as his earnings were approximately 40 times that of the average wage earner.

The Supreme Court determined that although the contract between Mr. and Mrs. Earl was valid, the court said that Mr. Earl was responsible to pay the tax on all his income. His wife was therefore not liable for any of the tax. The question of "are wages income?" had nothing to do with this case.

Nor is the *Brushaber Case* authority for this issue, as Brushaber was about taxes on stock dividends from a federally chartered railroad corporation. None of these cases put the "are wages income?" question before the court.

Now let's suppose a hypothetical. Suppose the "are wages income?" question had been put before the Supreme Court. Would the nine justices have sat around a table, debated the issue, and then voted on it? No, they wouldn't, as they are without power to make such a determination. What the justices would have done would have been to examine the historical record to discover what the intent of the American People was when they purportedly ratified the 16th Amendment.

Consequently, the only other place we can look for this authority is where each of the three branches of government would have had to look in the first place before any such tax was levied or enforced. It is to **We The People**. Had the "wages are income" issue actually been presented to the Supreme Court in any of the early income tax cases, the Supreme Court would have had to go to the same sources I went to as I did the research for this book.

The starting point would naturally be the Congressional Record. I found one quote from one Congressman that would be supportive to the government's claim that wages are income. There were hundreds of quotes opposed to this view. The last 61 pages of this book contain a sampling of these quotes. As you will see from the following quote, the one Congressman who was supportive of the "wages are income" contention was clearly not an authority on the subject, and we can therefore impeach his testimony.

> **"Mr. BARTHOLDT. I would tax an income of $100, say, at 1 percent, making the laboring man with an income of $100 pay 1 cent to the Government and the laboring man having an income of $1,000 pay 10 cents to the Government. This 10 cents represents to him as much as the thousands and thousands of dollars which the millionaire contributes to the Government....**
>
> **"Mr. CLARK of Missouri. The gentleman got his arithmetic wrong. One percent on $100 is $1, not 1 cent." 44 Cong. Rec., 4415 (1909).**

Other than the above quote from this Congressman who can't do math, there were no other statements made in support of the idea that wages or salaries would be taxed by the 16th Amendment. It simply was not an issue debated.

Failing to find any evidence to support the government's contention that wages are income in the Congressional Record, we can look other places. If you've read this far, you will know that we've discussed numerous newspaper articles, law journal articles, journals on political economy, magazine articles, law dictionaries and so on. Nowhere did I find in these other sources were the American People demanding that a tax be placed on their wages and not on their consumption. The evidence is simply not there.

If there is no evidence, then the conclusion is simple. There is not, and never has been, any delegation of authority from **We The People** to the government for the collection of an unapportioned direct tax on the wages and salaries of the American People. **We are being Taxed without Our Consent !**

Therefore, the government's claim that the infamous words from the *Stratton, Doyle* and *Eisner Cases*, that "Income may be defined as the gain derived from capital, from labor, or from both combined" means that the labor-equals-income argument is **wholly without foundation.** There is no evidence to support the government's interpretation of this quote.

Tax Court, District Court and Appellete Court decisions that rely on these misinterpretations of the *Brushaber* and *Eisner Cases* are nothing more than junk-law.

Until all labor is done by robots, corporations will continue to derive income from labor, as labor is commonly used in the normal course of business. Furthermore, unincorporated businesses and small time entrepreneurs will also derive income from labor. Within the context of these three cases the Supreme Court was right; income may be derived from labor. This doesn't mean that labor equals income for the American Citizen living and working in the several States of the Union. Write your Congressman and tell him **No Taxation without Our Consent.**

(Note: In the geographical areas where Congress has exclusive legislative authority, Congress may define income or wages to be anything it wants. Congress may do the same for employees of the federal government regardless if whether they live within or without the several States.)

But maybe I'm wrong. Maybe in the few thousand hours I spent researching the historical record I missed the evidence supportive of the contention that the American People were demanding that their wages be taxed in lieu of their consumption. If the government is right and I'm wrong, then somewhere in some government file cabinet this evidence must exist. Maybe the government can rebut the argument made by this book with a report entitled "Constitutional Income: Wages and Salaries are Included." Were the government to produce such a report, it may, perhaps cite and reference the evidence in support of its current position that wages and salaries are taxable as income.

## Confusion in the Courts

It is very unfortunate that attorneys and judges have a habit of writing in a style using double negatives and run-on sentences. Sometimes it is nearly impossible to figure out what they are saying. This is the situation with the *Brushaber Opinion*. Had this opinion been written more clearly, we would not have the confusion over the income tax issue we have today. In order to understand the *Brushaber Opinion*, one needs to read its briefs and oral arguments. Only then will you know what questions were laid before the court.

I believe even the appellate judges of the circuit courts are confused. The First Circuit Court of Appeals said:

> **"The 16th Amendment eliminated the indirect/direct distinction as applied to taxes on income." United States v. Turano, 802 F.2d 10, 12 (1st Cir. 1986).**

We saw in our discussion on the *Brushaber Case* that this determination by the First Circuit is simply not true. The Supreme Court said the two classes of taxation, that begin direct and indirect taxes, remained intact. The Supreme Court also said that the 16th Amendment created no new type of tax. The elimination of the "indirect/direct distinction" for income taxes would have created a new type of tax. The First Circuit is out of harmony with the Supreme Court.

The Second Circuit said:

> **"Therefore, the Sixteenth Amendment, along with the preexisting taxing power created by Article I, section 8 of the Constitution, provides Congress with the necessary authority to impose a direct, non-apportioned income tax." United States v. Sitka, 845 F.2d 43, 46 (2nd Cir. 1988).**

The issue underlying the above statement was also squarely before the Supreme Court, and the Supreme Court rejected the claim. Secondly, Congress four times rejected attempts to pass an income tax amendment that would have provided for a direct tax in the nature of an income tax. Twice the rejection came in the form of shooting down a proposed amendment, (S.J.R. #25 and S.J.R. #39), and twice on July 5, 1909, Congress rejected this as it voted on the 16th Amendment. The Second Circuit is simply wrong, more junk-law.

The Third Circuit said:

> **"An income tax is a direct tax upon income therein defined." Keasbey & Mattison Co. v. Rothensies, 133 F.2d 894, 897 (3rd Cir. 1943).**

No! The only authorized income tax in an indirect tax.

The Fourth Circuit said:

> **"The tax is, of course, an excise tax, as are all taxes on income...." White Packing Co. v. Robertson, 89 F.2d 775, 779 (4th Cir. 1937).**

As long as the Fourth Circuit is talking about income taxes that are "inherently indirect," as Seligman put it, they're right.

The Fifth Circuit said:

> **"The Supreme Court promptly determined in *Brushaber*... that the Sixteenth Amendment provided the needed Constitutional basis for the imposition of a direct non-apportioned income tax." Parker v. Commissioner, 724 F.2d 469, 471 (5th Cir. 1984).**

I read every brief, every motion, and the Supreme Court's opinion for the *Brushaber Case.* This is not what the Supreme Court said. Earlier in this chapter you read what the Supreme Court determined. The Fifth Circuit outright misquotes the Supreme Court.

The Sixth Circuit said:

> **"*Brushaber* and the Congressional Record excerpt do indeed state that for constitutional purposes, the income tax is an excise tax." United States v. Gaumer, 972 F.2d 723, 725 (6th Cir. 1992).**

This statement taken alone is perfect and correct.

The Seventh Circuit said:

> **"The Amendment allows a tax on 'income' without apportionment, but an unapportioned direct tax on anything that is not income would still, under the rule of the Pollock case, be unconstitutional." Commissioner v. Obear-Nester Glass Co., 217 F.2d 56, 58 (7th Cir. 1954).**

Again, this statement taken on its face alone is perfect and correct as long as "income" is given its constitutional meaning.

The Eighth Circuit said:

> **"The cases cited by Francisco clearly establish that the income tax is a direct tax, thus refuting the argument based upon his first theory. See Brushaber v. Union Pacific Railroad Co., 240 U.S. 1, 19 (1916) (the purpose of the Sixteenth Amendment was to take the income tax 'out of the class of excises, duties and imposts and place it in the class of direct taxes)". United States v. Francisco, 614 F.2d 614, 619 (8th Cir. 1980).**

Here the Eighth Circuit has it absolutely backwards. The problem was the *Pollock Court*, in 1895, took income taxes on unearned income, gain and profit out of the classification of indirect taxes, and placed them in the classification of direct taxes. This decision, being offensive to the American People, was overturned by the 16th Amendment. When the Supreme Court ruled on the *Brushaber Case*, they ruled opposite of what the Eighth Circuit said they did. What the 16th Amendment did was to insure that income taxes on net income would remain in the classification of indirect taxes.

The Ninth Circuit said:

> **"[T]he Sixteenth Amendment is broad enough to grant Congress the power to collect an income tax regardless of the source of the taxpayer's income." citations omitted. U.S. v. Buras, 633 F.2d 1356,1361 (9th Cir. 1980).**

According to the Supreme Court in the *Brushaber Case*, the 16th Amendment only provides authority to collect an income tax when the tax is "inherently indirect," and for such a tax one may not consider the source when determining whether or not the tax is direct or indirect. But for income taxes that are inherently direct, there is no authority for their collection under the 16th Amendment. Income taxes that diminish only the income and leave the source whole are inherently indirect. Income taxes that diminish the source, absent a privilege, are direct taxes.

The Ninth Circuit also said:

> **"The Sixteenth Amendment conferred no power upon Congress to tax incomes from any source....This amendment did, however, relieve Congress of the necessity of apportionment among the states of income taxes which would be direct taxes, such as taxes on real or personal property based on the ownership thereof." Fairbanks v. Commissioner, 191 F.2d 680, 681 (9th Cir. 1951).**

This is all screwed up. First of all, taxes on property because of ownership diminish the property and are direct taxes. Taxes on income diminish only the income; the source (property) is left whole. There is a huge difference. Secondly, the 16th Amendment did not relieve Congress of the requirement of apportionment for direct taxes. All the 16th Amendment did was to say that when only income was diminished by the tax, one could not consider the type of source of the income in an effort to determine whether the tax was a direct tax or an indirect tax. That was the *Pollock Rule*. The *Pollock Rule* was struck down by the 16th Amendment. Any and all direct taxes must still be apportioned when levied within the several States. There are no exceptions to the apportionment rule.

The Tenth Circuit said:

> **"For seventy-five years, the Supreme Court has recognized that the Sixteenth Amendment authorized a direct non-apportioned tax upon United States citizens throughout the nation, not just in federal enclaves, see *Brushaber...*" United States v. Collins, 920 F.2d 619, 629 (10th Cir. 1990).**

Junk-law again!

The Eleventh Circuit said:

> **"All are agreed that an income tax is a direct tax on gain or profits...." Bank of America National T. & Sav. Ass'n. V. United States, 459 F.2d 513, 517 (Ct.Cl. 1972).**

Well, this is half true as long as the word "direct" is not being used in the Constitutional sense. A Constitutionally indirect tax on income does fall directly on the gain or profit and when the source is not diminished by the tax, it remains an indirect tax.

Finally the Tax Court said in *Abrams v. Commissioner:*

> **"Since the ratification of the 16th Amendment, it is immaterial with respect to income taxes, whether the tax is a direct or indirect tax. The whole purpose of the 16th Amendment was to relieve all income taxes when imposed from apportionment and from a consideration of the source whence the income was derived." *Brushaber v. Union Pac. R.R. Co.,* 240 U.S. 1 (1916). See *Hayward v. Day*, 619 F.2d 716 (8th Cir. 1980). Abrams v. Commissioner, 82 T.C. 403, 406-7 (1984).**

By now you should be able to see the error here. The Tax Court is wrong. The Tax Court is not respecting the prior rulings of the Supreme Court. The *Brushaber Case* doesn't say what the Tax Court claims it says. Direct taxes must still be apportioned among the several States. Only income taxes which are inherently indirect may be levied under the authority of the 16th Amendment. For many in the judicial system, this is not human error, it is intentional and therefore deserves the label "junk-law."

So we can see that there is confusion in the courts. It is obvious that the circuit courts are not following the Supreme Court. It could be they simply don't understand the total picture of this income tax issue. Admittedly it is complex. Or it could be that they are so intimidated by the bureaucracy, they hand down unjust decisions based on fraudulent legal analysis. It is my hope this book will help restore truth and the rule of law to America on this most important issue.

Lastly we should address the Supreme Court case *Chas. H. Steward Mach. Co v. Davis* wherein the court said:

> **"(E)mployment for lawful gain is a 'natural' or 'inalienable' right, and not a 'privilege' at all. But natural rights, so called, are as much subject to taxation as rights of less importance. An excise is not limited to vocations or activities that may be prohibited altogether....It extends to vocations or activities pursued as of common right." 301 U.S. 548, 580-1 (1937).**

On its face this quote seems out of bounds, but the tax being discussed was the social security tax. The Social Security Administration has admitted that it is not mandatory that one join the social security program. After all, one must **apply** to receive a **benefit**. If Americans want to make such choices and subject themselves to the accompanying tax liability, they should be free to do so. That is, as long as they understand that joining the program was voluntary and by choice. Afterall, indirect taxes in the form of excises are avoidable. If, on the other hand, Americans join this voluntary program because they were taught to believe it was mandatory, then fraud exists.

And lastly, if it is optional and voluntary to join the Social Security program, then those who had the freedom to join should also have the freedom to unjoin.

# Chapter 9
## How Do They Do It?

***"Government is not reason, it is not eloquence, it is force! Like fire, it is a dangerous servant and a fearful master."***

***—George Washington***

Today most of the problems we have in government are not due to defects in our Constitution but are the result of the defects of men and their creative attempts to circumvent the Constitution. It is time for the American people to put an end to the political trickery of each of the three branches of government. Now is an appropriate time for us to amend the Constitution to plainly make illegal the tricks used to strip us of our birthright. Chapter Ten proposes *The People's Sovereignty Amendment* which has been designed to return us back to limited constitutional government.

The fact that this chapter bears the title "How do they do it?" speaks loudly as to how far we have come from a government that is "Of the People, by the People and for the People." If we have to theorize and speculate how it is that our government is taxing us out of up to half our earnings, then for all practical purposes we are not a democracy, we are not a constitutional republic, but instead we have slipped into a sophisticated form of tyranny.

***"I believe there are more instances of the abridgement of the freedom of the people by gradual and silent encroachments of those in power than by violent and sudden usurpations."* James Madison, 4th President and "Chief Architect of the Constitution."**

We live in a world where there are multiple jurisdictions. When most of us think of "jurisdictions," we think in geographical or subject matter terms. For example, you're speeding on the freeway, there are red and blue flashing lights far behind you and it's only one mile to the state line; are there choices that go through your mind? Or suppose your teenager gets a ticket for fishing without a license while fishing in your backyard swimming pool that you personally stocked with fish; is there a question of geographical or subject matter jurisdiction?

There is another type of jurisdiction that most of us are unaware of. This is personam jurisdiction. It is jurisdiction over a person. Not all people who live in the same area fall within the same jurisdictions.

Think of the Mormon Church. They have carved the United States into geographical areas, the smallest being called "wards." All of us live within one of these Mormon wards. But does the Mormon Church have jurisdiction over you even though you live within one of their wards? Yes and no. Yes, if you have voluntarily joined the Mormon Church, and no if you haven't.

There are other churches that have done what the Mormons have done giving us multiple layers of "church" jurisdictions which overlay our land. But not all of us are subject to all, one, or even any of these various church jurisdictions.

The same thing occurs in the political world. We have multiple political jurisdictions which overlay the same geographical area. No, I am not talking about city, county, state and national jurisdictions which cover the same geographical area yet differ in subject matter. What I am talking about is parallel political realities. The parallel political realities is something the courts and the politicians want to keep hidden from you. This arrangement allows them to fleece the flock while making you think they have constitutional authority to do so. Well, the government usually does have constitutional authority to do what they want. The question is which Constitution are we talking about—the organic handwritten Constitution of 1787—or the Constitution which functions as the bylaws of the political corporation?

If you are 35 years old or older, you may remember the *Star Trek* episode where Captain Kirk is caught between two dimensions, each one representing a separate reality. The focus of that episode was for the space ship Enterprise to position itself at the right time and place when Captain Kirk would cross back over into the reality where he came from so that the crew of the Enterprise could snatch him back.

Just as Captain Kirk was caught between two separate realities that occupied the same space and time, so are we caught between two separate political realities that occupy the same space and time. When you are born into this great land of America you become the Posterity our forefathers spoke of in the Preamble of our organic Constitution. You are by right entitled to life, liberty and the pursuit of happiness secured by our organic founding documents, the Declaration of Independence and the original handwritten Constitution of 1787.

Unfortunately for you, you quickly make choices proclaiming to the world that you do not want to live in the political reality secured by these organic legal documents, but instead you prefer the cradle-to-grave security of the political corporation. The evidence that you have chosen to live under the political corporation, stripped of your organic constitutional rights, begins with your signature on your birth certificate. Well, it's really not your signature, it's your footprint, but it is your acknowledgment that you agree to be a good taxpayer and help pay off the huge bankruptcy that president Woodrow Wilson got us into. This happened back in 1913 when he signed the Federal Reserve Act. (Remember, the Federal Reserve is not federal and has no reserves.)

There is other evidence that you prefer to have government take care of you from cradle to grave, and that you wish to forfeit your organic constitutional rights for this benefit. For example, you went to the government to get a driver's license—a voluntary act, but mandatory if you want to live in the corporate reality. As such, you help support the governmental organizations which will later break your door down because you spanked your children. Of course, most of us are unaware of this.

When our Declaration of Independence secured "liberty" for us, it protected our right to travel whenever and wherever we wanted uninhibited by government. As long as we travel on those highways which are owned in common by the People, and we travel in our private capacity (not commercial), government has no standing to require us to get a driver's license. Remember that a license is permission to do something that is otherwise illegal. To do so is an infringement of your constitutional right to liberty. Whether or not having some way to regulate driving is wise is an entirely different issue. I frankly think it is, but let's not strip ourselves of our birthright in order to do so.

The fact that you choose to get a driver's license from the political corporation is evidence that you do not wish to live under the organic Constitution, but instead you choose to live under the political corporation's bylaws, otherwise known as its constitution.

The same is true of the marriage license. Marriage is an institution created by God, not by government. Government has no right to license it. When you voluntarily get a marriage license, you are actually entering into a three-party contract. (Marriage licenses are voluntary for those who live under the organic law, but mandatory for those who want to live under the political corporation and wish to have access to the government candy store.) The parties to the contract are government, husband and wife. One of the terms of this contract is that the offspring of the marriage is the property of the government. This gives the government a flimsy lawful authority to intervene if they don't like how you have been raising "their" children. Those we have hired to be our public servants to run the agencies of government have become our masters!

It should be noted that getting a driver's license does not make you liable for income taxes, although it does make you liable for the state motor vehicle code. Similarly, a marriage license does not make you liable for income taxes, either, but it does subject you to a myriad of family law statutes which are not unconstitutional, they are nonconstitutional, i.e., part of the corporation body politic.

The federal government incorporated on February 21, 1871 (41st Congress, Session III, chapter 62, page 419 of the Statutes at Large, and 28 U.S.C. 3002 15) and uses the term "United States" when referring to this political corporation. Sound confusing? Well, it is meant to be. It is hoped by those we elected to be our public servants that you will make all the right choices (wrong choices if you love liberty) to place yourself under the jurisdiction of the political corporation. When you do so, by allowing yourself to be licensed for everything you do, the licensor—the bureaucracy—becomes the master and you, the licensee, becomes its subject. What was originally intended to be a citizen/public servant relationship has become a bureaucrat/master—or—licensee/slave relationship.

When the British General Cornwallis surrendered to General Washington at Yorktown in 1781, during the surrendering ceremony the British band played the song "The World Turned Upside Down." You see, this was the first time the People would be the sovereign and those chosen to be the political leaders would actually be public servants. Never before had this occurred. It was a truly Christian approach to government following the example of Christ, who himself was a leader, yet said "The Son of Man did not come to be served, but to serve." (Matthew 20:28*)* When the people of the world voted with their feet and came to America by the boatload, they confirmed that this Christian philosophical approach to government is the best system of government ever to exist on the face of this earth.

> ***"The highest glory of the American Revolution was this: it connected in one indissoluble bond the principles of civil government with the principles of Christianity."*** **John Quincy Adams, 6th President of the United States.**

But it has been the generations of our grandparents, our parents and us that have given our sovereignty away to the bureaucracy. Soon we will commit the ultimate political error when we give whatever sovereignty we have left to the United Nations. This process is being encouraged and orchestrated by the central bankers of the world. It is happening as you read this book.

According to researcher Richard Standring, there are five U.S. Constitutions and seven Internal Revenue Services'. We also know that there are approximately 450 separate and unique definitions of the term "United States" within federal and state law. If you thought there was only one U.S. Constitution and one IRS, you are naive. The deception is complex, and those of us who make up the citizenry really don't know how many layers to the onion this system has.

When a judge asks you, "You live in this country don't you?" Your answer should be, "Sir, your question is much too vague for me to answer. Which one of the 450 definitions of the term 'United States' do you mean when you use the word 'country?'" This is an important question as we learned from Chapter 4 that the tax laws apply differently in different areas. The jurisdictional implications to this question are huge.

As it turns out, this is an old trick. Those who signed the Declaration of Independence complained in that document "to a candid world" that King George "...has combined with others to subject us to a Jurisdiction foreign to our Constitution, and unacknowledged by our Laws; giving his Assent to their Acts of pretended Legislation." King Solomon said: "There is nothing new under the sun." *Ecclesiastes 1:9.*

The Internal Revenue Code, Title 26, contains at least 12 different definitions of the term "United States." The definition of "United States" found at 26 U.S.C. 4612 (a)(4) states:

> **United States. (A) In general. The term "United States" means the 50 States, the District of Columbia, the Commonwealth of Puerto Rico, any possession of the United States, the Commonwealth of the Northern Mariana Islands, and the Trust Territory of the Pacific Islands.**

This definition is the one used to define where various excise taxes are applicable within subchapter A of chapter 38 of Subtitle D. Many of the taxing statutes for excise taxes link to this definition of "United States." Excise taxes are relatively easy to impose. The constitutional rule that must be followed is that excise taxes be uniform throughout the United States. This constitutional rule does not single out the "several States." Therefore, the same excise tax may be levied within the several States and the possessions and territories at the same time. There are no extra hoops, like apportionment, to jump through.

It is my opinion that the term "50 States" found in 26 U.S.C. 4612 (a)(4) means the "several States of the Union." Any taxing statute that relies on this definition of "United States" would be levied any place the United States had any type of political jurisdiction, including the organic states, federal states, possessions, territories and enclaves. Any of the excise taxes tied to section 4612 would be constitutional.

The default definitions of the terms "United States" and "State" for the Internal Revenue Code are found at 26 U.S.C. 7701 (a)(9) and (10). Here the United States is defined as:

**(9) United States. The term 'United States' when used in a geographical sense includes only the States and the District of Columbia.**

**(10) State. The term 'State' shall be construed to include the District of Columbia, where such construction is necessary to carry out the provisions of this title.**

It is my opinion the word "State" above refers to the political corporation states, the federal states, the possessions and the territories and not the organic constitutional several States of the Union. A member of Congress told me personally that the word "State" here did not mean the several States of the Union nor was there any tax on wages within the several States. If this member of Congress was right, then Title 26 becomes fully harmonized with the organic Constitution in accordance with the arguments set forth by this book.

What follows is a definition of the word "State" from Title 23, section 101 of the United States Code. Title 23 deals with Highways. The Constitution give Congress the power to build and maintain highways at Article 1 section 8 of the Constitution. There is therefore no need for Congress to play games with this definition of the word "State" as Congress already has all the jurisdiction they could ever want on the issue.

**(32) State. The term "State" means any of the 50 States, the District of Columbia, or Puerto Rico.**

What follows next is another one of the unique 450 definitions of the term "United States" out of Title 28, the federal criminal code.

**(15) "United States" means –**
**(A) a Federal corporation;**
**(B) an agency, department, commission, board, or other entity of the United States; or**
**(C) an instrumentality of the United States.**

At this point you should be wondering how a Citizen could commit a crime against a federal corporation. Some have theorized that these crimes are civil with criminal pentalities.

The political corporation states are the states that have all the nonconstitutional programs to take care of its franchisees/slaves from cradle-to-grave. They are instrumentalities of the political corporation that governs the District of Columbia, a.k.a. the "United States." They exist along side and in the same time and place as the organic constitutional states, the several States of the Union. Unfortunately, all of these nonessential programs are now deeply rooted in our law, in our bureaucracy, and in our minds. Plus, these programs have been, and continue to be, largly financed by borrowing.

We learned in the first eight chapters of this book that a tax on wages and salaries, payable by the wage or salary earner, is a direct tax and that the 16th Amendment does not provide authority for an unapportioned direct tax. We also learned when any tax can be linked to a privilege, it will be deemed by the courts an excise tax as excise taxes are much easier to levy than direct taxes.

Through trickery the government has managed to turn a "sow's ear into a silk purse;" i.e., it has converted that very difficult direct tax on wages and salaries into an excise tax on a privilege. I have two theories on how they did it: The first is that your election to live your life as a franchisee of the political corporation is a privilege, one that you have voluntarily accepted so that you can receive all of the benefits from the government candy store. This candy store is not open to those who exist under the organic Constitution as the *de jur* government has no authority to offer candy to anyone. When our mothers taught us to never take candy from strangers, they should have also taught us to never take candy from the government.

The government will then take you to court and assert you are a "resident" of such and such a state. A member of the Posterity of **We the People** is an "Inhabitant" of one of the several States of the Union. A "resident" of a state is actually a franchisee/slave of the political corporation state. If you don't immediately object to being called a "resident," your goose is cooked. As a "resident" of the political corporation, the government could levy an excise tax on the air you breath; after all they are taking care of you from the cradle to the grave and your existence is therefore a privilege.

My second theory as to how a direct tax on wages and salaries has been converted to an excise tax on a privilege is in the acceptance of the exemption allowances and the various deductions offered by the Internal Revenue Code. The 16th Amendment provides authority to place an excise tax on unearned income and annual business profits severed from their source. There is no constitutional requirement that government offer anyone any deductions or exemptions in calculating the tax due. Now if you accept the "benefit" of these deductions and exemptions, even though your wages and salary have been lumped in with your unearned income, gains and profits, you are now receiving a privilege offered by government and the whole thing becomes an excise tax. Under this logic, if you were to forego taking the exemptions and deductions, then you could exclude wages and salaries from your taxable income as, absent a privilege (benefit), a tax on these would be a direct tax. Adam Smith called it a capitation tax. A capitation tax is a species of a direct tax.

In 1913, the first taxing statute offered to Congress under the authority of the 16th Amendment delineated these deductions and exemptions as "benefits." The precise language proposed for the statutes was:

> **"...authorized and required to deduct and withhold from such annual gains, profits, and income such sum as will be sufficient to pay the normal tax imposed thereon by this section, and shall pay to the officer of the United States Government authorized to receive the same;....In all cases where the income tax of a person is withheld and deducted and paid or to be paid at the source, as aforesaid, such person shall not receive the *benefit* of**

> **the *exemption* of $4,000 allowed herein unless he shall, not less than 30 days prior to the day on which the return of his income is due, file with the person who is required to withhold and pay tax for him an affidavit claiming the *benefit* of such *exemption*; nor shall any person under the foregoing conditions be allowed the *benefit* of any *deduction*....But in each case the *benefit* of the *exemption* and the *deduction* allowable under this section may be had by complying with the foregoing provisions of this paragraph [emphasis mine]." 50 Cong. Rec. 1237-8 (1913).**

By taking the **"benefit"** of the exemptions and deductions, what would have been a direct tax on wages and salaries is now an indirect tax on a privilege. Omit wages and salaries from the equation, don't take any deductions or exemptions, and what you have left is an indirect tax on unearned income and profit.

If you believe the inflation rate, based on the Consumer Price Index, averaged 3.4% per year between 1914 (the year we got fiat money) and the year 2000, the $4,000 exempted from the tax in 1913 would be worth $74,000 today. In 1913 any wages added into the pot as "taxable income" were exempted out by the $4,000 exemption (at least $74,000 in today's dollars). So no matter how you look at it, the first taxing statute was definitely an indirect tax as from a practical sense; wages and salaries were exempted out of "taxable income."

Furthermore, it is theorized that, when persons elect to live their lives under the political corporation, and elect to receive all of the benefits of the nonconstitutional programs, they have accepted the privilege of changing their status from that of a Citizen to a citizen. They are no longer an Inhabitant of one of the several States, but are instead a resident of the political corporation. They are no longer an elector, instead they are a voter. If tried for a crime, they are not an accused, they are a defendant. They do not enjoy the constitutional right to a trial by jury, instead they get a jury trial if so allowed by statute. And on it goes.

I believe this is how we have been entangled in all of these nonconstitutional processes. If you love freedom and liberty, you will agree with me this is not right. If you are not of this mind set, then the political corporation has given you heaven on earth, the best security man has to offer. Remember how the children of Israel complained to Moses in the desert about how good they had it as slaves in Egypt, and how they wanted to return?

Where do you stand? Would you rather enjoy the benefits and security of slavery, or do you want to be free?

There is a third argument we should address. That is the code section 861 argument. It is believed by tax researchers that the Internal Revenue Code only authorizes income taxes from "sources" as this is the term used in the 16th Amendment. The government claims anything that is listed in section 61 of the code is taxable. But what is listed in section 61 are "items," not "sources."

The thinking is that the income from an "item" is taxable only when that "item" is part of a taxable "source." Section 861 lists the taxable sources. According to other tax researchers, the taxable sources under section 861 generally are related to international and foreign commerce (including U.S. possessions and territories) when earned by American Citizens living in the several States. For a thorough analysis of section 861, go to **www.taxableincome.net.**

You'll notice that these sources do not involve one's right to exist as a member of the Posterity of **We the People** living and working in one of the several States of the Union. What is being taxed are therefore privileges upon which an excise tax can be levied. The section 861 argument fully harmonizes the Constitution with the 16th Amendment and the conclusions put forth by this book. It is scandalous that **We the People** cannot get our servant, the federal government, to explain exactly how this income tax is levied and who and what are being taxed.

## The Flat Tax

There are various "flat tax" proposals being offered today as an alternative to the 8,000-page Internal Revenue Code with its 11,000-page accompanying regulations we all suffer under. The fact that the Congress and the IRS have gone to such great lengths to confuse us with such a voluminous tax code should raise a red flag that there is something fundamentally wrong. It is immaterial whether or not the income tax is a graduated tax, with lots of deductions and exemptions, or a flat tax with few or no deductions or exemptions. As long as the tax is on wages and salaries and the tax is an unapportioned direct tax, there is no constitutional authority for it (at least when the tax applies to Citizens of the several States).

A flat tax is just a different flavor for the same thing. When the tax diminishes the wages and salaries of a natural person, it is still a direct tax and must be apportioned among the several States. Although for the political corporation states, those that are instrumentalities of the District of Columbia, a.k.a. the "United States," a flat tax would be okay under their bylaws as anyone who is a part of the "body politic" of that political corporation is such by privilege. It is difficult to conceive of a more direct tax than a tax on the wages and salary a man earns to feed his family. Such a tax system is feudalistic as it taxes one's right to exist.

While we consider the advisability of a flat tax, let us briefly revisit what the 16th Amendment does and does not do. We must do this in order to understand whether or not any flat tax proposal is constitutional or unconstitutional. Some of this material we have been over before, but it bears repeating as it is precisely the point of this book.

The following quote is from the Senate debates in 1913 when the first income taxing statute authorized by the 16th Amendment was being considered.

> **Mr. TAVENNER. "Mr. Chairman...I have made as extended inquires as anyone could make, and I believe that 90 percent of the people of the whole United States, regardless of their politics, race, religion, color, or creed are heartily in favor of an income tax which proposes a tax on wealth in lieu of the present system, which provides for the raising of revenue by taxing exclusively the clothes on a man's back, and the other things that people must wear, eat, and use in order to live.**
>
> **"Not only the poor man, from whose bending back some of the burden of taxation is to be lifted by means of this bill, favors the measure. I am in a position to say that many fair-minded men of wealth residing in my own district, men who will be required to pay a considerable tax on their incomes by virtue of the income-tax provision of this bill, have the proposition that a man should be taxed according to his ability to pay and according to the benefits and privileges he receives under the Government is fair and just.**
>
> **"I am not prejudiced against wealth. Any man who has honestly acquired wealth shows but an evidence of his industry, intelligence, and skill, and deserves the respect of all. But I do contend that men possessing wealth should pay, and are able to pay, more taxes than their less fortunate brothers who own only the clothes upon their backs, and possibly their household furniture, and whose weekly wage is scarcely enough to enable them to provide for their families from week to week, let alone to lay anything by for a rainy day.**
>
> **"Mr. Chairman, the income tax is part of the Democratic plan to reduce the ever-increasing cost of living in this country. It means the carrying out of the program prom-**

ised in the pre-election campaign last fall, namely, to take some of the tax off the necessaries of life, such as sugar, woolens, cottons, beef, and lumber, and to make up for the loss of revenue thus sustained by the Government by placing a tax upon incomes. It is estimated that this amount of taxation will raise approximately $100,000,000, and that this amount of taxation will be taken off the vital necessaries of life.

"But, Mr. Chairman, to tax wealth and incomes, according to the standpatters and protectionists, is class legislation. The fact is, however, that the present system of taxing the necessaries of life while permitting wealth to go untaxed is class legislation of the grossest sort. Is it not passing strange that those who complain of an income tax as class legislation were never heard to complain of the existing class legislation which taxes the hats, coats, and shirts of the masses almost 71 percent, while not requiring men like Rockefeller, Carnegie, and other millionaires to pay a single penny of taxation on their swollen personal fortunes to the National Government?

"The income tax is a recognition of the demand of the masses for a square deal in taxation, which they are not now receiving in either State or Federal taxation. Under the fiscal systems in vogue in most of the States the wealthy and powerful classes find ways to evade taxation, and are constantly succeeding, in one way or another, in shifting the chief weight of taxation from those most able to bear it to the shoulders of those weaker, poorer, and less able to protect themselves. So much for the chances of the small taxpayer in matters of State and local taxation. But the worst is yet to come. What about Federal taxation? In the raising of revenue to run the National Government, wealth is not asked to contribute anything whatever. Practically the entire expense of

**the Government are met with funds raised by taxing the things people eat, wear, and use." 50 Cong. Rec. 1253 (1913).**

Again we see what the purpose of the 16th Amendment was. It was to tax investment income from real or personal property and profits of business. This was the same tax that the *Pollock Case* was all about. It was not to tax the wages or salaries of the working man.

I know a waitress who works in a family restaurant where you can buy dinner for $9. The government automatically taxes her eight percent on her total till as the government assumes she gets tipped on every check. All her checks are tallied each night and her "employer" takes out of her paycheck 8 percent of her total till for the night to account for her "tip income" (If someone left her a 16 percent tip, half of that tip would go to government). But, if someone doesn't leave her a tip at all, it actually costs her to provide service to that customer. Her "employer" then bundles all her tickets together for the night, puts them in a box and saves them for seven years. This woman is a single mom and can barely make ends meet. Is this what the American people said they wanted when they demanded an income tax amendment to the Constitution? Or is this a government of greed and insanity?

Now let's revisit the Congressional Record in the year 1913 as they were again debating the first income tax statutes and see what Congress understood the word "income" to mean.

**Mr. WILLIAMS. "Here is the language, and I think if it read this way and the words 'and income' are left out, it never would have struck the gentlemen as unobjectionable in any respect:**

**"That, subject only to such exemptions and deductions as are hereinafter allowed, the net income of a taxable person shall include gains profits, and income -**

**"Now leave out the word 'income,' the repetition of which has confused - derived from salaries, wages, or compensation - For What?**

**"For personal service of whatever kind and in whatever form paid, or from - What else?**

**"Professions, vocations, businesses, trade, commerce, or sales or dealings in property, whether real or personal, growing out of the ownership of use of or interest in real or personal property -**

**"And, then, again -**

**"also interest, rent, dividends, securities.**

**"There is not the slightest lack or clearness in it, to my mind, unless it grows out of putting a double definition upon the word 'income,' and I see no objection to striking out the word 'income,' if you want to strike it out." 50 Cong. Rec. 3776 (1913).**

The point of this discussion was that it was not the wages of the man that was in and of itself the "gain or profit." It was the application of the labor by the business owner for the purpose of realizing a gain or profit in business that was to be the "income" upon which the tax would be levied. Wages and salary are not gain. Wages and salary are not profit. Because the proposed statute already had the words "gain" and "profit" in it, adding the word "income" was redundant.

Suppose you are the owner of a gas station and you have to pay an "income tax" on the business. Do you derive income only from the sale of gasoline, tires and accessories? Or do you also derive income from the labor your mechanic provides and the monies you charge for his services when he repairs a customer's car? The statute and the debates make it clear that you will be responsible to pay a tax on the gain and profit you make off the mechanic's labor, too. But the tax is not on the mechanic himself as this would be a tax on the mechanic's capital. It would be a capitation tax. Because it would diminish him, it would be a direct tax.

As we saw in the case of *Wilcox v. County Commissioners,* labor is only a component of a greater whole that produces income. The Supreme Court relied on this definition for their ruling in *Stratton Ind. v. Howbert.* The following is how the *Wilcox Court* defined "income":

> **"The income meant by the statute is the income for the year, and is the result of the year's business. It is the net result of many combined influences: the use of the capital invested; the personal labor and services of the members of the firm; the skill and ability with which they lay in, or from time to time renew their stock; the carefulness and good judgement with which they sell and give credit; and the foresight and address with which they hold themselves prepared for the fluctuations and contingencies affecting the general commerce and business of the country. To express it in a more summary and comprehensive form, it is the creation of capital, industry, and skill." Wilcox v. County Commissioners, 103 Mass. 544, 546 (1870).**

The *Wilcox* definition of "income" is in perfect harmony with the understanding of the American People and their intent as to the sources to be taxed by the 16th Amendment.

The people of America simply did not think the 16th Amendment was ever going to tax the wages or salary of a working man. Neither did the members of Congress who supported it. Quoting again from the Congressional Record in 1913:

> **Mr. SHERMAN. "The earnings of any person for any occupation or profession would, if not spent in like manner, become principal. If by professional effort any person should earn a given sum annually and he spends half of it, he saves the other half. The half so saved in**

**turn becomes principal. That principal is property. The savings from the income by professional effort or by any form of skilled labor or unskilled by hand becomes property. At the end of any given period that saving is a principal, and any income derived from it [the principle] is an income from property, not an income from the earning capacity or the personal ability of the taxpayer in question...."**

**Mr. CUMMINS. "Our authority is to levy a tax upon incomes. I take it that every lawyer will agree with me in the conclusion that we cannot levy under this amendment a tax upon anything but an income. I assume that every lawyer will agree with me that we can not legislatively interpret the meaning of the word "income." That is purely a judicial matter. We can not enlarge the meaning of the word "income." We need not levy our tax upon the entire income. We may levy it upon part of an income, but we cannot levy it upon anything but an income." 50 Cong. Rec. 3842-3 (1913).**

What we see here is the same logic as in the *Waring v. City of Savannah* case from 1878 where the labor of a man was the principle or tree. Any fruit produced by the tree, leaving the tree intact and whole, was income. In other words, in 1913 Congress understood there was a difference between what we call today "earned income" and "unearned income." A tax on the first, which diminished the source, was a direct tax; and a tax on the latter, which only diminished the income and left the source whole, was an indirect tax.

We also note that Congress understood they were without authority to determine what the word "income" meant. And today the Courts are without authority to determine what the word "income" means as it is a word used in the Constitution. All the Courts can do is to **discover** what the word "income" means as it is **We the People**, at the time the 16th Amendment was ratified, who determined forever the meaning of the words within that Amendment. And that definition is now a historical fact, unchangeable by any present day politician or judicial officer.

In a letter dated June 12, 1823 from Thomas Jefferson to William Johnson, Associate Justice of the Supreme Court, Jefferson was warning of the abuse that would take place if his advice in the following words was not taken:

> **"On every question of the construction of the Constitution let us carry ourselves back to the time when the Constitution was adopted, recollect the spirit manifested in the debates, and instead of trying what meaning may be squeezed out of the text, or invented against it, conform to the probable one in which it was passed."**

Correctly, the Supreme Court of the United States has ruled that the 16th Amendment does not provide authority for an unapportioned direct tax. This very assertion by today's lower courts, (which is of course erroneous) that the 16th Amendment does provide authority for a constitutional and unapportioned direct tax on incomes, was presented as argument to the Supreme Court by both the government and by Brushaber in the *Brushaber Case*.

Brushaber said in his brief:

> **"The evident purpose of this amendment was not to abandon the former policy of safeguarding the several sections of the Union against disproportionate taxation, but merely to substitute an apportionment according to 'incomes from whatever source derived,' in lieu of a *per capita* apportionment." Brief for Appellant at 10, Brushaber v. Union Pacific R.R. Co., 240 US 1 (1916).**

In the same case, the Government argued:

> **"Income taxes, at least on income derived from real or personal property, are direct taxes, and therefore not subject to the uniformity rule, EXPRESSLY prescribed by the Constitution." id., Brief for the United States at 11.**

So both *Brushaber* and the government argued the 16th Amendment provided authority for a constitutionally direct tax in the nature of an income tax exempted from the rule of apportionment. In other words, both parties argued that the 16th Amendment provided an exception to the direct taxation clauses of the Constitution. The question was squarely before the Supreme Court. The Supreme Court ruled they were both wrong! "That the contention that the Amendment treats a tax on incomes as a direct tax although it is relieved from apportionment and is necessarily therefore not subject to the rule of uniformity...thus destroying the two great classifications [of taxes] which have been recognized and enforced from the beginning, is wholly without foundation." Brushaber v. Union Pacific R.R. Co., 240 US 1, 18 (1916).

*Harvard Law Review* said:

> **"In *Brushaber v. Union Pacific Railroad Co.*, Mr. Chief Justice White, upholding the income tax imposed by the Tariff Act of 1913, construed the Amendment as a declaration that an income tax is "indirect," rather than as making an exception to the rule that direct taxes must be apportioned." The Income Tax and the Sixteenth Amendment, 29 Harvard Law Review 536 (1915-6).**

In the case of *Brushaber v. The Union Pacific R.R. Co:*

> **"...The (16th) amendment, the court said, judged by the purpose for which it was passed, does not treat income taxes as direct taxes but simply removes the ground which led to their being considered as such in the Pollock Case, namely, the source of the income. Therefore, they are again to be classified in the class of indirect taxes to which they by nature belong." Ramon Siaca, The Federal Income Tax Law of 1913: Construction of the Sixteenth Amendment, 1 Cornell Law Quarterly 298, 301 (1915-6).**

Today the lower courts tell us that the 16th Amendment provides for an unapportioned direct tax on wages and salaries thereby creating a new type of tax not subject to either to the rule of apportionment nor the rule of uniformity. This is in direct opposition to the above editorials from the law schools of the Cornell University and Harvard University, and in direct opposition to the Supreme Court.

> **"Thus, in the matter of taxation, the Constitution recognizes the two great classes of direct and indirect taxes, and lays down two rules by which their imposition must be governed, namely: The rule of apportionment as to direct taxes, and the rule of uniformity as to duties, imposts and excises. Pollock v. Farmer's Loan & Trust Co., 157 U.S. 429, 557 (1895).**

> **"The income from an investment is that which it earns, remaining itself [the investment] intact." Cornell Univ. v. Davenport, 30 Hun., 177, 184. (Cited in Stratton's Independence v. Howbert, 231 U.S. 399.)**

Commenting on the idea the 16th Amendment modified the direct taxation clauses of the 16th Amendment and created a new category of taxation, the Supreme Court stated in the *Brushaber Case:*

> **"This result, instead of simplifying the situation and making clear the limitations on the taxing power, which obviously the Amendment must have been intended to accomplish, would create radical and destructive changes in our constitutional system and multiply confusion." Brushaber v. Union Pac. R.R. Co., 240 U.S. 1, 12 (1916).**

> **"Acts of Congress are to be considered and applied with and not to thwart the purpose of the Constitution." Phelps v. U.S., 274 U.S. 341, 344 (1927).**

Just as the intent of Congress should be followed when construing a statute, so must the intent of the People, in their sovereign capacity, be followed when construing an amendment to the Constitution.

> **"The poor man does not regard his wages or salary as 'an income.'" Governor A.E. Wilson (Kentucky) on the Income Tax Amendment, New York Times, part 5, page 13, February 26, 1911.**

At the time of the ratification of the 16th Amendment, "incomes" were earned only by the rich. Some called them the "idle rich." Everyone else was either a farmer, a wage earner or worked for a salary. The latter did not consider themselves to have "an income."

The historical record shows us that the Supreme Court got it right in these early income tax cases. The 16th Amendment provides authority only for taxes on incomes that are inherently indirect. Taxes on incomes that are inherently direct are without the scope of the 16th Amendment. There is a finite boundary line that separates an indirect income tax from a direct income tax. The difference is that an indirect income tax does not diminish the source of the income, whereas a direct income tax; i.e., a tax on wages, salaries or gross income, does diminish the source of the income.

Regardless of what the courts say, the American People intuitively know this tax on wages and salaries is a direct tax and not one the People would ever wish to impose on themselves. They also know that something has gone astray in the imposition of this tax on our people. And so the controversy will continue to rage on until:

> **"No question is ever settled, until it is settled right." Frank Warren Hackett, The Constitutionality of the Graduated Income Tax Law, 25 Yale Law Journal 427, 442 (1916).**

> **"If your Honors please, no statute and no decision inconsistent with the Constitution can stand. A century of error cannot overrule the Constitution. The people are not to be deprived of rights imbedded in the Constitution by erroneous precedents. Those rights may slumber, but nevertheless they live and breathe. Where would we be today if the rule of precedent had controlled our forefathers? Is the Constitution to be enslaved by any such technical doctrine as *stare decisis*, and thus manacled with parchment chains? When Franklin stood at the bar of the English Commons ought he to have been satisfied to abandon the claims of the colonists because Mansfield, Thurlow, Eldon and Boston-born Copley could have demonstrated to him that precedent upon precedent fully sustained the right and the power of Parliament to tax the colonists without representation?" Opening Argument by Mr. W. D. Guthrie on behalf of Appellants, Pollock v. Farmers' Loan and Trust Co., 158 U.S. 601 (1895).**

Looking at the *Brushaber Case* again, we note in his complaint that Brushaber claimed he was "a citizen of the State of New York and a resident of the Brough of Brooklyn, in the City of New York." He also averred that the defendant, Union Pacific Railroad Co., was "a corporation duly organized and existing under and by virtue of the Laws of the State of Utah, and a citizen of the State of Utah, and has its executive offices and a place of business at No. 165 Broadway, in the Borough of Manhattan, City of New York...."

The *Brushaber Case* was decided by the Supreme Court on January 24, 1916 and on March 21, 1916 the Treasury Department issued Treasury Decision No. 2313 concerning the *Brushaber Case* which said on page 1:

> **Under the decision of the Supreme Court of the United States in the case of Brushaber v. Union Pacific Railroad Co., decided January 24, 1916, it is hereby held that income accruing to nonresident aliens in the form of inter-**

> **est from the bonds and dividends on the stock of domestic corporations is subject tot he income tax imposed by the act of October 3, 1913.**
>
> **The responsible heads, agents, or representatives of nonresident aliens, who are in charge of property owned or business carried on within the United States, shal make a full and complete return of the income therefrom on Form 1040, revised, and shall pay any and all tax, normal and additional, assessed upon the income received by them in behalf of their nonresident alien principles."**

Bundled with the *Brushaber Case* were the *Tyee Case* and the *Thorne Case*. In all three cases the plaintiffs were citizens of the State of New York. Based on T.D. 2313, one must conclude that a citizen of one of the states is a nonresident alien to the United States, a.k.a. the District of Columbia. Remember that the definition of the term "state" found at 26 U.S.C. 7701 (a)(10) only specifically mentions the "District of Columbia." A member of Congress told me privately that Idaho was not a state within this definition.

Unraveling what the Treasury Department was up to with their T.D. 2313 is possibly the key to understanding how they're sticking us with this unapportioned direct tax.

Columbia Law Review, in its June, 1916 issue, has an interesting article about T.D.2313 and its history. It seems that before the Supreme Court's *Brushaber Decision* the Treasury Department visited the issue of whether or not the income accruing to a nonresident alien's was taxable under the first income tax act of 1913.

Treasury Decision 2017, issued August 25, 1914 reads, "Interest on bonds of domestic corporations and dividends on stock of domestic corporations owned by non-resident aliens, and whether such bonds and stock be physically located within or without the United States, are not subject to the income tax."

Treasury Decision 2162, issued February 24, 1915, reads similarly, "Interest from bonds and dividends on stock of domestic corporations, owned by non-resident aliens, are not subject to the income tax, whether such bonds and stock are physically located within or without the United States or whether they are in the possession of agents, or trustees in some fiduciary capacity, in the United States or otherwise."

Both of these Treasury Decisions concerned the Tariff Law of 1913 (the income tax portion of the act) and were issued before the *Brushaber Decision* came down from the Supreme Court. Both were based on two official opinions issued by the Attorney General.

> **"I am of the opinion that the quoted provision does not lay a tax upon the interest accruing on bonds of the character specified when held and owned by a nonresident foreigner, and that this is true irrespective of whether they are unsecured or secured by a mortgage upon real estate in this country, and also irrespective of where the written bonds are in fact kept or interest payments thereon are made. Respectfully, J.C. McReynolds." 30 Opinions of the Attorney General 230, 231 (1919) issued October 23, 1913.**

The second official opinion was issued by the Attorney General on July 15, 1914. It said much the same thing. "It is my opinion, therefore, shares of stock of domestic corporations owned by nonresident aliens are not "property...in the United States" within the meaning of the act of October 3, 1913, and dividends accruing therefrom to such nonresident aliens are not subject to any tax under said act." ibid., 273.

How could all this be when the *Brushaber Case* had nothing to do with nonresident aliens? The Columbia Law Review article struggles with this same point.

> **"Comprehensive as was the decision in that case, the opinion in no way refers to non-resident aliens, the facts of the case did not present the question of the intent of**

> **the law or the power to impose a tax on such income, the matter was not referred to in the argument of counsel, and there was no attempt by the Supreme Court, either in this case or in any of the others [cases bundled with *Brushaber*] which have been before it involving the present Income Tax Law, to pass on those questions." Amos J. Peaslee, Taxing Incomes of Foreign Investors in American Stocks and Bonds, 16 Columbia Law Review 465, 466 (1916).**

Before government had such an insatiable appetite for money, it used to be the general custom that a person did not owe a duty to pay a tax unless a particular government offered a benefit to the taxpayer - and usually the benefit was protection. This opinion was held world-wide, and it was the general custom of the time that a citizen owed a tax only to the government who protected him. Judge Cooley, whom we have quoted before, wrote,

> **"A state can no more subject to its power a single person or a single article of property whose residence or legal *situs* is in another state, than it can subject all the citizens or all the property of another state to its power. The accidental circumstances that it may happen to have the means of reaching one and not the rest can make no difference; there must be an interest in the subject matter of the tax; there must be between the state and the tax-payer a reciprocity of duty and obligation, and these, in contemplation of law, would be wholly wanting in the case supposed." ibid. 471.**

As our government won't answer basic questions about our federal income tax, we can only speculate what happened to cause the Treasury to issue T.D. 2313. I believe the federal government thought the 16th Amendment provided for an unapportioned direct tax exempted from the apportionment clauses of the Constitution. This is what they argued in the *Brushaber Case*. It would have given them a new power - a new tax. When the Supreme Court ruled contrary to this, the Treasury Department and the IRS must have realized that the 16th Amendment was much narrower in scope and authority than they had first assumed. As the Supreme Court said in the *Peck Case* - 'there is no new tax.'

Remember that the apportionment rule does not apply outside of the fifty States. "In discussing the jurisdictional extent of the power of the United States to impose taxes we are not concerned with any constitutional limitations, because so far as territorial jurisdiction is concerned, there are none." ibid. 470.

What may have happened after the *Brushaber Decision* was that the government conspired as to how they were going to get the new tax denied them by the Supreme Court. Possibly what happens today is through a myriad of declarations on our part, we Citizens unknowingly declare ourselves to be territorial citizens, not protected by the Constitution. Of course this is a fraudulent activity on the part of our own government, but it does offer an explanation as to how the system might work today.

If true, then the IRS and the courts assume we are all territorial citizens who are somehow beneficiaries of privileges and no longer sovereign Citizens of the fifty several States. As such, they may levy an unapportioned direct tax on us. At least they think then can, and so far they have been getting away with it. But this is just a theory as more work is needs to be done in this area.

Whether the income tax is a graduated tax or a flat tax, as long as it is levied on wages and salaries it is a direct tax. According to Adam Smith, the income tax, as it is currently applied, is a capitation tax. Therefore, an unapportioned flat tax levied within the several states on wages and salaries is unconstitutional.

There is a draconian element to the flat tax scheme. Any flat tax arrangement will likely do away with the need to file returns as everyone will be treated the same and there will be no need for taking advantage of any of the former deductions and exemptions. With everyone paying the same rate, all taxes could be paid electronically. A flat income tax will provide the opportunity for a gigantic leap forward in the process of eliminating cash and ushering in a system of total control and total enslavement of our people.

This is an example of the classic case thesis, anti-thesis and synthesis. Government creates a problem, an oppressive tax code, and then offers a solution that seems better on the surface - a flat tax. In reality, the solution is much worse than the *status quo*. Then the people, like sheep, accept the solution only to find out they are worse off than they were before. The flat tax should be opposed by all people at all costs. Once we have a flat tax system, we will move much faster into a cashless society.

# Chapter 10
## The People's Sovereignty Amendment

### The Solution

> **"A wise and frugal government which shall restrain men from injuring one another, which shall leave them otherwise free to regulate their own pursuits of industry and improvements and shall not take from the mouth of labor the bread it has earned."**
>
> **—Thomas Jefferson, First Inaugural address, March 4, 1801.**

While our founding fathers were great and wise men, they were not perfect. They first gave us the Articles of Confederation, which didn't work. It took about 10 years for them to get on with writing the Constitution we have today. This Constitution provides for the best system of human government the world has ever seen. But it is not perfect, primarily because the men who operate our government are not perfect. That is why we have built into our government a system of checks and balances. The framers of the Constitution were students of history and understood that all goverments are predisposed to abuse of power. The battle for freedom must be fought by every person in every generation. Otherwise, governmental power will incrementally grow, and freedom will incrementally disappear.

> **"We have no government armed with the power capable of contending with human passions unbridled by morality and religion. Avarice [greed], ambition, revenge, or gallantry [debauchery], would break the strongest cords of our Constitution as a whale goes through a net. Our Constitution was made only for a moral and religious people. It is wholly inadequate to the government of any other." John Adams, 2nd President.**

As our government grows in size and as the growing population of our nation fills in the open lands, we are seeing the effect of "more rats in a box." Adding to this is the incredible advances in technology and the ability to know everything and track anything about each other. We are now faced with new and serious challenges to our freedom and liberty. The time is now to take the initiative and fight to maintain those precious gifts given to us by our forefathers.

I propose we amend the Constitution with what I call the **"People's Sovereignty Amendment."** Under this amendment, it would become both impractical and nearly impossible for the federal government to tax the wages and salaries of the Citizens of the several States, while leaving intact the original taxation clauses of the Constitution. The "People's Sovereignty Amendment" does this and at the same time accomplishes the goals of the People when they originally demanded the 16th Amendment. The "People's Sovereignty Amendment," unlike the 16th Amendment, uses unambiguous terms not subject to manipulation.

Remember it was the goal of the People (1909) to make accumulated wealth pay for the benefit wealth received from government. It was not a "soak the rich" scheme. Wealth essentially had a free ride and wealth, being organized, fought the income tax amendment tooth and nail. When those of the wealth class realized they would have to cave in, they were very forward thinking. They crafted the 16th Amendment in an ambiguous way so it could be manipulated later. By an expansion of the word "income" (not allowed by the rules of construction) those who were to get tax relief by the 16th Amendment are now fraudulently being taxed by it. They also managed to bring in the Federal Reserve Act at the same time as the income tax. The two schemes working together would allow the Federal Reserve Bank to pump a lot of debt based money into the system while harvesting out those same dollars through the income tax, thus keeping inflation low and maximizing the creation of debt.

The numbers of those benefitting from this new scheme are fewer than those who were benefitting during the time of the protective tariff. The former are the central bankers of the world and the insiders who do business with them. When the Federal Reserve was formed in 1913, it was alleged that eight families (five of them are European) owned the stock of this private bank (it's not federal and it has no reserves). Today, the rest of us find ourselves in the exact position as those people at the turn of the last century who were heavily taxed on what they ate, wore and used. The same thing is true today as it was then, except our money is taxed before we get it, instead of taxed when we spend it. Still the effect is the same as it is getting harder for the average person to afford the things we eat, wear and use.

Just as the Republican party at the turn of the last century attempted to convince the people that the manipulated tariff was good for America, by raising wages and protecting American jobs; so today we have the politicians of both the Democrat and Republican parties trying to tell us that "free trade" is good for us and has brought prosperity to America. But there is a growing body of unemployed, underemployed, impoverished and bankrupted Americans who are not buying this anymore.

Because we have almost eliminated tariffs under our many "free trade" agreements, the source revenue to run the government has been shifting from tariff taxes and excise taxes to the taxes collected on wages, salaries and incomes of working Americans. Personal income taxes and social security taxes make up over 80 percent of the federal government's revenue. The Republicans were deceiving the American People about the protective tariff in 1900. Today both the Republicans and the Democrats are doing the same concerning the free trade agreements. These free trade agreements reduce tariff, make the world safe for multinational corporations, and shift the tax burden onto both earned and unearned incomes. It is those who work for a living that are heavily taxed, while those who create money out of thin air or manage the international corporations benefit from this system. With such a huge monthly trade deficit, we would do our nation good to raise tariffs to a level where our trade was in balance. Much revenue for the support of government would be collected in the process while bringing tax relief to American families.

Thomas Jefferson said that the People should "Bind government with the chains of the Constitution." In that spirit, I propose we amend the Constitution with the following language:

## Amendment No. 28

**Section 1.** Repeal of the 16th Amendment. The sixteenth article of amendment of the Constitution of the United States is hereby repealed.

**Section 2.** Income Tax. The Congress shall have the power to lay and collect indirect taxes of uniform rate on severed profits and unearned income.

**Section 3.** Direct Taxes. Taxes on wages, salaries and occupations, being direct, shall be apportioned among the several States according to population.

**Section 4.** Taxing Statutes, Bills, Treaties. Taxing Statutes must be written in simple form with plain wording such that those who pay the tax can understand the statute. Every bill shall embrace but one subject which subject shall be expressed in the title. Treaties are inferior to the Constitution, the Constitution being the Supreme Law of the Land.

**Section 5.** Sovereignty, Juries. Sovereignty is retained by the People. There is no immunity for civil Officers or their delegates. In all suits, the People as Jurors retain authority to determine the law and the facts. When convened by the consent of one-tenth of the Electors of any County (or Parish), grand juries shall have power to administer oaths and issue subpoenas.

**Section 6.** State's Rights, Oaths, Term Limits. The Legislatures of the several States may repeal any law or bill passed by Congress when two-thirds of the Legislatures shall by vote determine to do so. No elected or appointed Official, Who has taken an oath required by this Constitution, may serve in any other public or quasi-public position, or any private capacity with substantial connection to government, while in service in their elected or appointed position. No Person may serve more than two terms as Senator and no more than four terms as Representative.

The first goal of this proposed 28th Amendment is to establish the purposes of the masses of Americans when they demanded a sharing of the tax burden with the accumulated wealth of the nation. On the tax issue, the intent of this proposed 28th Amendment is the same as the intent of the 16th Amendment. The difference is this proposed amendment uses unambiguous terms not subject to manipulation.

This Amendment does not seek to "soak the rich," but only to have those who benefit from government pay for the support of government. The inability to graduate the income tax will insure that this be the case. It would also make nearly impossible the taxing of wages and salaries as these taxes would have to be apportioned.

Although the latter is true even under the 16th Amendment, we have seen in this book how the government today ignores this constitutional requirement of apportionment. This proposed language would not allow them to get away with it any longer. Providing authority to tax wages and salaries is necessary though as it may need to be resorted to in time of emergency.

Repealing the 16th Amendment without replacing it is dangerous in my opinion. The original Constitution gave Congress a plenary power of taxation. Congress has always had the power to tax wages and salaries. At the time the American People were demanding the 16th Amendment, the Democrat party made a monumental mistake by allowing the Republicans to write the amendment. The Democrats should have written it and published it with their party platform in the 1908 presidential campaign. Because of this oversight, we ended up with vague language that continues to haunt us to this day. It is incumbent upon those of us who understand this problem to offer a viable remedy.

It is my opinion that if the 16th Amendment were declared null and void, we would revert to *Pollock* insofar as income taxes on unearned income, gain and profit. For taxes on wages and salaries, we would revert back to *Springer*. As I argued earlier, I believe both these cases had bad decisions, especially the *Springer Case*. The tax on unearned income would then become a direct tax, and the tax on earned income would then be an indirect tax. In both cases, we would have precisely the opposite of what it should be! I believe Bill Benson's conclusion, in his book *"The Law That Never Was,"* is true that the 16th Amendment was never properly ratified. But if we rid ourselves of the 16th Amendment, without replacing it with something better, we may find ourselves worse off than before. Nobody really knows, we can only speculate.

When income taxes on wages and salaries are eliminated and taxes on unearned income cannot be graduated, not only will wealth have to pay for the benefits it receives from government, but the tax revenue of the federal government will be so greatly reduced that the poor will no longer be able to receive benefits from government for which they don't pay for. The government will have to abandon all of its "nonessential" programs. Every human has a duty to our Creator to be charitable to our fellow man. This duty should never be delegated to government. Our 28th Amendment will make it difficult for politicians to buy votes from the poor with someone else's tax dollars. Government will have to return to its constitutional limitations as it won't have enough money to involve itself in mischief outside of its constitutional boundaries.

The practice of government taking from one person to buy a vote from another is a violation of the "Laws of Nature and Nature's God." It amounts to legalized plunder. Ultimately behind every law is the sheriff's pistol. Don't pay the taxes you owe and eventually the sheriff will show up at your door, pistol in hand. To promote the practice that government should tax one person to give a handout to another is to legalize theft at the point of a gun—the sheriff's gun.

> **"The Results of Legal Plunder. No society can exist unless the laws are respected to a certain degree. The safest way to make laws respected is to make them respectable. When law and morality contradict each other, the citizen has the cruel alternative of either losing his moral sense or losing his respect for the law. These two evils are of equal consequence, and it would be difficult for a person to choose between them." Frederic Bastiat, The Law, p. 12-13 (Foundation for Economic Education, Inc. 1996) (1850).**

Remember how 1,000 years ago, the bureaucracies of organized religion attempted to control the masses by withholding the Scriptures from them and conducting religious ceremonies in foreign languages. They made religion complicated so that the masses became dependant on the religious bureaucracy for their spiritual needs as a means of controlling them. This exact form of tyranny is occurring today in America with our complicated tax code. There is nothing new under the sun. Section 4 of the proposed "Peoples Sovereignty Amendment" would prevent our tax laws from being used for this purpose.

Section 4 would also preserve our Constitution as the Supreme Law of the Land, as it should be. Somehow the Supreme Court has in effect managed to rule that our Constitution can be superceded by international treaties. Today we have treaties in place, or in the pipeline, that encroach on property rights for the benefit of migratory birds; that affect the rights of parents to spank their children in order to provide "the children" with "rights," and a myriad of other draconian treaties. Every right we have will soon be superceded by some United Nations treaty if we don't defend these rights now. Otherwise we will have "global governance" and George Bush's "New World Order," most of which is already in place. This is an end run around the Constitution not anticipated by the founding fathers.

Section 5 will preserve to the People the jury powers our system intended them to have from the beginning. After all, the jury serves as the ultimate civilized check on the power of government, second only to the check on governmental power provided by the 2nd Amendment. Today, government has done all it can to reduce the power of the jury. Judges tell us the jury is allowed to judge only the facts and it is up to the judge to determine the law. If the People are ultimately sovereign, when did they yield this power to judge the law to the judicial department of government? The People didn't. The judicial department of government usurped it.

Our traditions of law and government come from England. The first document upon which our laws and traditions are based is the *Magna Carta* from the year 1215. Chapter 39 of the *Magna Carta* states:

> **"No free man shall be taken, imprisoned, disseised, outlawed, banished, or in any way destroyed, nor will We proceed against or prosecute him, except by the lawful judgement of his peers and by the law of the land."**

The "law of the land" is today what we call "due process." It was an acknowledgment that there was a higher law than the king's law, and it therefore placed the king himself under what later became known as "the laws of Nature and of Nature's God." It was understood by Englishmen that "No person shall be convicted of an unjust law." This formalized the People's right to judge both the law and the facts. After all, how could you have an "unjust law" if you didn't first have over zealous government officials writing unjust laws?

The People's right, as jurors, to judge the law is absolutely fundamental to the People's ultimate sovereignty over their own government. Lose the ability to judge the law, as we have had it hidden from us today, and government gets out of control. These rights don't come easy. King John signed the *Magna Carta* on the meadow at Runnymede while the barons held a sword to his throat. The barons had assembled their forces on that field and were prepared for war. The fact that King John signed it only under threat of war is proof that the *Magna Carta* placed the law above the government. What the barons were willing to die for we let slip away because we weren't paying attention.

The People would also be able to convene a grand jury independently under this Amendment without being dependant on some elected official or bureaucrat to call for a grand jury to be assembled. We have seen time and again how the grand jury process has been manipulated by those who should themselves be the ones investigated.

Section 5, by constitutional amendment, overturns the decision of the United States District Court for the District of Idaho (not the same as the "state of Idaho") when the court found that a federal government employee may murder an American Citizen as long as he had punched the time clock that morning and was still on duty. A grand jury, called by the People, would put a stop to such bad judicial behavior. On the issue of "sovereign immunity" and the idea "the king can do no wrong" the Supreme Court had this to say in the following case:

> **"Counsel for the claimant,...makes a very ingenious argument...That the maxim of English constitutional law, that the king can do no wrong, is one which the courts must apply to the government of the United States, and that therefore there can be no tort committed by the government.**
>
> **It is easy to see how the first proposition cannot have any place in our system of government.**
>
> **We have no king to whom it can be applied. The President, in the exercise of the executive functions, bears a nearer resemblance to the limited monarch of the English government than any other branch of our government, and is the only individual to whom it could possibly have any relation. It cannot apply to him, because the Constitution admits that he may do wrong, and has provided a means for his trial for wrong-doing,...by the proceeding of impeachment.**
>
> **It is to be observed that the English maxim does not declare that the government, or those who administer it, can do no wrong; for it is a part of the principle itself that wrong may be done by the government power, for which the ministry, for the time being, is held responsible; and the ministers personally, like our President, may be impeached; or, if the wrong amounts to a crime, they may be indicted and tried at law for the offense.**
>
> **We do not understand that either in reference to the government of the United States, or to the several States, or of any of their officers, the English maxim has an existence in this country." Langford v. U.S., 101 U.S. 341, 342-3 (1879).**

Today's legal doctrine of "sovereign immunity" for government officials flies in the face of this 1879 quote from the Supreme Court.

Section 6 gives back to the states the power over Congress the states lost with the 17th Amendment. It will also prevent congressional dynasties by implementing term limits. It will serve to mitigate the insanity that occurs within the beltway of Washington, D.C. No longer will Congress be able to manipulate the states with federal money and the strings they attach to it. The states will again have a veto power over Congress. The average citizen will be able to take his most grievous complaints against the federal government to his state legislator, who is much more accessible to him than is a member of Congress. A state legislator once told me that he didn't think the resolutions they send to Congress are worth the paper they are written on. This would no longer be the case if this proposed 28th Amendment becomes part of the Constitution.

And lastly, the restriction on positions that may be occupied by our elected officials will serve to prevent them from wearing multiple hats. In Congress, one minute the members are voting for a measure in their capacity of representative or senator under the organic handwritten Constitution of 1787 for the United States of America. Then a minute later they are voting on a measure in their capacity as officers of the political corporation known as the "United States" created in 1871. Then there is the Secretary of the Treasury, who is also governor of the International Monetary Fund (a private corporation), and so on. Where does a man's loyalty lie when he is serving two masters? Such conflicts of interest would not be allowable under the People's Sovereignty Amendment.

Even if the proposed amendment were to be ratified, it would only be words on paper unless actively enforced by the People. History has shown that, in the absence of oversight from the People, government will become oppressive.

## What You Can Do

First of all, don't put your faith in men, and especially don't put your faith in politicians. One politician will claim he is for big government and the next one will claim he is for limited government, when in fact both are for the Federal Reserve Bank and for global government. On the issue of national sovereignty, there is no difference between the Republicans and the Democrats. The competition between the two parties is just a diversion so that we don't realize we are actually losing our country.

There is a project I would like to pursue. This project is an investigation of the legislative debates that occurred while the 16th Amendment was ratified. Bill Benson and company did a similar investigation which is the subject of Mr. Benson's book *The Law That Never Was*. This project is different in that it will focus on what the intent of the legislatures was in passing the 16th Amendment as well as their understanding of the meaning of the word "income."

We have already seen the answer to these two questions in this book. I just want to pile the evidence higher and deeper. I have done this investigation in the state of Nevada. The journal for the Nevada legislature at the time did not record debates, but only the passage of bills. So no clues were found there. I also looked for committee reports or minutes from committee hearings, but these were not saved back in 1911 when the Nevada Legislature voted on the 16th Amendment. I did investigate the microfiche records for the two local newspapers, *The Carson City Daily Appeal* and the *Reno Evening Gazette*. What I found was no mention in any article of the state's ratification of the 16th Amendment. It was not news. *The Carson City Daily Appeal* had a minuscule reference to it in the type size you normally see the dog racing results reported on the sports page. This entry was so abbreviated the reader wouldn't have a clue as to what it was referring.

Another clue as to the importance of the passage of the 16th Amendment came from a lengthy article which contained the text of Governor Oddie's 1911 State of the State speech to the Nevada Legislature. This speech was given at the same time that the Nevada Legislature was considering the 16th Amendment. Gov. Oddie spent considerable time speaking about unfair taxation, yet never mentioned the 16th Amendment. One can only conclude that the lack of interest in the 16th Amendment was because it did not affect the People of Nevada. They realized it was not going to tax the thousands of miners who worked for wages just over the hill from Carson City in the Virginia City silver mines. These miners obviously understood that the 16th Amendment was only going to tax the accumulated wealth of those who lived in New York City, Boston, Philadelphia, etc., otherwise passage of the amendment would have been news.

I don't have time to go to each of the 50 states to do this research. But you have time to research your own state, or the records of the major newspapers in your state. You can report your findings to me at:

**www.constitutionalincome.com**

You can also check the findings of other people in the country doing similar research at this site.

Don't be sheeple. Turn off the TV, and start researching and studying the law so you can give to your Posterity what our founding fathers gave to us.

Bureaucracies are like weeds; they grow until they die, or until some outside force cuts them back. Congress and our state legislatures are part of the problem. The majority of legislators today would rather violate the Constitution than have a bad day in the newspaper. The American People never consented to this tax as administered. We are being **"taxed without our consent."** This feudal system we suffer under will only be removed when the People throw it off. The income tax on wages and salaries won't go away because someone made a good argument against it. It will only be blown away by the political winds. If you want it to go away, then get busy and become part of that political wind.

The task of throwing off this slave tax will require the collective efforts of tens of thousands or perhaps millions of people. Your help is needed. Only by working together can we restore limited constitutional government and liberty to America.

**Post Script:** What is Constitutional Income? It is net income or annual profit from unincorporated businesses severed from the source. It is also passive annual net income from accumulated wealth as in stocks, bonds, real estate or any other investment. (PH).

# ENDNOTES

## Chapter One: Constitutional Taxation

No Notes

## Chapter Two: A Brief History of "Income" Taxation

1. In the Appellant's briefs for the Pollock Case, counsel for Pollock went into great detail as to the improprieties of Hamilton's conduct during the Hylton proceedings. Hamilton was a federalist and wanted a strong central government. Counsel for Pollock speculated that out of the 125 carriages that Hylton owned "not kept for hire but for use of his own family; 124 of them must have been for use in his castles in Spain." Closing Argument of Appellants, Pollock vs. Farmers' Loan and Trust Co., 157 U.S. 429 (1894).

2. *The Law Practice of Alexander Hamilton*, Vol. IV, pg. 330.

3. *An Inquiry Into One Of The Constitutional Restrictions On The Revenue Powers Of The United States*, by George Ticknor Curtis, Harper's New Monthly Magazine, pg. 356, August, 1866.

4. Albert Gallatin, a member of the House of Representatives from Pennsylvania, introduced the resolution which called for this report. Mr. Gallatin was later Secretary of the Treasury and the author of "Sketches on the Finances of the United States.

5. *The Decline (and Fall?) of the Income Tax*, by Michael J. Graetz, 1997.

6. Many other authorities exist as to why the unconstitutionality of the Civil War income tax was overloaded. See also: The Proposed Income Tax, The Nation, Pages 404-5, November 30, 1893. "The revenue derived [from income taxes] during the [Civil] War is

no criterion whatever. At that time the taxpayers generally cooperated with the collector zealously. Public opinion compelled them to do so. The Nation's life was at stake. Those who were not in the field felt a double obligation to supply the means to support those who were there."

7. Seligman, The Income Tax, supra at 471.

8. Springer's income was $51,255 from his law practice and $161 interest from U.S. bonds and treasury notes. Bill of Exceptions, Exhibit B at 22-23, Springer v. U.S., 102 U.S. 586 (1880).

9. For some reason Springer waited until his Supreme Court trial to submit his first brief. Springer did not assert that he earned wages or a salary but instead that he had a business profit and professional earnings. Springer's failure to assert that he earned a salary or a wage probably proved fatal to his case. Springer was also somewhat careless in his brief having made the following statement: "(i) A tax upon salaries is a direct tax. It falls wholly upon the payer. To call it an indirect tax would do violence to the meaning of the words and would simply be ridiculous. It is unnecessary to cite authorities." Brief for Plaintiff at 6. Springer v. U.S., 102 U.S. 586 (1880).

10. In the second Pollock case Mr. Choate, attorney for Mr. Pollock, argued: "I have examined the exceptions in the case of Springer, as they appear upon the bound records, and I will show to your Honors that within that rule, the established, the universal, the binding rule upon the subject, there was no possibility of the Court's deciding in that case the question to which I refer. Here we have the bill of exceptions, and here we have his return, and it is a very interesting return--$54,504 as a lawyer, $161 as a holder of bonds. Let us see what the exception was...The first one is the only one which relates to the subject. "1. That the tax on the income, gains and profits of the defendant, assessed upon him, as appears by the evidence in this case, was a direct tax within

the meaning of the Constitution of the United States, and that, in order to constitute such a tax a valid claim upon the defendant, it should be apportioned among the several States the same as representatives in Congress are." Now, I say that that exception, within that rule, was too broad, that he could not and did not, even before the Judge at Circuit, by that exception, raise the question whether, as to his $161 of income from bonds, the tax was a direct tax, much less did it point to any such question before the appellate tribunal, so as to either enable or require this Court to pass on that question. This Court had no right to decide such a question upon the exception taken, and he had no right to ask them to decide it. He waived his point, if he had one, but Mr. Springer in waiving the point he had or might have had, cannot give away all the rights of the people of America in other hearings before this Court." Rehearing Closing Argument by Mr. Choate at 62-63, Pollock v. Farmers' Loan and Trust Co., 158 U.S. 606 (1895).

11. *The American Journal of Tax Policy*, Vol. 2, pg. 240 (1983); Hicks, *The Populist Revolt* (1931).

12. *The American Journal of Tax Policy, supra* at 245.

13. *Harvard Law Review*, Vol. 20, pgs. 285-6 (1907).

14. 26 C.F.R. 1.1-1, *Cook v. Tait*, 265 U.S. 47 (1923).

15. The state of Washington cases include *Culliton v. Chase*, 25 P.2d. 81 (1933) and *Jensen v. Henneford*, 53 P.2d. 607 (1936).

16. From Oregon: *Redfield v. Fisher*, 292 P. 813 (1930).

17. From Tennessee: *Jack Cole v. MacFarland*, 337 S.W.2d. 453 (1960).

18. From Arkansas: *Sims v. Ahrens*, 271 S.W. 720 (1925).

19. From Mississippi: *Vicksburg v. Mullane*, 106 Miss. 199, 63 So. 412 (1913).

## Chapter Three: Why was an Income Tax Necessary?

1. In the Pollock Case the Attorney General for the United States Richard Olney understood that the purpose of the income tax was to tax the accumulated wealth of the "wealthy people of this country" as the idea was to shift the tax burden of consumption which bore heavily on the poor and onto accumulated wealth via the income tax. "The only discrimination in our tax laws that will reach wealthy men as against the poorer classes of people is the income tax. There is no other tax on property levied by the United States of America. The tax on legacies and successions, which was in the nature of a property tax, is about to be repealed by the agreement of the committees of both Houses; and the income tax is the only tax levied by us that bears upon property in any shape or manner. All the rest of our taxes, both internal and external, are taxes on consumption. Now, according to every true theory of taxation, a large portion of the taxes ought to fall upon property or income derived from property. * * * I do not find fault with them because they complain of it; but if they would see that it was their property and their rights and their income that was saved by the operation of the war, and that most of the people who pay the taxes on consumption necessarily pay nine-tenths of all the taxes; the property holders and wealthy people of this country ought not to complain if we deem it necessary to maintain this tax at five per cent instead of, as we propose, at three per cent." Brief for the United States at 94-95, Pollock v. Farmers' Loan and Trust Co., 157 U.S. 429 (1894).

## Chapter Four: Pigeon Holes for Taxpayers

1. Herbert W. Titus, God, Man, and Law: The Biblical Principles, Institute of Basic Life Principles, 1998.

2. Exodus 18:13-26

3. There are some authorities that extend the uniformity requirement for indirect taxes to the possessions and territories.

## Chapter Five: Pigeon Holes for Taxes

1. The Association was first called "National Tax Association" but temporarily changed its name to "International Tax Association" when individuals from Canada attended. Mr. Foote was president of the International Tax Association.

2. Albert Gallatin was raised in France, was a member of the Constitutional Convention, a member of Congress and Secretary of the Treasury. On November 12, 1796 he published his famous work entitled "Sketch of Finances of the United States." Mr. Gallatin fully accepted Smith's distinction between indirect and direct taxes while rejecting the French Physiocractic limitation that direct taxes were only capitation taxes and taxes on land. Adam Smith himself also spent two and one-half years in France attending many meetings with the French Physiocratics.

3. Max West was a professor of economics at Columbia University and a contemporary of R. E. Seligman. Professor West provided an expert witness brief for the Pollock Case entitled The Teachings of Political Economists Defining Direct and Indirect Taxes.

4. At the time these industries were monopolies.

5. In the government's Petition for Rehearing after the conclusion of the first Pollock Case, Mr. Richard Olney, Attorney General for the United States, argued: "That such inequalities must result is practically admitted, the only suggestion in reply being that the power to directly tax realty and personalty was not meant for use as an

ordinary, every-day power; that the United States was expected to rely for its customary revenues upon duties, impost and excises; and that it was meant it should impose direct taxes only in extraordinary emergencies and as a sort of dernier resort." Petition for Rehearing at 2, Pollock v. Farmers' Loan and Trust Co., 157 U.S. 489 (1894). In his oral argument for the Pollock Case, Mr. Guthrie, attorney for Pollock said: "The people were told in almost every convention called to consider the adoption of the Constitution that direct taxes would not be laid except in times of war or extraordinary emergencies, and they were assured that duties, imports and excises would suffice for the ordinary requirements of the government." Opening Argument on Behalf of Appellants at 54, Pollock v. Farmers' Loan and Trust Co., 158 U.S. 601 (8195).

## Chapter Six: The 16th Amendment

1. This was submitted by Senator Brown (Nebraska) to the Senate on June 17, 1909.

2. Congress could by statute define the earned income of a government employee to be "wages." Then Congress could levy an indirect tax on these "wages" as this would be a tax on a privilege; the privilege being employment by the federal government. Such a tax is entirely constitutional.

3. *Thorne v. Anderson* is an unplublished case. The case was heard in the October 1915 term of the Supreme Court and carries docket number 394.

4. If Congress identifies the privilege as being taxed, then the rule of uniformity applies. But if the source exists by privilege, and Congress fails to identify the privilege in the taxing statute, then it is not the privilege that is being taxed and the rule of apportionment applies.

5. "An act to reduce taxation (yeah right!), to provide revenue for the government, and for other purposes," passed August 15, 1894.

## Chapter Seven: Income: The Meaning of the Word

No Notes

## Chapter Eight: Where's the Foundation?

1. This statement is from exhibit A in the Springer Transcript of Record. Exhibit A was a schedule of revenue and expenses in the form of an income statement and showed $51,255.08 of net income.

## Chapter Nine: How Do They Do It?

No Notes

## Chapter Ten: The People's Sovereignty Amendment

No Notes

# APPENDIX

## Glossary

**apportionment.** To distribute or allocate proportionally. The determination of the number of members of the U.S. House of Representatives [and share of direct taxes] according to the proportion of the population of each State to the total population of the United States. (Webster's).

**capitation tax**. "The private revenue of individuals, it has been shewn in the first book of this Inquiry, arises ultimately from three different sources: Rent, Profit, and Wages. Capitation taxes, so far as they are levied upon the lower ranks of people, are direct taxes upon the wages of labor." Smith, Adam, Wealth of Nations, pgs. 534, 540 (Prometheus Books, Amherst, New York 1991) (1776).

**direct tax.** Direct taxes fall directly on the person or property taxed. The person or property is taxed solely because the person or property exists. The person or property is diminished by the tax. The tax can not be shifted or avoided. It is not a tax on consumption, on an event, on an activity nor on a privilege.

**indirect tax.** Indirect taxes are either avoidable taxes or taxes that can be passed on. Indirect taxes may be avoided by either refraining from the event, activity or privilege that is taxed, or from refraining from the consumption of the article taxed. Constitutionally, indirect taxes include excises, duties and imposts.

**republican form of government.** "A government constructed on the principle that the supreme power resides in the body of the people. A government which derives all its powers directly or indirectly from the people and which is administered by persons holding their offices for a limited period of time or during good behavior." (citations omitted.) Ballentine's Law Dictionary, (3d ed. 1969).

# Congressional Record Quotes

The following quotes are from the summer of 1909 and are the income tax debates taken from the Congressional Record. The purpose of their inclusion in this appendix is to pile the evidence higher and deeper. The evidence being the legislative intent and the understanding of the people as to its purpose. That purpose being that only net income from personal property or net income from real property was to be taxed by the authority of the amendment. Wages and salaries are outside the scope of the 16th Amendment.

Mr. BAILEY. But knowing, as we all do know, that it is necessary for the Government to raise a vast sum of money to support its administration, my judgement is that a large part of that money ought to be raised from the abundant incomes of prosperous people rather that from the backs and appetites of people who, when doing their best, do none too well. 44 Cong. Rec. 1351 (1909).

The VICE-PRESIDENT. SEC.- . That from and after the 1st day of January, 1910, there shall be assessed, levied, collected, and paid annually upon the gains, profits, and income received in the preceding calendar year by every citizen of the United States, whether residing at home or abroad, and by every person residing in the United States, though not a citizen thereof, a tax of 3 per cent on the amount so received over and above $5,000; and a like tax shall be assessed, levied, collected, and paid annually upon the gains, profits, and income from all property owned and of every business, trade, or profession carried on in the United States by persons residing elsewhere. The tax herein provided for shall be assessed by the Commissioner of Internal Revenue and collected and paid upon the gains, profits, and income for the year ending the 31st of December next preceding the time for levying, collecting, and paying said tax. 44 Cong. Rec. 1352 (1909).

Mr. CUMMINS. I favor an amendment which will accomplish justice throughout the United States. I answer the Senator from Maryland further in this way: the Senator from Maryland further in this way: The amendment which I have offered provides that the tax shall be levied upon all the dividends received from corporations. It is to be levied not only upon all the dividends received from corporations, but it is to be levied upon all undivided surplus or undivided profits of corporations. In that way it reaches every penny that is accumulated by a corporation in the way of net income.

Now, mark you the reason that I prefer to reach the individual directly rather than the corporation is the one I have so repeatedly expressed. If you tax the corporation alone, or if you tax the corporation upon its entire net income, suppose that I were receiving from that corporation and from other sources an income of $100,000—a most impossible hypothesis, but I nevertheless assume it for the moment—and the Senator from Maryland was receiving an income from all sources, partially from the dividends of corporations, of $5,000— 44 Cong. Rec. 1423 (1909).

Mr. SMITH of Michigan. I should like to ask the Senator from Iowa just how he proposes to reach this net income—whether in the form of surplus or undivided profits, where the advantage to the stockholder is in the book value of his stock, or in a suspense account that may not even take the form of surplus? Does the Senator propose to reach that value by some inquisitorial means? 44 Cong. Rec. 1423 (1909).

Mr. CUMMINS. Just wait a moment. Precisely; the individual citizen. It provides that every corporation shall make a report showing its gross income and its net income, showing the amounts that it has paid in the way of interest, in the way of dividends, showing what the amount of the undivided profits of the year are, and also showing the distributive share of each stockholder in the undivided profits, and that is added to the income of the individual precisely as the income that he has actually received in money. 44 Cong. Rec. 1423 (1909).

Mr. SMITH of Michigan. If we are to have an income-tax law, it should be uniform, and it should apply to all people alike, whether natural or artificial, and in proportion to their incomes. 44 Cong. Rec. 1424 (1909).

Mr. BACON. I do not propose now to enter during the debate of the details, but I wanted to bring the attention of the Senator from Iowa to the fact that, with some of us a least , the common ground upon which we base the advocacy of an income-tax law is not that there shall be an increase of revenue, as was suggested by the Senator from Rhode Island in his speech on Monday, but that even if there should be no increase of revenue it may be so readjusted through the enactment of an income-tax law that a large part of the burden of the revenue may fall where it does not now rest, upon the wealth of the country, and that it may be taken off where it now rests in such an intolerable burden, from the masses of the people, destroying their efforts to secure a comfortable living for themselves and their families .44 Cong. Rec. 1429 (1909).

Mr. BACON. I confess that when the Senator from Iowa rose in his place this morning to advocate an income tax, I expected to hear a most instructive and, to me, a most gratifying disquisition upon the suggestion that the income tax was one which should be laid and which should have its greatest foundation in the great necessity to shift the burden of taxation from the shoulders of the ordinary consumers, those who are so little able to bear it, and should rest it in part, at least, so far as the machinery and the constitutional power of this Government may permit, upon the shoulders of those who have the great wealth of the country and who, under our peculiar system of government, bear no appreciable part in the support of the Government resting upon consumers and being almost per capita, regardless of the wealth and ability of the respective citizens to bear each his part.

Therefore, I desired to ask the Senator from Iowa whether of not, in his judgment, the ground for the imposition of the income tax in this particular juncture was rested upon the necessity for an additional revenue, or whether it was rested upon the importance of shifting the burden of taxation from the great masses of consumers, so far as we may be able to do it, to rest it in part, at least, upon the shoulders of those who have the wealth of the country. I wanted to know which, in the opinion of the Senator from Iowa, is the more important consideration, he having given his entire time to the one and having entirely omitted the other. 44 Cong. Rec. 1429 (1909).

Mr. CUMMINS. Simply because if I could change the situation I would so rearrange and readjust these schedules as to decrease the revenue derived from the custom-houses and place it where it should belong—upon those fortunate people who enjoy large incomes. 44 Cong. Rec. 1429 (1909).

Mr. BROWN. I want to suggest to the Senate this afternoon just briefly that if we take everything as true as stated by the Senator from Texas, and if we accept his conclusion as absolutely right, that the decision of the court in the Pollack case was wrong, I ask you, Senators, of what avail that would be to the country or with what satisfaction could it be received? Suppose it be true that we are convinced as Senators that the decision of the court was a mistake, does it help us? Does it help to place the burdens of taxation upon those who are earning the large incomes of the country? 44 Cong. Rec. 1568 (1909).

Mr. BROWN. Now, then... I want to appeal first to those of us who believe in passing a law which shall reach the luxurious incomes of this country and ask them to help pass this resolution that the Constitution may have in it a section that can not be misunderstood. When we have an income-tax law passed, we want the law to be enforceable and to be operative. 44 Cong. Rec. 1569 (1909).

Mr. BROWN. But when the people of this country find that courts are changing their minds on a subject in which they are interested and which they want to have settled, then I contend that it is the duty of Congress to give them an opportunity to settle it themselves by amending the Constitution. 44 Cong. Rec. 1569 (1909).

Mr. BROWN *(Quoting from the dissenting opinion of Justice Harlan in the Pollock case)*.

It tends to reestablish that condition of helplessness in which Congress found itself during the period of the Articles of Confederation, when it was without authority by laws operating directly upon individuals, to lay and collect, through its own agents, taxes sufficient to pay the debts and defray the expenses of government, but was dependent, in all such matters, upon the good will of the States and their promptness in meeting requisitions made upon them by Congress.

Why—

Says the Justice—

do I say that the decision just rendered impairs or menaces the national authority? The reason is so apparent that it need only be stated. In its practical operation this decision withdraws from national taxation not only all incomes derived from real estate, but tangible personal property "invested personal property, bonds, stocks, investments of all kinds," and the income that may be derived from such property. This results from the fact that by the decision of the court all such personal property and all incomes from real estate and personal property are placed beyond national taxation otherwise than by apportionment among the States on the basis simply of population. No such apportionment can possibly be made without doing gross injustice to the many for the benefit of the favored few in particular States. Any attempt upon the part of Congress to apportion among the States, upon the basis simply of their population, taxation of person property or of incomes would tend to arouse such indignation among the freemen of America that it would never be repeated.

Now—listen to the Justice—

When, therefore, this court adjudges, as it does now adjudge, that Congress can not impose a duty or tax upon personal property, or upon incomes arising either from rents of real estate or from personal property, including invested personal property, bonds, stocks, and investments of all kinds, except by apportioning the sum to be so raised among the States according to population, it practically decides that, without an Amendment of the Constitution—two-thirds of both Houses of Congress and three-fourths of the States concurring—such property and incomes can never be made to contribute to the support of the National Government. 44 Cong. Rec. 1569,1570 (1909).

Mr. BROWN. Congress is without power to levy the taxes on this vast volume of property, even though Congress might desire to pass such a law.

Mr. President, it ought to make the blood run to our faces when we stop to think that there is not another enlightened nation on the face of the earth that does not have and exercise the power to levy taxes on this kind of property except ourselves. What is there about this Republic that it should not be clothed with all the rights and powers and prerogatives enjoyed by every other sovereign nation on the face of the earth? 44 Cong. Rec. 1570 (1909).

Mr. BROWN. It is the theory of the friends of the income-tax proposition that property should be taxed and not individuals. I do not believe the fathers ever contemplated that income taxes must be apportioned according to population, but the courts have said that they did. I am here to-day presenting an amendment to the Constitution which will compel the courts to announce the contrary doctrine. 44 Cong. Rec. 1570 (1909).

Mr. BORAH *(Quoting from the biography of John Sherman)*.

While the expenses of the National Government are largely caused by the protection of property, it is but right to require property to contribute to their payment. It will not do to say that each person consumes in proportion to his means. That is not true. Everyone can see that the consumption of the rich does not bear the same relation to the consumption of the poor that the income of the one does to the wages of the other. * * * As wealth accumulates this injustice in the fundamental basis of our system will be felt and forced upon the attention of Congress. 44 Cong. Rec. 1680 (1909).

Mr. BORAH. And another great leader of that era used this language:

There is not a tax on the books so little felt, so absolutely unfelt in the payment of it as this income tax by the possessors of great fortunes upon whom it falls. There is not a poor man in this country, not a laborer in this country but who contributes more than 3, more than 10, more than 20 per cent of all his earnings to the Treasury of the United States, under those very laws against which I am objecting, and now we are invited to increase their contributions and to release those trifling contributions which we have been receiving from incomes heretofore. 44 Cong. Rec. 1680 (1909).

Mr. BORAH. As we contend—those who favor this measure—and as General Harrison said, it is but proper that wealth bear its fair proportion of the burden of government. 44 Cong. Rec. 1681 (1909).

Mr. BORAH. Coming closer home, ex-President Roosevelt, in his message of December 3, 1906, which I read again for fear that it is not remembered , said :

The National Government has long derived its chief revenue from a tariff on imports and from an internal or excise tax. In addition to these there is every reason why, when next our system of taxation is revised, the National Government should impose a graduated inheritance tax and, if possible, a graduated income tax. The man of great wealth owes a peculiar obligation to the state, because he derives special advantages from the mere existence of government. Not only should he recognize this obligation in the way he leads his daily life and in a the way he earns and spends his money, but it should also be recognized by the way in which he pays for the protection the state gives him. On the one hand, it is desirable that he should assume his full and proper share of the burden of taxation; on the other hand, it is quite as necessary that in this kind of taxation, where the men who vote the tax pay but little of it, there should be clear recognition of the danger of inaugurating any such system save in a spirit of entire justice and moderation. Whenever we, as a people, undertake to remodel our taxation system along the lines suggested, we must make it clear beyond peradventure that our aim is to distribute the burden of supporting the Government more equitably than at present. 44 Cong. Rec. 1681 (1909).

Mr. BORAH. I favor an income tax not for the purpose of putting all the burdens of government upon property or all the burdens of government upon wealth, but that it may bear its just and fair proportion of the burdens of this Government.

We believe that every tax system based upon consumption should be supplemented by a system which taxes property and the wealth of the country; not for the purpose of inciting class feeling, but simply calling upon the great interests of the Nation to share that part of the burden of government for which they receive an unquestioned benefit. 44 Cong. Rec. 41682 (1909).

Mr. BORAH. I am not about to discuss the question of the necessity of these ships; that is for another day; but I do say that if we are to build new ships and to continue to compete with the naval building of the world that expense should be visited to some extent at least upon the property and the wealth of this Nation. 44 Cong. Rec. 1683 (1909).

Mr. BORAH. But if it be true that we must continue to do so, upon what basis and upon what theory can men say that the whole burden should rest upon the men who pay practically as much when worth $500 as the man who is worth $500,000,000? Take a part of the burdens off the backs and appetites of men and put it upon the purses of those who will never miss it, those who enjoy the pomp and circumstances of glorious war—without the war. 44 Cong. Rec. 1683 (1909).

Mr. BORAH. The tariff tax—and I am a believer in the American protective policy—reaches at last most heavily the man of limited means. It is passed from the importer to the general merchant to the consumer. When you are taxing personal property, every cow, every horse, every animal, every piece of property that the man of limited means has is found, but the undiscovered millions locked in safe-deposit boxes never pay their proportion of taxes. I favor a system that will get them coming and going, if you can, for that is the only way you can get them at all. 44 Cong. Rec. 1683 (1909).

Mr. BORAH. The economic definition, or the definition given of direct taxes by the economic writers, was a tax which could not be shifted, a tax which must be paid by those against whom it is laid, a tax which must be responded to by the property upon which the charge is made, and which could not be shifted to property or to someone else other than the party against whom the tax was laid. This was illustrated in the Hylton case in the particular statute which was involved. There the tax was laid in one clause of the statutes against the carriage which was used personally by the proper party owning it, and, secondly, carriages used for hire. In one instance the owner must necessarily pay for it. In the other instance the owner might transfer the charge to the party who paid for the use of the carriage. That illustrates the difference between a direct tax and an indirect tax as defined by the economic writers.

This is one of the contentions which has been made in regard to an income tax or the definition of a direct tax from the beginning of the discussion of this matter. It was presented in the first place in the Hylton case. It was re-presented in Seventh Wallace in the Pacific Insurance case. It was re-presented in Eighth Wallace in the Veazie Bank case. It was re-presented in Scholey *v.* Rew in Twenty-third Wallace, and re-presented again in the Springer case. In all these different briefs, which were filed by able counsel, this particular proposition was amplified and urged. It was contended that the framers of the Constitution being familiar with Smith and Turgot and the other economic writers as to what they considered an income tax or a direct tax had followed the definition given by those writers. 44 Cong. Rec. 1694 (1909).

Mr. BORAH. I place my advocacy of the income-tax proposition upon a higher plane than that of raising a little revenue for the Government for the next few years. I believe it involves a great constitutional power, one of the great powers which in many instances might be absolutely necessary for the preservation of the Government itself. I believe that the Constitution as construed is the same as granting an exemption to the vast accumulated wealth of the country and saying that it shall be relieved from the great burden of taxation. I do not believe that the great framers of the Constitution, the men who were framing a government for the people, of the people, and by the people, intended that all the taxes of this Government should be placed upon the backs of those who toil, upon consumption, while the accumulated wealth of the Nation should stand exempt, even in an exigency which might involve the very life of the Nation itself. This can not be true; it was never so intended; it was a republic they were building, where all men were to be equal and bear equally the burdens of government, and not an oligarchy, for that must a government be, in the end, which exempts property and wealth from all taxes. 44 Cong. Rec. 1701(1909).

Mr. BAILEY. Although it is not pertinent to this discussion, I have no hesitation in declaring that a tax on any useful occupation can not be defended in any forum of conscience or of common sense. To tax a man for trying to make a living for his family is such a patent and gross in justice that it should deter any legislature from perpetrating it.

I do not hesitate to say that every occupation tax in America ought to be repealed, because it is a tribute exacted by sovereignty from a man because of his effort to make a living for himself and his family. I do, however, heartily subscribe to the tax upon corporate franchises, because they are the creations of the State and often possess a tremendous value. A franchise of any corporation is valuable. If it were not, the incorporators would not seek it. The value of many has never yet been measured in dollars. Therefore, when the State creates a corporation and endows it with faculties that are so valuable, it should be taxed. 44 Cong. Rec. 1702 (1909).

Mr. BAILEY. But, sir, does the Federal Government protect no right? A costlier one than any State safeguards. The very men with these colossal fortunes are the ones who travel over the world, and about them they carry the American flag, always for their protection. Go and consult the expenditures of the Government. What does this army and what does this mighty navy, whose ships now vex the waters of every sea, cost the American people? More than $200,000,000 a year to maintain them. This vast sum is spent to protect the rights of American citizens at home and abroad. How few of the men who pay this tax on consumption ever invoke the Government's great power to protect them while they travel in a foreign land! Not one of them in ten thousand, because their lean purses do not permit them to indulge in the luxury of foreign travel. It is the rich and prosperous for whose protection these ships and these battalions are sometimes needed. 44 Cong. Rec. 1702 (1909).

Mr. BAILEY. The rights protected by the Federal Government are as essential. And I might also say as sacred, as those protected by the States. If the States lay the cost of the protection which they afford upon the property of men, why should not the Federal Government do likewise? Why is it more just to compel men to contribute according to their wealth to support the state administration than it is to compel them to support the federal administration?

I go further than the Senator from Idaho has gone. I believe not that wealth ought to supplement the tax which consumption pays, but I believe wealth ought to bear it all. I think it is a monstrous injustice for the law to compel any man to wear a suit of clothes and then tax him for buying it. I think it is not right, when God made us hungry, and in obedience to His law we are compelled to appease our appetite, to charge us because we must keep could and body together by taking food. I believe that the Government ought no more to tax a man on what he is compelled to eat and wear than it ought to tax him on the water he drinks or upon the air he breathes. I believe that all taxes ought to be laid on property and none of it should be laid upon consumption.

Mr. President, there is one addition to the property tax that I would make. I would compel a man whose earning power from brain exercised in one of the professions or from inventive genius is great to pay on his income beyond a certain point. When a lawyer like the Senator from New York can earn at the bar, of which I am glad to say he is the honored head, $150,000 every year, I think he ought to be made to pay the Government a tax on that earning power, because in taking from him the small tribute which the law exacts we subtract no comfort from his home. I believe that any man in law or medicine or any other employment in life who exhibits an earning capacity far beyond the necessities of his home ought to be compelled to pay the Government which protects him in the exercise of his talents and in the accumulation of this wealth. He ought to be willing to pay, and I am willing that he should be made to pay. But save and except only this earning capacity of talent or of genius, I would lay every dollar's worth of the Government tax upon the property of men and not upon the wants of men.

None of us, except the simple Democrat of the old-fashioned school, have all we want, but many of us have all we need. After we have satisfied our needs, then the Government has a right to take its toll. 44 Cong. Rec. 1702 (1909).

Mr. BAILEY. While our budget of expense will increase, our most powerful manufactures *(sic)* will continue to outgrow the need for a protective tariff and the great labor unions will protect the wages of our workingmen.

The protective system will remain, but it will be supplemental for revenue purposes by federal taxation upon inheritances and incomes. It is not a socialistic scheme for the redistribution of wealth. It is a plan for an equitable distribution of burdens. There are 7,000,000 families of wage earners in the United States living upon a medium wage of $436 a year and 5,000,000 farmers whose average income is about $350 a year. The vast majority of American families live on $500 or less per year. In the great iron and steel industries, in 1900 , the income of the family was about $540 a year, and in 1905, $580 a year. The cost of living has increased from $74.31 in 1896 to $107.26 in 1906; coal increased in price $1 per ton; manufactured commodities advanced 32 per cent. Under these circumstances, it seems to me that where competition has been destroyed and the market price of the commodity is maintained at a high price by a trust the tariff on that commodity should be materially reduced, if not entirely removed, and that the large incomes, both of individuals and of corporation, should be required by an income tax to bear a larger share of the burden of federal taxation than they do now. 44 Cong. Rec. 1962 (1909).

Mr. DEPEW. There are 15 States with 30 Senators in this body whose aggregate population differs only a few thousand from that of the single State of New York with two Senators. New York has one-seventh of the property of the country. It has one-twelfth of the population. Yet, under an income tax, it would pay 33 per cent of the burdens of the Government. 44 Cong. Rec. 2103 (1909).

Mr. BAILEY. That answer would suffice if we did not have an onerous government to support. But the Senator from Rhode Island can not forget that with eighty years of history behind us—eighty glorious years; eighty years of peace, contentment, and marvelous progress—when the rude alarm of that great war called this country to arms, the expenditures of the Federal Government were only about $60,000,000—a frugal government; a happy people, of simple tastes and habits—and we were expending the sum, then sufficient, now considered paltry, of $60,000,000. Eighty years we lived, we prospered, we were honored abroad and content at home, and yet the expenditures for the federal administration took but $60,000,000 from the energies and from the savings of the American people.

In these last fifty years or less we have multiplied that expenditure from $60,000,000 to $600,000,000, and, not content with that wasteful extravagance, we have now multiplied six hundred million by almost two.

As against the $60,000,000 which the Government was spending in 1861 we have a burden now of more than a billion every year, and yet the Senator from Rhode Island seems to forget that a burden can be as great in time of peace as it is in time of war. Who would have prophesied that the Republican party, born in a protest against what it called the arrogance and wealth of a class, would ever have so forgotten its primitive lessons that now its great leaders stand here and denounce those of us, or, if they do not denounce us, they denounce our protestations against this modern extravagance?

If the Senator from Rhode Island will go back to the earlier and the better, the simpler, and happier days of this Republic and retrench these expenses, I will agree to withdraw the income-tax proposition. In other words, if he will lift the burden under which the toiling and consuming masses are stooping to-today, I will not quarrel with him about how he lifts it. I protest against the injustice which lays upon the people who toil, and who toil, thank God, without much complaint, this enormous burden of a billion dollars every year.

Mr. President, if you will add what our towns, our cities, our counties, and our States are spending, it amounts to more than the value of our cotton and our wheat and our corn crops all combined. This vast sum would be too much for any kind of a government, and for the kind which you are now giving the people it is a criminal waste. 44 Cong. Rec. 2334 (1909).

Mr. BAILEY. For the only law that would conform to the decision of that court would be a law that exempts the incomes arising from colossal fortunes and taxes only the incomes that arise from the exercise of brain and muscle. A good many people would escape the tax if it were laid on the exercise of brain who would have to pay it if it is laid on the income of property. 44 Cong. Rec. 2335 (1909).

Mr. BAILEY. Surely it is as fair to tax a man on an enormous income as it is to tax him on a moderate appetite, and, as between your tariff schedules that tax men on what they eat and wear, and an income tax which assesses them according to what they own, I think the people of this country will have small difficulty in choosing. 44 Cong. Rec. 2447 (1909).

Mr. CUMMINS. So we pass on through the bill, and when we reach that part of our work I believe there will be no doubt in the minds of Senators that we will need some revenue from an income tax. We can then determine better than at any other time whether the tax shall be 2 per cent or 3 per cent or 1 per cent. 44 Cong. Rec. 2448 (1909).

Mr. BAILEY. I not only would make it better in that I would make the duties lower, but I would make it better still in that I would lift from the backs and the appetites of the toiling millions of this Republic and lay a large part of the burden of this Government upon the incomes of those who could pay the tax without the subtraction of a single comfort from their homes. 44 Cong. Rec. 2455 (1909).

Mr. BAILEY. Gentlemen, go ask them; put it to them. Do you believe they are truthful men? Ask them how the vote would stand, and they will answer you as I now declare, that nine men out of every ten believe this is a wise and a just and an equal system of taxation. If it is, you may postpone it, but that is all you can do. You can not ultimately defeat it. You have no chance to reduce the expenditures of the Government, and therefore your only chance to meet these enormous and increasing expenditures is to lay a part of the burden upon the incomes of the rich. 44 Cong. Rec. 2455 (1909).

Mr. NEWLANDS. As the administrative expenses of the Government, amounting to over $600,000,000 annually, are to be paid by taxes on consumption, derived from internal revenue and customs, it is but fair that the additional burden, made necessary by needed public improvements, should be imposed upon wealth; and a tax on the surplus incomes over and above $5,000 annually, gradually increasing with the income, is a tax upon that form of wealth which can best stand the burden. 44 Cong. Rec. 2457 (1909).

Mr. HUGHES. I now call attention to another plank of the Democratic platform, because it would seem that planks in the Democratic platform are not only the subject of thought by Democratic Senators, but are giving concern to Republican Senators and find their way in some mysterious manner into the executive chamber at the White House. It contains this language:

We favor an income tax as part of our revenue system, and we urge the submission of a constitutional amendment specifically authorizing Congress to levy and collect a tax upon individual and corporate incomes, to the end that wealth may bear its proportionate share of the burdens of the Federal Government. 44 Cong. Rec. 3444 (1909).

That is not all, Mr. President. I sat here and listened with pleasure to the reading by the senior Senator from Indiana [Mr. BEVERIDGE] of extracts couched in clear and forceful English announcing the position of the President-expectant of the United States at that time in construction of the Republican platform. I shall call attention also to some expressions upon the income-tax law and the propriety of bringing to the attention of the Supreme Court again the constitutionality of such an act uttered by the same distinguished author in an address delivered before the Buckeye Club at Columbus, Ohio, August 19, 1907. He said:

A graduated income tax would also have a tendency to reduce the motive for the accumulation of enormous wealth, but the Supreme Court has held an income tax not to be a valid exercise of power by the Federal Government. The objection to it by from a practical standpoint is its inquisitorial character and the premium it puts on perjury. In times of great national need, however, an income tax would be of great assistance in furnishing means to carry on the Government, and it is not free from doubt how the Supreme Court, with changed membership, would view a new income-tax law under such conditions. The court was nearly evenly divided in the last case, and during the civil war great sums were collected by an income tax without judicial interference and, as it was then supposed, within the federal power. 44 Cong. Rec. 3445 (1909).

Mr. CUMMINS. That ours proposes a tax upon all the large incomes, whether they are individual or corporate, while the amendment, if we are to be advised by the papers and the influences which are now controlling, proposed by the Committee on Finance, is an income-tax amendment, to be imposed only upon the stockholders of corporations, whether their incomes be large or whether they be small. Here is an issue joined, and my suggestion now is for unanimous consent to decide that issue in a fair, clear vote between the proposal that will be made by the committee and the proposal already before the Senate. 44 Cong. Rec. 3484 (1909).

Mr. HUGHES. But if gentlemen on the other side believe otherwise and claim more revenue is necessary, not for an economical administration of public affairs, but for the purpose of carrying out

Republican political schemes—some of which you now have under advisement—then, I say, that instead of raising the revenue from the poor, from the producers and the consumers of the country, you should raise this additional revenue by a tax on the trusts and the accumulated and idle wealth of the land. That would be fairer, more equitable, and more consistent.

....I am in favor of making the idle wealth, the monopolies, and all these great trusts, giant corporations, and selfish syndicates do what the Republican party by law compels the toilers, the producers, and the consumers to do, and that is to pay the taxes—pay their just share of the expenses of the Government.

By a graduated corporation tax and a graduated inheritance tax we would lift the tax burdens from the farmers, the workingmen, and the consumers and place them where they justly belong, besides establishing publicity and to some extent preventing the watering of stocks and the centralization of wealth.

....What question is under consideration? The question of revenue—a question which involves the consideration of every subject that may justly be taxed. It involves the consideration of the equality of burdens—of the proper apportioning of burdens. It involves a consideration of the question whether a portion at least of this extraordinary tax levied for the purpose of carrying on a war justified by wealth should not be imposed upon wealth, particularly when under existing conditions the accumulated wealth of the country has for years practically escaped taxation.

I present no indictment against wealth as such. There are two classes of wealth in this country. One class—the majority, as I believe—consists of law-abiding persons who are willing to bear their fair proportion of the obligations of government; who are willing to sustain their fair proportion of government burdens; not eager to obtain exemption; not eager to obtain special privileges; not eager to utilize the functions of government for their own advancement.

Then there is another class of wealth—the lawless and the predatory wealth of the country—which seeks special exemptions, which seeks special privileges, which seeks to evade and escape the burdens of taxation, which seeks to pervert to its own advancement the functions of government. It is that form of wealth which brings conservative wealth under discredit and creates the discontent that finds its vent in communism and socialism. 44 Cong. Rec. 3761 (1909).

## TAXES ON INCOMES

Mr. CLAY. Mr. President, if the Senator's position is consistent, the very minute that we adopt the corporation tax raising $50,000,000, the Senator will turn to the woolen schedule—and I know of no subject that needs more attention at the hands of the Senate and the Finance Committee than the sugar schedule—and cut the duties on the necessities of life equal to the amount that will be produced by the corporation tax.

Mr. President, I expect to vote in favor of an income tax. If I knew that you were going to put $60,000,000 into the Treasury and not reduce the duties on the necessaries of life, I would say that you were unnecessarily taxing the people. 44 Cong. Rec. 3929 (1909).

Mr. CLAY. I will vote for an income tax, because I believe it to be right, and I would continue to battle before the country to induce the country to send Representatives to Congress who would enact it into a law and who would reduce the tariff duties on the necessities of life in proportion to the amount raised by an income tax.

I want to ask the Senator a question. If we are to raise $50,000,000 per year by a tax on corporation dividends, does the Senator think that such a tax is a vicious assault upon the protective system; and, second, if this bill, as it stands, will produce enough revenue to support the Government and we adopt the corporation tax, raising $50,000,000, does not the Senator think we ought to take up some of the other schedules of this bill and reduce the duty in proportion to the amount that we raise by the corporation tax?

Mr. ALDRICH. Does the Senator from Georgia want an answer?

Mr. CLAY. I would not have asked the question if I did not.

Mr. ALDRICH. I shall vote for a corporation tax as a means to defeat the income tax.

Mr. CLAY. I think that is an honest statement. 44 Cong. Rec. 3929 (1909).

Mr. DIXON. President Roosevelt in his message to Congress on the 4th day of December, 1906—and I want the junior Senator from Idaho to listen to this—said, in reference to inheritance and income taxes:

There is every reason why, when our next system of taxation is revised, the National Government should impose a graduated inheritance tax, and if possible, a graduated income tax. The man of great wealth owes a peculiar obligation to the State, because he derives special advantages from the mere existence of government. 44 Cong. Rec. 3945 (1909).

Mr. OWEN. Mr. President, I do not agree with the Senator from Montana [Mr. Dixon] that the psychological moment is at hand for the adoption of the inheritance tax. I have not the slightest idea that there is any probability of the programme laid down by the committee being changed in any respect. But I am in thorough accord with the view of the Senator from Montana in regard to the wisdom and propriety of an inheritance tax. I favor, equally, the income tax But I regard the inheritance tax as a matter of far greater importance, and that it ought to be added to our permanent fiscal system, not only for the purpose of raising revenue, but for the further and more important purpose of abating the increasing danger of the accumulations of fortunes swollen beyond all reason, which now constitute a menace to the stability of our finance and of our commerce and to the liberties of the people of the United States and of the civilized world.

I suggest to the Senate a progressive inheritance-tax amendment, which I ask the Secretary to read... 44 Cong. Rec. 3950 (1909).

Mr. OWEN. Where do the city laborers under protection come in as joint heirs of modern prosperity?

What part of this wealth created by labor is theirs?

They have no real estate, no live stock, farm machinery, manufacturing machinery, railroads, or under any visible classification. The only thing that they can have under this tabulation is clothing and a little personal property.

And yet the products of the labor in our specified manufacturing industries of 1905 reached a total of $14,802,147,087, for 5,470,321 wage-earners, whose product was therefore worth $2,708 per capita.

These people received $2,611,540,532 in wages (Stat. Abst. U.S. 1907, p. 144), or $479 per capita.

This $479 each must feed and shelter and clothe and educate and provide leisure and the joyous participation in the common providences of God for an average of three people, or about $160 each per annum, or about an average of $13.33 per month. 44 Cong. Rec. 3950 (1909).

Mr. President, it takes a human being of the first magnitude to administer an estate of $10,000,000 with wisdom and efficiency. No human being can properly consume the income of such an estate, which, at 5 per cent, will make an income of $500,000 per annum, $1,366 per diem—about a hundred dollars an hour for every waking hour.

Since such vast sums of money can not properly used by the individual in the gratification of any just personal needs, and since its possession frequently leads to the wildest extravagances, to the establishment of false standards of life, and often leads to harmful dissipation and vice, and sometimes even to the corruption of our legislatures, or our administrative offices, and of the judiciary itself in the crafty ways by which we all know human beings can be misled, a wise public policy should establish a system of government which will restore to the people so much of the swollen fortunes developed by our modern methods as justice demands.

No thoughtful student will deny that these gigantic fortunes represent values created by the labors and the activities of our people. No man can deny the moral righteousness of restoring to the people by legacy duty that which they have created and which has been taken from them under legal processes and by fair legal means, in the best view of the case, and by crafty, unfair, and illegal means in the worst view of the case. 44 Cong. Rec. 3951 (1909).

Mr. OWEN. I call the attention of the Senate to this important fact in considering this matter, that whenever a fortune grows very large the owner of that fortune can easily transfer his residence from a State which has an inheritance-tax law, and in that manner evade it. For that reason it is of the highest importance that the Federal Government should lay its hand upon the inheritance tax and upon the gigantic fortunes which are build up under our system of laws permitting monopoly to grow and flourish in this country, so that, at the death of the ambitious individual who has profited by our system, the people of the United States may have restored to them that which has been created by their labor. 44 Cong. Rec. 3953 (1909).

Mr. OWEN. When this policy shall have been adopted by the people of the United States, it will check the very dangerous accumulations of gigantic fortunes which now comprise a serious menace to the people of the United States. Where a single fortune reached a thousand millions and an annual income of fifty millions, increasing, as it must, in compounding geometric ratio and being typical, it is obvious that such an unequal distribution of the proceeds of human labor is not only unjust, unwise, but is dangerous to the peace and stability of the world.

Fifty millions of annual accumulations in one hand means the deprivation of many millions of people of a part of their slender earning, and the accumulated force of all the demands of all of the great fortunes of the country with their total exactions, means the impoverishment of the weaker elements of society by artificial exaction, depriving them of their reasonable opportunity to the enjoyment of life, of liberty, of the pursuit of happiness, and the enjoyment of the fruits of their own industry. 44 Cong. Rec. 3953 (1909).

Mr. CUMMINS. The issue, Senators, is plain and simple. I do not intend to hide behind any technicalities. I do not intend to be disturbed by mere names. I intend, if I can, to penetrate to the very heart of the thing; and I want to begin what I have to say by making it clear that the income-tax amendment proposed by the Senator from Texas [Mr. BAILEY] and myself rests as a burden only upon those natural and artificial persons with incomes of more than $5,000; but the income tax presented by the Finance Committee, and explained so clearly by the Senator from California [Mr. FLINT], rests upon the incomes of all the stockholders of our corporations, whether such stockholders be rich or poor, with little or great incomes, and upon many members of insurance companies, without regard to their ability to bear these additional burdens.

....This tax proposed by the committee is not fair; it is not equal; it does not distribute the burdens of government as they ought to be distributed; it does not put upon the shoulders of those who can best bear the weight of this great structure; but, without any regard to ability to pay or bear, it puts the burden on a certain class of men, namely, those who have invested their capitol in the stock of corporations. 44 Cong. Rec. 3955 (1909).

Mr. CUMMINS. Mr. President, I repeat that I do not wonder it is somewhat difficult to secure a quorum this morning, because it is uncomfortable in every sense. The weather is disagreeable. The amendment we are considering ought to make people uncomfortable. We are told by the morning's paper that the distinguished chairman of the Finance Committee has gone upon a sea voyage. I hope that it is true, for he has not only earned a rest during the last few weeks, but after the acknowledgment which he made yesterday to the Senate with respect to his motive in bringing forward the amendment we are now considering he needs the inspiration and the recuperation of a sea voyage. I would want to take a trip lasting about a thousand years if I should be compelled to make a confession of that sort with respect to a bill brought forward by myself. I will give some attention to that particular phase of the matter a little bit later. 44 Cong. Rec. 3959 (1909).

Mr. CUMMINS. I have sometimes thought that the propositions for reductions in the army, in the navy, and in the civil establishment can be traced to the same source that was yesterday uncovered by the Senator from Rhode Island, when he declared that the purpose of this amendment is simply to defeat the income tax amendment. 44 Cong. Rec. 3964 (1909).

Mr. CUMMINS. When you ask them to choose between placing the burden of government upon wealth, upon those who enjoy incomes of more than $5,000, and placing the burden of government upon the necessities of life, or even upon the luxuries of life, which they must buy abroad, they will not be slow in answering the question thus put to them. So I say that every protectionist, every man who desires an ally for protection, ought to stand firm for the adoption of some permanent supplement to our revenue.

Nor is the income-tax law inconsistent with the doctrine maintained by Senators upon the other side of the Chamber. Standing, as they do, for a tariff for revenue, it is still true that an income tax, levied upon those who ought to bear the burdens of government, those who are able to bear the burdens of government, will meet even that principle more perfectly than to levy duties upon the things that the people must use, and impose the weight of government only by the rule of consumption. It is consistent with the doctrine of protection, and it is consistent with the doctrine of a tariff for revenue. It bears just the same relation to both that our internal-revenue taxes bear to taxation at the custom-house.

I intend to consider presently the constitutional situation; but I want now, if I have been successful in showing that you are to be met with a deficit, to ask how are you going to meet it? You can not meet it by direct taxation. You know as well as I that the people of the United States would not submit for a single year to a tax levied according to the rule of apportionment. I care not whether direct taxes include something more than land. I care not what they include; but the Senate knows—every Senator knows—that the time has passed forever at which the Government of the United States will lay any tax by the rule of apportionment. Wealth and population have so far separated themselves in the United States that no man is or will be venturesome enough to suggest that a permanent income of the United States be raised by a tax levied according to the population of the several States.

If, therefore, you are not to adopt some form of direct taxation, you are remitted to some form of indirect taxation; and what shall it be? If it is your duty to provide for sixty millions or seventy-five millions or one hundred millions of dollars to meet the necessities of the Government in the next few years, how will you do it? You must adopt one of three general forms of taxation. 44 Cong. Rec. 3968 (1909).

Mr. CUMMINS. Senators, I can not conceive how there can be objections to the justice of an income-tax law. It places the burdens where they belong; it discards unproductive property and unprofitable labor, and exacts but a small percentage of gains and profits and earning actually received. It is impossible to conceive of any injustice in taking a little part of a surplus in hand over and above a most liberal allowance for the maintenance of a family. It exacts not a penny that is in fact needed for either the necessities, the comforts, or the luxuries of life. 44 Cong. Rec. 3969 (1909).

Mr. HEYBURN. The tax provided for in the amendment under consideration by the Senator is an excise tax. It is a tax, a proportion, cut out of something. 44 Cong. Rec. 3969 (1909).

Mr. CUMMINS. Of course now even that has passed away. As I said long ago, there never will be a Congress, unless the very life of the Nation is at stake, that will levy a direct tax. A tax upon land levied now would be intolerable, distributed among the States according to their population. You will never read in the whole future history of the United States a suggestion with respect to levying a direct tax, and whatever taxes Congress does employ must be indirect taxes. Therefore the term "direct taxes" should be limited to the fewest possible objects. So the court in the Hylton case decided that direct taxes embrace nothing but poll taxes and taxes upon land with its improvements. 44 Cong. Rec. 3973 (1909).

Mr. CUMMINS. What is the general income tax? It is a tax laid upon every income, whether of individuals or of corporations, that exceeds $5,000. It is fair; it is just; it makes all men under like conditions contribute equally to the support of the Government. What is the amendment which is proposed by the committee? I shall not now attempt to describe it in technical language. I describe it in commonplace language. With our amendment, every man who had an income of more than $5,000 or every corporation that had an income of more than $5,000, would have been compelled to have paid 2 per cent upon the income in excess of $5,000 for the support of the Government.

And what does the committee amendment mean? Needing a revenue, as we do need a revenue, it proposes that every man who has a share of stock in a corporation, whether he has an income of a hundred dollars or a million dollars, shall pay a part of the expenses of the Government because he is a shareholder in a corporation. 44 Cong. Rec. 3975 (1909).

Mr. BRANDEGEE. I understood the Senator from Iowa to state that the proposed committee amendment is not really a tax upon corporations, but is a tax upon the stockholders or upon the dividends of the corporation. If that is so, is not the same thing true of the proposed income tax upon corporations contained in the Senator's proposed amendment?

Mr. CUMMINS. It is, with this difference: In the amendment I propose if the total income of the shareholder does not reach $5,000, he is then not taxed. It preserves the central, fundamental idea of an income tax. In the case proposed by the committee, if a poor devil has 1 share of stock in a corporation, and it is all the income he has, he is nevertheless taxed. My desire is to relieve the incomes of men to the extend necessary to maintain their families, to support and educate their children, because I believe that they owe a higher duty to their families than they owe to the Government.

Mr. GALLINGER. Mr. President–

The PRESIDING OFFICER. Does the Senator from Iowa yield to the Senator from New Hampshire?

Mr. CUMMINS. I do.

Mr. GALLINGER. The Senator meant to day, I assume, that if the income in the first place added to other items of income does not aggregate $5,000, the man is not taxed?

Mr. CUMMINS. Precisely—in our case?

Mr. GALLINGER. Yes.

Mr. CUMMINS. That is true. Possibly I ought to correct that. I had it in my mind. The effect of our amendment is that no tax is laid upon a person unless his income from all sources exceeds $5,000; while in the proposal of the committee the tax is laid upon the income of every shareholder of a corporation that has a net income of more than $5,000, without regard to the extent of the individual income, whether that is the only income the shareholder receives or whether he receives other income from different sources.

That is the injustice of this proposal. It is not in accord with the humane civilization of this age. It is not in accord with the modern thought. It totally disregards every advance we have made in these years toward relieving those who are unable to bear the burdens of government from a greater share than is necessary, and giving them, as I said before, the opportunity to devote the first of their energies, the first of their income, the first of their earnings, to a dearer and more sacred object than the maintenance of the Government, viz, the maintenance of their citizenship and the support of their families. 44 Cong. Rec. 3975 (1909).

Mr. CUMMINS. It is very easy to point out the distinction to one who listens with open mind. To one who hears with a determination to arrive at a certain conclusion, it is utterly useless for me to point out either the distinction or to reconcile the differences. However, there is no inconsistency in the attitude I assume in regard to the income of individuals. I believe all income-tax laws ought to be imposed only upon the incomes of individuals, because corporations are simply the instrumentalities for creating and passing property from the artificial body to the possession of its members, and all the wealth of the country would be so taxed. 44 Cong. Rec. 3978 (1909).

Hon. J.P. DOLLIVER,
Washington, D.C.
**DEAR SENATOR:**

...The writer has always understood the economic principle of an income tax to be that when an individual's income became sufficient to support himself and family in a high degree of comfort any further increase of that income—which could only serve the purpose of luxury or more extensive investment—should be subject to a special tax for the common good; in short, the surplus income of one would be taxed to relieve a similar burden upon the scant income of another.

Very truly, yours,
**SECURITY TRUST AND SAVINGS BANK,**
Charles City, Iowa, June 24, 1909 44 Cong. Rec. 3982 (1909).

---

Hon. A. B. CUMMINS.
Washington, D.C.
**MY DEAR SENATOR:**

I feel that it is the duty of every citizen to express himself upon the proposed corporation income tax. It seems to me that of all the unfair propositions that was ever proposed, this one takes the cake. While personally I would not be in favor of an income tax, still, an income tax upon all income, it seems to me, would be "a king" compared to the corporation income tax which is proposed.

In every progressive community at the present time a large part of the business which is a benefit to the community and to the laboring man is conducted by corporations. These corporations are in almost every instance backed and supported by the men who believe in keeping their money at work for the good of his city. In order to do this he must invest his money in corporations doing business in his city.

There is another class of men in every community who have amassed fortunes, which they see fit to hold and only use for their own personal benefit to see how much "per cent" they can receive upon it, who never take any interest in the community and never do anything which will benefit anybody except themselves.

Yours, very truly,

**BETTENDORF METAL WHEEL COMPANY**

*Davenport, Iowa, June 21, 1909* 44 Cong. Rec. 3982 (1909).

Mr. BORAH. But I want to inquire first, Mr. President, who is to pay the tax we are about to levy? It has been given out to the country, and has been somewhat extensively assumed, that this is another means of placing a tax upon the wealth of the country; that by this process of singling out corporations we will reach the wealth of the land rather than place a tax upon consumers, or that great body of American citizenship which now bears its undue proportion of the taxes of the country. I am very frank to say that if I were convinced of that one proposition as stated by those who support this tax—that it will reach the wealth of the country—I should support it as a temporary measure, for the purpose of wiping out the deficit that now confronts us. I would not support it as a permanent measure, for the reason that I know that it can not and will not reach that already earned, now inactive, wealth which pays practically no tax, and never will if certain influences in this country can have their way. But as I am convinced beyond all question that by this means we are about to proceed, under a thin guise of doing otherwise, to place another heavy burden and tax upon those who already bear an unjust and undue proportion of the burdens of the Government, I prefer, rather than to support the tax, to go back to the statesman-like view announced by the Senator from Rhode Island in the opening of this tariff debate. That is to say, if we can not by the tariff bill raise sufficient revenue to run the Government, I should resort to extreme measures of retrenchment in expenditures rather than place this extra burden upon the great mass of American citizenship. ....My enthusiasm has arisen out of the proposition that it will enable us to distribute the already great burden of government between consumers and wealth. But if we are now to lay a tax—as I believe we are about to do—which will finally rest not upon wealth, but upon consumption, then I go back to the principle announced by the Senator from Rhode Island, and say that it is our duty as Senators to accept his statement that it is our duty as Senators to accept his statement that if there is not sufficient revenue to run the Government we must retrench. For, to my mind, it is almost a moral crime to place an additional expense upon the very people who are today bearing the great burdens of government. 44 Cong. Rec. 3985 (1909).

Mr. BORAH. Yet while the interested American people are looking on, thinking that we are trying to get a tax upon wealth, we are solemnly engaged in putting this burden where it will not be confined to corporations, but will all be charged to those who deal with them, by adding the tax to the price or reducing wages. 44 Cong. Rec. 3986 (1909).

Mr. BORAH. While the Senator does not seem to appreciate the fact, he has submitted here a reason why every Senator ought to support an income tax and should oppose this corporation tax, because it does not lie within the ingenuity of man to place the burden of taxation, as it should be placed, with equal force upon wealth and consumption, in spite of anything and all we may do. Our system of taxation is based upon the principle that the incident to the tax finally reaches the low man, the bottom man, in this cruel and merciless system of ours. The only thing we can do is to mollify it as much as it is possible to do, and we can only mollify it by taxing those things where they cannot shift it. But instead of undertaking to tax things where they can not shift it, we always exempt them from taxation and put it where they can shift it.

Unquestionably the great trusts of this country have transferred their taxes to the consumer. Unquestionably the great corporations of this country have transferred their taxes to the consumer to a very large and alarming extent. The men who do not transfer their taxes and can not transfer them are the uncounted holders of uncounted millions of bonds whom we are exempting from this proposed law at the present time. 44 Cong. Rec. 3987 (1909).

Mr. BORAH. I want to call the attention of the Senate to the fact, however, that there are a great many people in this country today enjoying incomes that they did not make a single dollar of; that they do not even furnish sufficient brains to take care of for any reasonable length of time, and have to have guardians appointed. They ought to pay some of the expense of the Government also.

There are vast incomes that the people who are enjoying them did not make any more than the unborn children made the property of their parents. 44 Cong. Rec. 3987 (1909).

Mr. BORAH. I do not want the Senator from Utah to forget that this contest in this Senate Chamber is not over the raising of a small temporary revenue, but it is over the proposition of whether we shall change the great principle of taxation in this country and place a part of the tax where it can not be shifted to the common citizenship of the country. We are not going to go back, Mr. President, to the owls and bats. Rather than to say we shall not put a part of this tax where it can not be shifted, we shall continue this contest until the uncontrollable wrath of the American people shall waken us to the fact that the great disparity between wealth and poverty in this country arises more out of our system of taxation than it does from the so-called "trusts." When you can put all the burden of government in one place, it is not long before you have that condition of affairs, whether it is in a republic or a monarchy, where the great masses are bearing the burden and the few are living upon the efforts of the masses.

Mr. President, to illustrate further, our system of taxation had its origin in the period of feudalism, when the tax was laid upon those, and those only, who could not resist the payment of it. That was the first tax under our present taxing system. The plan then was, as stated by a noted writer—and it was earnestly argued in those days—that it was a proper distribution of the burdens of government that the clergy should pray for the government, the nobles fight for it, and the common people should pay the taxes. The first fruits of that system, and the first modification of that system, were had during that economic and moral convulsion which shook the moral universe from center to circumference–the French revolution. Historians dispute to-day as to the cause of the French revolution. If you would know the cause, you will not find it in the days transpiring with the fall of the Bastile; you will not find it in the days when Robespierre, drunk with human blood, leaned against the pillars of the assembly, as he listened to his own doom. It is back of that. It is in those immediate years preceding, when the burden of government had become intolerable, when the stipends paid to the miserable satellites of royalty had become criminal, when bureaucracy reached out into every part of the nation and bore down upon the energies and the industries of the common man; and when, Mr. President, 85 per cent of that fearful burden was collected from the peasantry of France, which forced them from their little homes and farms into the sinks and dives of Paris, where the French revolution was born.

The history of taxation is well worthy of the attention of those who believe that, in order to maintain a republic, we must always have at the base of our civilization an intelligent , free, and, to some extent, an unburdened citizenship. No, Mr. President, we will not repeal all taxes,; but we will distribute the burdens; though we may not do it this session, and I do not suppose we will, we will do it before this fight is over.

....Whether from one motive or another, the result of it is that the great corporations, controlling the great industries in this country, are standing side by side with the Committee on Finance in support of this proposition in preference to the income tax. Why? Because they can transfer this tax; while that class of men, that vast amount of wealth to which the Senator from Iowa [Mr. CUMMINS] called attention, can not transfer. 44 Cong. Rec. 3989 (1909).

Mr. BORAH. That is one of the objections; but that is the slightest objection, in my judgment. The great objection is that it reaches a class of people, burdens a class of people who are already overburdened with taxation, and does not reach the class of people who ought to pay the tax and who ostensibly we seek to reach. 44 Cong. Rec. 3994 (1909).

Mr. BORAH. In other words, the Senator rather than to breach the rule of courtesy which would pass this great question up to the Supreme Court, rather than to tread upon that delicate ground, so called, would continue to levy this tax upon those who are now bearing the burden, would continue to leave the burden already there, and then levy more. Why would it not be better to consider a little the interests of the people and not quite so much the dignity of the court? 44 Cong. Rec. 3994 (1909).

Mr. BORAH. But, Mr. President, I am in deadly earnest about this proposition. I believe the income tax to be absolutely essential to preserve the harmony between wealth and consumption which is necessary in order to preserve the golden thread of equality which lies at the base of republican forms of government. Moreover, I believe—using the expression in as respectful a manner as I can—that, whether so designed or not, this tax is in effect a subterfuge for the defeat of that great measure. Therefore Senators will not blame me if, in my humble way, I gather up what proof I can as to both the justice of the income tax and the injustice of this tax, in order to do what I can to see that my party does not assume this responsibility. 44 Cong. Rec. 3996 (1909).

Mr. BORAH. In the first place, I do not claim that an income tax is a panacea for all the evils that afflict the race. I do not claim that it will adjust all the iniquities of taxation. I only claim that it will reach that class of wealth which to-day does not in my judgment pay its proportion of taxation, and will reach that class of wealth which can not shift the tax to the consumer.

It has been said many times that the income tax should be regarded purely as a war measure; that it was regarded by the Republican party as a war measure; and that it was repealed after the war closed because it was regarded as a war measure. In my judgment, in the light of history, that is an incorrect interpretation of the facts. It was repealed in 1870. It was repealed after a vigorous protest upon the part of the very greatest leaders of the Republican party. It was repealed by a bare margin of one vote. It was repealed at a time when Sherman, Morton, Garfield, McCreary, Howe, and all that class of men were standing forth in its defense, not as a temporary war measure, but as a permanent part of the revenue system of the United States. The men who had seen it in operation, who knew how it was administered, who knew the effect of its administration, and whose power to judge can not be questioned, insisted that the repeal of the income tax was unjust, as Morton said, to the great mass of the American people. You will look in vain through the arguments of those men to find an argument sustaining it upon the theory that it should be used only in times of stress.

It was repealed, Mr. President, by means of that power, of that influence , regardless of party lines, which has stood like a solid phalanx against its reenactment. It was repealed because of the fact that there were those who believed that it was better to levy the entire burden upon consumption than to levy any part of it upon wealth. What the reason for believing it was I will leave for those to judge who care to look into the debate.

Mr. McCreary, at the time of its repeal, said:

Mr. Speaker, there is another consideration which, to my mind, is entirely conclusive against the abolition of the income tax. It is the only mode by which a large part of the wealth of this country can be taxed at all. * * * Abolish the income tax and the man who has his fortune in those bonds, and so forth, will continue to receive his interest and contribute nothing to the support of the Government, either state or national.

General Garfield said:

Whenever a man terminates his active career in life and becomes a mere capitalist, living upon the profits of his wealth invested in some permanent form that man's income should pay a tax.

Senator Morton, of Indiana said:

If the wealth is in the hands of the few, there is where the tax should come from, because they have got it. 44 Cong. Rec. 3997 (1909).

Mr. BORAH. Let me submit this final question, then, to the friends of the income tax: Suppose we reject this income-tax amendment upon the theory that the decision of the Supreme Court is correct. That decision receives our indorsement, and if it can be made final, our action would have that effect. Then suppose we go into the campaign with the States and 12 States decide against the amendment. Then the fight is over, and the accumulated wealth of this country has won the greatest victory in the history of republican government.

Mr. President, in conclusion I want to urge, with all the power at my command, that those who consider an income tax from the standpoint of a revenue-producing proposition, after we have reached the point beyond which consumption can bear no greater burden, tear away the great equitable and moral basis upon which our whole contention rests. If we were compelled to rest it upon the argument of expediency we would still be upon solid ground, for even now, while we are in the full tide of national growth and development and in a time of peace, we have a deficit of a hundred million dollars, which, it seems to me, the incomes of this country could well afford to wipe out. The time will not soon come, if we care to test the system to its utmost, when we can not raise enough revenue under our present system to maintain the Government, for men must eat, and civilized men must clothe their persons; but it is unjust and unfair, tyrannical, and, to my mind, brutal to hold on to a system of taxation which continues to put all the burden, the ever-increasing burden of government, the maintenance of our army, of our navy, upon what we must eat and upon what we must wear, and nothing upon the great incomes which fools so often flaunt in the face of the poor and which lead to all kinds of extravagance and public demoralization. There is no possible justification for such a system, except the bias and stubbornness of custom and precedent on the one hand and the viciousness of greed on the other. 44 Cong. Rec. 3999 (1909).

Mr. BORAH. But it is said to be socialistic. The great and honored lawyer, Joseph Choate, the pride of two hemispheres, hard pressed for legal arguments against the tax in the Pollock case, turned and denounced the tax as socialistic—socialistic to lay a fair tax upon wealth, to sustain and keep in operation a great constitutional government. When the State or the Government sees fit to lay a tax which may take 30 per cent of the income, the fruits of the labor, of the man of ordinary means, that is the exercise of constitutional power.

But when you lay a tax of 2 per cent upon incomes, so slight a burden that it would scarcely be felt, that is socialism. Man's intelligence should not be so universally discredited. 44 Cong. Rec. 3999 (1909).

Mr. ROOT. In 1906, there was a special committee of the House of Commons raised for the purpose of reexamining the whole subject, and they reported in 1907, and upon their report the British system has been largely modified, and they reported a different scale of imposition upon the incomes that were earned and which were therefore part capital from that which they imposed upon incomes coming from invested capital.

It is not just, and it is universally recognized by the people who have thought carefully and deeply upon this subject that it is unjust, to take a man who is in the enjoyment of a few years of earning capacity—it may be ten or twenty or thirty—when he is turning into money his brains and his nerves and his life; when, if he is wise, if he has a grain of common sense, if he possesses those qualities that we all of us wish to foster and encourage among our people, he will be laying up a portion of that income against the days of his age and his illness and the wants of his family, and impose upon that income, the part that he lives on and the part that he is accumulating as capital, the same imposition that is put upon the income that his neighbor gets from invested securities that last forever. Now, I say the latest and the most considerate treatment of the subject of income tax makes a careful distinction between those two.

Mr. President, it has so happened that in the development of the business of the United States the natural laws of trade have been making the distinction for us, and they have put the greater part of the accumulated wealth of the country into the hands of corporations, so that when we tax them we are imposing the tax upon the accumulated income and relieving the earnings of the men who are gaining a subsistence for their old age and for their families after them. 44 Cong. Rec. 4003 (1909).

Mr. ROOT. But the income-tax provision has a $5,000 exemption for individuals. I agree that the income that is necessary to a decent and comfortable living, the income that is necessary to enable an American citizen to clothe and feed and house and educate his children, should be exempted from the imposition of an income tax, just as farming implements necessary for the continuance of his support ought to be, and are, exempted from execution. But when you pass beyond that limit, sir, you are entering upon dangerous ground. 44 Cong. Rec. 4004 (1909).

Mr. ROOT. Mr. President, the provision to which I have referred as the "corporation tax" saves all of the income tax that is constitutional and can be enforced. It avoids the evils of the income-tax provision; it avoids drawing the Supreme Court of the United States through the mire and brambles of political controversy; it avoids the possibility or the probability of creating in the eyes of the world a conflict between two branches of our Government; it avoids the injustice of imposing the same duty upon the toiler, who is earning and laying up the capital for his future years, and upon the possessor of accumulated wealth. I assert, sir, that the income-tax provision as it stands is unwise, unjust, unconstitutional. I assert that the corporation-tax provision is constitutional, is just, and is wise; that it is adapted to the purposes for which it is designed; that it is free from the objections that gather around the broader measure. 44 Cong. Rec. 4005 (1909).

Mr. ROOT. Our people are separating into three classes: The men who work, who are laying up out of their earnings provision for the future, and on whom the hand of the taxgatherer should be laid most lightly; the owners of land, the farmers and other landowners, whom it is universally acknowledged that it was the intention of the fathers of the Constitution to protect by the provisions regarding the apportionment of direct taxes; and the possessors of the stored-up wealth of the country, which is being invested in the corporations that are doing the business of the country. And by the simple course of dropping out from this income-tax measure the parts that are unconstitutional under the decision of the Supreme Court, that are unjust according to the acknowledged judgment of all students of the income tax, that are incapable of enforcement within such a time as to relieve the deficiency that may be before us and by saving the tax upon the stored-up wealth of the country invested in corporations, called an "excise," we shall have accomplished the great object of the income tax. 44 Cong. Rec. 4006 (1909).

Mr. BAILEY. I believe that in earning an income by personal service every man consumes a part of his principal, and that fact ought always to be taken into consideration. The man who has his fortune invested in securities may find in a hundred years, if he spent his income, that fortune still intact, but the lawyer or the physician or the man engaged in other personal employment is spending his principal in earning his income. That fact ought under every just system of income taxation to be recognized and provided against. 44 Cong. Rec. 4007 (1909).

Mr. CLAPP. It is not my purpose, either, to enter into a long discussion of the income tax. I listened with great interest to the Senator from New York and to the objections which he raised against an income tax. One of his objections was the objection which in late years has been developed in English study of economy, between taxing the early energies of the individual and the accumulated fortune which the individual may in later years have laid by. I challenge the Senator from New York, or any other Senator, to point out where and how that defect is cured in this proposed so-called "corporation tax," for, so far as it reaches corporations, so far as it lays its hand upon any individual either by diminishing the income of a stockholder or by the transfer of the tax to the consumer purchasing of the corporation, it lays it with equal weight upon the man who is struggling to secure a competency and the man who has obtained a competency, because it makes no discrimination between the rich stockholder or the stockholder of moderate means, nor between the rich or poor consumer.

Not only does it fail to make such discrimination, but absolutely exempts the man who has gone still further in the process of accumulation and has laid his accumulated savings in the form of bonds. 44 Cong. Rec. 4008 (1909).

Mr. BACON. Now, if the Senator will pardon me a moment, we recognize that the general language "invested personal property" would cover not only investments in bonds and things of that kind, to which the Senator has alluded, but would cover investments in all other kinds of personal property. If I understand the Senator correctly, his idea is that the intention of the court was that absolutely idle property, upon which men live without effort by simply clipping coupons, was intended by the law to be beyond the reach of Congress to tax, whereas all the property which goes into the great activities of life may be subjected to onerous taxation. Is that the view of the Senator?

Mr. ROOT. I think, under the decision in the Pollock case, the property which the Senator speaks of as idle, which is only idle for the investor–

Mr. BACON. That is what I am speaking about.

Mr. ROOT. Of course, it is the representative of somebody else's activity, and I think it is protected against taxation now according to the rule of apportionment, while the other, being incidentally employed in connection with the business of life, is subject to an excise tax or duty, whatever it may be called, which is free from the rule of apportionment.

Mr. BACON. The result is that this property which is thus represented by bonds is practically to be exempted for all time from taxation, because if that interpretation is correct, bonds could only be taxed through apportionment, and we know that on account of conditions which have been explained here in this argument taxation through apportionment is practically impossible.

It will never be resorted to because of its gross inequality; one section would be so much more taxed per capita than another, and one particular locality so much more under direct apportionment than it would be under an ad valorem. Then the natural and necessary result is that the property which I have denominated as idle property, and which I do not think I have incorrectly denominated, is to be for all time exempted from taxation whereas the class of property which enters into the great activities of life, and out of which our prosperity is to be developed is the property which will be exclusively hereafter burdened with taxation.

I speak of the investment of bonds, and so forth, as the idle property. In a sense, or course, it has been created by great industry and great labor, but taxation at last falls upon the man who owns the property, and the man who owns the bonds and who is himself not engaged in the industry which produces the interest out of which he lives is absolutely to escape, so far as that particular investment is concerned, though he lives upon the use of the labor of others. For myself I am not willing to subscribe to any proposition which will lead us to so very undesirable a result as that.

The PRESIDING OFFICER. The question is on agreeing to the amendment offered by the Senator from Rhode Island [Mr. ALDRICH].

Mr. ELKINS. I will ask the Senator from New York, if he is in charge of the measure, if 1 per cent would not be enough instead of 2? I should like to have somebody answer as to the amount of revenue that would be derived from 2 per cent and the amount to be derived from 1 per cent. I do not see any member of the committee here, and I should like to have the Senator from New York state if any attention has been drawn to the matter as to how much revenue would be produced with 2 per cent and if we could do with 1 per cent. 44 Cong. Rec. 4035 (1909).

Mr. BRISTOW. I have also a letter from a gentleman engaged in the dry goods business, and in that letter he says:

Is it fair and consistent with the American idea of fairness and a "square deal" to tax our net earnings—taxes which will come out of the dividends to our stockholders, very many of whom are men in very moderate circumstances and working every day for a living and the support of their families-simply because we are doing business under a charter, while a neighbor doing business as an individual or under a copartnership is entirely free from said tax? And further, does the proposition reach the very wealthiest citizens, such as Rockefeller and Carnegie, whose holdings are not in stocks of corporations, but in bonds? 44 Cong. Rec. 4036 (1909).

Mr. CUMMINS. The Senator's next objection to the general income-tax amendment was that it had a tendency to array the East against the West, especially that part of the income-tax provision which exempted incomes not in excess of $5,000. Again, I believe he did scant justice to the intelligence and the patriotism of the American people. I believe that we are strong enough to rise above these accidents in the distribution of wealth. It happens that a great proportion of the accumulated wealth of the United States lies within a narrow compass of our country geographically; it happens that these vast and swollen fortunes, in which many thinking men and many profound statesmen find a menace to our institutions, lie in the eastern portion of our territory. It is naturally so, because in the East is found the cradle of our business, and the progress and the development of the West are but the children of the activity and enterprise of the East. There is no prejudice in the portion of the country from which I come either against wealth, or against wealth because it finds its home chiefly along the eastern border of our land. If, however, we are to tax wealth—if that be our purpose—we must tax it where we find it. It can not be removed from the East to the West; and if we are always to allow wealth to escape, if we are to allow it to shift, if you please, the burden that it ought to bear in the affairs of government, because to tax it is to impose burdens greater in the East than in the West, then we will never tax wealth in proportion to its distribution. 44 Cong. Rec. 4037 (1909).

Mr. CUMMINS. Any corporation that divides its investment into capital derived from bonds and from capital stock is a good illustration of the point I am endeavoring to make. The men who invest their money in bonds are the conservative men, the men who do not want to share the vicissitudes and the dangers of business, the men who are not willing to incur the risk and hazards of an enterprise carried on for profit; and they, therefore, take the bonds of corporations. The income arising from those bonds is the very sort of income which the Senator from New York declared, and declared very wisely and very truly, should bear a tax and a heavy tax, or at least a heavier tax than the incomes that arise from the sagacity and the business shrewdness of the men who are engaged in the particular enterprise.

....But, not only so, there is another kind of capital that is taxed here, which I am sure the Senator from New York will see in a moment ought not to be taxed under any such provision. I mean the capital of insurance companies. An insurance company—I refer now to the mutual insurance companies, and nearly all insurance companies are mutual insurance companies—has no money except that which is paid into it by its policy holders—not one penny. The tax that is sought to be placed upon that capital by this amendment is a tax upon the premiums paid by policy holders, in order to do what? Either to gather a fund which may support them in their old age or to protect their families against want after the provider is gone. Every dollar that this amendment extracts, or will extract, from men who pay premiums for life insurance, for accident insurance, for fire insurance, is just so much more laid upon these people, who, of all others, ought to be tenderly dealt with in devising systems of taxation. Therefore I am not ready to admit that the amendment offered by the Senator from Texas and myself is subject to the criticism suggested by the Senator from New York; and certainly I am not willing to admit that the amendment for which he stands sponsor remedies the defect so pointed out.

I pass to my objections to the amendment, and I want to record them just as emphatically as I can. I know that we are making an issue in this measure. I know it is an issue which will be fought out among the people of the United States. It will never be settled until it is settled right, because we are about to ignore the vital principles of organized society.

I am opposed to the measure reported by the committee because it discriminates unfairly and unjustly between the people of the United States and because it lays its burdens, not upon those who are able to bear them, but upon all who happen to be shareholders in corporations, without regard to their ability to pay or the extent of the property which they may have accumulated. I am opposed to it because it serves the purposes of the mighty corporations of the land. I have not heard that any of them have lifted up their voices in opposition to this measure, and they ought not to. Why? Because it is to take the place of one which would not only tax the net incomes of the corporations themselves, but would follow into the hands of the rich and the great the fortunes which they have accumulated either through individual or corporate enterprise.

I do not wonder that a man like Morgan is in favor of this measure, for although his corporations will bear some part of this taxation, his own vast fortune will be untouched. I do not wonder that a man like Harriman should favor this measure rather than the general income tax: because the part of his great fortune, which has been segregated from the corporations in which he is interested, lies beyond the operation of this law. I do not wonder that all these conspicuous examples of riches and of financial power should favor this measure; because while it taxes some part of their investment in a corporate way, it leaves untouched the very part that the American people are most interested in reaching and subjecting to the power of taxation. And the reason these great corporations are not protesting against this measure is that they are all dominated and controlled by the men who, by virtue of this substitution, will escape the taxation that we seek to impose upon them by virtue of the general income-tax law. It is a perfectly natural support; it is a perfectly natural approval. I am not criticising the motives of anyone; I am simply analyzing a situation which must be as obvious to the casual observer as it is to the deepest thinker. 44 Cong. Rec. 4038 (1909).

Mr. HUGHES. We can not legislate in that way. I know the feeling to which I have referred. I know its extent, and I think I am dealing only fairly with the people when I say it has its limitation. I know full well that those who have used this form of organization until they have gathered together in vast and almost countless millions profits coming through privilege and favored legislation have withdrawn them in such manner from such corporations that they will utterly and entirely escape this tax.

Mr. President, the "Laird of Skibo" will continue forever in his Marathon race with his millions, haunted by the fear that he may die a rich man, without relief by taxation, if this is the only kind of taxation indulged in by the Federal Government. You are not reaching, nor intending to reach, nor has there been a suggestion made here that by this legislation you will reach those whom, we were told, it was the especial desire of our former President to reach; those whom, we were told by President Taft in at least two speeches, it was his desire to have taxed, and those who the Members of this body, of all parties, have so often united in proclaiming should be subjected to their fair share of the burdens of taxation. They have escaped hitherto, and they escape now. And yet the Senator from Maryland avowed, in answer to the Senator from Iowa, that it was in the power of this Government to lay an occupation tax upon all persons and firms and corporations in this country, and thereby to include in the tax which would be collected under such law and under the Bailey-Cummins amendment the income which is the proceeds of the untaxed accumulated wealth, not the precarious incomes which we were yesterday told ought to be exempt, but the piled-up and secured and safe and untaxed accumulations in this country which are not invested in corporation stocks, unless in exempted holding companies. These fortunes, these incomes, still escape; they go yet untaxed. 44 Cong. Rec. 4046 (1909).

Mr. HUGHES. One objection to the Bailey-Cummins amendment offered here was referred to by the Senator from Iowa [Mr. CUMMINS], and that is that the income tax would lay a large burden upon certain enumerated States. My response to that also is that they have the wherewithal to pay that tax. The remainder of the country has paid its tribute for a century into these coffers, coerced, and induced to this contribution by the exactions of an unjust system of revenue, and now when this wealth has been piled up mountain high as a result of this discriminating and unjust revenue legislation, the very fact that it is large is used here as an argument why it should not pay its proportionate part of the taxation of the country. 44 Cong. Rec. 4047 (1909).

Mr. NEWLANDS. Our legislation, both with reference to revenue and publicity, should be concentrated upon those forms of wealth that have become most oppressive and upon those forms of wealth with reference to which the greatest abuses have existed; those forms of lawless wealth that have brought the law-abiding wealth of the country itself into discredit. There will be no difficulty in raising ample revenue from such sources. 44 Cong. Rec. 4048 (1909).

Mr. NEWLANDS. Without much inquiry into the law, I then stated that grave danger existed as to the constitutionality of the tax imposed by this amendment; that if it should be regarded as a tax upon occupations, then the question would be raised that it was not a uniform tax; that to tax an occupation in the hands of an artificial person and not to tax it in the hands of a natural person might be regarded as a denial of that uniformity called for by the Constitution; that if it should be regarded as a tax upon the privilege of being a corporation, the power to be and the power to do, the question might be raised as to our constitutional power to tax such a franchise, the creation of a sovereign State acting within its jurisdiction.

It is true that the Supreme Court has declared that that uniformity need be only a geographical uniformity; but the question of classification is always a question upon which hair-splitting decisions can be made. 44 Cong. Rec. 4049 (1909).

Mr. NEWLANDS. If we do that, we shall avoid the inconvenience of taxing all the small corporations of the country, and we shall confine our taxation to these great combinations of capital whose profits have been enormous, whose ability to bear is greater than that of any other class of the community, and whose abuses have awakened the attention of the country and demand legislative cure. The substitution of the corporation tax for the income tax seems to be a foregone conclusion, so far as present action is concerned; but I shall hope that when the bill as amended is before the Senate such amendments will be made as will free the small corporations from its operation, will place the combined wealth of the big manufacturers and corporations under national burdens, will furnish the statistical information necessary to rectify trust and tariff abuses, and, above all, such amendments will make the tax imposed identical with that which has already so successfully stood the test of the courts. 44 Cong. Rec. 4049 (1909).

---

WOOSTER, OHIO, June 29, 1909
Hon. CHARLES DICK,
***United States Senate, Washington, D.C.***

**DEAR SIR:**

In your consideration of the proposed corporation tax we wish to urge you favorably to consider the exemptions made in the President's recent message. This tax, if placed upon the local building and loan companies, would certainly work hardship to the many thousands of wage-earners who are its patrons.

Very truly, yours,

**THE WOOSTER BUILDING AND LOAN ASSOCIATION CO., *J. W. HOOKE,* Secretary.** 44 Cong. Rec. 4054 (1909).

---

*MARIETTA, OHIO, June 29, 1909.*
*Hon. CHARLES DICK,*
*Washington, D.C.*

DEAR SIR:

Representing 1,500 stockholders—for the most part small wage-earners that can ill afford such a penalty upon their thrift—we earnestly request your assistance in securing the exemption of building and loan associations from the operation of the proposed corporation tax.

Respectfully,
**THE PIONEER CITY BUILDING AND LOAN COMPANY,**
**WM. H. H. JETT, President.**
**J. S. H. TORNER, Vice-President.**
**S. J. HATHOWAY, Second Vice-President.**
**FRED W. TORNER, Secretary.**
**J. C. BRENAN, Attorney.**
**J. M. WILLIAMS.**
**D. G. BORGL.**
**C. L. BAILEY.** 44 Cong. Rec. 4054 (1909).

---

*WAVERLY, OHIO, June 29,1909*
*Hon. CHARLES DICK,*
*Washington, D. C.*
DEAR SENATOR:

I noticed in last Sunday's paper that the bill introduced in the Senate proposes to tax all corporations 2 per cent on their net earnings, which will include building and loan companies. The State of Ohio has probably the largest number of building and loan companies of any State in the Union, and has more money invested in such companies. Three-fourths of this money was placed in such companies by the frugal laboring man and woman. A 2 per cent tax on the net earnings of such companies will put them out of business or bring about an increased rate of interest to borrowing members. The law now in this State requires at least 5 per cent of the net earnings of such companies to be set apart as a "contingent fund" for contingent losses. I am the attorney for a local company at this place, and our company has only been able to pay a semiannual dividend of 2 _ per cent. Not many other companies pay any better. They can not unless they exact an unreasonable rate of interest. You can see what a tax of 2 per cent on the net earnings would do to such companies. I could see no serious objection to the bill recommended by the President, for he proposed that building and loan be exempt. Companies earning less than $5,000 ought to be exempt. The measure anyway, like an income tax, is odious to the average man and will prove to be very unpopular with the people, and such measures ought not to be resorted to in times of peace. I hope you can see your way clear to help defeat this bill so far as it will apply to building and loan companies.

Very respectfully,

**F. E. DOUGHERTY.** 44 Cong. Rec. 4054 (1909).

---

***TROY, OHIO, June 29, 1909.***
***HON. CHARLES DICK,***
***Washington, D. C.***

*DEAR SIR:*

At the regular meeting of the People's Building and Savings Association Company last evening I was directed by the unanimous vote of the directors to write you to use your influence and vote to secure for building associations the exemptions in the proposed corporation tax suggested by President Taft.

Our own deposits represent almost entirely the savings of the wage-earners of this city, and speaking for the directors, who, with one exception, are Republicans, and for myself, a member of the same party and an officeholder by virtue of my membership in it, I do not believe that the Republican party can afford to place a tax upon the thrift of this class of people, while ignoring the opportunities presented by the income tax to lay the burden upon those best able to bear it, and who for the most part escape their just proportion of the Nation's taxes.

Whether it is just or not, there is a feeling that our party has not kept faith in revising the tariff upward, and to impose a direct tax, like that proposed by the corporation tax, would appear to the people only as another evidence of our party's and our representatives' indifference to that great majority—the common people.

I am writing this because I believe that not only natural justice, but party expediency, demands that for the balance of the session of Congress the Republican party should father only such legislation as will remove the feeling that I speak of and make the wage-earner feel that his voice has penetrated Washington and that the party will protect his modest savings from the excise man.

Very truly, yours,

**J. C. FULLERTON, Jr.** 44 Cong. Rec. 4054 (1909).

---

***CINCINNATI, OHIO, July 1, 1909***
***Senator CHARLES DICK,***
***Washington, D.C.:***

We protest against the passage of the proposed bill taxing the net income of corporations. As common stock can receive no dividends until bonds and preferred stocks are cared for, it in effect places the burden entirely upon the holders of common stock, who are usually those actively engaged in the building up of their industry and of such moderate means that it is necessary that they take the risks of the business for the chance of securing greater rate of income. It leaves untouched those securities which are most generally held by people of large fortunes. It is peculiarly unfortunate at this time that this burden should bed thrown upon the common-stock holders owing to the growing disposition upon the part of corporations to interest their workmen more closely with them through ownership of common stock in the corporation, as common stock reflects the increased efficiency and not the preferred. That workingmen will avail themselves of such opportunity, I might mention this company has had such plan in effect for twelve years, and its employees other than its officers own in excess of $2,000,000 worth of its stock, every share of which is common. We ask that your efforts be exerted against its passage.

**THE PROCTER & GAMBLE COMPANY,**
**WILLIAM COOPER PROCTER, President.**
44 Cong. Rec. 4055 (1909).

---

***CINCINNATI, OHIO, June 23, 1909***
***Hon. CHARLES DICK,***
***Senate, Washington, D.C.:***

We earnestly hope you may see your way clear to assist in securing exemption of life insurance companies from proposed tax on net incomes of corporations. Life companies now bear a heavy burden of taxation in all States and Territories, out of proportion to that paid by other corporations. All these taxes fall on the policy holder or on the beneficiary of insurance, a class of citizens, as a rule, least able to bear such exactions. Letter follows.

**JESSE R. CLARK,**
**President, the Union Central Life Insurance Company.**
44 Cong. Rec. 4055 (1909).

---

***DELAWARE, OHIO, June 29, 1909.***
***Hon. CHARLES DICK,***
***United States Senate, Washington, D.C.:***

On behalf of members of building and loan association of Delaware County, Ohio, we respectfully urge that you use your best efforts to exempt these savings institutions of the wage-earners from proposed corporation tax, as was the case in the old income-tax law and the Spanish-American war stamp act.

**THE FIDELITY BUILDING ASSOCIATION AND LOAN COMPANY,**
**D.H. BATTENFIELD,** ***President.***
**PEOPLE'S BUILDING AND LOAN COMPANY,**
**C. RIDDLE,** ***President.*** 44 Cong. Rec. 4058 (1909).

---

***YOUNGSTOWN, OHIO, June 29, 1909.***
***Hon. CHARLES DICK,***
***United States Senate, Washington, D.C.:***

Proposed tax on corporations will be disastrous to building associations. Ten thousand working people in this city would suffer. Exempt the associations.

**THE HOME SAVINGS AND LOAN COMPANY** 44 Cong. Rec. 4058 (1909).

---

*YOUNGSTOWN, OHIO, June 30, 1909.*
*Hon. CHARLES DICK,*
*United States Senate, Washington, D. C.:*

Proposed corporation tax will work a hardship to building associations. In former acts of this nature they have been exempted and they should be exempt now. Working people everywhere will benefit by their exemption.

**J.R. WOOLY,**
**Vice-President Home Savings and Loan Company.**
44 Cong. Rec. 4058 (1909)

---

*CLEVELAND, OHIO, June 28, 1909.*
*Hon. CHARLES DICK,*
*United States Senate, Washington, D.C.:*

We solicit your earnest endeavor to exempt building and loan associations from the corporation tax, as in this case the burden would fall upon thrifty working men and women trying to pay off mortgages on their houses.

Cleveland Savings and Loan Company, William R. Creer, Secretary; The Cuyahoga Savings and Loan Company, Davis Hawley, president; The Equity Savings and Loan Company, H.W.S. Wood, president; The Economy Building and Loan Company, O. J. Hodge, president; The Cleveland West Side Building and Loan Company, **Jacob Haller, secretary.** 44 Cong. Rec. 4058 (1909)

---

***YOUNGSTOWN, OHIO, June 23, 1909.***
***Hon. CHARLES DICK,***
***United States Senate, Washington, D.C.:***

Building and loan associations should be exempt from proposed corporation tax. Similar acts in the past have always exempted them. Such exemption would benefit 400,000 wage-earners in Ohio alone.

***JAMES M. MCKAY,***
***Vice-President Ohio Building Association League.***
44 Cong. Rec. 4058 (1909).

---

***DAYTON, OHIO, June 27, 1909.***
***Hon. CHARLES DICK,***
***Washington, D. C.:***

We urge to use your efforts to exempt mutual building and loan associations from income tax. Seven thousand wage-earners and small savers in this association alone would thus be taxed.

**AMERICAN LOAN AND SAVINGS ASSOCIATION** 44 Cong. Rec. 4058 (1909).

---

***BELLAIRE, OHIO, June 28, 1909.***
***Hon. CHARLES DICK,***
***Senate Chamber, Washington, D.C.:***

Over 5,000 working people ask you to oppose bill to tax incomes of building associations.

**THE BUCKEYE SAVINGS AND LOAN CO.,**
**By W.G. MCCLAIN,** ***Secretary.*** 44 Cong. Rec. 4058 (1909).

---

*DAYTON, OHIO, June 27, 1909.*
*Hon. CHARLES DICK,*
*Washington, D. C.:*

On behalf of 50,000 wage-earners who have their savings in the Dayton building associations you are urged to consider the justice of having building associations exempted from the operation of the proposed tax on corporations.

*MONTGOMERY COUNTY BUILDING ASSOCIATION LEAGUE,*
***S. RUFUS JONES, President.*** 44 Cong. Rec. 4058 (1909).

---

*CINCINNATI, OHIO, June 26, 1909.*
*Hon. CHARLES DICK,*
*United States Senate, Washington, D.C.:*

Three hundred and twenty-five thousand building and loan association members in Ohio respectfully urge you to secure proper exemption from proposed tax on corporations. Congress has always granted building and loan associations exemptions from the operation of previous taxes on income. The proposed tax, if it includes building and loan associations, will be unjust and a tax on the thrift of the wage-earners.

**AMERICAN BUILDING ASSOCIATION NEWS,**
**H.S. ROSENTHAL,** ***Editor.*** 44 Cong. Rec. 4059 (1909).

---

Mr. BACON. One great objection to the amendment offered by the Senator from Rhode Island, representing his committee, is the fact that it does not go far enough. The tax which is proposed reaches only a very small part of the particular class of wealth which it is designed to tax for the purpose of raising this needed revenue. I say needed revenue. It seems there is a division of opinion upon that subject.

....The desire to reach the bonded interests of the country would be very much more generally shared by the people at large than the desire to reach simply the stocks of corporations. The excise tax in the various cases where it has been imposed has been a tax upon a privilege or a right, or upon the exercise of certain business.

...the ground upon which I base this amendment is that if a privilege can be taxed as an excise tax, a legal right can also be the basis for an excise tax, and the right to hold bonds is as legitimate a subject-matter of taxation as a right to exercise the business through the exercise of which these bonds are to be ultimately paid in the hands of the bondholders.

....If, however, the right to hold bonds is a taxable right, one which can be taxed under the exercise of the excise power, then the effort to convert the stock of corporations into bonds, and thus escape the tax contemplated by this section of the bill, will be defeated. 44 Cong. Rec. 4062 (1909).

Mr. BACON. I am in favor of taxing corporations, but I am also in favor of taxing other accumulated wealth as well as corporations, such as bonds, and so forth. 44 Cong. Rec. 4063 (1909).

Mr. OVERMAN. I am in favor of taxing corporations, and also of taxing wealth. I want all to bear equal burdens. 44 Cong. Rec. 4065 (1909).

Mr. McLAURIN. I desire to look into this. I do not say that I shall vote against this proposed amendment, but I shall offer to amend the constitutional amendment by striking out the words "or other direct" in one place, and by striking out the words "and direct taxes" in another. The Constitution will then confer all the power which is provided for in the joint resolution and also free Congress from a great many other embarrassments. 44 Cong. Rec. 4067 (1909).

Mr. STONE. Mr. President, I desire to consume about ten minutes or so of the valuable time of the Senate to say a few words respecting the resolution proposing an amendment to the Constitution, authorizing the imposition of an income tax. I wish to read a declaration contained in the Democratic national platform which was promulgated at Denver in 1908. It is as follows:

We favor an income tax as part of our revenue system, and we urge the submission of a constitutional amendment specifically authorizing Congress to levy and collect a tax upon individual and corporate incomes, to the end that wealth may bear its proportionate share of the burdens of the Federal Government. 44 Cong. Rec. 4106 (1909).

Mr. BROWN. There are several Senators who want to talk, and I think I will yield the floor. I hope that all these amendments may be voted down. I believe that the joint resolution is drawn simply; it is drawn in language that is not susceptible of two or three constructions; it vest the power in Congress to lay and collect income taxes; and that is the proposition we want to adopt. 44 Cong. Rec. 4115 (1909).

Mr. MONEY. We can feel quite sure that an act of such far-reaching importance, that touches the pockets of very many rich people, is not very likely to become a part of the organic law of our Republic or of our confederation. 44 Cong. Rec. 4115 (1909).

61st Congress, 3d Session — SENATE — Document No. 705

# SHALL THE INCOME-TAX AMENDMENT BE RATIFIED

ARTICLE BY

## HON. NORRIS BROWN

UNITED STATES SENATOR FROM NEBRASKA

IN

THE EDITORIAL REVIEW

*APRIL, 1910*

PRESENTED BY MR. BORAH

December 14, 1910.—Ordered to be printed

WASHINGTON
GOVERNMENT PRINTING OFFICE
1910

# SHALL THE INCOME TAX AMENDMENT BE RATIFIED?

BY NORRIS BROWN, United States Senator from Nebraska.

[Printed in the Editorial Review of April, 1910.]

The American people have been given by Congress few opportunities to amend the Constitution. While the people have the right to amend the Constitution without having the proposed amendment first submitted by Congress they have never exercised that right. The Constitution may be amended in two ways. If the legislatures of two-thirds of the several States petition Congress for a convention to propose amendments it is the duty of Congress to call the convention; but never in the history of the country has this method been followed. The existing fifteen amendments to the Constitution have all been adopted by the other method provided in the Constitution, namely, by the action of Congress by a two-thirds vote of both Houses proposing amendments which were submitted to the several States and ratified by the legislatures of three-fourths of the States. Congress has been very slow to propose amendments. While it is true that Members of Congress have introduced several thousand resolutions since the Constitution was adopted, proposing various amendments thereto, only eighteen resolutions so offered have ever received the two-thirds vote of both Houses necessary to submit an amendment during all these years. The first ten amendments were proposed by the First Congress and were ratified by the States.[1] The same Congress proposed two other amendments which failed of ratification.

The eleventh amendment was proposed by the Third Congress and was ratified in 1798. The twelfth amendment was proposed by the Fifth Congress and by the proclamation of the Secretary of State in 1804 was declared to have been ratified by the legislatures of three-fourths of the States. The thirteenth amendment was proposed by the Thirtieth Congress in February, 1865, and was declared ratified in December of the same year.[2]

[1] The first ten amendments were ratified by the following States and the notifications of ratification by the governors thereof were successively communicated by the President to Congress: New Jersey, Maryland, North Carolina, South Carolina, New Hampshire, Delaware, Pennsylvania, New York, Rhode Island, Vermont, and Virginia. There is no evidence on the Journals of Congress that the Legislatures of Connecticut, Georgia, and Massachusetts ratified them.

[2] The States ratifying the thirteenth amendment were Illinois, Rhode Island, Michigan, Maryland, New York, West Virginia, Maine, Kansas, Massachusetts, Pennsylvania, Virginia, Ohio, Missouri, Nevada, Indiana, Louisiana, Minnesota, Wisconsin, Vermont, Tennessee, Arkansas, Connecticut, New Hampshire, South Carolina, Alabama, North Carolina, and Georgia.

The fourteenth amendment was proposed by the Thirty-ninth Congress in June, 1866, and was declared ratified in July, 1868.[1]

The fifteenth amendment was proposed by the Fortieth Congress in February, 1869, and was declared ratified in March, 1870.[2]

So it appears that Congress has proposed, up to the year 1909, seventeen amendments to the Constitution, fifteen of which were ratified and two rejected by the States. This emphasizes the disposition of the people to abide by the original Constitution amending it only when moved to do so by some extraordinary reason. It is evidence also that the framers of the original instrument builded so well and so wisely that but few amendments have been deemed necessary in order to carry out the high purposes of a representative form of government.

In July, 1909, Congress by joint resolution proposed the sixteenth amendment, which reads as follows:

> Congress shall have the power to lay and collect taxes on incomes from whatever source derived, without apportionment among the several States and without regard to any census or enumeration.

It is well to note that in the judgment of Congress this amendment should be ratified by the States; for it will be recalled that the resolution proposing the sixteenth amendment received the unanimous vote of the Senate and the almost unanimous vote of the House of Representatives. When a measure in Congress receives such support from the chosen representatives of the people of every State in the Union who are under every obligation to represent their constituents with wisdom and fidelity, it may safely be concluded that some imperative reason involving the rights of all the people controlled them. It is also conclusive evidence that the demand for the amendment is nation wide.

The same reason that controlled Congress if understood by the electorate of the country will compel the members of the legislatures of the several States to ratify the amendment. What is that reason?

The existing Constitution confers the power of taxation upon Congress and provides that the tax may be laid either directly or indirectly on all kinds of property.[3] But, it further provides, that if the

---

[1] The proclamation of the Secretary of State was unusual in that it said the fourteenth amendment had been ratified by three-fourths of the States in the following manner: Connecticut, June, 1866; New Hampshire, July, 1866; Tennessee, July, 1866; New Jersey, September, 1866 (and the legislature of the same State passed a resolution in April, 1868, to withdraw its consent to it); Oregon, September, 1866; Vermont, November, 1866. Georgia rejected it November, 1866, and ratified it July, 1868; North Carolina rejected it December, 1866, and ratified it July, 1868; South Carolina rejected it December 20, 1866, and ratified it July, 1868; New York ratified it January, 1867; Ohio ratified it January 1, 1867 (and the legislature of the same State passed a resolution in January, 1868, to withdraw its consent to it); Illinois ratified it January, 1867; West Virginia, January, 1867; Kansas, January, 1867; Maine, January, 1867; Nevada, January, 1867; Missouri, January, 1867; Indiana, January, 1867; Minnesota, February, 1867; Rhode Island, February, 1867; Wisconsin, February, 1867; Pennsylvania, February, 1867; Michigan, February, 1867; Massachusetts, March, 1867; Nebraska, June, 1867; Iowa, April, 1868; Arkansas, April, 1868; Florida, June, 1868; Louisiana, July, 1868; and Alabama, July, 1868. Georgia again ratified the amendment February, 1870. Texas rejected it January, 1867, and ratified it October, 1869. The amendment was rejected by Kentucky, January 10, 1867; by Delaware, February, 1867; by Maryland, March, 1867, and was not afterward ratified by either State.

[2] The record in the office of the Secretary of State discloses that the following States ratified the fifteenth amendment: North Carolina, West Virginia, Massachusetts, Wisconsin, Maine, Louisiana, Michigan, South Carolina, Pennsylvania, Arkansas, Connecticut, Florida, Illinois, Indiana, New York (and the legislature of the same State passed a resolution the following year to withdraw its consent from it), New Hampshire, Nevada, Vermont, Virginia, Missouri, Mississippi, Ohio, Iowa, Kansas, Minnesota, Rhode Island, Nebraska, Texas, and Georgia.

[3] The Congress shall have power "To lay and collect Taxes, Duties, Imposts and Excises, to pay the Debts and provide for the common Defense and general Welfare of the United States; but all Duties, Imposts, and Excises shall be uniform throughout the United States."—Sec. 8, art. 1, Constitution. (Hylton *v.* United States, 3 Dall., 171; Osborne *v.* Bank of the United States, 9 Wh., 739; Veazie Bank *v.* Fenno, 8 Wall., 533; Springer *v.* United States, 102 U. S., 586.)

tax is a direct tax it must be apportioned among the several State according to population.[1]

To lay a direct tax on any kind of property and apportion it among the several States according to population instead of according to value is admittedly so unjust and inequitable as to be acceptable to no one and therefore in effect impossible. The proposed amendment is a proposition to abolish the rule of apportionment among the States according to population so far as income taxes are concerned. It would not be necessary to eliminate this rule of apportionment except for the decision of the Supreme Court of the United States, in what is known as the Pollock case, decided in 1895, which held that a tax on incomes was a direct tax.[2] Until that decision Congress had exercised the right at different times in the history of the country to lay and collect taxes on incomes without apportionment, on the theory that such a tax was an indirect and not a direct tax. Up to that time the Supreme Court had sustained the doctrine that a tax on incomes was not a direct tax and therefore need not be apportioned among the States according to population. But when the court changed its mind and overturned the rule which it had for a century sustained, the Government found itself without power either in time of peace or war to tax the large incomes of the country without apportioning the tax among the States, for it must be admitted that the judgment of the Supreme Court bound Congress and the people.

The effect, therefore, of the proposed amendment, if ratified, will be to restore to the people and to the Government a power for many years exercised by them in national emergencies to tax income without apportionment. The restoration of this power so long enjoyed and so recently denied may become necessary to the life of the Republic. Whether the power shall be exercised, or when it shall be exercised, or whether it shall be exercised at all, are other questions entirely aside from the question of whether the Government shall be vested or stripped of the power. The amendment vests the power in the Government; without the amendment the Government is without the power.

The sole question, therefore, presented by the amendment, and the sole consideration involved in its ratification or rejection, is whether or not the United States, the foremost nation of the world, shall be clothed with this perogative of national sovereignty—the power to tax incomes according to their value and without regard to apportionment among the several States according to population. I do not regard the question as debatable. From every standpoint this Nation should be clothed with every power necessary to protect itself and to maintain itself under all circumstances and under all possible dangers. To deny this proposition is to put our Nation at a disadvantage with every other civilized nation of the globe. England has had and exercised at different times for more than a hundred years the power to tax incomes. It was first invoked as a war measure in the year 1798. At that time England needed the revenue in order to enable her to defend herself against the

[1] No capitation or other direct tax shall be laid unless in proportion to the census or enumeration hereinbefore directed to be taken.—Sec. 9, art. 1, Constitution. (License Tax Cases, 5 Wall., 462; Springer v. United States, 102 U. S., 586; Pollock v. Farmers' Loan & Trust Co., 157 U. S., 429; Nicol v. Ames, 173 U. S., 509; Thomas v. United States, 192 U. S., 363; Spreckles Sugar Refining Co. v. McClain, 192 U. S., 397.)

[2] Pollock v. Farmers' Loan & Trust Co. (157 U. S., 429).

aggressive Napoleon. William Pitt suggested that others sources of revenue having been impaired by the strain of war an income tax was necessary. Immediately after Napoleon's fall at Waterloo the tax was repealed. It was later reenacted and was in force in the early fifties of the last century, when Mr. Gladstone came forward with a scheme for its gradual repeal and its final elimination from the fiscal policy of that country at the end of five years. On that issue a campaign was waged and Gladstone's policy entered upon. However, before the expiration of the five-year period, the Crimean war came, and out of the national necessities occasioned by the war it became necessary for England to abandon the Gladstone policy and to retain the income tax. Again in 1874 Mr. Gladstone made a campaign on the issue of repealing the tax; but he was defeated at the election and the Disraeli administration came into power. No successful effort has ever been made to repeal the law since, or rather to change the policy of taxing incomes, for it will be remembered the English statute is reenacted every year, the rate of the tax levy being changed annually to meet the needs of the country. Under the operation of the law England taxed incomes amounting to more than $3,000,000,000 in the year 1908, $200,000,000 of which represented the salaries of the Government employees and incomes arising from investments in Government securities.

France is about to exercise the power, which no one questions she possesses, to tax incomes. The German States have for many years taxed incomes. So have the Cantons of Switzerland, the Netherlands, Austria, Sweden, Belgium, and Denmark. Italy has a very satisfactory system of laying an income tax, resembling in many ways the English plan. So far as current literature is able to advise us, there seems to be no serious sentiment in any of these countries that incomes should not be taxed. And yet, in this country there is apparently a determined intention in some quarters to deny to the Government even the power to tax incomes. If an income tax in the great nations named, having been laid by them in times of peace as well as of war, conduces to the general welfare of those countries as shown by trial and experience, will some one suggest what possible harm could come to the people of the United States by vesting our Government with the power merely. Should the Nation's distress ever make it necessary to exercise the power and such power should not be possessed, those who help to defeat the pending amendment will not be able to justify in their own consciences their efforts in that direction. This is not an argument in favor of an income-tax law. It is an argument in favor of an income-tax amendment to the Constitution, which lays no tax, promises to lay none, but simply and solely restores to the people a power many times sustained but finally denied by the courts. The exercise of the power can not become an issue until the power is restored.

Recently, the question has been raised by those who are opposed to the ratification of the amendment that with the amendment ratified the powers of the States will in some way be impaired and their strength and vitality, in some way not specified, destroyed. The objection is not sound. The amendment in no way changes the existing relation between the State and the Federal Government. Whether the amendment is ratified or not, the rights of the State as a State and those of the Federal Government in their relation to each other will remain the same. Each sovereignty is now wholly independent of the other in the exercise of certain governmental functions, and the proposed amendment neither adds to nor takes away from the independence now enjoyed by each. But it is the argument of some who oppose its adoption that the amendment will alter that relation by conferring upon the Federal Government the power to tax incomes arising from investments in State and municipal securities. I do not agree with that argument because the language of the amendment and the occasion for its submission by Congress and the Constitution itself do not warrant that interpretation. Under the existing Constitution the Federal Government is without the power to tax State or municipal securities, and the State is without the power to tax Federal securities. Each may tax its own securities, but neither is subject to the jurisdiction of the other in taxation matters. The proposed amendment in not the remotest degree suggests any change in that regard. Each sovereignty is left to the independent and exclusive privilege of taxing its own securities without interference by the other.

For the sake of the argument, let it be conceded that the proposed amendment will so modify this relation that the Federal Government will have the power to tax incomes arising from investments in State and municipal securities. Should that contention be true, an additional reason is given for the adoption of the amendment rather than its rejection; because under such interpretation all incomes would be subject to taxation. There would be no exceptions nor exemptions save, as Congress might, and, in my judgment should, except all incomes up to a certain amount, and the larger the income the larger the tax rate should be. The very fact that all incomes would be treated alike commands the approval of the average American citizen. Any favor in the matter of taxation is inherently obnoxious to every sense of justice. Some people are willing to suffer discrimination, socially or industrially or politically, but no one except the favored one will tolerate discrimination by the Government when it levies a tax.

The growing objection to the tax on consumption is vitalized by the fact that such a tax discriminates against those least able to pay the tax and in favor of those whose ability to pay the tax is unquestioned and whose protection from the Government is so much greater because their larger property requires and receives a larger measure of protection. When the Government seeks to lay a tax for its defense or its support on the incomes of the country, it should reach all incomes. If the income arises from an investment in lands, it should be taxed; if it arises from investments in manufacturing enterprises, in railroads, in banks, in newspapers, in the mercantile business, or in steamship lines, it should be taxed. Why should an income arising from an investment in State or municipal bonds not be taxed? Why should the holder of these securities enjoy his income free from any contribution to assist this Government, which protects him and his property no less than it protects other people owning another class of property? Why should he escape and other people be compelled to pay?

There must be some hidden reason for making an exception of the public-bond holder because none is easily apparent. If it be argued that the exception should be made not on account of the bondholder, but on account of the bond debtor—the State—the answer is, The same reason exists for the exemption of all incomes, those arising from investments in other securities as well as those arising from investments in public securities. On that theory, the man who loans money should be exempted from paying any tax on the note or mortgage, because the borrower, in the end, has the tax to pay. He pays the tax because he pays the interest. And yet in not a State in this Union are the owners of notes and mortgages, stocks or bonds, excused from the tax burden. If it be argued that the tax on incomes arising from investments in State securities would impair the borrowing capacity of the State, the answer is, It does not have that tendency or effect in any of the countries where such a tax is laid. The United Kingdom taxes the incomes arising from investments in public securities and she collects the tax in advance, retaining it out of the interest. The same is true of Italy. Indeed, in none of the foreign countries having income-tax laws is an exemption made of the incomes arising from investments in public bonds.

Nor has the borrowing capacity of any of these great nations suffered in any degree by reason of the tax collected on incomes arising from investments in public bonds. England, with a population scarcely more than half that of this country, has been able to borrow at 2½ per cent more than four times as much as the United States now owes. Italy, with scarcely more than a third of our population, has a public debt three times as large as ours. In no country taxing incomes from every source can evidence be found to sustain the fear voiced by some who oppose the amendment that such a law would have a tendency even to impair the credit of any State. The evidence all sustains the contrary doctrine.

Again, if it be true that an income tax could be so laid as to injure the States in any conceivable way, the ratification of the amendment does not mean that such a destructive tax ever would in fact be laid, for the reason that the law providing such a measure would have to be enacted by Congress. The membership of that body is chosen by home constituencies in every State and congressional district in the United States. Does anyone seriously suppose that any Member of either House of Congress could be found who would vote to tax his State or his congressional district out of existence? The record of Congress during the entire history of the Republic shows how vigilantly and persistently its Members have opposed every advance to impair the powers and the rights of the States. The severest and truest criticism ever passed on the Federal Legislature is the charge that, sometimes, Senators and Representatives legislate for their own several States and districts rather than for the good of the Nation as a whole. In a measure this criticism is justified. Will anyone suggest that a tariff law was ever passed except by the votes of those interested primarily in its effect on the industries locally at home, and, secondarily, in its effect on industries away from home? How frequently, indeed, do we find Members of Congress applying *the same economic principle differently* as the point of application may be near by or far away from the industries of the people who elected them. This habit of legislators to remember their own localities and faithfully to protect their interests against encroachment is deeply rooted everywhere. It has the moral support of every community and is as certain to control the votes of legislators in the future as it has in the past. No State will be desirous of having an income tax passed which could injure the State, and therefore no such law ever will be passed nor any attempt made to do so. To argue that Congress would or might undertake to destroy the States and thereby most certainly destroy the Union is too unreasonable and absurd to merit respectful consideration.

The people of the United States are, above every other consideration, loyal to the country. They look with suspicion on any argument directed to withold any power which is or may become necessary to the life and safety of the Nation. The future is full of possibilities. No man can tell how long the present happy and peaceful relations with foreign powers may continue. May they never end. But it is the duty of a patriotic people to be prepared for every emergency. This amendment is a preparatory measure. It appeals to patriotic impulses. It should prevail.

O

# Bibliography

## Books

Bastiat, Fredric, The Law, (Foundation for Economic Education, Inc.,1996) (1850).

Borah, William C., Income Tax, Univ. of Idaho Library (1910).

Cooley, Thomas M., A Treatise on the Law of Taxation (vol.1, 1903).

Cooley, Thomas M., Constitutional Limitations (7th ed., 1903).

Foote, Allen Ripley, The Power of Taxation Should be Regulated, State and Local Taxation, Second International Conference, International Tax Association, 203 (1909).

Foster, Roger, A Treatise on the Federal Income Tax Under the Act of 1913 (Lawyers Co-operative Publishing Co., 1914).

Grays, Michael J., The Decline (and Fall?) of the Income Tax, 1997.

Hart, Henry M.; Sacks, Albert, M. The Legal Process (Foundation Press 1994).

Hicks, The Populist Revolt (1931).

Holland, Vern, The Law That Always Was (F.E.A. Books, Tulsa, Oklahoma 1987).

Keenan, Kossuth K., Income Taxation (Burdick & Allen Publishers, Milwaukee 1910).

Loos, Prof. Isaac A.; Foote, Allen Ripley, The Division Between State and Local Taxation, State and Local Taxation, Second International Conference, International Tax Association 203 (1909).

Meador, Dan, By the IRS Book (self published, 7th ed. Dec. 1995).

Miller and Baar, 545 United States Tax Cases (Commerce Clearing House 1921).

Mullins, Eustace, The Secrets of the Federal Reserve (Bankers Research Institute, Staunton, Virginia 1993).

Seligman, Edwin R.A., The Income Tax (MacMillan Co., New York 1911).

Singer, Norman J., Sutherland on Statutory Construction (5th ed. 1992).

Skinner, Otto, The Biggest Tax Loophole of All (self published 1997).

Smith, Adam, Wealth of Nations (Prometheus Books, Amherst, New York 1991) (1776).

Titus, Herbert W., God, Man and Law: The Biblical Principles (Institute of Basic Life Principles 1998).

Wells, David Ames, The Theory and Practice of Taxation (D. Appleton and Co., New York 1907).

## Editorials and Newspaper Articles

Bad Tax Laws, Editorial, N.Y. Times, pg. 10, March 24, 1911.

Congress and the Constitution, The Nation, pg. 214, March 21, 1895.

Drama for Wage Earners, N.Y. Times, pg. 10, May 30, 1911

Gov. Fort Upholds the Income Tax, Relieving Burden on Poor, N.Y. Times, February 8, 1910.

Governor A.E. Wilson (Kentucky) on the Income Tax Amendment, N.Y. Times, Part 5, pg. 13, February 26, 1911.

Income Tax Voted in Alabama House, N.Y. Times, pg. 1, August 3, 1909.

Justice Brewer on Income Tax, The Wall St. Journal, July 23, 1909.

Mr. Aldrich's Surprise, Editorial, N.Y. Times, pg. 8, April 21, 1909.

Perfectly Plain and Bad Laws, Editorial, N.Y. Times, pg. 8, March 2, 1910.

The Gist of the Question, Editorial, N.Y. Times, pg. 12, May 3, 1910.

The Proposed Income Tax, The Nation, pg. 404-5, November 30, 1893.

The Rejected Amendment, N.Y. Times, pg. 10, May 5, 1910.

The Corporate Tax Sustained, Editorial, N.Y. Times, pg.10, March 14, 1911.

The Income Tax, Editorial, N.Y. Times, pg. 8, April 15, 1910.

The Income Tax, Editorial, N.Y. Times, pg.10, April 19, 1911.

# Congressional Records

Annals of Congress, 4 Cong. 2nd Sess., pg. 1898 , 1797

Congressional Record, Vol.44, pgs. 1351, 1352, 1353, 1420, 1423, 1424, 1429, 1568, 1569, 1570, 1680, 1681, 1682, 1683, 1694, 1695, 1698, 1701, 1702, 1962, 2083, 2086, 2093, 2094, 2095, 2103, 2334, 2335, 2447, 2448, 2455, 2457, 3309, 3344, 3377, 3391, 3444, 3448, 3484, 3761, 3900, 3929, 3936, 3938, 3940, 3941, 3943, 3945, 3947, 3950, 3951, 3953, 3955, 3959, 3968, 3969, 3972, 3973, 3975, 3976, 3977, 3982, 3985, 3986, 3987, 3988, 3989, 3994, 3995, 3997, 3998, 3999, 4003, 4004, 4005, 4006, 4007, 4008, 4013, 4028, 4035, 4036, 4037, 4038, 4039, 4041, 4044, 4046, 4047, 4048, 4049, 4054, 4055, 4056, 4057, 4058, 4059, 4063, 4065, 4067, 4106, 4109, 4115, 4120, 4229, 4232, 4233, 4235, 4237, 4238, 4390, 4393, 4396, 4398, 4399, 4409, 4412, 4414, 4415, 4416, 4417, 4418, 4420, 4421, 4423, 4424, 4433, 4435, 4436, 4666, 4682, 4959, 4960.

Congressional Record, Vol. 50, pgs. 1237,1238,1253, 3776, 3842, 3843.

Congressional Globe, 41st Congress, 2d. Sess., pg. 3993 (1870)., plus 38th Cong., 1st Sess., pg.1874 (1864).

Congressional Record, March 27, 1943, p. 2580.

Congressional Record, June 13, 1967, p. 15641.

House Reports No. 15, 61st Congress, 1st Session (1909).

House Reports No. 1040, 77th Congress, 1st Session (1941).

Senate Document No. 98, 61st Congress, 1st Session (1909).

Senate Document No. 365, 61st Congress, 2nd Session (1910).

Senate Document No. 367, 61st Congress, 2nd Session (1910).

Senate Document No. 705, 61st Congress, 3rd Session (1910).

Senate Document No. 171, 63rd Congress, 1st Session (1913).

Wilcott, Oliver, Direct Taxes, No. 100, 4th Congress, 2nd Session (1796).

# Law, Economic and Political Journals, Annotations

Amos v. Peaslee, Taxing Income of Foreign Investors in American Stocks and Bonds, 16 Columbia Law Review 465, 466 (1916).

Bird, Francis W., Constitutional Aspects of the Federal Tax on the Income of Corporations, 24 Harvard Law Review 32 (1911).

Bosley, William Bradford, The Constitutional Requirement of Uniformity in Duties, Imposts and Excises, 9 Yale Law Journal 164 (1900).

Bullock, Charles J., Direct and Indirect Taxes in Economic Literature, 13 Political Science Quarterly 442 (1898).

Burgess, John W., The Reconciliation of Government with Liberty, 31 Political Science Quarterly 43 (1916).

De Mott, Gary A., "STATE OF UTAH," another "State" in the nature of a municipal corporation and department of the state of Utah, unpublished paper (1999).

Freemen, Israel, Constitutionality of Federal Corporation Tax Law, 72 Central Law Journal 59 (1911).

Graves, Arthur C., Inherent Improprieties on the Income Tax Amendment to the Federal Constitution, 19 Yale Law Journal 505 (1910).

Hackett, Frank Warren, The Constitutionality of the Graduated Income Tax Law, 25 Yale Law Journal 427 (1916).

Harvard Law Review, Vol, 20, pgs. 285-6 (1907).

The Income Tax and the Sixteenth Amendment, 29 Harvard Law Review 536 (1915-6).

McDonough, Amending the Constitution of the United States, 76 Central Law Journal 335 (1913).

Minor, Raleigh C., The Proposed Income Tax Amendment to the Federal Constitution, 15 Virginia Law Register 737 (1910).

Morrow, Dwight W., The Income Tax Amendment, 10 Columbia Law Review 379 (1910).

Resort to Constitutional or Legislative Debates, Committee Reports, Journals, etc., as aid in Construction of Constitution or Statute, Annotation, 70 American Law Reports 5, 22-25.

Seligman, Edwin, R.A., The Income Tax, 9 Political Science Quarterly 610 (1894).

Seligman, Edwin, R.A., The Income-Tax Amendment, 25 Political Science Quarterly 193 (1910).

Sewell, Robert, The Income Tax: Is It Constitutional?, 28 American Law Review 808 (1894).

Siaca, Ramon, The Federal Income Tax Law of 1913: Construction of the Sixteenth Amendment, 1 Cornell Law Review 298 (1916).

The American Journal of Tax Policy, Vol. 2, pg. 240 (1983).

West, Max, The Income Tax and National Revenues, 8 The Journal of Political Economy 433 (1900).

Whitney, Edward, The Income Tax and the Constitution, 20 Harvard Law Review 280 (1907).

W.C.J., Constitutional Law: Income Tax: Sixteenth Amendment, 4 California Law Journal 333 (1915-6).

# Other Authorities

50 American Jurisprudence, 1st Statutes § 363.

American State Papers, Finance, Vol. 1, pgs. 414-441.

American State Papers, Vol. II, Pg. 887.

Ballentine's Law Dictionary (3rd Ed. 1969).

Beatles, Revolver, Apple Records 1 (1966).

Black's Law Dictionary (6th Ed. 1990).

Black, Campbell, A Law Dictionary (1910).

Curtis, George Ticknor, An Inquiry Into One Of The Constitutional Restrictions On The Revenue Powers Of The United States, Harper's New Monthly Magazine, p. 356, August, 1866.

Democrat party Presidential Platform (1908).

Judicial and Statutory Definitions of Words and Phrases (West Publishing Co. 1904).

Magna Carta, Chap. 39 (1215).

Treasury Decisions, 2017, 2162, 2313, Internal Revenue, Vol. 30 (1919).

Ecclesiastes 1:9 (New American Standard).

Exodus 18:13-26.

Jeremiah 1:5 (Authorized King James).

Luke 20:25 (New American Standard).

Mark 4:22 (New American Standard).

Matthew 20:28 (New American Standard).

Matthew 22:21 (New American Standard).

Psalms 139: 13-14 (New American Standard).

Romans 13:3-4 (Geneva Bible, 1st Edition, 1560).

# Table of Cases

Bank of America National T.& Sav. Ass'n. v. United States, 459 F.2d 513 (Ct.Cl. 1972).

Brushaber v. Union Pacific RR. Co., 240 U.S. 1 (1916).

Butchers Union Co. v. Crescent City Co., 111 U.S. 746 (1883).

Chas. C. Steward Mach. Co. v. Davis, 301 U.S. 548 (1937).

Chevron U.S.A. v. Natural Resources Defense Council Inc., 467 U.S. 837 (1984).

Collector v. Day, 78 U.S. (11 Wall.) 113 (1870).

Commissioner v. Obear-Nester Glass Co., 217 F.2d 56 (7th Cir. 1954).

Cook v. Tait, 265 U.S. 47 (1923).

Cornell Univ. v. Davenport, 30 Hun. 177 (N.Y. 1883).

Culliton v. Chase, 25 P.2d. 81 (Wash. 1933).

Downes v. Bidwell, 182 U.S. 244 (1901).

Eisner v. Macomber, 252 U.S. 189 (1919).

Equitable Trust Co. v. Prentice, 240 N.Y. 1; 164 N.E. 723 (1928).

Evans v. Gore, 253 U.S. 245 (1920).

Fairbank v. United States, 181 U.S. 283 (1901).

Federal Trade Commission v. Raladam, 283 U.S. 643 (1931).

Flint v. Stone Tracy Co., 220 U.S. 107 (1910).

Foster v. United States, 303 U.S. 118 (1938).

Hale v. Henkel, 201 U.S. 43 (1906).

Hale v. State Board, 302 U.S. 95 (1937).

Hylton v. United States, 3 U.S. (3 Dall.) 171 (1796).

Insurance Co. v. Soule, 74 U.S. (7 Wall.) 433 (1868).

Jack Cole v. MacFarland, 337 S.W.2d. 453 (Tenn. 1960).

Jensen v. Henneford, 53 P.2d. 607 (Wash. 1936).

Keasbey and Mattison Co. v. Rothensies, 133 F.2d 894 (4th Cir. 1937)

Langford v. United States, 101 U.S. 341 (1879).

Lawrence v. Wardell, 273 F. 405 (9th Cir. 1921).

Levi v. City of Louisville, 30 S.W. 973; 97 Ky. 394; 28 L.R.A. 480 (1985).

Loan Ass'n. v. Topeka, 87 U.S. (20 Wall.) 655 (1874).

Marbury v. Madison, 5 U.S. (1 Cranch) 137 (1803).

Mattox v. United States, 156 U.S. 237 (1895).

Maxwell v. Dow, 176 U.S. 581 (1900).

McColloch v. Maryland, 17 U.S. 316 (1819).

McCreery v. McColgan, 110 P.2d 1051 (Cal. 1941).

Merchants' L.&T. Co. v. Smietanka, 255 U.S. 509 (1921).

Miles et.al. v. Department of the Treasury et.al., 199 N.E. 372 (Ind. 1935).

O'Connell v. State Bd. of Equalization, 25 P.2d 114 (Mont. 1933).

Pacific Insurance Co. v. Soule, 74 U.S. 433 (1868).

Parker v. Commissioner, 724 F.2d 469 (5th Cir. 1984).

Parker v. North British Insurance Co., 7 So. 599; 42 La.Ann. 428 (1890).

Peck & Co. v. Lowe, 247 U.S. 165 (1917).

Penn Mutual Indemnity Co. v. C.I.R., 32T.C. 653 (1959).

Phelps v. United States, 274 U.S. 341 (1927).

Pollock v. Farmers' Loan and Trust Co., 157 U.S. 429 (1894); reh. 158 U.S. 601 (1895).

Redfield v. Fisher, 292 P. 813 (Or. 1930).

Sargent Land Co. v. Von Vaumbach, 207 F.423 (D. Minn. 1913).

Schholey v. Rew, 90 U.S. (23 Wall.) 331 (1874).

Sims v. Ahrens, 271 S.W. 720 (Ark. 1925).

Smith v. Hooper, 51 A. 844 (Md.1902).

Spreckels Sugar Refining Co. v. McClain, 192 U.S. 397 (1904).

Springer v. United States, 102 U.S. 586 (1880).

Stanton v. Baltic Mining Co., 240 U.S. 103 (1916).

Stratton's Independence v. Howbert Ltd., 231 U.S. 399 (1913).

Tyee Realty Co. v. Anderson, 240 U.S. 115 (1916).

United States Esp. Co. v. State of Minn., 223 U.S. 335 (1912).

United States v. United Mine Workers of America, 330 U.S. 258 (1947).

United States v. Collins, 920 F.2d 619 (10th Cir. 1990).

United States v. Turano, 802 F.2d 10 (1st Cir. 1986).

United States v. Francisco, 614 F.2d 617 (8th Cir. 1980).

United States v. Sitka, 845 F.2d 43 (2nd Cir. 1988).

United States v. Gaumer, 972 F.2d 723 (6th Cir. 1992).

United States v. Sprague, 282 U.S. 716 (1930).

Veazie Bank v. Fenno, 75 U.S. (8 Wall.) 533 (1869).

Vicksburg v. Mullane, 106 Miss. 199; 63 So. 412 (1913).

W.C. Peacock & Co. v. Pratt, 121 F. 772 (9th Cir. 1903).

Waring v. City of Savannah, 60 Ga. 93 (1878).

White Packaging Co. v. Robertson, 89 F.2d 775 (4th Cir. 1937).

Wilcox v. County Commissioners, 103 Mass. 544 (1870).

In re Armitage, 3 Ch. Div. 337 (1893).

# Index

## Symbols



## A

## B



## C

## D

## E



## F

## G



## H



## I

## J



## K



## L



## M

## N



## O



## P

## Q



## R



## S

## T

## U

## V



## W



## Y

***Constitutional Income: Do You Have Any?***

# ORDER FORM

**Please Print**

**Name** ______________________________________________

**Address** ____________________________________________

**City** ___________________________ **State** ____________

**Zip** ______________

**Phone (_____)** ________________

_________ copies of book at $20.00 each $ __________

Idaho residents add 6% sales tax $ __________

Total amount enclosed $ __________

***Quantity Orders:*** 5-9 books are $16.00 a book, 10-23 books are $14 a book, 24 or more books are $10.00 a book.

*(Shipping and Handling included in the cost of the book.)*

***Mail check or money order payable to Alpine Press***

***APLINE PRESS***
***1324 N. Liberty Lake Rd, PMB 145***
***Liberty Lake, WA 99019***